Market and Price Analysis
The Agricultural Industries

Market and Price Analysis
The Agricultural Industries

Dale C. Dahl
Professor of Agricultural and Applied Economics
Adjunct Professor of Law
University of Minnesota, St. Paul

Jerome W. Hammond
Professor of Agricultural and Applied Economics
University of Minnesota, St. Paul

McGraw-Hill Book Company

New York   St. Louis   San Francisco   Auckland   Bogotá   Düsseldorf
Johannesburg   London   Madrid   Mexico   Montreal   New Delhi
Panama   Paris   São Paulo   Singapore   Sydney   Tokyo   Toronto

Market and Price Analysis
The Agricultural Industries

1234567890   KPKP   7832109876

This book was set in Times Roman by University Graphics, Inc. The
editors were J. S. Dietrich and Matthew Cahill; the cover was designed
by Rafael Hernandez; the production supervisor was Angela Kardovich.
The drawings were done by Danmark & Michaels, Inc.
Kingsport Press, Inc., was printer and binder.

Library of Congress Cataloging in Publication Data

Dahl, Dale C
    Market and price analysis.

    Includes bibliographies and index.
     1.   Agricultural industries—United States.
2. Agricultural prices—United States. I. Hammond,
Jerome W. II. Title.
HD9005.D25   380.1′41′0973   76-26018
ISBN 0-07-015060-5

To Our Wives
Marie Hammond and Rosemary Dahl

Contents

Preface

The purpose of this text is to provide the reader with an understanding of the economic organization and operation of the food and fiber sector of the U. S. economy. We have attempted to fill a void that exists in the subject matter areas. Various texts provide good treatment of agricultural price analysis. There are also a number of texts that consider the various dimensions of the marketing system for agricultural inputs, farm products, and processing and distribution activities. On the basis of our teaching experience, we believe that there is a need for a text which aims to treat both topics comprehensively and analytically.

A complete analysis of the vast group of interrelated industries that represent the food and fiber sector is far beyond the scope of this text. Furthermore, such a study would be outdated shortly by continued and significant changes in products, business and institutional structures, and business and public policies. Therefore, we have presented materials that best exemplify fundamental economic structures and methods of analysis.

The text is intended for use in introductory courses in market and price analysis. Students would benefit from prior courses in the principles of economics (particularly microeconomics) and a basic course in college algebra.

We wish to acknowledge the encouragement of W. Burt Sundquist and our colleagues in the Department of Agricultural and Applied Economics of the

University of Minnesota. The department supported the effort that resulted in this text. We also express our appreciation to the following economists who reviewed all or part of the manuscript: Martin E. Abel (University of Minnesota), Harold F. Breimyer (University of Missouri), Willard W. Cochrane (University of Minnesota), Vernon R. Eidman (University of Minnesota), Ray A. Goldberg (Harvard University), Peter Helmberger (University of Wisconsin), James P. Houck (University of Minnesota), F. Richard King (University of Maine), Richard A. King (University of North Carolina), E. Fred Koller (University of Minnesota), Willis Peterson (University of Minnesota), V. James Rhodes (University of Missouri), James D. Shaffer (Michigan State University), and William G. Tomek (Cornell University).

Special thanks are due to Winston W. Grant, who prepared the index for this book, and to Pamela Gantzer, Sandra Fox, and Linda Davidson, all of whom typed various drafts of the manuscript.

Dale C. Dahl
Jerome W. Hammond

Chapter 1

Agricultural Markets and Prices

INTRODUCTION

Food and fiber from farming identifies the nation's largest industrial sector. Most of the $279.0 billion spent by U.S. consumers for food, beverages, clothing, and shoes in 1975 supported a vast array of interrelated business activities in the United States. Part of this money was paid to the petroleum industry for supplying fuel and the raw materials used by fertilizer and pesticide manufacturers. Some was paid to rural machinery dealers and feed and seed stores where farmers buy their production inputs. Livestock ranchers, farmers, truck gardeners, dairy workers, and cotton and wheat producers also shared in the expenditures of consumers. The farm product assembler, the food processor, the trucker, the warehouse worker, the commodity speculator, the wholesaler, the grocery retailer, the garment manufacturer, the restaurant owner—each took a portion of the total.

Consumers are concerned about the price they pay and the quality and availability of the farm-based products they buy. Frequently consumers feel economically helpless; food and clothing is priced by someone else, its quality is already established when they go to the market, and they may feel cheated if the item is not on the shelf or rack at the time and place they want to buy it.

Farmers have a similar feeling of powerlessness. The prices they pay for animal feed, machinery, fertilizer, and farm buildings are preset. And when the time comes to sell their products, farmers are told the price that they will receive. Sometimes the farm product price received is more than enough to offset the costs of inputs. Other times, it is not.

What is the nature of this food and fiber system that provides such results? How are food and fiber prices established? What causes them to go up and down? What forces set farm-input prices and the prices received by farmers? What are the costs of food and fiber manufacture and distribution? Are there excessive profits in the food processing industries? Is food and fiber transportation and handling inefficient and wasteful? Are commodity speculators professional gamblers, with the consumer and farmer always losing? Why does the government not help the consumer and farmer? Or is the government too involved in farming and consumer decision making now?

This book addresses these questions and many more like them. The answers are not always obvious and the solutions are frequently difficult. We will start with some basic definitions and fundamental descriptive approaches.

DEFINITIONS AND APPROACHES

The act of exchanging money for goods or services is such a commonplace event in our everyday lives that we tend to underplay its importance. But to the economist it is a matter of central significance.

Professor Kenneth Boulding provided us with an example transaction involving the purchase of two pounds of butter by a mythical Mrs. Jones.

> When Mrs. Jones buys her two pounds of butter, then, we observe first that there are two persons participating in the event, the buyer and the seller. We observe also that there are two physical objects involved. One is the butter, which passes from the possession of the storekeeper to Mrs. Jones. The other is the $1.60, which passes from the possession of Mrs. Jones to the storekeeper. An exchange, therefore, consists of two reciprocal transfers of ownership. At least three economic quantities are involved in the event: the quantity of butter (two pounds), the quantity of money ($1.60), and the *ratio* of these quantities, the $1.60 for two pounds, or, what is the same thing, 80 cents per pound. The ratio of the quantities exchanged is the *price,* or exchange ratio.[1]

The setting in which Mrs. Jones buys her butter is the inside of the store. For most people, this store or some other physical location where transactions occur is what is meant by the term *market.* But economists have a more elaborate definition:

> A market is *some* sphere, or space, where (1) the forces of demand and supply are at work, (2) to determine, or modify, price, (3) as the ownership of some quantity of

[1]Kenneth E. Boulding, *Economic Analysis,* vol. 1, *Microeconomics,* 4th ed., Harper and Row, New York, 1966, pp. 6–7.

good, or service, is transferred, and (4) certain physical and institutional arrangements may be in evidence.[2]

Mrs. Jones, the *buyer* of butter, is also a family purchasing agent for the household consuming unit. As a *demander* of butter she must take many factors into account. First, she must consider the *price,* or the exchange ratio between the quantity of butter and the quantity of money she will forego. The importance of this price in her decision further depends upon her food budget, the availability and price of substitutes to butter (such as margarine), her expectations about future butter price changes, and so forth. All of these considerations and more are the "forces of demand" at work in this simple transaction.

The storekeeper, the *seller* of butter, is called a *supplier.* In making the decision of how much butter to sell at 80 cents per pound, the grocer must first consider the *costs.* In addition to the amount paid to the dairy for the butter, the grocer must calculate the store rent, employee salaries, refrigeration expenses, and other costs of storekeeping. Then these costs must be allocated across all the goods the storekeeper sells to determine a *markup* or *margin* to add to the price originally paid to the dairy. But the storekeeper must also add a charge for his or her time and a return to the personal capital which the storekeeper has invested in the business. The return to the storekeeper's time is calculated by what the individual could earn in some alternative employment. This is called *opportunity cost.* The extra return to capital invested under risk is called *profit.*[3] All of these considerations made by the storekeeper, and there are undoubtedly more, are the "forces of supply" at work in this transaction.

Together, these forces of demand and supply determine or modify price—in this case, the price of butter. In the transaction, the act of exchanging butter for money also transfers ownership of the goods involved. Mrs. Jones becomes the owner of the butter and the storekeeper becomes the owner of the $1.60.

This single transaction takes place in one grocery store (where "certain physical and institutional arrangements are in evidence"), a single retail establishment among many where thousands of people like Mrs. Jones purchase consumer goods every day.

A single buyer and seller transaction, by itself, may be sufficient to define a "market." But a market is usually defined by a group of transactions. There may be many buyers and many sellers. Many products can be involved. The transactions may occur regularly or irregularly over time. And various kinds of physical and institutional arrangements may be in evidence.

Some buyers, like Mrs. Jones, *consume* the product they buy. Consumption is the act of using up the satisfaction-giving value or *utility* of a good. Other buyers, however, purchase a commodity as an intermediary. The commodity

---

[2]Willard W. Cochrane, "The Market as a Unit of Inquiry in Agricultural Economics Research," *Journal of Farm Economics,* vol. 39, no. 1, Feb. 1957.

[3]Note the words "extra return to capital." Total returns to capital consist of: (1) that return which one could get by investing one's capital elsewhere at the going rate of interest (the "opportunity cost" of one's capital), and (2) that extra return which is above the current rate of interest that encourages one to stay in the business of storekeeping.

may then be resold or employed as raw material in the manufacture of another product.

The end result of primary good production, assembly, storage, transportation, manufacture, and distribution is consumption. All of the intermediate steps from primary production to ultimate consumption are encompassed by the term *marketing.*

Agricultural market and price analysis, like the discipline of economics of which it is a part, is frequently subdivided in terms of solution processes to the applied *problems* addressed. From earlier acquaintance with other social sciences, you may know that social problems are identified when reality is at odds with the way we would like things to be. To "solve" such a problem it is necessary to (1) *describe* reality, (2) *analyze* (or understand) why things are as they are, (3) clarify what we want reality to look like (formulate our *goals*), and (4) develop and execute a plan *(policy)* to change the reality that exists into the state we desire.

Description of the marketing and pricing system for food and fiber, then, is our first point of departure in the serious study of market and price analysis. There are many (too many) aspects of the food and fiber system that can catch our eye. Market and price economists, after careful study of the food and fiber system, have developed useful ways of describing the events that take place in the assembly, storage, transportation, processing, and distribution of farm-related products.

The *marketing* of farm supplies and farm products can be viewed as a sequential series of steps, stages, or *functions* that need to be performed as the input or product moves from its point of primary production to ultimate consumption. It can also be viewed in terms of the firms and agencies performing these functions or in terms of how these institutions interrelate.

For descriptive purposes, the "steps of operation" (or, more commonly, "functions") have been classified in different ways by different authors. One current text on agricultural marketing separated the functions of marketing into nine categories: (1) buying (assembling), (2) selling, (3) storage, (4) transportation, (5) processing, (6) standardization, (7) financing, (8) risk bearing, and (9) market intelligence.[4]

Another descriptive approach classifies the firms and agencies (collectively called *institutions*) that perform the several marketing and pricing functions.

Other significant descriptive approaches have been suggested to classify the complex set of behavior patterns that characterize marketing middlemen as well. Shepherd and Futrell have recommended that markets and marketing activities be classified in terms of the dimensions of time, space, and form.[5] Kohls and Downey additionally suggest the classification of the behavior of marketing firms in terms of "systems" of market interrelationship. Yet another descriptive

[4]Richard L. Kohls and W. David Downey, *Marketing of Agricultural Products,* 4th ed., Macmillan, New York, 1972, p. 20.
[5]Geoffrey S. Shepherd and Gene A. Futrell, *Marketing Farm Products—Economic Analysis,* 5th ed., Iowa State University Press, Ames, Iowa, 1969, pp. 18–24.

framework is the so-called market structure analysis approach to market and price analysis. This approach and its descriptive and analytical applications are the subject of Chapter 12 of this text.

However described, this complex set of functions, institutions, and behavioral patterns are interrelated directly and indirectly in technical and economic terms. The nature of this interrelation is the subject of market and price analysis. If we can comprehend how the marketing system operates, we can address the very important question of why it operates as it does. The answer to "Why?" is the basic endeavor of all scientific inquiry. If we understand the underlying causes of structure and behavior, we can more accurately predict and sometimes control outcomes.

The method used to understand or answer the "why" questions about reality is called *analysis*. To analyze we must have some prior knowledge about the nature of the interrelationships among economic variables *(economic theory)*. And we must also have a grasp of certain *quantitative tools* (accounting, mathematics, statistics) that permit us to specify and state those interrelationships.

Once we have described how the food and fiber system is organized and operates, and after we have understood, by our analysis, why it is so structured and functioning, then we are in a position to do one of two things. First, we can try to *predict* what the system will look like and how it will behave in the future. This sequence of description, analysis, and prediction (or some part of it) is referred to as *positive economic analysis*.

Second, we could compare our reality to a postulated ideal and provide a study of the "means" by which we can change reality into something we consider better. This is called *normative economic analysis*. The means we study are also called *economic policy*.

Whether by directed policy or by a seemingly inexplicable set of forces, the economic sector and its food and fiber system subcomponent has undergone dramatic changes since this country was founded. Let us review some of these developments.

HISTORY AND DEVELOPMENT OF THE MARKETING SYSTEM

In the same way that the act of *exchange* serves as a basis for several fundamentally important concepts in market and price analysis, the act of *specialization* helps to explain the evolution and organizational configuration of the present-day food and fiber system. The concept of specialization was first generally explained by Adam Smith:

> To take an example, therefore, from a very trifling manufacture; but one in which the division of labour has been very often taken notice of, the trade of the pinmaker. . . .
> One man draws out the wire, another straightens it, a third cuts it, a fourth points it, a fifth grinds it at the top for receiving the head; to make the head requires two or three distinct operations; to put it on, is a peculiar business, to whiten the pins

is another; it is even a trade by itself to put them into the paper; and the important business of making a pin is, in this manner, divided into about eighteen distinct operations. . . . I have seen a small factory of this kind where ten men only were employed. . . . Those ten persons could make among them upwards of forty-eight thousand pins in a day. Each person, therefore, making a tenth part of forty-eight thousand pins, might be considered as making four thousand eight hundred pins in a day. But if they had all wrought separately and independently, and without any of them having been educated to this peculiar business, they certainly could not each of them have made twenty, perhaps not one pin in a day. . . .

This great increase of the quantity of work, which, in consequence of the division of labour, the same number of people are capable of performing, is owing to three different circumstances; first, to the increase of dexterity in every particular workman; secondly, to the saving of the time which is commonly lost in passing from one species of work to another; and lastly, to the invention of a great number of machines which facilitate and abridge labour, and enable one man to do the work of many.[6]

Adam Smith thought that specialization had limited application in the agriculture of his day. But during the past two centuries specialization served as the functional basis for dramatic evolutionary changes in the U.S. food and fiber system.

When this nation was born, farming was the dominant form of business activity. Each farm and farmer was economically self-sufficient. The typical operation produced its own food, shelter, and clothing. And the production unit was sustained by a continual "refeeding" of farm-produced fuel, animal feed, seed, fertilizer, and power back into the combined farm and household operation.

The first major advent of specialization was in the form of mechanical devices designed to perform repetitive tasks more efficiently. These machines included the cotton gin and cast-iron plow. These were followed by mowers, reapers, and eventually the mechanical thresher. Each of these discoveries made the farmer more productive—the farmer used less time and effort to produce more product.

Along with the technological revolution on the farm, there was a necessary "companion" revolution off the farm. This included the development of commercial handling, storage, processing, transportation, and distributive outlets for the farm-produced food and fiber.

One set of changes led to others. Older food-preserving techniques like drying, salting, and canning were improved. New methods, such as dehydration, quick-freezing, and precooking, evolved. Because each farmer was more productive, fewer people were required to produce our food and fiber. The result was a migration of people from the farm to urban areas.

Implied in these changes was a modification of the functions performed by the urban household, and later the farm household also. The homemaker looked

[6]Adam Smith, *The Wealth of Nations,* Modern Library Edition, book 1, pp. 4–7.

for time-saving and labor-saving aids too. Instead of personally preserving and preparing foods, the homemaker became increasingly dependent upon others to do it. Instead of weaving cloth and making garments, the homemaker came to depend upon fiber processors and manufacturers to offer ready-to-wear clothing.

In addition to the development of major food and fiber assembly, processing, and distribution industries, another phase of the off-the-farm technological revolution developed from the increasing tendencies of farmers to use inputs manufactured by off-farm firms for their on-farm production. Accordingly, there developed the farm machinery, feed, fertilizer, and farm-building industries that provide the modern-day farmer with production inputs and facilities. Throughout its evolution, agribusiness has existed in a decentralized state:

> Agribusiness has no center of control or direction. It has no president, no board of directors, and no central office. Instead, it consists of several million farm units and several thousand business units—each an independent entity, free to make its own decisions. In addition, there are hundreds of trade associations, commodity organizations, farm organizations, quasi-research bodies, conference bodies, and committees, each largely concentrating on its own interests. . . . In brief, today agribusiness exists in a vast composite of decentralized entities, functions, and operations relating to food and fiber.[7]

PREVIEW OF THE FOLLOWING CHAPTERS

This abbreviated background information provides us with a starting point in our quest to understand why the food and fiber system operates as it does. But before we delve too deeply into the reasons, we will descriptively review the general character of the food and fiber system and try to grasp the complexity of its parts. The agricultural markets and marketing systems are the subject of Chapter 2. Once we have an appreciation of the system and its subparts, we will review some fundamental but essential quantitative tools of analysis: accounting, mathematics, and statistical methods (Chapter 3).

We will then be ready to examine this sector of our economy. We will start by studying food and fiber consumption and the economic relations that underlie the changes which we observe in it (Chapter 4). Then we will proceed to investigate farm production and the factors that explain its changes (Chapter 5). Armed with knowledge about the *demand* for food and fiber and the *supply* of it by farmers, we will be in a position to explain *market prices* at various levels of the system (Chapter 6). But our analysis would be incomplete at this stage unless we focused analytical attention on the *marketing margin,* the difference in price between farm and retail price. Marketing costs and margins are the subject of Chapter 7.

We will not be content to merely explain prices over time and at various levels of the system. We will study how and why prices and markets vary over

---

[7]John Davis and Ray Goldberg, *A Concept of Agribusiness,* Harvard University Press, Cambridge, Mass., 1957, p. 6.

space (Chapter 8), the pricing mechanisms and institutions that deal with storage and uncertainty (Chapter 9), and price and market differences by product class and quality (Chapter 10). We also will be interested in understanding how farm producers and consumers communicate with each other and the role that market information plays in decision making by farm supply firms, farmers, marketing middlemen, and consumers (Chapter 11).

The economic behavior of agricultural market participants is heavily influenced by the number that interact and their relative size, the nature of the product they produce, and various other "conditions" that exist. This is the subject of *market structure analysis* (Chapter 12). Pricing and marketing practices are further explained by unique institutions, such as cooperatives and marketing orders, that have developed and become a major part of the system of markets involved in generating our food and clothing (Chapter 13). And there are numerous regulations in the form of statutes, court decisions, and administrative bodies at federal, state, and local levels that constrain or facilitate the movement of products through the marketing and pricing system (Chapter 14).

We will conclude our study of markets and prices by addressing the interesting marketing relationships that exist in economic development, both in the United States and elsewhere. Our conclusion, of course, is that agricultural marketing and prices play but one part in the long-term evolution of the entire economic system that constitutes a vital part of any society.

SUMMARY

The food and fiber sector of the U.S. economy is large and complex. Millions of consumers and farmers and hundreds of thousands of businesses are interrelated because they each play a role in producing, processing, assembling, storing, transporting, distributing, or consuming food and fiber. Each depends upon the other as a *buyer* or a *seller* of their goods or services.

The essence of the organization and behavior of buyers and sellers is found in each transaction process. Under specific conditions, a set of transactions define a *market*.

Market and price analysis involves economic description and theory, the application of quantitative tools, and possibly prediction and study of private and public policies.

The food and fiber system, as we know it today, is a relatively unplanned outgrowth of specialization and exchange over the past two centuries. Self-sufficiency has been replaced by complex interdependency.

QUESTIONS

1 Frequently, real or personal property must be "appraised" to determine its *market value*. What is market value? How might these appraisals be done?

2 Specialization and exchange serve as the analytical basis for many economic rela-

tionships and developments. In what way are these two concepts interrelated? Can you have specialization without exchange? Or vice versa? Why or why not?
3 Many off-farm agribusinesses have started to engage in some farming activities in the past two decades. Some retail chain stores have their own feedlots; some canning companies grow some of their own vegetables. This seems contrary to the earlier development of agribusiness. What explanation can you offer for this apparent change of events?

BIBLIOGRAPHY

Boulding, Kenneth E.: *Economic Analysis,* 4th ed., Harper and Row, New York, 1966, vol. 1 *(Microeconomics).*

Cochrane, Willard W.: "The Market as a Unit of Inquiry in Agricultural Economics Research," *Journal of Farm Economics,* vol. 39, no. 1, Feb. 1957.

Davis, John, and Ray Goldberg: *A Concept of Agribusiness,* Harvard University Press, Cambridge, Mass., 1957.

Kohls, Richard L., and W. David Downey: *Marketing of Agricultural Products,* 4th ed., Macmillan, New York, 1972.

Shepherd, Geoffrey S., and Gene A. Futrell: *Marketing Farm Products—Economic Analysis,* 5th ed., Iowa State University Press, Ames, Iowa, 1969.

Thomsen, Frederick L.: *Agricultural Marketing,* McGraw-Hill, New York, 1951.

Agricultural Markets and Marketing Systems

INTRODUCTION

The channels by which resources move through the farming sector and ultimately to consumers as food, fiber, and related products are varied, sometimes complex, and include hundreds of thousands of firms. A description of the major marketing channels for inputs and food and fiber products is the prime objective of this chapter. We hope to provide the reader with a broad view of the system and a picture of (1) how products move through the system, (2) the vast coordinating function that must be performed to match production decisions with consumer wants, and (3) the innumerable exchanges of goods that must be accomplished in allocating goods to all possible uses.

For purposes of our descriptive effort, the food and fiber system is divided into four segments. The first segment includes the farm-input industries—those firms that manufacture and/or distribute farm supplies and provide producer services to farmers. The second segment includes the hundreds of thousands of farming operations that combine land and other resources to produce raw food and fiber products. The third segment, the food and fiber product markets, is composed of those firms that assemble, store, transport, process, and distribute farm products and items made from them. The fourth and final segment of the

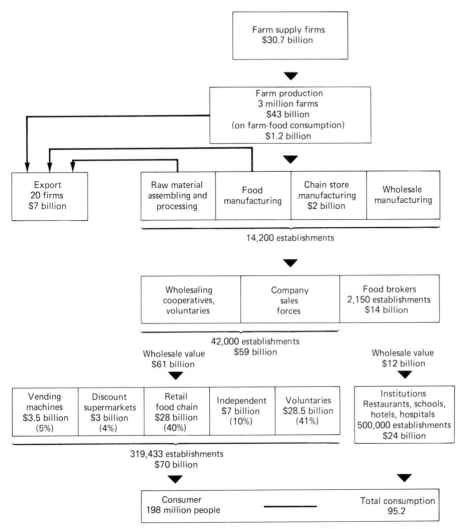

Figure 2-1 Functional organization of U.S. food agribusiness, 1967 (estimated). *Source:* Ray Goldberg, *Agribusiness Coordination,* Harvard University Press, Cambridge, Mass., 1968, p. 12.

food and fiber system includes the regulatory and facilitative services provided by government at federal, state, and local levels. Figure 2-1 illustrates, in a very aggregate way, the flow of products into the farming sector and the flow of products from that subsector through the product market to consumers as food products. Although the absolute values have changed since 1967, the relative importance of the various functional classifications of firms has probably not changed greatly. Farm supply firms, manufacturers, wholesalers, and distributors sold $30 billion of inputs to farming, which in turn sold $43 billion of farm-food products. In 1972 farm sales totaled $60.7 billion. Numerous processing, wholesaling, and retail firms were involved as the products moved to consumers. By the time all food products reached consumers in 1967, they had a value of $95.2 billion. Retail food and beverage expenditures rose to $116 billion by 1974.

The final distribution of food to consumers takes a variety of routes. The institutional trade (restaurants, hotels, hospitals, etc.) accounted for $24 billion of final consumption in 1967. Food chains were the largest single type of outlet, accounting for about 40 percent of all consumer sales.

In addition to the channels for food distribution, similar channels and sometimes the same channels exist for nonfood farm products. These include tobacco, wool, cotton, and feeds which move into export or back into the farming sector as an input into livestock.

Given this aggregate view of the food and fiber system, let us now review some economic dimensions of its major parts. We will proceed by describing the markets for farm inputs, the farming segment itself, and the food product markets, followed by a review of the market channels for fiber and tobacco. And we will conclude by outlining the government agencies that serve or regulate the food and fiber system.

FARM-INPUT MARKETS

One of the most significant and continuing changes in U.S. agriculture is the shift from nonpurchased to purchased inputs in farm production (Figure 2-2). In terms of total value, the quantity of all inputs has remained remarkably stable. It was about 12 percent higher in 1970 than in 1950. Nonpurchased input use declined by about 30 percent while use of purchased input has increased by 50 percent. In dollar terms, purchased input expenditures increased from $12.7 billion in 1954 to $19.9 billion in 1969. Farm machinery, fertilizer, and feed were the most important in value, accounting for more than 60 percent of total farm inputs. The 1973 farm-input expense for U.S. farmers was distributed as indicated in Figure 2-3.

Farm Machinery Industry

The production and distribution of farm machinery is a major economic activity in the United States, $10.4 billion in 1974. The total value of machinery shipments (other than tractors) by manufacturers exceeded $3 billion in 1971. Shipments of tractors of all types alone exceeded $2 billion.[1] Although the long-term trend in the market for farm machinery has been upward and will undoubtedly continue in that direction, it is characterized by significant short-term fluctuations. The long-term trend appears to be particularly sensitive to change in farm income, farm numbers and size, and technological change in farm production.

The movement of farm machinery to farmers is characterized by two rather distinct channels. One channel exists for the full-line and long-line machinery companies. Another exists for the short-line companies.

[1]*Statistical Abstract of the United States*, 1973, p. 732.

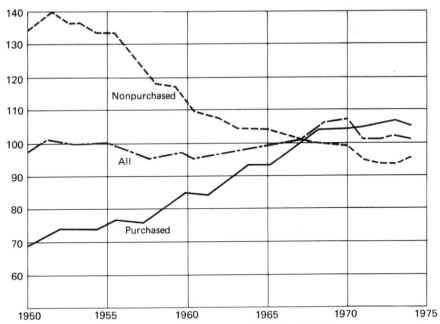

Figure 2-2 Indexes of farm inputs used, 1950–1974 (1967 = 100). *Source:* U.S. Department of Agriculture, *Changes in Farm Production and Efficiency: A Summary Report,* Statistical Bulletin 548, Sept. 1975, p. 29.

The full-line companies are those that produce tractors and a complete array of equipment powered by tractors. They also handle self-propelled equipment, attachments, and other machines. Short-line companies usually are quite specialized in terms of the type of mechanical device they offer for sale.

Figure 2-4 shows channels of distribution for the farm machinery of the two types of organization. Channels for full-line companies are relatively short. Wholesalers and manufacturers' branches usually market the products to farmers through franchised dealerships. On the other hand, channels for short-line companies are complicated because various levels of merchant and agent middlemen become involved. There is a relative absence of these institutions for full-line companies.

In 1967, the most recent census year, there were over 1,600 farm machinery and equipment manufacturers, an increase of 3 percent since 1963. At the retail level, some 16,200 dealerships exist throughout the United States.[2]

Fertilizer Industry

There are three main chemical substances necessary to crop nutrition: nitrogen, phosphate, and potassium. The extraction and manufacture of these products

---

[2]U.S. Bureau of the Census, *1967 Census of Manufacturers* and *1967 Census of Business.*

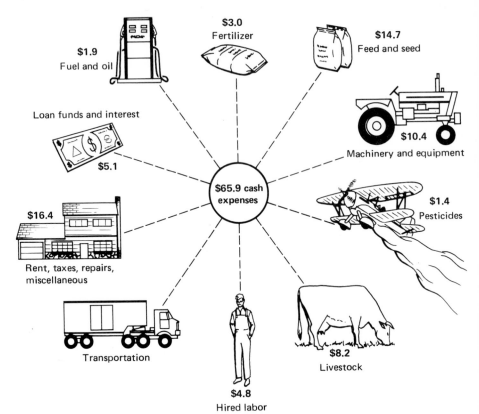

Figure 2-3 Farm-input expenses, 1973. *Source:* Economic Research Service, U.S. Department of Agriculture [NEG. ERS 855-74(11)].

serve as a basis for an industry that made sales in the vicinity of $4–6 billion to farmers in 1974.

The principal source of nitrogen is the atmosphere. Nitrogen is combined with hydrogen to produce synthetic ammonia. Natural gas is the major source for producing hydrogen; other sources include refinery gas, naphtha, fuel oil, coke, oven gas, water gas, and electrolytic hydrogen. Approximately 90 percent of U.S. ammonia production comes from natural gas.

Phosphorus is contained in small amounts in all rocks. Domestic deposits yielding a high proportion of phosphorus are found in Florida, North Carolina, Tennessee, Idaho, Montana, Utah, and Wyoming. Florida has approximately 38 percent of the U.S. domestic sources but supplies about 70 percent of total rock output; Tennessee has 2 percent of the reserves but supplies 12 percent; the Western states have 60 percent of the reserves and supply 16 percent.

Approximately 90 percent of domestic potassium production is from New Mexico mines; the remainder comes from California and Utah. Substantial quantities of potash are now imported from Canada.

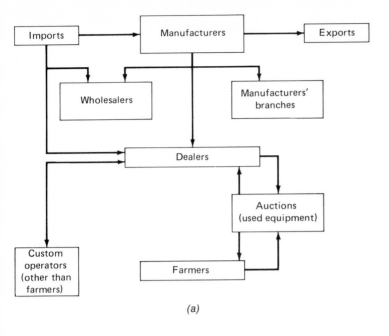

(a)

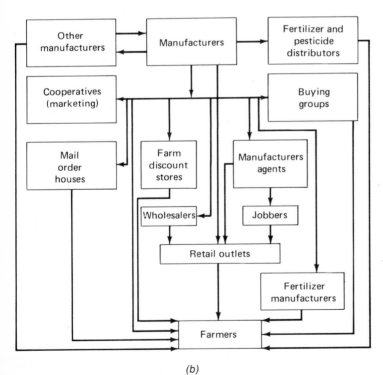

(b)

Figure 2-4 Distribution channels of farm machinery. *Source:* Economic Research Service, U.S. Department of Agriculture [NEG. ERS 5355-67(9) and 5356-67(9)].

Primary producers

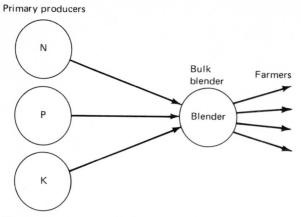

Figure 2-5 Production and distribution channels for bulk-blended fertilizer.

The fertilizer industry is comprised of all producers, processors, and mixers of fertilizer nitrogen, phosphate, potash, and sulfur. As plant-nutrient-bearing materials are carried from mine and factory to the farmer, phosphatic fertilizer producers occupy a pivotal position. Farmers buy more than 60 percent of fertilizers as mixtures containing at least two of the three principal plant nutrients. Much, but not all, of the mixing industry is vertically integrated with the production and processing of phosphate rock. Phosphate producers integrated with the mixing industry and other fertilizer mixers purchase most of the nitrogen and potash produced and sell it to farmers.

Substantial quantities of potassium-based fertilizers sold in the United States are imported from Canada. Potash imported from Canada to the United States is transacted through long-term contracts with several major fertilizer companies in the United States who also have control of the nitrogen and phosphate supplies.

The fertilizer industry in the United States has undergone dramatic changes in organization within the past 15 years. The fertilizer industry, as described then, really no longer exists. Nearly all of the fertilizer sold in the United States today is either in liquid or granular form, and much of it is sold as so-called straight materials. The blending or combining of the nitrogen, phosphate, and potassium materials is done largely at local levels in accordance with the particular nutritional requirements of farmers given their crop and soil situations (Figure 2-5).

As indicated previously, much of the fertilizer industry is integrated from manufacturing level through wholesaler level. There were substantial efforts made during the late 1960s by petrochemical companies to integrate forward to the retail end of the system (where sales are made directly to farmers). There was some disenchantment with the results. The farm-supply retail system in the United States is primarily held by agricultural cooperatives and long-established farm supply businesses. With the exception of farm supply cooperatives, most independent wholesalers and retailers have been squeezed out of the industry because of an overcapacity situation in the late 1960s. The resultant highly integrated operations from manufacturer to retailer are capable of retaining very tight control over the allocation and pricing of their product.

Feed Industry

Feeds and formula feeds are major inputs into livestock production. Farmers paid $7.1 billion for feed in 1969.[3] In the past, much of the feed input was used on farms where it was produced, but this has changed dramatically. In 1948–1950, approximately two-thirds of all feed grains were fed on farms where they were produced. By 1968–1970, only one-third was used on farms where produced (see Figure 2-6).

Feed grains moving off the farm may move directly to other farmers engaged in livestock and poultry feeding or they may go to assemblers. These assemblers may be country elevators or terminal buyers. Country elevators may be shipping

---

[3]Karl Meilke, "The Demand for Animal Feed, an Econometric Analysis," doctoral dissertation, University of Minnesota, 1973, p. 166.

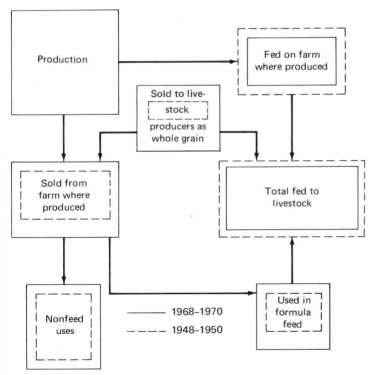

Figure 2-6 Relative change in the use of feed grains, 1948–1950 and 1968–1970. *Source:* Karl Meilke, "The Demand for Animal Feed, an Econometric Analysis," doctoral dissertation, University of Minnesota, 1973, p. 169.

Table 2-1   Production of Formula Feeds by Type of Feed, 1969

Type of feed	Tons	Percent
Complete feed		
Laying	11,263,530	19.8
Broiler	11,313,614	19.9
Turkey	2,589,016	4.5
Dairy	11,105,523	19.6
Beef[a]	11,549,963	20.3
Hog	5,832,074	10.3
Other	3,146,741	5.6
Total complete	56,800,461	100.0
Supplement feed		
Laying	1,255,544	11.1
Broiler	211,573	1.9
Turkey	275,865	2.4
Dairy	1,667,522	14.7
Beef[a]	3,338,797	29.5
Hog	4,255,335	37.6
Other	322,730	2.8
Total supplement	11,327,366	100.0

[a]Includes sheep feed.
Source: Karl Meilke, "The Demand for Animal Feed, an Econometric Analysis," doctoral dissertation, University of Minnesota, 1973, p. 169.

to terminal markets where the grains are sold into the export trade or to manufacturers of mixed feed. The relative importance of these changes are also illustrated in Figure 2-6.

Formula feed use doubled between the period 1948–1950 and 1968–1970. Formula feed manufacturing uses not only feed grains but byproducts of milling and oilseed processors. Dairy farms, beef feeders, hog producers, and poultry producers are all important users of mixed feed (see Table 2-1). Formula feeds account for about 44 percent of complete mixed and 15 percent of supplements.[4] They account for nearly 100 percent of total poultry feed.[5]

The structure of the feed manufacturing and distribution system is somewhat difficult to identify. Specialized feed manufacturers are common but many are diversified into livestock and poultry feeding, other grain merchandising and processing, and various kinds of farm supply, wholesaling, and retailing. With the exception of the integrated feeder operations, most mixed feeds move from the manufacturer through a local dealer or feed handler. The local dealers provide many services associated with feed grinding and mixing farmer's feed

[4]Ibid., p. 9.
[5]Ibid., p. 14.

grain, technical and nutritional advice and financing, and other supplies and services. Farmer cooperatives are an important part of the feed manufacturing and distribution system. It is estimated that they handle about 20 percent of the commercial formula feed business.[6]

Other Farm-input Industries

In addition to machinery, fertilizer, and feed, farmers spend substantial amounts of money on other production items and facilities. Farm buildings and fencing materials constitute a large category of farm expenditures, followed by farm credit, petroleum, and pesticides. Several categories, such as hand tools and veterinary supplies, comprise the smallest expenditures. The marketing channels of these farm-input industries is beyond the scope of this chapter, but references are provided at the end.

FARMING

There are numerous characteristics of the farm sector of our economy which are relevant and have implications for marketing and pricing processes. Some characteristics will be considered here and others will be treated as we describe and develop the techniques of supply and price analysis.

A dominant feature of the farm sector of the economy is the large number of firms involved. There were 2,786,000 farms in the United States in 1976 (see Table 2-2). The number of farms has declined almost continuously during this century, but farming is still essentially a competitively organized industry.[7] Farm numbers for any given type of enterprise—livestock, dairy, wheat, etc.—would certainly be less than this, but would still be in the thousands for the major farm types.

The family-type farm also dominates in American agriculture, as indicated by Table 2-3. The table shows that 62.5 percent of all farms in 1969 were operated by the owners. Another 24.6 percent were operated by part owners for a total of 87.1 percent. The dominance of the owner-operator goes back to at least 1900. Whether this kind of structure can be maintained with the developing asset requirement for an average farm seems to be an important question. It may require some major agricultural policy decisions.

The kinds of major farm production activities differ from one region to another (Figure 2-7). Feed grain and livestock predominates in the Corn Belt, and dairying predominates in the Lake states. Obviously, the kinds and location of marketing facilities are determined in large part by these geographic patterns. Change in geographic distribution brings about change in the marketing system.

---

[6]U.S. Department of Agriculture, *The Structure of Six Farm Input Industries,* ERS-357, Economic Research Service, 1968.

[7]Data in Chapter 5 will show that farm numbers have not decreased for all size categories of farms. In fact, numbers of farms with sales in excess of $50,000 annually have increased since 1950.

Table 2-2 Farms: Number, Total Land, and Average Land per Farm, United States, 1959–1976

Year	Number of farms	Total land in farms (1,000 acres)	Average land per farm (acres)
1959	4,104,520	1,182,563	288
1960	3,962,520	1,175,646	297
1961	3,825,410	1,167,899	305
1962	3,602,410	1,159,383	314
1963	3,572,200	1,151,572	322
1964	3,456,690	1,146,106	332
1965	3,356,170	1,139,597	340
1966	3,257,040	1,131,844	348
1967	3,161,730	1,123,456	355
1968	3,070,860	1,115,231	363
1969	2,999,180	1,107,711	369
1970	2,954,200	1,102,769	373
1971	2,908,950	1,097,300	377
1972	2,869,710	1,093,017	381
1973	2,843,890	1,089,530	383
1974	2,820,570	1,086,937	384
1975	2,808,000	1,086,025	387
1976[a]	2,786,000	1,084,671	389

[a]Preliminary.
Source: Agricultural Statistics, 1974, p. 420 and SRS Supplements.

Table 2-3 Farms: Classification by Tenure of Operator, United States, 1880–1969

		Tenure of operator				
Year	Number of farms	Full owners, %	Part owners, %	Managers, %	All tenants, %	Croppers (South only), %
1880	4,008,907	...	...	...	25.6	...
1890	4,564,641	...	...	...	28.4	...
1900	5,737,372	55.8	7.9	1.0	35.3	...
1910	6,361,502	52.7	9.3	0.9	37.0	...
1920	6,448,343	52.2	8.7	1.1	38.1	17.5
1925	6,371,640	52.0	8.7	0.6	38.6	19.9
1930[a]	6,295,103	46.3	10.4	0.9	42.4	24.1
1935	6,812,350	47.1	10.1	0.7	42.1	20.9
1940[a]	6,102,417	50.6	10.1	0.6	38.8	18.0
1945	5,859,169	56.3	11.3	0.7	31.7	15.5
1950[a]	5,388,437	57.4	15.3	0.4	26.9	13.1
1954	4,782,416	57.4	18.2	0.4	24.0	11.6
1959[a]	3,710,503	57.1	22.5	0.6	19.8	7.4
1964[a]	3,157,857	57.6	24.8	0.6	17.1	...
1969[a]	2,730,250	62.5	24.6	...	12.9	...

[a]Includes Alaska and Hawaii.
Source: Agricultural Statistics, 1974, p. 422.

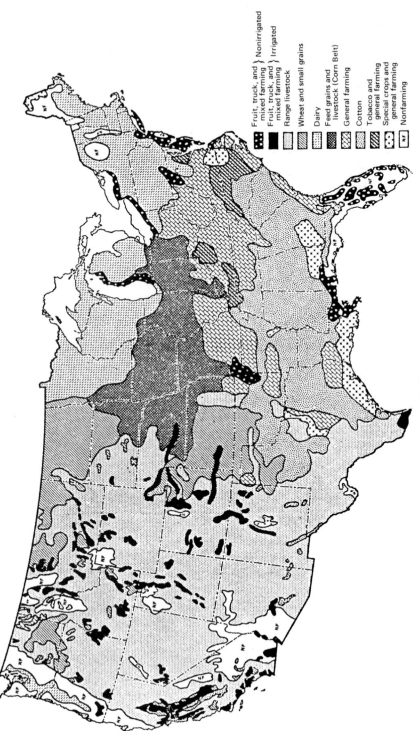

Figure 2-7 Major types of farming areas in 48 states. *Source:* W. W. Cochrane, *The City Man's Guide to the Farm Problem*, University of Minnesota Press, Minneapolis, 1965, p. 17.

Fruit, truck, and mixed farming } Nonirrigated

Fruit, truck, and mixed farming } Irrigated

Range livestock

Wheat and small grains

Dairy

Feed grains and livestock (Corn Belt)

General farming

Cotton

Tobacco and general farming

Special crops and general farming

Nonfarming

FOOD PRODUCT MARKETS

The entire food system from farmer to consumer involves a wide range of products and firms. The major groupings detailed here include the dairy industry, the livestock industry, the grain industry, and food wholesaling and retailing.

Dairy Industry

Every state in the United States produces milk. Concentration of production is greatest in the Northeast, the Lake states, and the Pacific Coast states. Total milk production has remained relatively stable since 1950. Total production was 116.6 billion pounds in 1950 and 115.6 billion pounds in 1975. Peak national production of 126.8 billion pounds occurred in 1964.

The dairy industry has two distinct major segments, each having somewhat different marketing and pricing problems. About one-half of all milk is used in fluid milk and cream products (see Table 2-4). Because of the perishability and high transport costs for these products, markets are geographically limited. Milk for most major metropolitan centers and surrounding areas is usually produced in the immediately adjacent areas. Thus, the production areas, called milksheds, are easily defined for Chicago, New York, Minneapolis-St. Paul, and other markets. Overlapping of supply areas does occur.

Almost all milk used in fluid products must meet special grade A health requirements of the state or municipality. It should be noted that although all fluid milk products must be produced from grade A milk, not all grade A milk is used in fluid products.

The other half of the nation's milk supply is used in the production of manufactured dairy products—butter, nonfat dry milk, cheese, ice cream, evaporated and condensed products, and others. The markets for these products, with the exception of ice cream, are essentially national in scope. Products from any one area can compete directly with products from any other area. The two largest manufacturing users of milk are butter-powder plants and cheese factories. Cheese, however, continues to expand relative to butter and nonfat dry milk. Manufactured products are produced from grade B milk—milk produced under less rigorous quality control than grade A—as well as from grade A milk that is in excess of fluid product demand.

Milk is assembled from farms principally by cooperatives who either deliver milk to proprietary bottlers and distributors or, in numerous instances, process and package the products themselves. Of the 39 major milk markets in the Midwest in 1960, over 80 percent of the milk emanated from cooperatively organized producers.[8] The percentage has likely increased since that time.

Heaviest concentration of manufactured dairy product production is in the Midwest, with Minnesota and Wisconsin leading in cheese, butter, and nonfat dry milk production. Cooperatives are also a dominant factor in production of

[8]Sheldon Williams et al., *Organization and Competition in the Midwest Dairy Industry,* Iowa State University Press, Ames, Iowa, 1970, p. 69.

Table 2-4 Use of Market Supply of Milk, United States, 1960–1975

Year	Fluid use	Creamery butter	Cheese American	Cheese Other	Creamed cottage cheese	Evaporated and condensed milk[a]	Dry whole milk	Frozen dairy products, net	Other factory products	Total factory products[b]	Miscellaneous[c]	Market supply of milk[d]
1960	46.5%	25.7%	8.5%	3.2%	0.9%	4.8%	0.6%	8.3%	0.4%	52.5%	1.0%	100%
1961	44.8	27.0	9.5	3.2	0.9	4.6	0.5	8.2	0.3	54.2	1.0	100
1962	44.9	27.8	9.0	3.1	0.8	4.2	0.5	8.2	0.3	54.0	1.1	100
1963	45.9	26.0	9.2	3.3	0.8	4.2	0.6	8.4	0.4	53.0	1.1	100
1964	45.6	25.9	9.5	3.5	0.8	4.2	0.5	8.5	0.5	53.5	0.9	100
1965	46.8	24.1	9.7	3.6	0.8	3.9	0.6	9.0	0.5	52.2	1.0	100
1966	47.8	20.4	10.5	3.9	0.9	4.1	0.6	9.1	0.5	50.0	2.2	100
1967	47.0	22.7	11.1	3.9	0.9	3.5	0.4	9.1	0.3	52.0	1.0	100
1968	47.6	22.1	11.3	4.2	1.0	3.5	0.5	9.8	0.4	52.5	-0.2	100
1969	47.1	21.1	11.3	4.4	1.1	3.5	0.4	9.8	0.4	52.0	0.9	100
1970	45.8	21.1	12.6	4.7	1.1	2.9	0.4	9.8	0.4	52.9	1.3	100
1971	45.0	20.8	13.1	5.0	1.1	2.8	0.4	9.6	0.5	53.5	1.5	100
1972	45.7	19.6	14.0	5.5	1.1	2.7	0.5	9.4	0.7	53.5	0.9	100
1973	46.5	16.5	14.9	6.0	1.0	2.6	0.5	9.8	0.6	52.0	1.6	100
1974	44.9	17.2	16.5	6.3	0.9	2.5	0.4	10.0	0.6	54.4	0.6	100
1975[e]	45.7	17.4	14.8	6.7	0.9	2.2	0.4	10.7	0.7	53.9	0.4	100

[a]Canned and bulk.
[b]May not add due to rounding.
[c]Minor miscellaneous uses and any inaccuracies of independently determined use items.
[d]Milk marketed by farmers, net imports of ingredients such as frozen cream, butterfat-sugar mixtures, and ice cream, and net change in storage cream.
[e]Preliminary.
Source: U.S. Department of Agriculture, *The Dairy Situation,* May 1976, p. 17.

manufactured dairy products. It was estimated that 50 percent of these products were manufactured by cooperatives in 1964.[9]

Price determination at the various levels of the marketing channels for dairy products involves a unique combination of central market price discovery, government administration of a discriminatory price system, a price support program, and individual and group negotiations. Minimum farm prices for manufacturing grade milk are established under the agricultural price support program. In all the major fluid milk markets, special administrative agencies use formulas to fix the prices that handlers must pay for milk in each of the uses. Wholesale prices for butter and cheese are determined by bids and offers on exchanges in Green Bay, Chicago, and New York. Other products are priced by negotiations between sellers and buyers. Retailers apply markup procedures to arrive at retail store prices. The impact of any firm or group of firms on the pricing process must be analyzed in the context of these various market institutions.

Livestock Industry

Meat products are the largest group of products in total consumer expenditures for domestically produced farm goods, accounting for 31 percent of all expenditures in 1973. They also accounted for the largest share of the food marketing bill (24 percent). Numerous kinds of agents are involved in providing the marketing services for meat: commission firms, brokers, feeders, slaughtering firms, specialized meat processors, food wholesalers, branch houses, the food service industry, and many others. Some agents provide marketing services for a wide range of food products; some specialize in one or a few functions for livestock and meat.

The movement of livestock from farms to the slaughtering plants is illustrated in Figure 2-8. The channels are similar for all livestock, but the data indicate the relative importance of alternative routes for slaughter cattle only. The diagram indicates that the producing sector has two major components: (1) farmers and ranchers that provide about 98 percent of all domestically slaughtered cattle, and (2) the feedlots which in 1972 finished 74 percent of all slaughter cattle. This latter segment has become more important as the industry has evolved. In 1963 only 58 percent of cattle moved through feedlots. It is very probable that the relatively low feed-grain prices which have persisted since World War II have stimulated this expansion. If recent feed-grain price increases hold, there could very well be a reversal of this trend.

Imports are a relatively minor source of slaughter cattle, accounting for 2 percent of the 1972 supply.

The channel which cattle take to the packing plants is dominated by direct country buying (72.2 percent in 1972). It is distinguished from the other two methods of sale in that the producer or feeder personally negotiates the sale. These direct sales may be made to: (1) the packing plant; (2) the buying stations of the packers; (3) the country agents of the packers; (4) country livestock

---

[9]Ibid., p. 82.

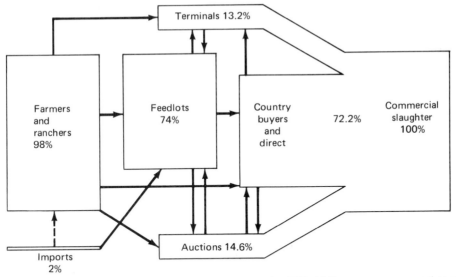

Figure 2-8 U.S. marketing channels for slaughter cattle, 1972. All figures are expressed as a percentage of the total commercial slaughter volume.

dealers; (5) order buyers, who are independent agents for other kinds of buyers who operate on a fee basis; or (6) other producers.[10]

Terminal markets, once the dominant institution for moving slaughter live-stock into the marketing process, accounted for only 13.2 percent of sales in 1972. There were 55 such markets in 1970. The once major terminal livestock market in the country, the Chicago Union Stockyards, has ceased operations. These kinds of markets are usually located at large railroad terminals and are usually adjacent to major slaughtering and packing houses. Producers ship their livestock to terminal markets where the sales are negotiated by commission firms. Buyers will be from the same groups as indicated for direct sales.

Auction markets accounted for 14.6 percent of slaughter cattle purchases in 1972. Percentages for sheep, lambs, and hogs are approximately the same. Since 1960 the sales shares for these classes have remained rather constant. The major change has been for calves, the percentage of sales through auctions increasing from 32.1 percent in 1960 to 60.7 percent in 1972.[11]

The slaughtering industry is characterized by a large number of firms. The federally inspected (FI) slaughtering plants (those inspected and therefore authorized to ship meat in interstate commerce) are geographically dispersed according to the density of livestock production. Data in Table 2-5 indicate practically no change in total plant numbers between 1963 and 1972. The table does show that the increase in numbers of FI plants is almost equal to the non-FI decrease. Undoubtedly some plants have shifted to a federally regulated status.

[10]John McCoy, *Livestock and Meat Marketing*, Avi, Westport, Conn., 1970, pp. 146–149.
[11]U.S. Department of Agriculture, *Packers and Stockyards Resume*, 1973.

Table 2-5 Number of U.S. Slaughter Plants by Type of Inspection and Size (Mar. 1, 1965–Mar. 1, 1970)

Year	Federally inspected	Nonfederally inspected			Total nonfederally inspected	All plants
		Large	Medium	Small		
1965	571	855	1,552	4,750	7,157	7,728
1970	726	567	2,596	3,845	7,008	7,734
Change 1965 to 1970 in number	155	−288	1,044	−905	−149	6
Change 1965 to 1970 in percentage	27.1	−33.9	67.3	−19.0	−2.1	0.1

Source: John McCoy, *Livestock and Meat Marketing,* Avi, Westport, Conn., 1970, p. 159.

Concentration of the meatpacking industry was once a major antitrust concern. In 1918 the five largest packers accounted for 70 percent of livestock slaughter in interstate trade. This figure had declined to 26 percent for the four largest packers in 1967 (see Table 2-6).[12] A number of factors accounted for this decrease: vigorous antitrust action that restricted the growth means of the major packers, increased direct country buying that reduced livestock volumes moving through terminal markets and therefore the quantity available to large packers, and the increased use of grading that permitted smaller packers to effectively compete. Monopoly and monopolistic practices appear much less of a threat now than in the past.

Distribution of meat and meat products from packing houses takes a number of routes. One route is to packer branch houses which are located in large population centers. McCoy reports that these houses, in addition to distribution to retail stores, do a considerable amount of breaking, processing, smoking, and curing.[13] Branch houses have decreased in importance as the large meatpackers have declined in importance. Large quantities of meat move directly from packers to the retail food chains. Chains perform many of the functions formerly provided by the branch houses. Additionally, independent wholesalers, brokers, and packer sales offices engage in moving meat to retailers and the hotel, restaurant, and institutional (HRI) trade.

Retail food stores are key agents in the channel for moving meat to households. Most sell directly to consumers but some retail stores also service the HRI trade. The HRI trade is very important in moving food to consumers. In 1969, 23.4 percent of all beef was moved into the HRI trade and 13.0 percent of all other meat moved through this channel.[14]

[12]McCoy, op. cit., p. 164.
[13]U.S. Department of Agriculture, *Separate Eating Places,* Statistical Bulletin 487, Economic Research Service, 1972, p. 7.
[14]Ibid.

Table 2-6 Census Concentration Ratios for Meat Slaughtering and Processing Firms, Industry Basis, 1947, 1954, 1958, 1963, and 1967

Year	Number of firms	Number of establishments	Value added by manufacture (million dollars)	Percentage of value added by manufacture Firms ranking			
				1–4	1–8	1–20	All firms
Meatpacking (SIC 2011)							
1947	1,999	2,154	$ 977	41	54	63	100
1954	2,228	2,367	1,397	39	51	60	100
1958	2,646	2,810	1,749	34	46	57	100
1963	2,833	2,992	1,908	31	42	54	100
1967	2,529	2,697	2,220	26	38	50	100
Meat processing (SIC 2013)							
1954	1,254	1,316	$334	16	24	35	100
1958	1,430	1,494	442	17	25	36	100
1963	1,273	1,341	563	16	23	35	100
1967	1,294	1,374	742	15	22	31	100

Source: John McCoy, *Livestock and Meat Marketing*, Avi, Westport, Conn., 1970, p. 165.

Grain Industry

The grain and oilseed economy encompasses a wide range of farm products and an even larger range of final products. Some of the establishments in the marketing channel handle a variety of products for which they are providing similar services. Country elevators are the initial sales outlet for almost all grains and oilseeds, and each handles all the grain and oilseeds produced in its assembly area. Other establishments in the channel are specialized as to commodity and function: flour milling, oilseed processing, baking, and cereal manufacturers to name a few.

Assembly   Country elevators are the principal buyers of farmer grains and oilseeds. It is estimated that approximately 90 percent of farmer soybean sales and 83 percent of farmer wheat sales are to country elevators.[15] Corn, oats, barley, sorghum, and other crops move into commercial channels largely via this route. In 1967, 6,477 country elevators were operating in the grain- and oilseed-producing regions of the United States. Table 2-7 shows that the number of elevators increased rather sharply between 1954 and 1963 and have since declined. The pattern was, at least partially, the result of the price support programs which stimulated large stockholdings by country elevators during the late 1950s; after this period, such price support programs declined.

Three types of organization patterns exist in the country elevator business: local independents (either proprietorship or corporations), local cooperatives, and line elevators (elevators that are branches of larger cooperative or corporate grain and oilseed firms). The local independents and cooperatives predominate at this level of the market.

Country elevators provide a variety of marketing services in addition to assembly from the farmer and forwarding to other buyers and users. They may clean, dry, and blend grains. Many market farm and farm supplies, such as seed, feed, fertilizer, fuel, and chemicals.

Terminal elevators and processors are the major outlet for commodities purchased by country elevators. Terminal elevators provide a variety of functions. A principal activity is the storing of commodities and the releasing of them throughout the year to the various outlets, feed manufacturers, millers, cereal and oil processors, and exporters. The holding of grains and distribution as needed throughout the year is an especially important function.

An important institution to all participants in grain marketing is the commodity exchange markets. These are places where trading occurs for the commodities. But more important, commodity exchange markets are the places where the price-making forces are evaluated in order to bring about the movements in price levels for the commodities. This institution and its operation will be considered in detail in Chapter 9.

---

[15]J. P. Houck et al., *Soybeans and Their Products,* University of Minnesota Press, Minneapolis, 1972, p. 39; and National Commission on Food Marketing, *Organization and Competition in the Milling and Baking Industry,* Technical Study 5, 1966, p. 9.

Table 2-7 Elevator Numbers in the United States

Year	Number of country elevators	Number of terminal elevators
1954	6,580	460
1958	7,000	690
1963	7,653	633
1967	6,477	767

Source: U.S. Department of Agriculture, *Market Structure of the Food Industries,* Market Research Report 971, 1972, p. 51.

Processing of Grains and Oilseeds A number of important industries process grains and oilseeds directly into consumer food and nonfood products or into products that are used in other food processing industries. Among the most important are millers, breakfast cereal manufacturers, brewers and distillers, and soybean crushers.

The number of firms, establishments, and the value of shipments for the major food-grain processing industries are listed in Table 2-8. Flour and meal millers are the largest users according to all of these measures. The National Commission on Food Marketing estimated that miller and cereal processors together utilized three-fourths of domestically used food grains and approximately one-half of total wheat production.[16]

The heaviest geographic concentration of the flour milling industry is in the North Central region of the United States; the area accounted for approximately 50 percent of total milling capacity in 1965. In this region, Minneapolis and Kansas City are the major centers of milling. Such major milling firms as International Multi-Foods, Pillsbury, and General Mills originated in the Minneapolis market.

The cereal processing industry is one of the most concentrated in American industry. Only 30 firms produced cereal preparations in 1967. The four largest of these accounted for 88 percent of industry shipment in that year (Table 2-8).[17]

The soybean processing industry is our largest domestic edible oil industry. It accounted for 80 percent of all edible oil production in 1969. Initial processing of soybeans results in two products, crude soybean oil and meal. The basic processing of soybeans is now almost exclusively a solvent extraction process. Further refining of the oil is necessary for use in other products.

The initial processing segment is controlled by a relatively small number of firms, 55 in 1970. The number of plants operated by processing firms has been essentially constant since 1961, with 131 plants in 1961 and 130 plants in 1970. Although expanding soybean production required additional crushing capacity throughout the decade, this was achieved by expansion of plant size rather than construction of new plants.

[16]National Commission on Food Marketing, op. cit., p. 1.

[17]U.S. Department of Agriculture, *Market Structure of the Food Industries,* Marketing Research Report 971, Economic Research Service, 1972, p. 27.

Table 2-8 Grain Mill Industries: Companies and Establishments, Value of Shipments, Value Added by Manufacture, and Capital Expenditures for Census Years 1954–1967

Item and Year	Grain mill industries					
	Flour and meal	Cereal prep- arations	Rice milling	Blended and prepared flour	Wet corn milling	Total
Number						
Companies						
1954	692	37	65	123	54	n.a.
1958	703	34	61	112	53	n.a.
1963	510	35	62	140	49	n.a.
1967	438	30	54	126	32	n.a.
Establishments						
1954	803	46	80	131	58	1,118
1958	814	43	72	117	59	1,105
1963	618	48	74	165	60	965
1967	541	45	68	148	45	847
Million dollars						
Value of shipments						
1954	$2,002.2	$365.7	$273.8	$267.2	$463.5	$3,372.4
1958	2,086.7	444.1	312.1	279.4	528.5	3,650.8
1963	2,176.5	625.1	423.0	434.0	622.4	4,281.0
1967	2,457.4	793.0	548.4	547.5	751.3	5,097.6

Source: U.S. Department of Agriculture, *Market Structure of the Food Industries,* Market Research Report 971, 1972, p. 53.

The Baking Industry   The commercial baking industry is the largest single user of flour in the United States. Approximately 41 percent of total wheat flour was channeled to this industry in 1965. The industry is characterized by several types of organizations: (1) wholesale bakers who produce bread and related products to sell to retail outlets, (2) grocery chain bakeries, (3) multioutlet retail bakeries, and (4) home service bakeries. The dominant organizational structure is the wholesale baker, which accounted for 86 percent of all industry shipments in 1967.[18]

Wholesaler bakers are of several business types: multistate corporations, cooperatively organized independent bakers, and independent bakers. Multistate corporations, of which there were nine in 1965, accounted for 40 percent of all commercial bread production.[19] Most of these companies trace their origin to mergers of many smaller companies in the early and mid-1920s.

The cooperative bakeries provide advantages of large-scale buying of equipment and supplies, managerial services, and common regional and national brand

[18]Calculated from data in *Market Structure of the Food Industries,* p. 56.
[19]National Commission on Food Marketing, op. cit., p. 50.

names. The independent member firms are thus in a stronger position to compete with the large corporations on a cost basis.

Grocery chain baking has been a significant factor in the market for years. Since 1958 they have accounted for approximately 10 percent of commercial bakery output. Chains undertook baking for a variety of reasons. They can substantially reduce amounts and costs of brand differentiation that are associated with the regional and national brands. The coordination of baking with demands results in less loss from stale bread. Efficiencies of bread delivery to stores and in-store handling reduce costs. The existence of chain store bakeries and the potential of additional integration has probably resulted in somewhat lower bread marketing margins that would otherwise be the case.

Food Wholesaling and Retailing

Food retailing brings together the products of dozens of market channels and industries and distributes them to the millions of households and eating establishments. With the exception of farming, food retailing has more firms than any other U.S. industry. In 1967 there were 254,469 food-store firms operating 294,243 food stores.[20] Food stores include grocery stores and specialized food stores, such as meat markets and retail bakery outlets. Grocery stores are by far the largest segment with 187,293 firms operating 218,130 retail grocery stores.[21]

The supermarket is the most significant unit in food retailing. Supermarkets, stores with more than $500,000 annual sales, account for more than 75 percent of total grocery sales even though they make up only 15 percent of store numbers. Stores with over $1 million annual sales made up 61 percent of all sales. These stores sell a complete line of food items and substantial quantities of nonfood items. It was calculated that the grocery store of the 1960s handled 6,800 items per store. Each brand or product variation is listed as an item; nevertheless, the number indicates the choices available to or required of each shopper. Nonfood items have totaled about 5 percent of supermarket sales since the mid-1950s.

Supermarkets, as well as many small grocery stores, are organized into food chains, usually defined as corporate entities that operate at least 11 stores. Grocery chains sold 50 percent of all groceries in 1967. They are usually engaged in performing the wholesaling function for many of their products, and in numerous instances they process some of their products. Chains are able to achieve many cost savings in food merchandising because of efficiency in use of equipment, wholesaling facilities, coordinating of processing, wholesaling, and retailing, and reduction of expensive product differentiation activities. Among the more widely known national chains are A & P, National, Safeway, and Kroger. A & P, the oldest chain store organization, traces its origin to the middle of the last century.

Within the chain store segment of food retailing, a few firms make the majority of the sales. The largest four have accounted for approximately 20

[20]*Market Structure of the Food Industries,* p. 92.
[21]Ibid.

percent of grocery store sales since 1954. The largest 20 chains made 40 percent of grocery sales in 1970.[22]

To more effectively compete with chain stores, independent wholesalers and retailers have affiliated to achieve some of the advantages of large-scale buying, group advertising, and other services. Two types of arrangements have developed. In some cases, independent retailers have cooperatively organized wholesale units to supply members with merchandise and services. The largest of the cooperative retailers is Certified Grocers of California. In the Midwest, Spartan Stores, headquartered in Michigan, and Fairway Foods, in St. Paul, are the largest.

Food wholesalers have affiliated with independent retailers to provide themselves with services in much the same manner as the corporate chains. These groups were developed as a response to the declining business of old line food wholesalers that were losing business to corporate chains and cooperative retailers. Many groups were organized in the 1920s and 1930s. IGA (Independent Grocers Alliance) and Red and White are two of the largest wholesale-sponsored retail groups. The wholesale-sponsored group together with the cooperative groups accounted for 45 percent of all grocery stores sales in 1970.[23]

Private-label merchandising under the retailer's own brand name is a common merchandising practice of food stores of all types. It is widely used for bakery products, dairy products, frozen fruits and vegetables, processed meats, coffee, and canned fruits and vegetables. The private-label product may be processed and packaged in the retailer's own manufacturing facilities or the retailer may contract with independent food processors to package under the retailer's own brand. In either case, one advantage of private labeling is that brand loyalty is transferred from the manufacturer to the retailer.

FIBER PRODUCTS MARKET

The major nonfood commodities produced by farmers include the cotton and wool fibers used in garment manufacturing and tobacco. This section briefly describes the structure of the cotton and tobacco industries in the United States.

The Cotton Industry

The market structure of the cotton industry is quite complex. Nearly 500,000 farmers produce cotton throughout the United States and sell it to ginning mills located in or near the production areas. Because of a substantial government price support program, a large portion of cotton produced by farmers becomes owned by the government through their Commodity Credit Corporation. Cotton merchants and warehousemen buy the cotton from local ginning mills and the government and sell it to the milling industry exporting to foreign countries and to various industries for intermediate productive activities (see Figure 2-9).

[22]Ibid., p. 96.
[23]Ibid.

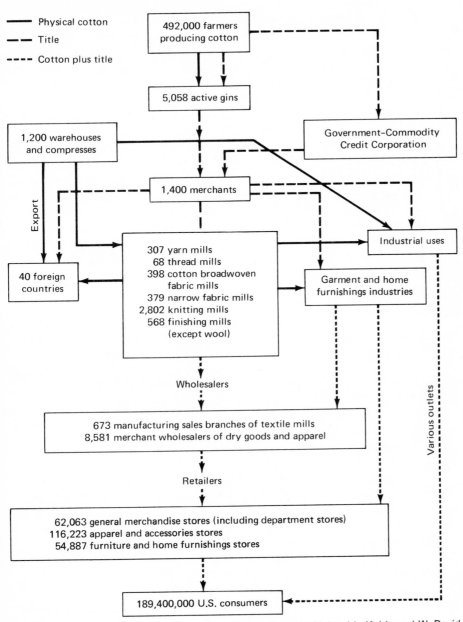

Figure 2-9 Market structure of the cotton industry. *Source:* Richard L. Kohls and W. David Downey, *Marketing of Agricultural Products,* 4th ed., Macmillan, New York, 1972.

Textile fabric production processes usually involve three stages: fiber preparation, yarn spinning and dying, and the weaving or braiding of yarn into gray or unfinished fabric to produce finished goods ready for cutting. Some degree of vertical integration is present in fabric manufacture but a substantial part of this industry is made up of independent dye processors and "converters." Independent dye manufacturers engage in custom dying services for yarn and fabric producers but converters buy the finished cloth and sell it to garment manufacturers and industrial users.

There also exists a substantial wholesaling and retailing industry substructure that handles different types of clothing. Clothing wholesalers sell to a broad range of retail establishments, including not only traditional ladies' and men's wear but also a large number of variety stores that handle many other kinds of consumer products as well.

An important adjunct to the cotton industry is the production of cotton seed which is rendered to produce oils and cotton seed meal. The oils are utilized for industrial purposes and for food industrial production processes, and the meal is largely consumed by livestock as feed.

The Tobacco Industry

Tobacco is a highly differentiated product in that each classification of tobacco has distinctive characteristics and uses. The classifications are based largely upon the type of curing process and the type of market to which the product will be directed. There are flu-cured, fire-cured, and air-cured tobaccos which are primarily used for cigarettes. There is tobacco classified as fillers, binders, and wrappers that are employed largely in cigar manufacture.

The government price support program plays an active role in tobacco marketing. Tobacco is produced on relatively small acreage plots and sold at local warehouses that use an auction sales method. Tobacco manufacturers walk, as a group, down the rows of tobacco at the warehouses and bid according to their needs. Tobacco not sold to the manufacturers is sold to the government Commodity Credit Corporation, which in turn sells it to exporters and manufacturers at a later stage. In addition to manufacturers' representatives, there are dealers and speculators in tobacco who buy at the local warehouse and later sell in the export or local manufacturing market (see Figure 2-10).

GOVERNMENT AND AGRICULTURE

Federal, state, and local governments are involved in the legislation and administration of a vast set of statutes, ordinances, and rules that restrict or facilitate the organization and operation of the food and fiber system. At the federal level, the U.S. Department of Agriculture (USDA) and the Food and Drug Administration (FDA) of the Department of Health, Education, and Welfare play major administrative roles. At the state level, there are similar governmental units that deal with the many "food laws" that are designed to protect consumers and farmers and to facilitate or restrain the processing and distribution practices of farmers

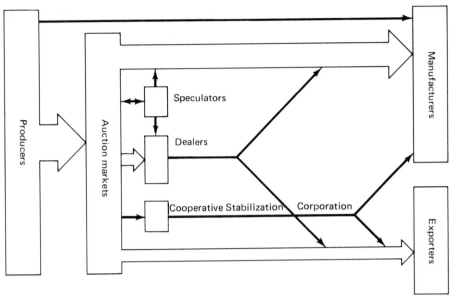

Figure 2-10   Tobacco marketing channels. *Source:* Richard L. Kohls and W. David Downey, *Marketing of Agricultural Products,* 4th ed., Macmillan, New York, 1972.

and middlemen. At county, city, and village levels, various organizations exist to further protect the health of the citizens and to discourage marketing abuses.

While it is impossible to neatly categorize these laws, the following grouping may be illustrative of the scope of this segment of the law: (1) agricultural price and income policies, (2) consumer protection laws, (3) agricultural tax and land use policies, (4) farm labor laws, (5) antitrust laws and the agricultural exemptions, (6) food industry regulations, (7) agricultural business organization legislation, and (8) agricultural research and extension policies.

The agricultural price and income policies of the federal government include the popular "price support" activities of the USDA as well as such income-supporting mechanisms as the food stamp plan, the school lunch program, and food dispositions to welfare recipients. Substantial bureaucratic structures exist at federal, state, and local levels to administer these programs.

The FDA works at national and regional levels to inspect food supplies and to assure quality standards. Also, the FDA administers labeling requirements for food products. The Federal Trade Commission (FTC) assures the consumer that product advertising is not fraudulent. Several agencies in the USDA offer inspection services for specific farm products to assure product quality.

The tendencies of farm incomes to exhibit "boom or bust" proportions has led to special income and property tax legislation for farmers at federal and state levels. Farmers are provided with certain opportunities to adjust their tax burdens and equalize them over time.

Land use policies are intimately bound up with environmental protection laws and the need for more space by urban dwellers and business units. Zoning and land use policies exist at federal, state, and local levels.

Farm labor, once primarily provided by farm family members, is increasingly provided by workers who specialize in this type of employment. Similar to other employees, they demand unemployment compensation privileges, union status, work safety, fringe benefits, and adequate wages. Accordingly, there has been a substantial increase in legislation and governmental activities for the farm laborer in recent years.

The antitrust laws of the United States are designed to limit the abuses of power by business in their pricing and marketing practices. Consumers are permitted to join in "class actions" to halt abuses by business organizations that violate U.S. antitrust policies. Legislatively, farmers and consumers have been regarded as the "oppressed" and have been accorded special exemptions and privileges in relation to these laws. In order to organize supply and marketing cooperatives, farmers were granted a conditional exemption from the antitrust laws. Under certain conditions, legislation has permitted farmers to fix prices and engage in collusive behavior for the purpose of protecting their income position.

Numerous food industry regulations exist at all levels of government. These laws regulate quantity and quality standards, require licensing of marketing firms to assure financial and technical capability, and establish rules for manufacturing and trading that assure "fairness" in business transactions. Other laws authorize the USDA and other governmental organizations to collect, summarize, and disseminate information about the operation of the food system through market reports, current price and quantity data, and special studies of different segments of the system.

Laws exist, most commonly at state levels, which restrict the type of business organizations that can engage in farming activities. The so-called anti-corporate farming laws usually permit the family farmer to operate his or her farm as a corporation, but the laws are designed to prevent large nonfarm business interests from entering and controlling farming activities.

Through the establishment of *land-grant colleges* and USDA research activities, the federal and state governments play a major role in carrying out agricultural research and extending the results to farmers so that they may incorporate them into the farming practices. Land-grant universities have resident colleges of agriculture, agricultural experiment stations, and a county-staffed agricultural extension service that reaches farmers throughout the United States.

SUMMARY

The food and fiber system in the United States is vast and complex. It includes (1) the farm-input markets, (2) farming, (3) the food product markets, (4) the fiber product markets, and (5) the governmental sector that relates to the food and fiber system.

The farm-input markets are dominated by the manufacture and distribution of farm machinery, fertilizer, and feed. Each has specialized marketing channels to reach the farmer customer. The farming component consists of nearly three million farms spread across the entire United States. The farms are quite specialized and vary in size and productivity.

The major food product markets include (1) the dairy industry, (2) the livestock industry, (3) the grain industry, and (4) the food wholesaling and retailing industry. These food industries vary in their structure, but each are involved in assembling, processing, storing, transporting, and distributing food products from farmer to consumer.

The major fiber product markets include cotton and wool as major sub-units. The cotton industry is complexly structured and includes moving and transferring cotton from the farm into clothing and industrial products at consumer and industrial levels. Tobacco, from its harvested state to cigarettes and cigar consumption, is a major industry in the southeastern part of the United States.

The government plays a major role in regulating the entire food system. Its laws have many purposes, including the assurance of healthful and safe foods, prevention of exploitation of consumers and farmers, price and income support, and technological progressiveness in the food and fiber industries.

QUESTIONS

1 Select a food product or food group and describe the processes and agencies involved in moving the product from farm gate to the ultimate consumer. Obtain estimates of the value of the farm product and the marketing costs in the final retail price.
2 Distinguish between purchased and nonpurchased farm inputs. What have been the trends in their relative importance in terms of total farm inputs? What has accounted for the divergent patterns?
3 What are the alternative methods of sale used by farmers in selling cattle? What is the relative importance of each method?
4 What kinds of organizations have developed in the food wholesaling and retailing industry to offset the market power and efficiencies of the large corporate food chains?

BIBLIOGRAPHY

Cochrane, Willard W.: *The City Man's Guide to the Farm Problem,* University of Minnesota Press, Minneapolis, 1965.
Houck, J. P., et al.: *Soybeans and Their Products,* University of Minnesota Press, Minneapolis, 1972.
Kohls, Richard L., and W. David Downey: *Marketing of Agricultural Products,* 4th ed., Macmillan, New York, 1972.
McCoy, John: *Livestock and Meat Marketing,* Avi, Westport, Conn., 1970.

Meilke, Karl: "The Demand for Animal Feed, an Econometric Analysis," doctoral dissertation, University of Minnesota, 1973.

National Commission on Food Marketing: *Organization and Competition in the Milling and Baking Industry,* Technical Study 5, 1966.

Statistical Abstract of the United States, 1973.

U.S. Bureau of the Census: *1967 Census of Manufacturers* and *1967 Census of Business.*

U.S. Department of Agriculture: *Market Structure of the Food Industries,* Marketing Research Report 971, Economic Research Service, 1972.

——: *Packers and Stockyards Resume,* 1973.

——: *Separate Eating Places,* Statistical Bulletin 487, Economic Research Service, 1972.

——: *The Structure of Six Farm Input Industries,* ERS-357, Economic Research Service, 1968.

Williams, Sheldon, et al.: *Organization and Competition in the Midwest Dairy Industry,* Iowa State University Press, Ames, Iowa, 1970.

The Tools of Analysis

Although price and market analysis has economic theory as its foundation, data and various mathematical and statistical tools are necessary to apply the theory to problems and/or policy formulation. Regardless of whether we are concerned with describing all or part of the marketing system, analyzing dimensions of its structure and behavior, or prescribing business and government policies, we deal with numbers. The numbers may be prices, product quantities, wages, or profits, to name a few. These numbers must be expressed in summary form and usually need to be related to other numbers for descriptive or analytical purposes.

To understand the market and pricing system for farm foods and fibers, we must therefore have an understanding of basic economic theory and certain quantitative methods. The economic theory appropriate to each of the remaining chapters in this book is reviewed at the outset or as a part of each chapter. This chapter is devoted to a review of selected quantitative methods used in market and price analysis. These include (1) some accounting concepts, (2) certain mathematical notions, and (3) basic statistical measures and techniques.

MARKETING ACCOUNTING

A major concern of accounting is the construction of useful categories of financial and related business data to provide the business executive with information relevant to his or her decision making. As we readily appreciate in our personal financial situation, it is important to keep track of our income, expenditures, indebtedness, and saving for both short-term and longer-run goals. Business similarly keeps track of these items through rather standard systems of accounting. State and national governments can and do keep accounts on state and national economic activity.

In account construction, we often specify *equalities* between accounting categories. For example, in the absence of borrowing and saving, our income *must identically equal* our spending. Why? Because, in this simple example, we cannot spend more than we receive in income, yet we will spend it all. In mathematical notation, we might say that

$$Y = E$$

where Y represents income and E stands for spending. Because $Y = E$ in all cases, we refer to this equation as an *accounting identity*.

Still in the absence of borrowing or saving, we may want to subdivide the income and spending categories into subcategories or accounts. With regard to income, we may subdivide it into: (1) a wage account, our income from working for a company; (2) an interest account, our income from some corporate bonds we hold; and (3) a rental account, our income from a dwelling we own and lease to tenants. If these are our only sources of income, we can express another accounting identity

$$Y = W + I + R$$

where W, I, and R refer to each of the income accounts listed above. Similarly, we may wish to subdivide (or construct accounts) regarding our spending.

We can also withdraw our *assumption* concerning no borrowing and no saving, which complicates our accounting framework some, but now we are coming closer to more realistic accounting practices. Most people, firms, and governments borrow money, and therefore we must develop accounts that reflect this in our system of accounting identities. Furthermore, most entities own homes (or have part ownership until a mortgage is retired), business equipment and facilities, and so forth. In addition, individuals and businesses (and occasionally, governments) *save* that surplus of income over current expenditures.

It immediately becomes clear that a complete accounting system for a household, business, or governmental unit can be very complex. But it is not the purpose of accountants to add to the difficulty of understanding our financial situation or any of those things that bear upon it. Rather, accounting attempts to simplify, by categorizing and summarizing, business data that would otherwise be almost incomprehensible.

Years of experience with all types of decision-making units have permitted accountants to develop basic "statements" that provide valuable information to consumers, business executives and government officials. The two most commonly used accounting statements are the balance sheet and the income statement.

The Balance Sheet

The essential characteristic of the balance sheet is its presentation of a "still picture" of how assets are equated (identically) with liabilities and net worth. Let us use the so-called balance sheet of agriculture as our example.

This balance sheet is an aggregation for the entire farming sector, not for merely a single farm firm.[1] The asset side of the balance sheet lists all resources owned and used in farming, such as farm land, buildings, livestock, machinery, equipment, and inventories. The closely related assets necessary for farming operations, such as household furnishings, financial reserves, and investments in cooperative associations, are also included. The liability side of the balance sheet lists total debt secured by farm real estate, non–real estate debts attributable to farming operations, and Commodity Credit Corporation loans to farmers. The equity item on the balance sheet is the difference between total assets and total liabilities.

The balance sheet of agriculture includes the farm assets and farm-related debts of nonfarm landlords. It does not include the nonfarm assets or nonfarm debts of this group. It also excludes farmers' investments in nonfarm businesses, life insurance cash values, and deposits in savings and loan associations.

Assets and liabilities of some agricultural enterprises are partially included and partially excluded. In broiler production, broilers not owned by the farmer are excluded. However, equipment, land, and facilities used in broiler production and owned or leased by the landlord are included in farm assets.

The specific accounts used in summarizing this financial information are shown, *as of January 1,* for selected years from 1940 to 1976 in Table 3-1. Note that farmers' assets are primarily in the form of real estate, valued on January 1, 1976, at more than one-half trillion dollars![2] In terms of our earlier stated accounting equation, assets of $589.8 billion identically equal liabilities of $90.7 billion plus farm net worth (proprietors' equities) of $499.1 billion that year.

The balance sheets on January 1 for each year are presented graphically in Figure 3-1. In this illustration we are able to see how balance sheets compare over time.

The Income Statement

An income statement, unlike the balance sheet, provides financial information on operations of the business *over a period of time.* The basic accounting identity is that profits (or losses) for a time period will exactly equal the total revenues gained minus total costs incurred for that period. In aggregate farm accounting, there are two kinds of income statements. One account system considers farm-

[1]This description of the balance sheet is based on U.S. Department of Agriculture, *Major Statistical Series of the U.S. Department of Agriculture: How They Are Constructed and Used,* vol. 6, *Land Values and Farm Finance,* Agricultural Handbook 365, Apr. 1971, p. 2.

[2]An interesting sidelight is that total farm assets far exceed the combined assets of all other manufacturing industries in the United States.

Table 3-1   Balance Sheet of Farming Sector in Billion Dollars, January 1, for Selected Years 1940–1976

Item	1940	1950	1960	1970[a]	1975[a]	1976[a,b]	Change 1975 to 1976	Change 1975 to 1976[c]
Assets								
Physical assets								
Real estate	$33.6	$ 75.3	$130.2	$206.1	$371.1	$422.3	$51.2	13.8%
Non-real estate								
Livestock and poultry	5.1	12.9	15.2	23.3	24.6	29.5	4.9	20.1
Machinery and motor vehicles	3.1	12.2	22.7	31.9	55.8	69.0	13.2	23.7
Crops stored on and off farms[d]	2.7	7.6	7.7	10.9	23.2	20.7	-2.5	-10.8
Household equipment and furnishings	4.2	8.6	9.6	10.1	15.4	17.0	1.6	10.2
Financial assets								
Deposits and currency	3.2	9.1	9.2	11.9	15.0	15.3	0.3	1.7
U.S. savings bonds	0.2	4.7	4.7	3.7	4.3	4.4	0.1	1.0
Investments in cooperatives	0.8	2.1	4.2	7.2	10.5	11.6	1.1	9.8
Total	$52.9	$132.5	$203.5	$305.1	$519.9	$589.8	$69.9	13.4%
Claims								
Liabilities								
Real estate debt	$ 6.6	$ 5.6	$ 12.1	$ 28.4	$ 46.3	$ 51.9	$ 5.6	12.1%
Non-real estate debt								
Excluding CCC loans	3.0	5.1	11.6	27.0	35.2	38.4	3.2	9.0
CCC loans[e]	0.4	1.7	1.1	2.7	0.3	0.4	0.1	12.1
Total liabilities	10.0	12.4	24.8	58.1	81.8	90.7	8.9	10.8
Proprietors' equities	42.9	120.1	178.7	247.0	438.1	499.1	61.0	13.9
Total	$52.9	$132.5	$203.5	$305.1	$519.9	$589.8	$69.9	13.4%
Debt to asset ratio (percent)[c]	18.9	9.4	12.2	19.0	15.7	15.4	...	...

[a]Includes Alaska and Hawaii.
[b]Preliminary.
[c]Computed from unrounded data.
[d]All crops held on farms, including crops under loan to CCC and crops held off farms as security for CCC loans. On January 1, 1973 the latter totaled $534 million.
[e]Nonrecourse CCC loans secured by crops owned by farmers. These crops are included as assets in this balance sheet.
Source: U.S. Department of Agriculture, *Balance Sheet of the Farming Sector, Supplement No. 1,* Agricultural Information Bulletin No. 389, Economic Research Service, April 1976, p. 2.

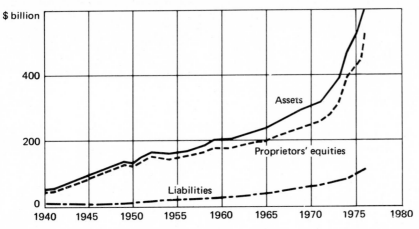

Figure 3-1 Balance sheet of the farming sector. Data are provided for 48 states through 1968 and for 50 states beginning in 1969; the 1976 data are preliminary. *Source:* Economic Research Service, U.S. Department of Agriculture.

ing as a business or industry and treats all U.S. farms as though they are a single farm. It measures gross farm income and production expenses. The difference is net income of farm operators. It is the return for several factors— their own labor (including unpaid labor), management, and capital investment in their farms and equipment. The second income account concept is personal income of the farm population. It includes income from both farm and nonfarm sources for people who live on farms. It measures incomes of farm laborers and persons living on farms, as well as farm operators.[3]

The farm income estimates are reported on an annual basis for the nation, for regions, and by states. Personal income estimates are reported only for the nation.

Table 3-2 provides an example of an aggregate farm income statement for the United States for selected recent years. Note the handling of the income accounts. Added together are cash receipts from farm marketings, government payments to farmers, and the value of home-consumed farm products and farm-dwelling rental values. The total is called *realized gross farm income* and is similar to our accounting term *total revenue*. Farm production expenses (like *total cost*) and inventory reductions are subtracted to provide a value called *net farm income*. Net farm income, however, is not equivalent to *profits* in general accounting terminology. This is the case because farmers usually do not value the time of their own (and their families') management and labor input, nor do they fully value the equivalent rental of their land and production buildings or the interest-earning value of their equity capital used in farming. A graphic representation of the farm income statement is presented in Figure 3-2.

[3]U.S. Department of Agriculture, *Major Statistical Series of the U.S. Department of Agriculture: How They Are Constructed and Used*, vol. 3, *Gross and Net Farm Income*, Agricultural Handbook 365, p. 1.

Table 3-2 Farm Income Components in Billions of Dollars, 1965–1975

Year	Marketing receipts	Government payments	Nonmoney and other income	Realized gross	Production expenses	Realized ne
1965	$39.4	$2.5	$3.6	$45.5	$33.5	$12.0
1966	43.4	3.3	3.9	50.6	36.4	14.1
1967	42.8	3.1	4.0	49.9	38.3	11.6
1968	44.2	3.5	4.0	51.7	39.5	12.2
1969	48.2	3.8	4.3	56.3	42.2	14.2
1970	50.5	3.7	4.4	58.6	44.6	14.0
1971	52.9	3.1	4.6	60.6	47.6	13.0
1972	61.0	4.0	4.9	69.9	52.4	17.5
1973	86.9	2.6	5.8	95.3	65.8	29.5
1974	93.5	0.5	7.1	101.1	73.4	27.7
1975	90.6	—	8.6	99.2	75.5	23.7

Note: Details may not add to totals due to rounding.
Source: U.S. Department of Agriculture, *1975 Handbook of Agricultural Charts*, Agricultural Handbook
491, Oct. 1975, p. 4 and *Agricultural Outlook*, AO—10, May 1976, p. 18.

The Supply and Utilization of Farm Commodities

Another frequently used accounting method in agricultural economics is to
balance total farm product supplies with total utilization.[4] The accounting equation used is:

[4]An important value of supply utilization tables is that they provide a quick and general view of
the sources of given products as well as total domestic and export uses.

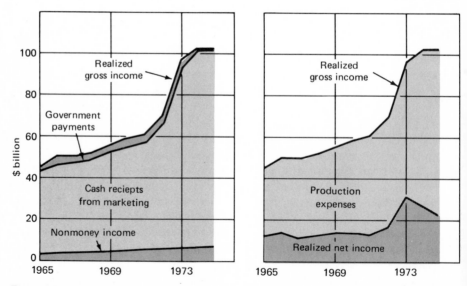

Figure 3-2 Farm income components. *Source:* Economic Research Service, U.S. Department
of Agriculture.

Net U.S. production + imports + stock change = food use
+ net nonfarm use + exports

This is referred to as the *supply utilization* accounting equation and is annually measured for major farm products and for each major product category. This marketing accounting equation combines the features of the balance sheet and financial statement techniques. Net farm production, imports, exports, and nonfarm use are measured over the year, but stock change is the estimated difference in stock levels as of January 1 in one year as compared to stock levels on January 1 of the following year.

Table 3-3 and Figures 3-3 and 3-4 show the supply utilization for U.S. food from 1960 to 1975. A significant conclusion provided by these data is that the United States is highly self-sufficient in food production relative to its uses.

MATHEMATICAL AND STATISTICAL CONCEPTS

Most students become acquainted with a number of elementary but fundamental mathematical ideas in the first few years of primary school. And these ideas are repeated and expanded upon through secondary schooling and into college.

Despite this exposure, many students "draw a blank" when they encounter mathematical statements in algebraic or geometric form. But the elementary mathematics used in this text should not cause concern for most students. To ensure this attitude, we will briefly review some elementary mathematical and statistical notions, using marketing and price economics for examples. We will discuss sets, simple graphics, averages, functions, slope, and equations.

Virtually everything can be classified into categories called *sets*. Those entities, elements, or factors included in a set have similar definitional characteristics. For example, we might regard all retail prices (prices paid by U.S. consumers) as a set. If we wanted to further subdivide our prices into prices of food, clothing, and so forth, retail food prices would be referred to as a *subset* of all retail prices. Similar subdividing can obviously result in subsets of subsets to the limit of reasonable use.

Sets or subsets also may be called *variables* or *constants,* depending upon whether characteristics of the entities or elements are capable of measurement, and these are capable of change and do, in fact, change. If the retail price of milk, for example, never changes (at least does not change during the period covered by our study), it would be regarded as a *constant*. If it did change, we would call it a *variable*. Since we have observed that the retail milk price changes over time, we would conclude that it is a *variable*.[5]

Having selected prices of a given product, for example, retail milk, what is the "makeup" of this subset? Presumably, it could include an exceedingly vast

[5]It should be observed that whether a set is a variable or a constant is intimately related to *time*. At a point in time, there are no variables, only constants. As we expand our time consideration from an instant to a minute, an hour, a day, a month, a year, and a decade, more and more constants become variables.

Table 3-3 Sources and Uses of Food Commodities in Billion Dollars, 1965–1975[a]

| | Sources | | | | Uses | | |
Year	Net production	Imports[b]	Stock change[c]	Total net utilization	Food use	Net nonfood use[d]	Exports[e]
1965	29.5	3.2	-0.2	32.5	27.4	0.9	4.2
1966	29.1	3.5	0.8	33.4	27.9	1.0	4.5
1967	31.4	3.5	-1.1	33.8	28.8	1.0	4.0
1968	31.5	3.9	-0.9	34.5	29.5	1.0	4.0
1969	31.6	3.5	-0.5	34.6	29.9	0.9	3.8
1970	30.9	3.7	1.1	35.7	30.2	0.9	4.6
1971	33.9	3.9	-1.4	36.4	31.0	0.9	4.5
1972	32.9	4.0	0.6	37.5	31.1	0.9	5.5
1973	33.6	4.1	0.8	38.5	30.3	1.0	7.2
1974	32.9	4.0	1.3	38.2	31.0	1.0	6.2
1975[f]	37.0	3.5	-2.5	40.5	38.0	1.0	6.4

[a]Quantities weighted by constant 1957–1959 farm prices. Domestic use allocated on the basis of value of processed products. Includes essentially all commodities having any U.S. food use.
[b]Includes shipments from U.S. territories.
[c]Farm (other than live animals), commercial, and government program holdings. Negatives indicate stock increases; positives signify withdrawals.
[d]Feed and seed use omitted from total commodities to avoid double counting of use through livestock.
[e]Includes shipments to U.S. territories.
[f]Preliminary.
Source: U.S. Department of Agriculture, 1975 Handbook of Agricultural Charts, Agricultural Handbook No. 491, Oct. 1975, p. 38.

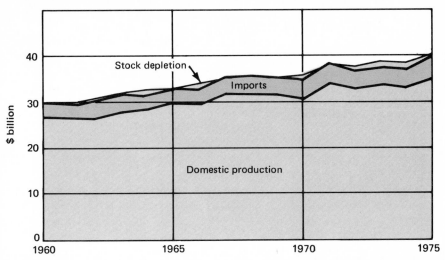

Figure 3-3 Sources of U.S. food. Dollar figures are based upon 1957–1959 farm prices. The import figures include shipments from U.S. territories, and the domestic production figures exclude feed, seed, and change in the live animal inventory. Data for 1975 are preliminary. *Source:* Economic Research Service, U.S. Department of Agriculture.

listing of individually observed and recorded prices in many retail markets. Thus, we may wish to further divide our subset so that we concern ourselves only with observed retail prices for milk of 2 percent butterfat in quart containers in St. Paul, Minnesota, during the first 15 days of January 1974. Even the collection of this more modest list of prices would be a major undertaking.[6]

Once the prices are in our subset, we must summarize this information to make it meaningful in any context. We could, for example, average the prices and/or report a range of observed values on a day-to-day basis. But even this seemingly simple procedure is beset with questions for us to answer. Should we report the most frequently observed price (the *mode*) or that price at the center of the *array* of prices from lowest to highest (the *median*)? Or should we add up the prices and divide by the number of our observations (the *mean*)? If we decide to calculate a mean average, should we somehow indicate the importance of observed prices by reflecting the quantities sold at each price (a *weighted average*)? The answers to these questions depend upon what our informational needs are—the kind of analysis we have in mind.

We could represent these prices *graphically,* as illustrated in Figure 3-5. Notice that *each* dot represents an observed (and recorded) price for a particular day in the month of January. The dot is called a *coordinate* and is identified by referring to the price and the day.

Prices are recorded on the vertical dimension of the graph (the *ordinate*) and days are recorded on the horizontal line (the *abscissa*). The same information

---

[6]A much more sensible approach would be to obtain a *sample* of these prices. We have done this here. But we will leave discussion of "sampling" to the following section of this chapter on statistical techniques.

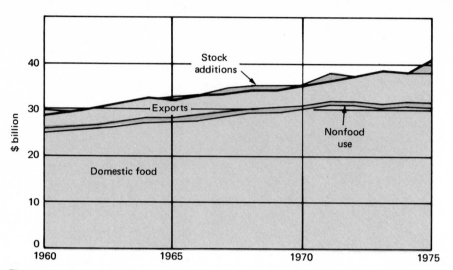

Figure 3-4 Uses of U.S. food products. Dollar figures are based upon 1957–1959 farm prices. Domestic food figures include military use, and nonfood use excludes feed, seed, and change in the live animal inventory. Data for 1975 are preliminary. *Source:* Economic Research Service, U.S. Department of Agriculture.

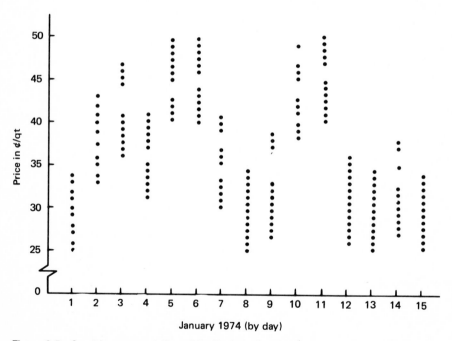

Figure 3-5 Graphic representation of St. Paul retail milk prices.

Table 3-4   St. Paul Retail Milk Prices

Date	Prices (¢/qt)				
	25–29	30–34	35–39	40–44	45–50
1	10	10			
2		2	4	4	
3			4	3	3
4		4	4	2	
5				4	6
6				5	5
7		4	5	1	
8	5	5			
9	3	4	3		
10			2	4	4
11				5	5
12	4	4	2		
13	5	5			
14	4	2	4		
15	5	5			
Σ	36	45	28	28	23

could be listed in tabular form. If this was done, we might find it convenient to aggregate our price information somewhat. For example, we could record our prices in groups or classes: the number of observed prices from 25 to 29 cents per quart, the number of prices from 30 to 34 cents per quart, and so forth. Organized in this manner, our table could be reduced to the last row of entries listed in Table 3-4.

It should be clear that we could have organized our prices into *classes* for graphical representation as well. But if we did this, we would have to make a choice. We could either represent *a price per class* for each day or we could compare price classes and the number of price observations per class.[7]

Usually, a price chosen to represent a class is the *midpoint* of the class. Since our classes are five cents in range (or *class interval*), the midpoints would be 27.5, 32.5, 37.5, 42.5, and 47.5 cents.[8] Representing midpoints of price classes would produce a graph similar to Figure 3-5 (with fewer dots), but this representation would provide little new or useful information.

If we selected the second procedure (price classes and number of price observations per class) to represent our price data, we could merely reverse the price class designation of our vertical axis to the horizontal axis and record number of price observations per class on the vertical axis. In the new graph, we could "lump together" the price observations for the entire 15-day period and record the information as in Figure 3-6.

The price data representation in Figure 3-6 is called a *frequency distribution*.

---

[7] Unless we wanted to use a three-dimensional graph.
[8] More precisely, the midpoints are 27.49999, 32.49999, and so forth.

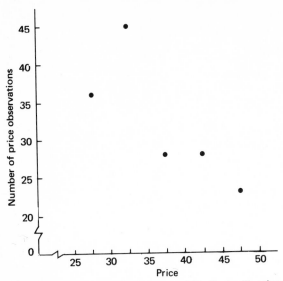

Figure 3-6 Frequency distribution of St. Paul milk prices.

In fact, it shows graphically how frequently (number of times) a price was recorded during the 15-day period in each price class. It should be clear that it was not necessary to record our prices in classes. Rather, we could merely have listed the frequency of our observation of each price recorded.

Another method for recording and representing the same data would be to show how the retail price of milk compares to the quantity of milk purchased from January 1 to January 15, 1974, in St. Paul. If we did so, we might see our data (coordinates) follow the graphical pattern shown in Figure 3-7.

You should recall from your principles of economics that this graphing of our data is *suggestive* of a *price-quantity relationship* called a *demand function*. You should be careful at this point, however, because this pattern may or may not represent a true demand function. Why? Because we must first define more precisely what economists mean by the concept of demand. And prior to the definition of demand, we must make explicit what is meant by the term *function*.

We said earlier that a variable is a set or subset which has a measurable characteristic that changes over the period of our observation of the characteristic. Such variables (like constants) may be stated in descriptive terms (milk prices), or they may be referred to in "shorthand" by a *symbol*. The symbol can be nearly anything, but frequently it is a letter of the English or Greek alphabet. For the milk prices in our example, let us use p as our symbol. This means that p will refer to "price of 2 percent butterfat milk in quart containers sold in St. Paul, Minnesota, during the period of January 1 to 15, 1974."

In Figure 3-7, we represented these prices on the ordinate axis and "the quantity or number of quarts of 2 percent butterfat milk sold in St. Paul during

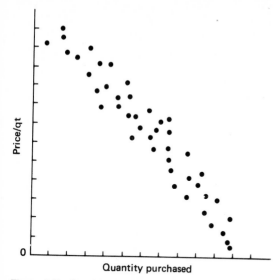

Figure 3-7 Graphic representation of retail price of milk in comparison to the quantity of milk purchased.

the period January 1 to 15, 1974," on the abscissa. Let us symbolically abbreviate this quantity by q.[9]

Are p and q somehow related? The data in Figure 3-7 suggest that at high prices lesser quantities were purchased, and at lower prices greater quantities were purchased. We might conclude that p *is related to* q in terms of the purchasing behavior of St. Paulites. If this is true, it would be called a *behavioral relationship*.

A relationship between these two variables could be expressed in general mathematical notation without expressing the exact relationship or correspondence. If we have information that causes us to believe that the value of q is related to (or determined by) p, the relationship could be expressed as $q = f(p)$. This does not mean that f is multiplied by p but rather that q is a function of p. A common distinction is that the variable in the parentheses is the independent variable and the other variable is the dependent variable. The value of the dependent variable is said to be determined by the value of the independent variable. Additional variables could be included in the parentheses, meaning that those included jointly determine the value of the dependent variable.

If the exact relationship between the variables is known, it can be stated in the form of an equation. In explicit form, it might appear as follows:

[9]It should be clear to the careful reader who has some mathematical background that a variable or constant need not be a set, but can be a measurable characteristic of a set, depending on how we define the set. In our example, we could define the set as all 2 percent butterfat milk in quarts purchased in St. Paul from January 1 to 15, 1974. The price, number of quarts, etc., are measured characteristics of this set.

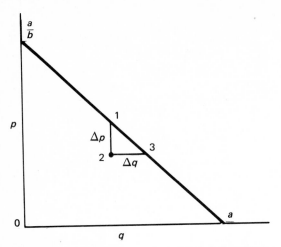

Figure 3-8 Graph of the mathematical relationship $q = a - bp$.

$$q = a - bp$$

The a, the minus sign ($-$), and the b have permitted us to make the general functional form $q = f(p)$ *explicit*. The a, which is the *intercept*, is the value of q when p equals zero. And b is the change that occurs in q as p changes. With the explicit equation, the value of q can be calculated for any value of p.

We might even observe that some limits to the relation exist. For price-quantity relationships, the limits could be that at some extremely high price no one in St. Paul would buy even a single quart of milk; at the other limiting extreme, if the price of milk were zero, St. Paulites would take milk in some very large, but specific, quantity. If we knew these limits, we could expand our mathematical expressions to reflect them. It could also be merely stated that neither price nor quantity can take on negative values.

The algebraic relationship can also be illustrated graphically. The mathematical relationship $q = a - bp$ is graphed in Figure 3-8. As mentioned previously, at some very high price a/b, no milk will be purchased ($q = 0$). At any price less than a/b, some milk will be purchased, but the quantity purchased is related to the price. Consider the points 1, 2, and 3 in Figure 3-8. When the price *decreases* from level 1 to level 2, the quantity purchased *increases* from level 2 to level 3. The change in quantity (Δq) is functionally related to a change in price (Δp). The b in the expression $q = a - bp$ is a *ratio of changes* in q and p, that is, $b = \Delta q / \Delta p$. The symbol b is called the *slope* of the line. Where this line intercepts the price axis (a/b), quantity is at zero.[10]

In general, when two variables are plotted against each other to explicitly illustrate their exact relationship, the dependent variable is indicated on the vertical axis and the independent variable is indicated on the horizontal axis.

[10]In the expression $q = a - bp$ if $q = 0$, then $0 = a - bp$, or $a = bp$, or $p = a/b$.

This implies, for the dependency implied in $q = a - bp$, that price is on the horizontal axis and quantity is plotted on the vertical axis. In economics this convention is often violated in plotting demand relationships. Quantity, although found to be dependent upon price, is almost *always* plotted on the horizontal axis. This convention leads to an inconsistency between the algebraic expression of the relationship and its graphic expression. Recall that the slope of a line is the ratio of the rise to the run, $\Delta q/\Delta p$, which equals b from the equation. But if price is plotted on the vertical axis and quantity is plotted on the horizontal axis, the slope is $\Delta p/\Delta q$. Thus the b of the demand function expressed by the slope of the conventional plotting of price and quantity is actually $1/(\Delta p/\Delta b)$.

The hypothetical functional relationship described above graphs a straight line (see Figure 3-8). It is an example of a *linear* relationship. We also may hypothesize or observe relationships that are not linear. They could be curves (curvilinear relations) or some other geometric form. All geometric forms can be represented algebraically. A few that may be appropriate for expressing economic relationships are illustrated in Figure 3-9.[11]

The graphic or algebraic relationships that exist between or among economic variables are fundamental to market and price analysis. If we can determine that one variable is functionally related to another, we *may* be able to infer *cause* and *effect*. If a change in price results in a change in quantity purchased, for example, we might infer that price changes cause purchasing behavior effects. Of course, we may be wrong in our inference. Many other factors can come into play in human behavior besides price. Therefore, we must be very careful in drawing conclusions about supposed cause-effect relationships to avoid the many pitfalls to logical reasoning.

Because many factors influence the behavior of individuals and their institutions (households, firms, governments, etc.), the data we gather, observe, and interrelate will usually not reflect the regularity of simple lines or curves. Instead, we will normally observe tendencies rather than absolutes. This is the reason why statistics plays an important role in economic analysis.

SOME STATISTICAL TECHNIQUES

The subject of statistics frequently is divided into two categories: descriptive statistics and analytical statistics. The primary purpose of descriptive statistics is to simplify data into useful summary measures or forms. The objective of analytical statistics is to provide logical methods for drawing inferences or conclusions based upon incomplete or sample information.

In the previous section of this chapter, you were introduced to some ideas basic to courses in descriptive statistics. These included frequency distribution, mode, median, and mean averages *(measures of central tendency),* and a brief reference to one measure of dispersion (the range). There are a few additional

[11]William Baumol, *Operations Research and Operations Analysis,* 2d ed., Prentice-Hall, Englewood Cliffs, N.J.

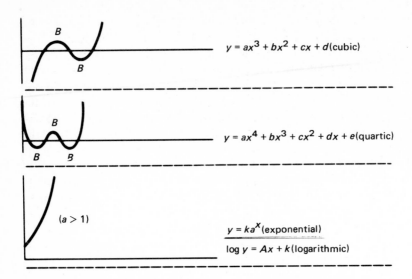

$y = ax^3 + bx^2 + cx + d$ (cubic)

$y = ax^4 + bx^3 + cx^2 + dx + e$ (quartic)

$(a > 1)$

$y = ka^x$ (exponential)

$\log y = Ax + k$ (logarithmic)

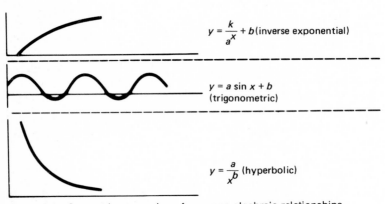

$y = \dfrac{k}{a^x} + b$ (inverse exponential)

$y = a \sin x + b$
(trigonometric)

$y = \dfrac{a}{x^b}$ (hyperbolic)

Figure 3-9 Geometric expression of common algebraic relationships.

techniques of descriptive statistics which we will present in this section. Thereafter, we will introduce a limited number of ideas concerning statistical analysis to complete this chapter.

Descriptive Statistics: Sampling

Once we have defined the set, we must acquire measurements of the characteristics that compose it. In our earlier example, we decided to name "retail prices of 2 percent butterfat milk sold in quart containers in St. Paul during the first 15 days of January 1974" as our set. At that point in our discussion, we assumed that we could acquire all of the prices (and quantities) that consumers paid each day during the half-month period. However, the job of obtaining all price and quantity observations would be a monumental task. It would be much more reasonable to obtain a sample of these prices. Why? Simply because of the expense involved. Imagine the resource requirements needed to obtain all prices and quantities. It would be necessary to station price reporters at every checkout lane in every retail establishment selling milk throughout the city for all hours that the businesses were open for a full 15 days! Despite the expense involved, we could be sure that some observational and recording errors would be made. Therefore, even if we spent a large sum of money in data gathering, we could not be certain that our data would be either complete or *reliable!*

The important question for us to consider, knowing that our price and quantity data will not be perfectly complete or reliable, is how complete or reliable must the data be to be useful to us. It really depends upon what relationship(s) we want to test and what our resource limitations are. In most cases, it is not necessary to have *all* the observations to obtain a reasonably accurate estimate. A balance must be struck between data reliability and survey cost.

A *sample* (subset of milk price and quantities) must be large enough so that summaries of the sample data describe or meaningfully represent the entire set of price and quantities sold (the population). From discussions with store managers, we might learn that prices normally do not change during any one day (but may be different from store to store) but that quantities sold follow a weekly pattern. Habits of consumers may be such that they buy lesser quantities on Sunday through Thursday and larger quantities on Friday and Saturday. Furthermore, we may learn that people buy larger quantities of milk at low supermarket prices once per week and then buy smaller quantities of milk at higher prices at neighborhood grocery stores during the week. These purchasing habits and many other factors can (and should) influence the design of our sample. We may, for example, want to station our reporters in supermarkets on Friday and Tuesday and in neighborhood groceries on Saturday and Monday. We may want to take price readings in different parts of the city and at different times of the day and night.

Our purpose in such preliminary interviews with storekeepers is to try to determine what habits and other factors should be taken into account to ensure a representative sample of all the retail milk prices and quantities sold in St. Paul for the period of analysis. To the extent to which we can identify this behavioral information, we may be more confident that the price-quantity information collected is descriptive of the entire population of prices and quantities.

Different sampling methods and sample sizes depend upon what we know a priori (beforehand) about the population. If we have no information at all, we may merely take a *random* sample. There is no neat formula that says we should select 5, 10, or 50 percent of the price-quantity observations. With a random sample, we randomly select stores that sell milk and then station our reporters there on randomly selected days in the hope that we would get a good representation of prices and quantities. If we know that milk prices vary only slightly among stores and from day-to-day, and that amounts purchased per consumer vary little, we could get by with a small sample size. If we know that prices and quantities purchased vary between supermarkets and neighborhood stores, we will want to *stratify* our sample to ensure a certain number of observations from each type of establishment.

Consider the price sampling problems encountered by the USDA:

> Collecting valid and meaningful price data—once a relatively simple operation—has become a terrifically complex procedure, and some lagging of this process behind the dynamic changes in marketing is inevitable. . . . Developing a complete sampling frame of all the agencies that participate in the marketing of farm products would be a tremendous task, one that far exceeds all the resources that have ever been available for this work. For most commodities, certain types of marketing channels are more or less clearly recognizable and account for most, or at any rate much of the total marketings, and it has been to these that efforts at data collection have been primarily directed.

> Prices received by farmers for products they sell are collected from various primary sources, but mostly from voluntary reporters. In general, price reporters may be classified in the following broad groups: (1) country merchants; (2) farm produce dealers at local shipping points; (3) country mill and elevator operators; (4) federal milk market administrators; (5) state milk control agencies; (6) managers of milk distribution or manufacturing plants; (7) cooperative marketing organizations; (8) country bankers; and (9) well-informed farmers.

> Most of the data on prices received are collected by means of a mailed questionnaire. To some extent, this is supplemented by enumerative checks of various types, depending on the commodities in question. Prices of beef cattle are being collected by enumeration of actual sales by commission firms and to buyers at auctions in a number of states.[12]

Descriptive Statistics: Index Numbers

It is relatively easy to calculate an average price for a given time period for a well-defined product, unit size, and geographic area. In our St. Paul milk example, we could merely add up our price observations on January 1 for each transaction and divide by the number of transactions. A shorthand way of stating this procedure is $\bar{p} = (\Sigma p)/t$. The bar over the p is frequently used to denote *average*. Thus, $\bar{p}$ means average price. The Greek capital letter sigma (Σ) is generally used to mean *sum of*. When it precedes p, it means the sum of all the recorded prices that day. t is shorthand for the number of transactions.

The simple average described above does not give any indication of the "importance" of each price in terms of the quantity that was transacted at that price. To reflect this, we would want to record the price and the quantity sold at each price to provide us with a set of *weighted prices* to add up. In this form, however, we would want to divide by the total quantity (number of quarts) sold

---

[12]U.S. Department of Agriculture, *Major Statistical Series of the U.S. Department of Agriculture: How They Are Constructed and Used*, vol. 1, *Agricultural Prices and Parity*, Agricultural Handbook 365, Apr. 1971.

rather than the number of transactions. Thus, a weighted average price would be expressed

$$(w)\bar{p} = \frac{\Sigma(pq)}{Q}$$

The sigma (Σ) refers to the sum of each price multiplied by the quantity transaction, and Q is the sum of the number of quarts of milk sold, $Q = \Sigma q$.

Once obtained, our weighted average price on January 1 may be compared to the weighted average price on January 15 in the form of a *ratio*. If $(w)\bar{p}$ on January 1 was 35 cents and $(w)\bar{p}$ on January 15 was 40 cents, we could compare these prices in terms of the ratio 40 cents:35 cents. We could further express the prices in percentage terms, letting the January 1 price be equal to 100 percent. If so, the ratio 40 cents:35 cents would be multiplied by 100 to yield 114.3. In this form, we would be expressing what is called a *price relative,* that is, one price relative to another. The price we relate to, 35 cents, is called the *base price* and the date, January 1, is called the *base period.* The weighted average price on January 15 is 114.3 percent of the weighted average price on January 1. If we kept January 1 as our base period, we could express price relatives for each of the other January days for which we have data as well.

Now we will complicate our statistical description problem somewhat. What if we had our reporters record not only milk prices and quantities but also price and quantity data for pork chops, 4-ounce containers of salt, and heads of lettuce? In a manner similar to milk, we could calculate weighted average prices for each of these food items and report price relatives separately for each product. Let us assume our January 1 and January 15 $(w)\bar{p}s$ for each product looked like this:

Product	Unit	(w)$\bar{p}$ January 1	(w)$\bar{p}$ January 15	Price relative
Milk	Quart	.35	.40	114.3
Pork chops	Pound	1.08	.93	86.1
Salt	4 ounces	.12	.13	108.3
Lettuce	Head	.49	.39	79.6

If you were asked whether the general price of *all four* items increased or decreased, what would you answer? You might retort: "It is not possible to answer such a question. Two items increased in price and two products showed price decreases." But this kind of question is asked regularly. It is usually in the form: What has been the general price change for food, or for *all meat,* or for *all prices received by farmers,* or for the *prices paid by farmers for production items?*

The answer to these questions is made by reporting an *index number* of prices. An index number is a tool that permits the averaging of prices of different items so that the index number can be compared with an earlier base index. Using our example of milk, pork chops, salt, and lettuce, let us see how it can be done.

One way would be to merely add up the prices for each product on January 1 and divide by four to obtain an average price for the items involved. If we performed the same operation for January 15 prices, we then could treat the resulting price averages as we did in calculating price relatives previously. But this procedure undoubtedly would provide us with information of little value. Why? Because as consumers, we may buy many quarts of milk but very few pork chops. The price of milk and the price of pork chops receive a weighting of importance greatly dissimilar to one's total expenditures for these items. This would even be true if we chose to take a simple average of their price relatives.

A method with which we can resolve this problem is to weight the price relatives in terms of their importance in the average person's food bill. To do this, we would need to make a sample survey of food expenditures to find out the amount that each consumer spends annually for milk, pork chops, salt, and lettuce. If we found that consumers spend 15 percent of their food budget on milk, 5 percent on pork chops, 0.1 percent on salt, and 1 percent on lettuce, we could use this information in constructing an expenditure-weighted price index that would be meaningful to the consumer.

A popular price index used is one in which expenditure weights are held constant (for the survey period) and the base period and subsequent period prices are multiplied by it. Let us assume that our expenditure survey was taken in December 1973. Our data for constructing the index would be as follows:

Product	Unit	(1) $(w)\bar{p}$ January 1, dollars	(2) $(w)\bar{p}$ January 15, dollars	(3) Expenditures weight, percent
Milk	Quart	.35	.40	15
Pork chops	Pound	1.08	.93	5
Salt	4 ounces	.12	.13	0.1
Lettuce	Head	.49	.39	1

Furthermore, let us use some abbreviations: $(w)\bar{p}_1$ = January 1 weighted average prices; $(w)\bar{p}_{15}$ = January 15 weighted average prices; and W_d = expenditures weights for December 1973.

The weighted price index in this case would be stated as follows:

$$I = \frac{\Sigma[(w)\bar{p}_{15}W_d]}{\Sigma[(w)\bar{p}_1W_d]} (100)$$

The calculation procedure we follow would be to multiply .35 × 15, 1.08 × 5, .12 × 0.1, and .49 × 1 to obtain a sum of 11.15 for January 1. Then we multiply .40 ×

15, .93 × 5, .13 × 0.1, and .39 × 1 for a sum of 11.05 for January 15. We divide the January 15 sum by the January 1 sum and multiply by 100 to obtain our price index, 99.1.

Complicated? Somewhat. But now we have compared price changes over a 15-day period in terms that are meaningful to most consumers. If the price of milk increased by a nickel, it would be 150 times more important to the average person than if salt prices increased by five cents!

There are many ways to weight index numbers.[13] For example, we can hold prices constant (as we did expenditures above) and measure quantity change over time. The important lesson to be learned with index numbers is that you *can* compare apples and oranges *in some ways*.

Index numbers are widely used. The consumer price index (CPI), also called the cost of living index, is the most widely known. The "price received by farmers" index is frequently used in agricultural economic analysis and parity computations.

For all price indexes, it is necessary to determine the base period for prices, the base period for the quantity weights, and the items to be included. It is not necessary to use the same base period for price and quantity weights. For the index of prices received by farmers, 43 farm commodities are included; quantity weights are the average quantities of each commodity marketed for the years 1971–1973. Subgroup indexes are computed for all crops, livestock, and products in addition to the all-farm products index. The current price-base year is 1967 = 100.

In addition to the farm price index or the 1967 base year, price indexes on the 1910–1914 base period are calculated. The marketing weights for this index are the average quantities marketed during the period 1924–1929. This index series is used in calculating parity prices for many farm commodities. The parity price has been used in establishing support prices for many farm commodities.

Descriptive Statistics: Fitting Lines

Another kind of "averaging" is to represent a group of coordinates by a single geometric line or curve (or algebraic expression). As noted earlier, recorded

[13]The weighting period may be the same as the base period for prices. The form

$$I = \frac{\Sigma(p_1 q_0)}{\Sigma(p_0 q_0)}$$

is called a Lasperes index. The results are *biased* (too heavily weighted) to the earlier period. The other extreme

$$I = \frac{\Sigma(p_1 q_1)}{\Sigma(p_0 q_1)}$$

is called a Paashe index, but it is biased in the other direction. A compromise is the so-called Fisher index, which averages the weighted bias by selecting a "middle" weighting period. In practice, most weights are based upon survey periods and are updated by new surveys from time to time. The index user (analyst) should check the weighting period to assess the possible bias implicit in the index being used.

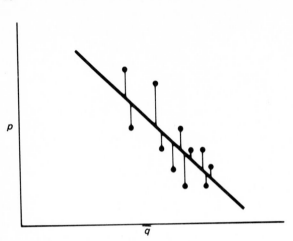

Figure 3-10 The line is "fitted" so that summed vertical distances of points above the line to the line are equal to the sum of the vertical distances of points below the line to that line.

economic data associating two variables rarely make up a *locus* of points that forms a neat line or curve. Rather, the data (as in Figure 3-7) are dispersed, but they suggest a specific relationship. We could leave the data in this form, but usually we want to simplify them by drawing a single line that seems to "fit" the data by averaging out its dispersion. We can do this *visually* by merely drawing a line through the data, taking care that the combined vertical distances of all data on one side of the line (to the line) equal the distances on the other side, as in Figure 3-10. This diagram implies that price is specified as a function of quantity. If quantity is in fact a function of price, then the statistical fitting would require fitting a line that minimizes the horizontal squared deviations of the observations from the line. This line-fitting procedure for two variables can be done mathematically by means of *simple regression analysis*.

The line average we obtain from our fitting is frequently regarded as an approximation of the functional relationship hypothesized (for example, in demand theory here). We can test the "goodness of fit" (how close the data come to the line) and measure the slope in absolute numbers or percentage terms. We can fit many kinds of lines using simple regression analysis. We may want to discern a *trend* or *cycle* in prices over time (*time series analysis*). We may want to fit a frequency distribution. And so forth.

With the exception of very short periods of time, the data we record may lie all over our graph, without an easily discernible pattern. Why? Because, in demand behavior, more than price affects the quantities purchased. The *incomes* of the consumers may change, their *tastes* may vary, the *price of substitutes* can change, and people's *expectations* about prices or product availability may alter. If these variables, as well as price, change during the period of our analysis, we will need to find a way to take this into account. To do this, we will have to simultaneously consider all the variables that affect quantities demanded. We would no longer be able to draw freehand lines and would be forced to use *multiple regression techniques*.

In multiple regression, instead of simply stating $q = f(p)$, we would have to expand the function to $q = f(p, y, pr, t, e, \ldots)$, where y = income, pr = price of substitutes, t = taste, e = expectations, and so forth. By holding y, pr, t, and e constant, we can estimate the degree to which changes in p influence q. Similarly, holding p, pr, t, and e constant, we can estimate the degree of influence of income changes on quantity change, and so forth, until we have estimated the net effects of each of the variables on quantity. The analytical technique becomes more complex but it permits us to explain the influence of the several variables on quantities of product purchased.

Analytical Statistics: A Note

The descriptive statistical techniques noted above are used both to describe and empirically analyze economic phenomena. But statistical analysis is the drawing of inferences or conclusions based upon incomplete information. It deals with conclusions that are based upon *probabilities*. Any sample of a population (or universe) may or may not reflect the characteristics of the population. How can we be sure? There is no complete assurance. We can, however, test the "chance" that the sample is representative or not.

A frequently used example of probability is the flipping of a coin. At each flip, the coin will come up heads or tails. If we assume that the coin is balanced in weight on each side (and it does not land and stand on edge!), we would expect the flips to turn out one-half heads and one-half tails. Yet in practice, we might flip a coin 100 times and find heads come up 55 times and tails 45 times. Does this single experience show that our 50-50 hypothesis is wrong? Not at all. It merely demonstrates that probability outcomes based upon our reasoning may not always be duplicated in practice. We may, time permitting, wish to flip the coin 10,000 times and record the results. If we did, we may find the results more consistent with our original expectations. But we could not be sure of 5,000 heads and 5,000 tails. Why? Because there is a "random factor" involved.

This random factor can occasionally create unusual results. If we are sampling milk prices and quantities, we may just happen to record a purchase made by a person in charge of a school party—say, 10,000 quarts at a high price. Imagine what this purchase would do to our averages and conclusions! Such a purchase may happen only once a year, but, alas, it happened between January 1 and 15, 1974, in St. Paul!

This demonstrates that the conclusions we reach must be in terms of probabilities. We may be very incorrect because of our samples but not because we are considering the incorrect variables or because we have not carefully designed our sample. We were wrong because of a chance happening which we could not reasonably anticipate.

Random error creeps into most statistical measurements. Statisticians have therefore developed tests, based upon probabilities, of a measure being incorrect. Frequently, when empirical measures are presented, you may see references to *tests of significance*. These are expressions of how much faith (probabilistic-type) you can place in the results.

SUMMARY

This chapter has reviewed a limited number of fundamental quantitative methods used in market and price analysis. The purpose was not to be exhaustive or complete in the treatment. However, a firm grasp on the ideas presented here will make subsequent chapters easier to read and understand.

QUESTIONS

1 Describe the aggregate "farm income" account for agriculture. What does it show and how does it differ from the standard profit and loss statement for a farm business?
2 Supply utilization tables for U.S. agricultural products provide what kind of information?
3 What is the meaning of the term *behavioral relationship?* What behavioral relationships are of concern to agricultural economists? How might you express or illustrate a behavioral relationship?
4 In the construction of price indexes for groups of products, what is the purpose of weighting the price relatives by quantities purchased or produced rather than computing a simple average of the price relatives?
5 For what purposes would you use descriptive statistics in agricultural economics? For what purposes would you use analytical statistics? Give examples.

BIBLIOGRAPHY

Baumol, William: *Operations Research and Operations Analysis,* 2d ed., Prentice-Hall, Englewood Cliffs, N.J.

U.S. Department of Agriculture: *Major Statistical Series of the U.S. Department of Agriculture: How They Are Constructed and Used,* vol. 1, *Agricultural Prices and Parity;* vol. 3, *Gross and New Farm Income;* vol. 6, *Land Values and Farm Finance;* Agricultural Handbook 365, Apr. 1971.

———: *Statistical Reporting Service of the U.S. Department of Agriculture Scope, Methods,* Miscellaneous Publication 967.

Waugh, Frederick V.: *Graphic Analysis: Application in Agricultural Economics,* U.S. Department of Agriculture, Agricultural Handbook 326, Nov. 1966.

Chapter 4

Consumption
and Demand

The end result of all farm-input manufacturing and distribution, production activities on the farm, and the processes of assembly, storage, transportation, processing, and wholesale and retail trade in food and fiber is *consumption*. The attitudes of consumers toward farm-produced food and fiber play a key role in the operation of the complex system of interrelated industries that compose the food and fiber sector of the U.S. economy. It is appropriate then that we begin our study of market and price dimensions of this sector by looking at what and how much of these products consumers buy, how their eating and clothing habits have changed over time, and the economic rationale that underlies their purchasing decisions. The economic rationale is *demand theory* and it is used to show *why* consumption patterns and trends are what they are. We will show measures of the demand for food and fiber and what these measures mean in terms of public policy and private business decision making. And, finally, we will demonstrate how consumer demand is related to farm-level demand.

CONSUMPTION

Americans spend a great deal of money on food and clothing. In 1974 people living in the United States used 27 percent of their income after taxes on these items—some $261 billion. Of this amount, 19.8 percent was spent on food alone. Not all the food and fiber was produced on U.S. farms, but most of it was. For example, the U.S. *imported* about $3.5 billion but *exported* $6.4 billion in 1975. Export dollars are measured at the farm level. Measured at the retail level, what we import in food makes up less than 10 percent of what we eat.

Food consumption can be measured in many ways: by the *pounds* of food we eat, by the *calories* we get from the food, or by the *amounts* we spend for food at home, in eating places, or in institutions.

Table 4-1 shows the per capita (per person) poundage consumption of food products in the United States for every tenth year since 1910. Several interesting trends stand out. First, notice the changes in total pounds of food consumed per person. With the exception of 1940, Americans have consumed less pounds of foods per person for every succeeding decade recorded. Compared to 1910, each of us is eating about one-half pound *less* food per day. Why? Look at how the *composition* of our diet has changed. Total meat consumption has increased, but we eat less potatoes and cereals. Our diets are less bulky than in the earlier decade.

Another reason for the decrease in poundage is that we are consuming fewer calories per person than we did in 1910. Figure 4-1 shows that caloric intake for the average American is approximately 5 percent less than what our grandparents consumed each year in the 1909–1913 period. We are less physically active now than people were 65 years ago; therefore, our energy requirements are considerably less.

Despite this reduction in poundage and calories, however, we spend considerably more for the food we eat today than ever before. If we weight our food by its retail price (prices held constant), we obtain the food consumption index. If we weight our food by its farm price (prices held constant), we obtain the food use index. Both of these indexes of food consumption per person have increased in the face of the reduction in pounds and calories. Why? One reason is because our tastes and preferences have changed from eating less expensive foods to more expensive foods, or perhaps our preferences have not changed but income increases have enabled us to obtain more expensive foods. The foods we favor require more resources to produce than those for which we have less preference. We might gain the same nutritional value from cereals (wheat, barley, etc.) as we do from beefsteak, but the production of beef requires that the beef cow eat the cereal and then we eat the animal. The result is added expense in farm production to satisfy our desires.

Another reason for the rise in the retail price-weighted quantity index of food consumption is the increase of our demands for food services. Years ago, most homemakers baked their own bread, canned their own vegetables, and sliced their own potatoes. Today we demand that these and other services be performed for us. We want meat that is ready for the grill, quickly prepared frozen dinners, and so forth. Also, we are not content to wait for the fruit season anymore; therefore, processors freeze or can these items so that they can be purchased year round. All of this costs a large amount of money and it helps to

Table 4-1 Per Capita Consumption of Selected Food Products in the United States, 1910–1970

	1910	1920	1930	1940	1950	1960	1970
Meat (carcass weight)							
Beef (lb)	70.4	59.1	48.9	54.9	63.4	85.2	113.7
Veal (lb)	7.2	8.0	6.4	7.4	8.0	6.2	2.9
Lamb and Mutton (lb)	6.5	5.4	6.7	6.6	4.0	4.8	3.3
Pork (lb)	62.3	63.5	129.0	73.5	69.2	65.2	66.4
Poultry (eviscerated weight)							
Chicken (lb)	15.5	13.7	15.7	14.1	20.6	29.2	41.4
Turkey (lb)	...	...	1.5	2.9	4.1	6.2	8.1
Eggs	306.0	299.0	331.0	319.0	389.0	334.0	319.0
Fats and oils							
Butter (lb)	18.3	14.9	17.6	17.0	10.7	7.5	5.3
Margarine (lb)	1.6	3.4	2.6	2.4	6.1	9.4	11.0
Potatoes and cereals							
White potatoes (lb)	198.0	140.0	132.0	123.0	106.0	102.0	118.6
Sweet potatoes (lb)	26.2	29.1	18.3	16.2	12.1	6.3	5.5
Wheat flour (lb)	214.0	179.0	171.0	155.0	135.0	118.0	110.0
Fruit							
Fresh fruits (lb)	137.9	145.4	133.6	142.1	107.4	97.5	80.8
Canned fruits (lb)	3.6	9.4	12.8	19.1	22.0	22.9	22.6
Frozen fruits and juices (lb)	...	...	0.53	1.28	4.28	9.1	9.8
Total food consumed (lb)	1615.0	1565.0	1555.0	1568.0	1525.0	1470.0	...

Source: U.S. Department of Agriculture, *Consumption of Food in the United States, 1909–1952,* Agricultural Handbook 62, Sept. 1953, and succeeding AMS supplements.

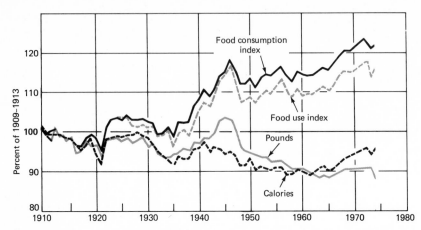

Figure 4-1 Four measures of per capita food consumption. Food consumption index is the re-tail-weight equivalent, weighted by constant retail prices. Food use index is the farm-weight equivalent, weighted by prices received by farmers; the index is adjusted to the level of the food consumption index in 1924 (1924 = 103.8). Calories are those available for consumption at the retail level, and pounds are the retail-weight equivalent. Figures for 1974 are preliminary. *Source:* Economic Research Service, U.S. Department of Agriculture, Neg. ERS 5520-75 (11).

explain the increase in the price-weighted food consumption index in Figure 4-1. The difference between the food use index recorded in that figure and the food consumption index is an indication of the change in the food services associated with the food we consume.

The per capita food consumption trends illustrated in Table 4-1 are graphically shown in Figure 4-2 for major food groups. The changes in the food groups differ substantially from those for the total food consumption. The interesting trend in fruit and vegetable consumption is not that it increased slightly until World War II and then, with the exception of melons, modestly declined, but that there has been a shift away from fresh fruits to canned and frozen fruits and juices over the 60-year period.

The substantial increase in per person coffee consumption up to World War II, followed by a decline and leveling off in the later 1950s and 1960s, shows both a change in preferences and a reduction in real price. Carbohydrates (cereals and bakery products) have become a less important part of our diet. Sugars and sweeteners have become more important. This may be partly the consequence of lower prices. Potato consumption declined until about 1953 and has increased since then. The increase is largely the result of new potato products which have increased the total demand for potatoes. The impact of these new products is illustrated in Figure 4-3. Potato chips, frozen french fries, and various processed potato products for snack foods followed changing daily eating habits concurrent with the advent of television and increased eating away from home.

A shift of food intake emphasis from morning to evening showed up in egg consumption trends, as you would expect. Egg consumption per person was erratic but steady until the mid-1930s; it then increased during the major war years (when animal protein was scarce). After about 1953, egg use dropped as evening "snacking" increased.

Dairy product consumption has been erratic but steady, demonstrating a gradual decline since World War II. Part of the reason for this "apparent" decrease is in the consumption measure itself. All dairy products are converted, on the basis of their fat content, to a "wholemilk equivalent" that has approxi-

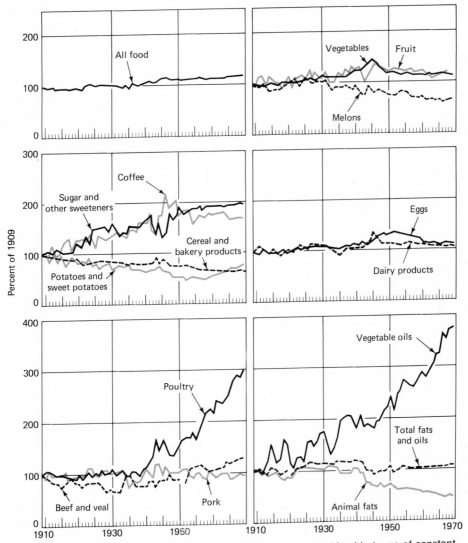

Figure 4-2 Trends in per capita food consumption. Items are combined in terms of constant retail prices. Butter is included with both dairy products and fats and oils. *Source:* Economic Research Service, U.S. Department of Agriculture, Neg. ERS 4017–69 (10).

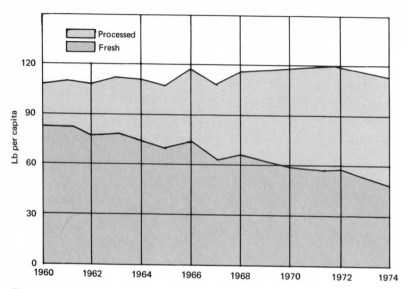

Figure 4-3 Fresh and processed (fresh weight equivalent) potato consumption. Fresh potatoes include small quantities used for flour. Figures for 1974 are preliminary. *Source:* Economic Research Service, U.S. Department of Agriculture.

mately 3.5 percent *butterfat,* and butterfat consumption has been decreasing along with other animal fats. However, this is partially the result of a shift to low-fat items, such as skim milk, 2 percent milk, and nonfat dry milk. Thus, consumption in pounds of product has declined less. But some dairy products, such as cheese, have shown substantial increases.

Generally, meat consumption has increased greatly since 1910. Consumers in the United States currently eat about one-half pound of meat per day, compared to less than one-quarter pound in 1910. Beef makes up the largest part of our meat diet, but pork and chicken are also important (see Table 4-1). Pork consumption decreased more rapidly than beef increased from 1930 to 1960 on a per capita basis. Some experts believe this to be the result of excessive amounts of fat in pork, but it was also caused by a general change in tastes and preferences over this period.

Vegetable fats have increased in significance in the average American diet, replacing the less desired animal fats used in earlier years.

Figure 4-4 relates the story of fiber consumption in the United States. Synthetic fibers, such as rayon, nylon, and dacron, have replaced much farm-produced cotton as the material for clothing. Wool usage has been most dramatically reduced, but cotton is still important in garment manufacturing. Tastes, preferences, and relative prices usually are offered as explanations for the change.

Consumption trends over many years or from month to month are partially *explained* by the factors affecting consumer and producer decision making. The factors that influence consumer purchasing are the subject of demand theory.

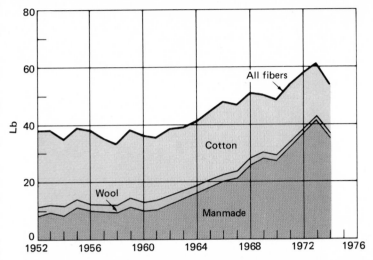

Figure 4-4 U.S. domestic consumption of fibers, per capita. Mill consumption is adjusted for fiber equivalent of trade balance in textile manufactures. All fibers does not include flax and silk. Figures for 1974 are preliminary. *Source:* Economic Research Service, U.S. Department of Agriculture, Neg. ERS 4376–75 (9).

DEMAND

The theory of consumer demand is rooted in the physiological and psychological needs of individuals. Their purchasing behavior may, at times, be or *seem* to be irrational to the casual observer, but what people buy, how much they purchase, and where and when they choose to make consumer expenditures *usually* has a rational basis. Let us first examine some seemingly "noneconomic" aspects of consumer choice.

Consumer Choice

Experiencing hunger pangs, you enter a small cafe for lunch and are confronted by a menu that offers hamburgers, cheese sandwiches, and hot dogs as their only fare aside from a modest beverage list. You must make a choice. One choice, of course, is to leave the cafe and go somewhere else, but let us assume that you do not have enough time between classes to walk to another restaurant. What will you choose to eat? Obviously it will depend on your "tastes" for these items and your "preferences" in ranking them. Let us say that you prefer hamburgers to cheese sandwiches or hot dogs. Why do you have such a preference?

The answer lies in your past experiences. Some of the reasons may be due to the "conditioning effect" instilled in you by your parents. They may also prefer hamburgers and you have learned to like best what they like best. And your preferences may have been influenced by your friends or a bad taste experience with cheese sandwiches or hot dogs. Or your preferences may have been shaped by a previously good taste experience with a hamburger at this cafe, or an

Table 4-2   Total and Marginal Utility of Hamburgers

Number of hamburgers	Total utility (utils)	Marginal utility (utils)
0	0	
		100
1	100	
		75
2	175	
		35
3	210	
		10
4	220	
		0
5	220	
		−20
6	200	

advertising poster in the window as you walked in, or a number of other psychological, sociological, or physiological reasons *unique to you.*

Some economists believe that you could *measure* the differences in your own tastes and preferences among hamburgers, cheese sandwiches, and hot dogs for the *number* of each type consumed under given conditions. The measure they suggest is the *util,* a vaguely defined "unit of satisfaction" that you expect from eating the hamburger. *How much* satisfaction you gain from the hamburger will depend on the degree of your hunger, how good the hamburger tastes, and your preconditioned attitude toward hamburgers. Let us assume that you have skipped breakfast, and the hamburgers are small and utterly delicious! How much satisfaction (utility) will you get out of that hamburger? Quite a lot! Let us arbitrarily assign 100 utils as a measure of your satisfaction from eating *one* little hamburger.

But you are still hungry after eating only one hamburger. So you decide to have another one. Will you get the same amount of satisfaction from the second hamburger? Perhaps, but probably not. Because your hunger has been partially satisfied, you still enjoy the second little hamburger, but its worth is less than 100 utils to you. Rather, it provides only 75 units of satisfaction. Still hungry, you decide to purchase a *third* little hamburger. Chances are you will get quite a bit less utility from that one than from hamburgers 1 and 2—let us say about 35 utils. Depending upon how much of a glutton you are, you might eat even more than three. But eventually you would get so stuffed with hamburgers (or so embarrassed by people watching you) that you would receive no satisfaction from another hamburger. Let us examine the utility you gained from eating hamburgers with respect to both total utility and extra utility from each additional hamburger. These data are listed in Table 4-2.

You should note two aspects of your behavior. First, the total utility you get from eating hamburgers increases rapidly with the first hamburger and then slows down (but continues to increase) until you have eaten four hamburgers. At four hamburgers you have reached a *peak* of satisfaction that cannot be increased by eating another hamburger! And if you eat more, you will experience dissatisfaction and your total utility will start to decrease!

Second, notice the column "marginal utility." This relates the utility for each succeeding hamburger you eat. From zero to one hamburger you obtain 100 utils of satisfaction, from one to two you get 75, and so forth. The word *marginal* refers to the next or incremental unit. In this table, your marginal utility decreases as you eat more and more hamburgers. This is called the *law of diminishing marginal utility*. You knew about this law long before you read this book, because you have experienced it yourself. And you recognize that it has a physiological and psychological basis. You also can begin to see how it helps to explain why people will buy more at lower prices.

Let us return to the cafe. While you are devouring your hamburgers, another person sits down next to you, examines the menu, and orders a hot dog. Obviously, she has exhibited a preference for hot dogs over hamburgers and cheese sandwiches. Does this make her "wrong" and you "right"? Of course not. You have your tastes and preferences and the other person has her own. Both of you are acting rationally; you just have different preferences.[1] And the other person may rate (in utils) the hot dogs she consumes differently than you do. The first one may be worth 300 utils to her, the second only 15, and a third −150! This teaches us that no two people are alike in tastes and preferences. Nevertheless, we can be fairly certain that all people experience the law of diminishing marginal utility.

You might be saying to yourself at this point that this is an interesting way to explain what we all experience, but that it is foolish to try to assign utils to our satisfaction because utility cannot really be measured. That is a matter of debate. Some people believe that you can measure satisfaction, and they are called cardinal utility believers. Others say the best a person can do is *rank* these preferences (ordinal utility), and still others think that it is how people actually behave that counts (revealed preference). Regardless, most people feel that utility plays a significant role in human behavior. For economists it plays an especially important role in relation to price.

The Theory of Demand

Demand is a behavioral relationship that describes how much product will be purchased at different prices *under a carefully defined set of conditions. Consumer demand* refers to the purchasing behavior of one or more buyers who will consume (use up) the utility of a product. *Intermediate demand* refers to the price-quantity purchasing behavior of buyers who obtain the product for resale or use it as raw material in a manufacturing process. If we add up the individual demands of buyers at any one market level, the aggregate is called the *market demand*. Let us first discuss consumer demand and then consumer market demand.

The first question that may be raised at this point is: How are consumer preferences, described in the last section, translated into consumer demand? It

---

[1]Despite this, it is always surprising how people "put down" others for their preferences, simply because they do not conform with their own or some other "accepted" standard!

should be obvious that the feasible choices available to the individual are limited by the individual's income and the prices charged for goods or services. It also seems reasonable that we will want to purchase and consume such that total satisfaction (utils) is maximized. Using only the data from the previous example, this would indicate that satisfaction is maximized when four hamburgers are consumed, assuming that our income is sufficient to buy four hamburgers. If we purchased additional hamburgers, total satisfaction would be reduced even though income is sufficient to buy more. But our reasoning would lead us astray except under very restrictive circumstances. Why? It is not merely the amount of utility from hamburgers that we want to maximize but the total utility from all goods and services that we can buy with our given income. The consumer makes a choice on how much of a given product to purchase with his or her income in mind. Also, the consumer is mindful of other uses for this money as well. If we had made our cafe example more realistic, we would have placed a "budget constraint" in the example. Let us do that now. Instead of having an unlimited amount of money, suppose that you have but one dollar and that hamburgers cost 25 cents each. Before you spend your last two bits on that fourth hamburger, you may need to consider an alternative use for the quarter. Assume that the amount represents bus fare home. Now you must ask yourself: Will I get more satisfaction by eating a fourth hamburger or riding the bus home? The bus ride at the end of a tiring day may give you more satisfaction than one more hamburger. If so, you will rationally decide to stop eating after three hamburgers and save the last 25 cents for your bus fare!

There are two lessons rather than one in the preceding example. The first lesson is that your disposable income directly influences the amount of a given product you purchase. But the second lesson, and the less obvious one, is that your purchasing is also influenced by the availability and prices of other products. In reality, you not only have to choose between bus rides and hamburgers but among thousands of products that you possibly can purchase. Thus for each consumer, there is an income constraint and a whole range of alternative purchases that can be made. Some alternatives may be complementary in terms of total satisfaction (you may want to buy a coke with your hamburger), or other alternative purchases may be substitutes for the hamburger (such as the hot dog or cheese sandwich). Even though you have a preference for hamburgers, you might choose a cheese sandwich as a substitute if it were priced low enough.

The preceding discussion indicates that many choices and decisions are necessary for most of us to maximize our satisfaction. The general rule guiding maximization of satisfaction is that given a level of income, it should be allocated among all possible choices such that the marginal utility per dollar of expenditure on each good and service is equal to the marginal utility per dollar of expenditure in every other use.[2] Algebraically, the rule can be stated for all goods or services *A* to *N:*

---

[2]An excellent discussion of this theory of consumer behavior is presented in Willis L. Peterson, *Principles of Economics: Micro,* Darcey, 1971, pp. 20–22.

$$\frac{\text{Marginal utility of good } A}{\text{Price of good } A} = \frac{\text{marginal utility of } B}{\text{price of } B} = \cdots$$

$$= \frac{\text{marginal utility of } N}{\text{price of } N}$$

Why does this procedure result in maximum satisfaction? This can be illustrated by examining a situation where the equality does not hold. Suppose that a consumer is allocating expenditures such that the marginal utility per dollar spent in the restaurant is 30 and the marginal utility spent on entertainment is 50. By shifting a dollar's worth of expenditure from restaurant food to entertainment, total satisfaction could be increased by 20 utils. Consumer utility from food consumption would be decreased by 30 utils, but this is more than offset by increased utility, 50 utils, from the dollar spent on entertainment. Because of the existence of diminishing marginal utility for all goods and services, shifting of additional expenditure between the two may increase total utility, but by a lesser amount for each succeeding transfer. As long as the marginal utilities per dollar of expenditure are different, total satisfaction can be increased by reallocation of expenditures.

Given this discussion, we must state the price-quantity purchasing behavior of an individual consumer subject to some assumptions about income and the price of related products. There are assumptions other than income and related product prices which we must recognize as well. Your behavior is subject to your hunger and psychological makeup at a particular time or during a particular time period at a specified place. The price-quantity relationship is generally formulated under the assumption that all other factors affecting consumption are constant. Furthermore, the decision is assumed not to be affected by expectations that prices, availability, income, or other factors will change.

Consumer demand is thus expressed as the relationship between price and quantity purchased of (1) a well-defined product, (2) at or during a particular time, and (3) at a particular place or over a specified geographic area. This assumes that the following factors remain unchanged: (1) consumer disposable income, (2) prices of substitute products, (3) prices of complementary products, (4) expectations of future prices and income, and (5) tastes and preferences. In a general form we could state this as:

$$Q_D = -f(P \mid Y, P_S, P_C, E, T)$$

where Q_D = quantity demand
f = function of
P = price
$\mid$ = holding following variables constant
Y = income
P_S = prices of substitutes
P_C = prices of complements

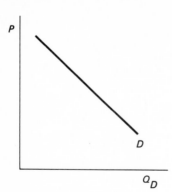

P

D

Q_D

Figure 4-5 Own-price demand curve slopes downward and to the right.

E = expectations
T = tastes and preferences

Because of the principle of diminishing marginal utility, the price-quantity relationship is always negative. Geometrically, this means that the demand curve slopes downward, as illustrated in Figure 4-5.

Notice that in algebraic notation we omitted the assumptions about product definition, time, and location. These are "implied," that is, you are expected to know them without having to see them in notation form. The geometric representation of demand leaves out all of the assumptions noted above. But they are implied and you should always read these diagrams with them in mind.

The expression $Q_D = f(P \mid Y, P_S, P_C, E, T)$ is called the *own-price relation of demand*. If we switch some of these symbols around, we can also state other relations. $Q_D = f(Y \mid P, P_S, P_C, E, T)$ is called the *income relationship of demand*. P_S and P_C are frequently combined into P_R. The expression $Q_D = f(P_R \mid P, Y, E, T)$ is a cross-demand relationship. Other demand relations are also possible.

The income relationship may be either negative or positive. If your income increased to allow you $1.25 for lunch and a bus ride, you might consume that fourth hamburger and not change your expenditure for bus rides. If your income increased substantially, you might choose to go someplace else and eat steak!

When an income increase results in an increase in quantity purchased, the product is called a *normal* or *superior good*. If the increase in income calls forth a decrease in the product purchased, the item is called an *inferior good*. Diagrammatically, the distinction is illustrated in Figure 4-6.[3] Lard (pork fat) is an example of an inferior good; beefsteak serves as an example of a superior good.

The cross-demand relationship simply states that as the price of one product increases or decreases, the quantity demanded of a related product will increase

---

[3] The alert student may have noticed that Q_D has been recorded on the ordinate axis rather than on the abscissa in contrast to the P and Q_D relation. The usual practice is to put the *dependent* variable on the ordinate axis and the *independent* variable on the abscissa.

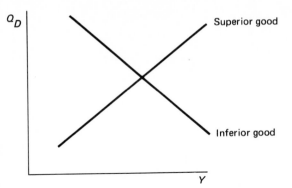

Figure 4-6   Income demand curves illustrate a superior and an inferior good.

or decrease, depending upon how these products are related in consumer decision making. If the price of cheese sandwiches decreases, this may result in fewer hamburgers being sold. This phenomenon would indicate that hamburgers and cheese sandwiches are substitutes. If the price of hamburgers decreased, this might encourage an increase in the sale of cokes. If so, these products are complements. Diagrammatically, this distinction is illustrated in Figure 4-7.

ELASTICITY OF DEMAND

We explained in Chapter 3 that each line or curve can be represented algebraically. For example, we can express a straight-line demand relation as $Q_D = a - bP$, leaving unstated for the moment the implied assumptions we stressed. If we were able to measure Q_D and P and knew the limits of the relation to obtain the value of a, we could determine the value of b. The term b, you recall, is the reciprocal of the slope of the graphed demand relation. The slope of this relation, measured in absolute terms, is the change in price divided by the change in quantity, $\Delta P / \Delta Q$. Although the slope is correctly stated in terms of our

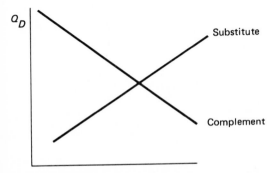

Figure 4-7   Cross-demand relationships for a substitute and a complementary good.

earlier geometry, it is not accurate in terms of our algebraic statement of demand (see Chapter 3). The algebraic slope is $b = \Delta Q / \Delta P$.

Responsiveness of demand is indicated by the slope of the demand curve. However, comparison of slopes for different demand curves for different products leads to problems. As long as slope is measured in absolute terms, its value will depend upon the units of measurement of P and Q_D, which makes comparisons of slopes of different demand functions relatively meaningless. The slope may be expressed in changes in bushels, hundredweights (cwt), tons, pounds, or kilograms as compared to dollars, lire, rubles, or other currency. To resolve this comparison problem, economists have adopted the standard practice of expressing change in quantity and price in percentage terms. A percentage change in hundredweights relative to a percentage change in dollars can be directly compared to a percentage change in kilograms relative to a percentage change in yen. These percentage change ratios of quantity to price are called *own-price elasticities*. Algebraically,

$$E_p = \frac{\text{percent } \Delta Q_D}{\text{percent } \Delta P}$$

where Δ means change.[4] Notice that the "effect" variable Q_D is in the numerator and the "causal" variable is in the denominator.

For a specific change along a demand curve, such as moving from point 1 to point 2 in Figure 4-8, the elasticity can be calculated (see the formula beneath Figure 4-8).

To avoid the problem of obtaining a different elasticity, depending upon whether the starting point is P_1, Q_1 or P_2, Q_2, a standard procedure is to use the arc-elasticity formula. This formula yields an elasticity at a point midway between the two observations. It involves the use of an average of the quantities and an average of the prices rather than the initial quantity and prices. Algebraically, it is stated as follows:

$$E_p = \frac{Q_1 - Q_2}{Q_1 + Q_2} \frac{P_1 + P_2}{P_1 - P_2}$$

In the same manner as we have expressed own-price elasticity of demand, we can express income elasticity of demand:

$$E_Y = \frac{\text{percent } \Delta Q_D}{\text{percent } \Delta Y}$$

and cross elasticity of demand:

---

[4]The student familiar with calculus can see that *slope* can be stated dQ/dP and that price elasticity at point (A_i, P_i) is $E_p = (dQ/dP)(P/Q_i)$.

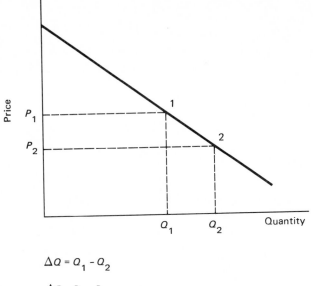

$$\Delta Q = Q_1 - Q_2$$

$$\Delta P = P_1 - P_2$$

Therefore, $E_p = \dfrac{Q_1 - Q_2}{Q_1} \dfrac{P_1}{P_1 - P_2}$

Figure 4-8 Measuring the price elasticity of demand.

$$E_c = \frac{\text{percent } \Delta Q_D}{\text{percent } \Delta P_R}$$

The actual computational procedure may include average values as in the arc elasticity described above.

Because the own-price curve always slopes downward to the right, E_p will always have a negative value, ranging from 0 to minus infinity ($E_p = 0 \rightarrow -\infty$). If the value of E_p ranges between 0 and -1 ($E_p < 0 > -1$), we call the price-demand relationship *inelastic*; if $E_p = -1$, it is called *unitary elastic;* and if $E_p < -1$, it is called *elastic.*

These measures can be directly related to the direction of change in total market revenue from changing price. If the demand is elastic, total revenue increases as price decreases. If demand is inelastic, total revenue decreases as price decreases. If demand has unitary elasticity, total revenue does not change in response to price changes.

Income elasticity can be negative or positive in value. If $E_y > 0$, the product under consideration is a superior good; if $E_y < 0$, the product is an inferior good. Cross elasticity may also be negative or positive. As an approximation, if $E_c > 0$, the goods being compared are *substitutes;* if $E_c < 0$, the products are *complements.*

An interesting feature about these three elasticity measures is that under special but not unusual circumstances, they will add up to 0 for a given product. Thus, $E_p + E_y + E_c = 0$.[5] This relation is of particular value to the economist who may have estimates of two of these values but not the third.

There are other important demand elasticity measures. The *price flexibility* coefficient is approximately equal to the inverse of the own-price elasticity coefficient. It is

$$F = \frac{\text{percent } \Delta P}{\text{percent } \Delta Q_D}$$

and is used to study price changes that result from changes in the quantity marketed.

The concept of total price elasticity is sometimes used. Whereas own-price elasticity is a measurement of changes in quantity demanded when price changes—holding all other factors, such as income and related product price, constant *(ceteris paribus)*—total price elasticity is a measure of quantity change in relation to price change—while allowing other factors to vary *(mutatis mutandis)*. Thus, in practice, a change in the price of *A* causes a movement along the demand curve for *A*, and additionally it changes the demands for product *B*, *C*, etc. Given fixed supplies of *B*, *C*, etc., their prices will change, causing changes in the demand for *A*. The price for *A* will change again in addition to the original adjustment. In general, the total elasticity for a given product will be less elastic than the more standard *ceteris paribus* concept of demand.

DEMAND ESTIMATION

In actual practice, one usually does not have an easily identifiable demand curve from which elasticities can be calculated. Observed prices and quantities are the results of a dynamic, everchanging system. Nevertheless, the static demand theory that we have just described is a basic starting point for any analysis or measurement of demand. As stated by Waugh:

> The first step in any statistical analysis should be to set up some sort of theoretical model describing how the markets for a commodity work. The model generally starts with a listing of factors that are believed to affect the supply, demand, and price of the commodity. Diagrams are often helpful in portraying various interrelationships.[6]

The model may be complex, with several equations representing a number of supply-demand relations, or it may be rather simple, with one equation representing demand.

[5]This is known as the Slutsky-Schultz relation, the mathematical proof of which is beyond the scope of this book. The logic of the relation merely suggests that products which have many or close substitutes also have more price elastic demands, or that those products which are strongly superior when incomes increase, even if there are few substitutes, may be price elastic.

[6]Frederick V. Waugh, *Demand and Price Analysis,* U.S. Department of Agriculture, Technical Bulletin 1316, Nov. 1964, pp. 6–7.

Finally, the model should be put into a form that can be fitted by statistical techniques to determine if it is consistent with the observed data. To set up a good model for measuring the demand for any commodity, the researcher must have an intimate understanding of the markets for that particular commodity. The routine fitting of the same model to cotton, beef cattle, and canned peas is poor research method.[7]

Once the variables that determine demand for a given product and the mathematical form of the relationship among the variables have been selected, the researcher is in a position to use observed data to fit the relationship. Two types of data are used in estimating demand relationships. One is cross-section data, observations on a sample of consumers at a given point in time. The observed consumption difference between consuming units is the basis for estimating the price and income relations.[8] Cross-section data from samples on panels of consumers are usually rather expensive to obtain and they are not regularly available.

The most regularly available data for food and agricultural products are the time-series data on average consumer purchases and prices. The quantity data for annual consumption are computed by dividing the total annual domestic disappearance of food or fiber by the population. The resulting figure is the average annual consumption for an average consumer. Total prices are reported on a monthly and an annual basis by two branches of the U.S. government; the BLS of the Department of Commerce reports retail food prices and the SRS of the Department of Agriculture reports farm prices. Since food prices normally vary from year to year, the differences are used to estimate demand relations.

The particular methods of estimation are beyond the scope of this text. A common method of determining the line (curve) of best fit for either the cross-section or time-series data is the regression analysis that is briefly described in Chapter 3. Other techniques are available.

EMPIRICAL DEMAND ESTIMATES

A considerable amount of research has been devoted to estimation of demand relationships for food products. One of the more comprehensive studies of demand was performed by P. S. George and G. A. King at the University of California.[9] They estimated price elasticities, all cross-demand elasticities, and income elasticities for 49 foods. Their results for 14 food products and all nonfood purchases are presented in Table 4-3. In this table the direct price elasticity for each product is entered where the row and column intersect. All

[7]Ibid.

[8]At a given point in time, prices of foods do not usually differ significantly from one consumer to another while incomes do vary. Consequently, much of the cross-section demand analysis is directed at estimating the relationship of food consumption to income and demographic variables, not price.

[9]P. S. George and G. A. King, *Consumer Demand for Food Commodities in the United States with Projections for 1980,* Giannini Foundation Monograph 26, California Agricultural Experiment Station, Mar. 1971, pp. 1–2.

Table 4-3 Retail Demand Elasticities for Selected Farm Products

| | 1 percent change in the price of: | | | | | | | | | | | | | | | |
Percent quantity change column	Beef	Veal	Pork	Lamb and mutton	Chicken	Eggs	Butter	Marga-rine	Fresh milk	Cheese	Sugar	Oranges	Bread	All foods	Nonfood	Income
Beef	-0.6438	0.0280	0.0826	0.0454	0.0676	0.0013	0.0003	0.0002	0.0028	0.0008	0.0009	0.0004	0.0036	-0.3896	0.0996	0.2899
Veal	0.3593	-1.7177	0.1977	0.0660	0.1736	0.0074	0.0018	0.0011	0.0153	0.0042	0.0050	0.0022	0.0198	-0.7943	0.2032	0.5911
Pork	0.0763	0.0141	-0.4130	0.0602	0.0355	0.0026	0.0006	0.0004	0.0053	0.0015	0.0017	0.0008	0.0069	-0.1793	0.0459	0.1335
Lamb and mutton	0.5895	0.0661	0.8914	-2.6255	0.2336	0.0040	0.0010	0.0006	0.0083	0.0022	0.0027	0.0012	0.0107	-0.7675	0.1963	0.5712
Chicken	0.1971	0.0436	0.1208	0.0546	-0.7773	0.0023	0.0006	0.0003	0.0047	0.0013	0.0016	0.0007	0.0061	-0.2398	0.0613	0.1785
Eggs	0.0102	0.0027	0.0111	0.0019	0.0033	-0.3183	0.0036	0.0022	0.0307	0.0085	0.0101	0.0043	0.0396	-0.0737	0.0189	0.0549
Butter	0.0019	0.0017	0.0003	0.0011	0.0003	0.0076	-0.6524	0.1605	0.0072	0.0020	0.0024	0.0010	0.0093	-0.4274	0.1093	0.3181
Margarine	0.0119	0.0030	0.0133	0.0021	0.0039	0.0162	0.4245	-0.8465	0.0000	0.0025	0.0030	0.0014	0.0117	0.0000	0.0000	0.0000
Fresh milk	0.0064	0.0021	0.0050	0.0015	0.0016	0.0107	0.0014	0.0002	-0.3455	0.0007	0.0008	0.0004	0.0031	-0.2736	0.0700	0.2036
Cheese	0.0041	0.0020	0.0032	0.0013	0.0011	0.0095	0.0011	0.0002	0.0013	-0.4601	0.0055	0.0026	0.0215	-0.3344	0.0855	0.2489
Sugar	0.0109	0.0028	0.0120	0.0020	0.0036	0.0154	0.0022	0.0005	0.0069	0.0077	-0.2419	0.0018	0.0154	-0.6432	0.0110	0.0321
Oranges	0.0035	0.0018	0.0021	0.0012	0.0008	0.0083	0.0011	0.0001	0.0000	0.0044	0.0015	-0.6632	0.0325	-0.3500	0.0895	0.2605
Bread	0.0119	0.0030	0.0133	0.0021	0.0039	0.0162	0.0024	0.0006	0.0078	0.0081	0.0042	0.0065	-0.1500	0.0000	0.0000	0.0000
All foods	-0.0420	-0.0062	0.0250	-0.0060	-0.0091	-0.0039	-0.0056	0.0003	-0.0247	-0.0093	-0.0020	-0.0055	-0.0039	-0.2368	-0.0606	0.1763
Nonfood	-0.0217	-0.0008	0.0317	-0.0008	-0.0086	-0.0103	-0.0025	-0.0015	-0.0214	-0.0059	-0.0070	-0.0033	-0.0276	-0.2253	-1.0179	1.2432

Source: P. S. George and G. A. King, *Consumer Demand for Food Commodities in the United States with Projections for 1980.* Giannini Foundation Monograph 26, California Agricultural Experiment Station, Mar. 1971, pp. 46–51.

other intersections show cross elasticities with the exception of the last column, which contains the income elasticities for the 15 items. Thus, the direct elasticity of demand for chicken is −0.7773, the cross elasticity of demand for chicken with respect to the price of pork is 0.1208, and the income elasticity of demand for chicken is 0.1785.

Table 4-3 illustrates a basic characteristic of the demand for food. For the most part, the price demand for foods tend to be inelastic ($-1 < E < 0$). Only two of the foods listed in the table have an elastic demand. Demand for food is also relatively unresponsive to income changes. This is reflected in the low-income elasticities, all less than 1. The inelastic nature of demand for food characterizes not only retail demand but also farm-level demand. This means that small volume harvests are associated with high return (revenue) and large volumes are associated with smaller revenues.

ANALYTICAL USES OF DEMAND RELATIONS

We are now ready to use our demand theory and estimated demand relations. We will deal with an actual problem presented to one of the authors a few years ago.

The American Lamb Council, a producer organization, has, as one of its purposes, the promotion of greater per capita consumption of lamb in the American diet. A representative of this organization presented the following information and problem:

> Lamb consumption per person in the U.S. has regularly decreased over the past decade. We [the council] have tried to advertise it as a beneficial, low-cost pre-serving meat and have gone to considerable expense preparing pamphlets and demonstrations of how it can be prepared in a variety of nourishing and tasty ways. But despite our efforts, lamb per capita consumption continues to decline. *Why* is it decreasing? If we knew the answer we might redirect our promotional efforts to get at the causes.

Can demand theory help in the analysis of this "real-life" problem? Let us see what we can do. First, let us record the information presented to us. Per capita consumption of lamb is listed in Table 4-1. From 1960 to 1970, per capita lamb and mutton consumption decreased from 4.8 to 3.3 pounds per person per year, a 31 percent decline. Our theory has indicated a number of factors that will affect consumption. Let us first determine if the *real price* of lamb and mutton changed between 1960 and 1970. And if so, how? Could the decrease in lamb consumption have been explained by a real price increase? To discover this we must find the annual average price of lamb and mutton in 1960 and again for 1970. Can we obtain this information? Where? The USDA maintains price statistics for many products, as does the Department of Commerce. Their data show that the 1960 annual average lamb price was 72.3 cents/pound and the 1970 price was 105.5 cents/pound. But this is not the *real* price. If we take inflationary changes

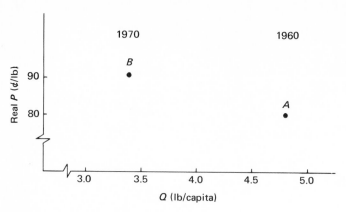

Figure 4-9 Demand curve points for lamb.

in all prices into account (adjusting actual price by the CPI, 1967 = 100), we find that the real prices were 81.5 cents/pound in 1960 and 90.7 cents/pound in 1970, as stated in 1967 dollars. Knowing this, we can plot these two points on a graph illustrating price and quantity, with point A in 1960 and point B in 1970 shown in Figure 4-9.

Now we must ask the question: What is the own-price elasticity of demand in each of those years? Why do we ask this question? Because we want to try to reproduce the demand functions as best as possible to see if the price change explains the consumption decline or if the demand curves have shifted. The study by George and King shows an own-price demand elasticity of −2.63 for lamb and mutton. This information permits us to draw the demand functions through our coordinates because we can convert elasticity to slope (see Figure 4-10). The price rise of 11.3 percent from 1960 to 1970, all other things constant, would have caused lamb consumption to decline 29.7 percent to 3.4 pounds per capita. These were calculated by substituting in the price elasticity formula:

$$E_p = \frac{\text{percent } \Delta Q}{\text{percent } \Delta P}$$

$$-2.63 = \frac{\text{percent } \Delta Q}{12.9 \text{ percent}}$$

Therefore, percent ΔQ = 29.7, and 29.7 percent of 4.8 is 1.4. Graphically, this means a shift along the demand curve in Figure 4-10 from point A to point C. Actually, we ended up at point B, which would imply that the demand curve also shifted to the left slightly during this period. Now we might conclude at this point that most of the change in consumption was due to price, but we may also be interested in what caused this demand curve to shift. The cause could be any one of the factors that we examined earlier: changes in income, prices of related products, expectations, or basic consumption habits of the population.

Let us investigate each of these factors. What about income? We know that

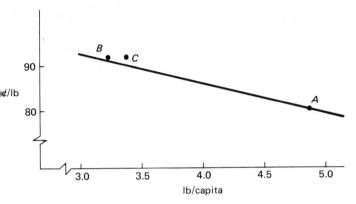

Figure 4-10 1960 demand curve for lamb drawn through point *A*.

real income per person increased during those 10 years. In fact, it increased by 30.4 percent. Thus, if lamb and mutton are an inferior good, we might explain part of the decrease by the real income increase. But the George and King studies show lamb and mutton to be a superior good! It has a positive income elasticity of 0.5712. This means that the increase in real income should have caused an *increase* of 17.4 percent in per capita lamb consumption. Translating this into pounds, holding all other factors constant, would have meant a 0.8 pound per capita increase. Starting from 3.4 pounds, we are now back to 4.2 pounds per capita. We are now considerably farther from explaining the change than by merely considering the price of lamb. Something else must have been at work.

What about changes in the real price of substitutes and complements? First, we must determine what products are substitutes for lamb or mutton and what products, if any, are complements. The George and King studies can help us again. Beef, pork, veal, and chicken are identified as having significant positive cross elasticities with lamb and mutton. So now we must obtain 1960 and 1970 retail prices for these substitutes, adjust for inflation, and see what has happened to the real price of these substitutes. We find that the real price of beef and veal increased slightly, pork remained approximately the same, but chicken prices decreased by about 50 percent.

The beef and veal price *increases* would have caused lamb consumption to *increase,* so that is not our answer. Nor did the change in pork price have much, if any, influence. But the chicken price decrease *would* have an effect on lamb consumption, causing it to decrease! Again, how much of an effect? The cross elasticity from Table 4-3 between lamb quantities and chicken prices was 0.2336. Let us put this information into our E_c formula:

$$E_c = \frac{\text{percent } \Delta Q}{\text{percent } \Delta P}$$

$$0.2336 = \frac{\text{percent } \Delta Q}{\Delta 50 \text{ percent}}$$

Therefore, percent ΔQ = 11.68 percent.

Given that 1960 consumption was 4.8, 11.68 percent of that figure would be a 0.551-pound decrease that could be explained by reduced chicken prices. Thus, after allowing for the impact on its own price, income, and substitute prices, lamb consumption would have been about 3.7 pounds per capita. But lamb consumption decreased from 4.8 to 3.3 pounds, a decline of 1.5 pounds per person. We have part of the answer but not all of it! Something else offset the decline caused by increased lamb prices and decreased poultry prices. About 0.2 pounds of the decrease must be caused by something else. Could it be "expectations?" Not over a 10-year period. This variable is meaningful only in short-run situations.

The only category left is consumer tastes and preferences. A change in tastes or preferences must account for the largest part of the consumption decline. But our investigation cannot conclude here if we really want to help the Lamb Council. *Why* did tastes or preferences change? To study this change, we will need to know more about lamb consumption. What kind of people eat lamb, where is it consumed, when is it eaten, and how is it prepared? A household food consumption survey of U.S. families is taken approximately every 10 years. Here are a few facts of interest.

More women than men eat lamb.

Older people seem to have a greater preference for lamb than younger people.

More lamb is consumed by high-income than by low-income families.

Lamb is eaten more regularly by people with greater formal education.

More lamb per person is consumed in coastal areas than in the Midwest and the South.

Most lamb is eaten as an occasional evening meal rather than as a lunch or snack.

These facts about lamb consumption suggest several hypotheses to be analyzed and tested.

The analysis of demand for a given product can lead to a systematic explanation of why changes have occurred. Furthermore, it may be used to design policies and programs or to determine the feasibility of programs to increase consumption. Obviously, the Lamb Council cannot do much about chicken prices, but it might indicate the groups at which to direct promotional programs.

The foregoing has been an exercise in *demand analysis,* the use of demand theory and measurement to arrive at a needed conclusion. It is only one example of how *economic analysis* is performed.

DERIVED DEMAND

Up to this point we have discussed *consumer demand.* It is obvious that, at other levels of the marketing system, there are purchasers of intermediate farm-

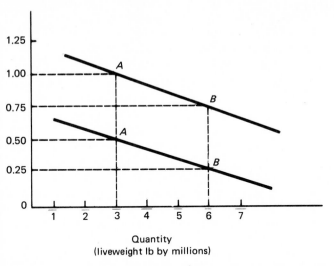

Figure 4-11 Measuring the price elasticities of demands at the retail and farm levels.

produced products. At each of these levels there are demanders and suppliers. But what is the nature of this *intermediate demand?* Is it related to consumer demand? And if so, how?

In market and price analysis, we refer to consumer demand as the primary demand because it is to this demand that all other demands in the system relate. The intermediate level demands are called *derived demands* because they are derived from the primary or consumer demand.[10]

It is possible to directly compare demand curves at two levels of the marketing system *only if* we express the quantities at one level in terms of quantities at another level. In the study of the food and fiber sector, we usually express quantity in terms of the *farm-level equivalent* at all levels. For example, if we wanted to compare the demand for sirloin steak with the farm-level demand, we would have to recognize that only about 10 percent of the beef carcass is made up of this type of steak and that the carcass represents only about 56–57 percent of the liveweight of the beef animal on the farm. There is a set of conversion factors that we can refer to for this purpose.[11]

Given our ability to express demands in terms of equivalent price and quantity units, we can draw demand curves for two or more market levels on the same diagram. Figure 4-11 illustrates hypothetical demand relations at two market levels. In this figure, D_R is the retail (or consumer) demand and D_F is the farm-level demand. D_R would also be referred to as the primary demand and D_F would be called the derived demand. The difference between these two demands is the marketing costs associated with each quantity of product demanded. In the

---

[10]Another economic use of the term *derived demand* is in conjunction with estimating the marginal value product from a production function. This is discussed in Chapter 5.

[11]U.S. Department of Agriculture, *Conversion Factors and Weights and Measures for Agricultural Commodities and Their Products,* Statistical Bulletin 362.

example, the marketing cost is constant at 75 cents/pound regardless of tne quantity marketed. Note that in the diagram D_R and D_F are as parallel as they will be for any product with a constant farm-to-retail marketing period. This means that both lines have the same *slope*. Are the price elasticities of the two also equal? Absolutely not. Slope does not equal elasticity. Let us examine *why*.

Recall that E_p = percent ΔQ/percent ΔP. In practice we would measure elasticity at a point on the lines or over a range of price and quantity changes. Let us assume that we start at retail demand point A and that an increase in supplies at that level causes a movement of equilibrium price and quantity along the curve to point B. This will be recorded as a ΔQ of about 3 million pounds and a ΔP of about 25 cents/pound. At the farm level, a movement from A' to B' also means a ΔQ of 3 million pounds and a ΔP of 25 cents/pound. Thus, as we said earlier, the slope of both demand lines is the same:

$$\frac{\Delta P_r}{\Delta Q} \text{ for } D_R = \frac{\Delta P_f}{\Delta Q} \text{ for } D_F$$

But E_p is not $\Delta Q/\Delta P$. It is the percentage change in Q divided by the percentage change in P. How do we calculate that? Over the range of price and quantity change, with the arc-elasticity formula, we take the average of the two P's or Q's as the base to which we relate the change. In algebraic notation

$$E_{pr} = \frac{\text{percent } \Delta Q}{\text{percent } \Delta P_r} = \frac{\Delta Q}{\Delta P_r} \left(\frac{\overline{P_r}}{\overline{Q}} \right)$$

At the retail level, $\Delta A/\Delta P$ is 3/25 cents, $\overline{P}_r$ is $(1.00 + 0.75)/2 = 0.875$, and $\overline{Q}$ is $(3 + 6)/2 = 4.50$. Thus,

$$E_{pr} = \frac{3}{-0.25} \left(\frac{0.875}{4.50} \right) = -2.33$$

At the farm level, $\Delta Q/\Delta P$ is 3/25 cents, $\overline{P}_f$ is $(0.50 + 0.25)/2 = 0.375$ and $\overline{Q}$ is $(3 + 6)/2 = 4.50$. Thus,

$$E_{pr} = \frac{3}{-0.25} \left(\frac{0.375}{4.50} \right) = -1.00$$

The price elasticity of the retail-level demand is always greater (in absolute terms) than the price elasticity of the farm-level demand across the same quantity range when the demands are parallel. In fact, if the demands are parallel, we can generally state that

$$E_{pf} = E_r \left(\frac{\overline{P_f}}{\overline{P_r}} \right)$$

As you might guess, demands may not be parallel over all quantity ranges. But we shall not discuss the topic further here since it is one of the subjects of Chapter 7. What we can point out, though, is that knowledge of the relationship between primary and derived demands permits us to estimate intermediate demand elasticities if we know primary demand elasticities, and vice versa. This has allowed economists to estimate farm-level demand elasticities after calculating retail-level estimates.

SUMMARY

Per capita consumption of food products in the United States has exhibited significant change over time. To explain the causes of some of these changes, we have reviewed and explained some of the concepts of consumer demand and their measurement. This included consideration of the own-price and quantity relationships, income demand relationships, and cross-demand relationships. The responsiveness of quantities demanded to changes in those factors and the measurement of responsiveness was described. Relationships of demand elasticities at different market levels were analyzed. The use of demand theory and measurements to analyze a specific change in demand were illustrated.

QUESTIONS

1 Describe the impacts of changes in incomes, changes in prices of other products, and changes in tastes and preferences on the demand for a given food product.
2 What have been the changes in U.S. food consumption patterns for major food groups since 1910? What are some of the possible causes of these changes?
3 Use the elasticities in Table 4-3 to analyze the consumption (1960–1970) changes for one of the products included in that table. Use the procedure described on pages 78 through 84.
4 Suppose you are advising a government on the consequences of a price support program for farm products. What would be the value of demand elasticity for the product?
5 Comment on the following statements. The demand elasticity for veal at retail is −1.7. One would expect, therefore, that the demand at farm for calves is also elastic.
6 Would you expect the income elasticity of demand for food to increase or decrease as income increases? Give the rationale for your answer.

BIBLIOGRAPHY

George, P. S., and G. A. King: *Consumer Demand for Food Commodities in the United States with Projections for 1980,* Giannini Foundation Monograph 26, California Agricultural Experiment Station, Mar. 1971.
Peterson, Willis L.: *Principles of Economics: Micro,* Darcey, 1971.
U.S. Department of Agriculture: *Conversion Factors and Weights and Measures for Agricultural Commodities and Their Products,* Statistical Bulletin 362.
Waugh, Frederick V.: *Demand and Price Analysis,* U.S. Department of Agriculture, Technical Bulletin 1316, Nov. 1964.

Chapter 5

Agricultural Production and Supply

INTRODUCTION

The production activities of farmers involve answering three basic questions: *What* commodities should I produce? *How much* of these will I produce? And *how* will I produce them? How farmers arrive at these answers is not readily discerned from observing the myriad of farm jobs they undertake.

One response to the above questions, and one not completely without validity, is *tradition*. But despite the tendency on the part of farmers to do things as they have in the past, major changes have occurred. Soybean production, which was a relatively insignificant 5 million bushels in 1924, is now in excess of 1.2 billion bushels per year. There has been a large shift of cotton production from the South to the Southwest since the turn of the century. Some of the major changes in the way farm products are produced are illustrated by large decreases in farm numbers and the continued adoption of new machinery and equipment.

If we question farmers further as to why they have made changes in levels of production of a given crop or product, and as to why they change the way they have produced the product, most farmers would likely respond that they changed because it increased profits. Most farmers are maximizers, and in this respect they resemble the consumer that we described in the previous chapter. In fact, farmers are both profit-maximizing producers and utility-maximizing consumers.

They use the return from the farm for consumption and savings. The greater the profit, the greater the satisfaction from consumption and savings. Maximization of profit is a basic assumption of production theory. This objective, together with given prices and technological production constraints, leads to the supply behavior of the farm firm. The translation of these behavioral patterns into an industry supply curve will be considered in the following two sections. First, we will consider the optimum use of a single-variable input. Then we will move to the more general output decision of the individual farm. This will lead to a better understanding and a basis for analysis of the aggregate production relation for a given product or for the entire farm sector.

SINGLE-VARIABLE RESOURCE PROBLEM

In analysis of the production process, the period of time under consideration usually has an impact on decisions and outcomes. To deal with this problem, economists have defined three time periods for analysis. These time periods are tied to the degree of resource fixity during the production process. The *immediate run* is a period in which none of the resources can be varied, and the *short run* is a period of time in which some of the resources can be varied and some are fixed. The *long run* is a period of time that permits all of the resources used in the production process to be varied. It is a period in which new firms can enter the industry or an existing firm can exit.

In agriculture, the questions raised about supply are often of a short-run nature. What will happen to next year's supplies of wheat, corn, and milk at certain prices? What will increased energy prices do to the U.S. farm outputs? These questions usually assume some fixed resources. Thus, let us begin our analysis with a very simple short-run decision.

A Milk Production Function

Consider a farmer with a production plant composed of buildings, land, and equipment. Even the labor of the farmer is a fixed input as long as the farmer continues in farming. These resources have to be used for production, where they are now employed, or not at all. Once the crop is planted, use of only a few inputs can be altered: fertilizer, chemicals, and cultivation for most crop enterprises and rates of feeding for most livestock enterprises. But at what levels should the farmer use these variable inputs?

Although the farmer usually has a number of variable inputs for which the optimum level of use must be simultaneously determined, the principles of the decision can be illustrated by considering just one variable input. The data for our example are drawn from actual dairy feeding experiments by the Iowa State Agricultural Experiment Station.[1] The experiment involved observation of

[1]E. O. Heady, N. L. Jacobsen, J. P. Madden, and A. E. Freeman, *Milk Production Functions in Relation to Feed Inputs, Cow Characteristics and Environmental Conditions,* Research Bulletin 529, Agricultural Extension Station, Iowa State University, Ames, Iowa, July 1964.

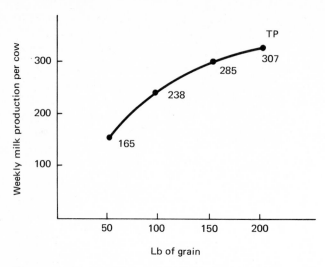

Figure 5-1   Weekly milk production per cow for alternative levels of grain feeding.

weekly milk production per cow associated with different levels of hay and grain use.

The data plotted in Figure 5-1 show weekly milk production associated with four levels of grain feeding: 50, 100, 150, and 200 pounds per week. These points are connected by a solid line. All other inputs, including the quantity of hay, were held constant. Hay was fixed at 100 pounds per week. One could assume that an actual farm has produced enough hay to feed at this rate. The observations indicate that increased grain feeding leads to higher milk production.

The Marginal Product

Although total milk production (TP) increases over the range of these grain feedings, Figure 5-1 shows that successive 50-pound increments in grain yield successively smaller additions to output. This illustrates a basic principle of economics: the law of diminishing marginal physical product. This law, generally stated, is that as successive units of a variable input, grain in this situation, are added to a fixed resource (the dairy cow, hay, building space, etc.), the additional increment to production will eventually decrease. The increment per unit of input is defined as the marginal physical product (MPP). Thus, it was calculated for the experiment that the 51st pound of grain increased milk production by 1.70 pounds, the 101st by 1.19 pounds, the 151st by 0.69 pound, and the 201st by 0.19 pound. Plotting these marginal physical products and connecting them with a line yields a relation with the characteristics of the curve in Figure 5-2.

At very low levels of use of the variable input, it may be possible to obtain increasing marginal physical product. At very high levels, marginal physical product may be negative, which indicates that total product is declining. The relevant range for determining optimum use is the declining segment of the MPP curve above the 0 axis. More detailed analysis of the characteristics of the marginal physical product curves are discussed in most intermediate economics theory textbooks.

The optimum level of feeding per cow can be determined in several ways given the prices of milk and grain. Here, we will use the marginal approach to optimum use of a variable input. First, however, we will make an assumption about milk and feed prices. We will assume that the milk producer represented by the experimental results is operating in a purely competitive market when selling milk or buying grain. This means that the prices of milk or grain per unit are the same regardless of the quantity that the milk producer buys, produces, or sells. For this example, we will assume a milk price of $6 per hundredweight, or 6 cents per pound, and a feed price of $4 per hundredweight, or 4 cents per pound.

Value of the Marginal Product

Calculation of the values of the marginal physical products at each level of use provide the basic information for determining optimum use. The values of additional units of feed (denoted at VMP) are calculated by multiplying MPP by product price *Pm*. The values are listed in Table 5-1 for the four levels of input use. Because MPP of the input is a declining function of quantity, VMP of the resource is also a declining function of quantity. Now, given the price of feed (4 cents per pound), consider the four levels of use listed in the table. At 50 pounds of grain per week, an additional pound of grain will produce 10.2 cents in additional revenue. This is sufficient to cover the cost of the additional feed (4 cents) and contribute 6.2 cents to profit or to cover fixed costs, thus increasing

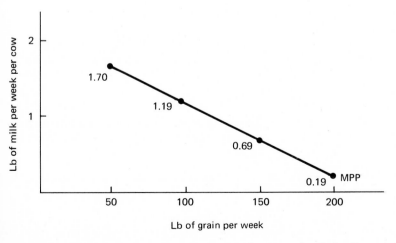

Figure 5-2   Marginal physical products of alternative rates of grain feeding per dairy cow.

Table 5-1   Value of Marginal Product for Alternative Levels of Grain Feeding

Pounds of grain	MPP of grain in pounds of milk	Price of milk in dollars per pound	VMP of grain dollars per pound (MPP × *Pm*)
50	1.70	0.06	0.102
100	1.19	0.06	0.071
150	0.69	0.06	0.041
200	0.19	0.06	0.011

profits or reducing losses. At 100 pounds of feed per week, an additional pound of feed will bring 7.1 cents in additional revenue. The cost of obtaining it is still only 4 cents. Obviously, this amount should be fed. At 200 pounds of feed, the additional revenue from using another unit of feed is 1.1 cents, but the cost is still 4 cents. Profits are now being reduced or losses increased. It appears that at these prices, the optimum level of feeding is slightly over 150 pounds per week. Graphically, this can be determined by the intersection of the horizontal dashed line at a feed price of 4 cents per pound and the VMP, as indicated in Figure 5-3.

A change in the price of feed will change the optimum feeding level. Suppose feed prices rise to $7 per hundredweight, or 7 cents per pound. Now, the optimum level of feeding falls to a little over 100 pounds per week. Again, this can be determined graphically, or it can be determined by using Table 5-1. You may now have deduced that the VMP curve is a kind of demand curve—the individual firm demand curve for the input. If the assumption of profit maximization holds, each point on the curve indicates the amount of feed that should be purchased at alternative feed prices.

Average and Marginal Costs

The technical production relationship between levels of inputs and outputs can also be translated into the individual firm supply curve for the product. Again, we will use the results of the dairy feeding experiment. In developing the supply relation, we hold the feed price constant at the $4 per hundredweight level.

Two unit cost–output relationships can be derived from the production relation with a fixed input price: the average variable costs of production and the marginal costs of production. Since grain is the only variable input in this example, the average variable cost is calculated by dividing total feed costs by total output for each level of output.

$$AVC = \frac{\text{price of input} \times \text{quantity of variable input}}{\text{quantity of output}}$$

The data and calculated value of AVC are presented in Table 5-2 and plotted in Figure 5-4. For the four milk output levels, AVC varies from 1.2 cents per pound

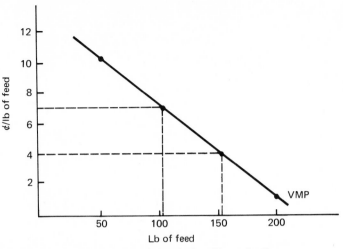

Figure 5-3   Value of marginal of grain in milk production.

of milk to 2.6 cents per pound. This measure does not readily indicate the level of optimum output, but it does indicate whether the firm should operate to minimize losses when product price is less than total average costs (variable plus fixed). As long as the price of milk exceeds the average variable costs of production, the farmer can pay for the variable input plus covering at least some of the fixed costs that are incurred, regardless of whether the firm operates or not.

Marginal cost (MC) of production for any given level of output is the additional total cost of producing an additional unit of output. Since fixed costs are the same regardless of the level of production, fixed cost does not enter into marginal cost. Thus, total costs of production vary only as variable costs vary. Marginal cost can be calculated by dividing the change in total costs at a given output level by the change in total output. Because the feed price (the variable input price) is the change in total cost, and since the change in total output is the MPP for a one-unit change in input use, the feed price can be divided by MPP to obtain MC for an additional unit of output:

Table 5-2   Costs Associated with Alternative Levels of Weekly Milk Production per Cow

Total milk production (lb/week)	Total grain (lb/week)	Price of feed ($/lb)	Average variable cost per pound of milk ($/lb)	Marginal cost per pound of milk ($/lb)
165	50	0.04	0.012	0.024
238	100	0.04	0.017	0.034
285	150	0.04	0.021	0.058
307	200	0.04	0.026	0.210

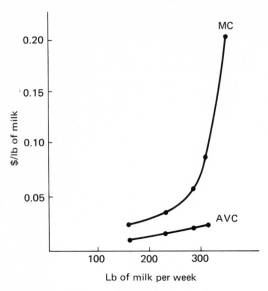

Figure 5-4 Average variable costs and marginal costs of milk production.

$$MC = \frac{\text{price of variable input}}{MPP}$$

The MC for four levels of output are listed in the last column of Table 5-2 and plotted in Figure 5-4, and they show a rapidly increasing relationship. The upward slope of the curve is the result of the law of diminishing marginal physical productivity.

Supply Curve

What level of milk production should be selected? Let us assume as before a milk price of $6 per hundredweight. If the farmer selected an output of 165 pounds, the farmer would be receiving an average return of 4.8 cents in excess of the variable costs. Obviously, it is not optimal to produce at this level. By expanding production per cow by 1 pound, the farmer can increase revenue by 6.0 cents while increasing costs by only 2.4 cents, thus increasing profits or reducing losses. Maximum contribution to profits or fixed costs can be achieved by producing slightly in excess of 285 pounds of milk per week at the point where the price of milk just equals MC. Note that this level of output with the given milk and feed price is consistent with the input level selected when considering the problem from the input side.

Selection of another milk price and holding feed price constant yields another optimum output level. It can be determined by equating MC of the output with the price of milk. The MC curve can therefore be considered as the supply curve for milk when each cow is considered a production unit.

COST-CURVE APPROACH TO FIRM DECISION MAKING

The preceding example has been highly simplified to illustrate the derivation of an input demand curve and a product supply curve where only one input is variable. Farms, however, are not one cow or one acre. Numerous inputs are involved and once a farm unit has been established, the farmer may have a substantial number of inputs that are variable and many that are fixed. Nevertheless, the decisions on the optimum use of each variable input are governed by the principles described above.

Production Costs and the Level of Production

Cost curves for production units are commonly used to illustrate the production and supply decision of the individual firm. Given the technical production relationships for a firm and the input prices, costs associated with any given level of production can be calculated. Such costs for a hypothetical 500-acre wheat farm are presented in Table 5-3. The production relation assumed for these costs is characterized by diminishing marginal physical productivity of the variable inputs. Total, average, and marginal costs are presented for this firm.

The average and marginal costs plotted in Figure 5-5 exhibit characteristics that are common to cost curves for any firm which encounters diminishing MPP. Average fixed costs (AFC) decline continuously as output increases because a fixed total amount is allocated to a larger and larger output. Average variable costs (AVC), the total variable cost divided by output, first declines and then rises. Average total costs are the sum of AFC and AVC.

Marginal cost of any given output, which was defined in the last section, is the cost of obtaining an additional unit of output. It may have a declining

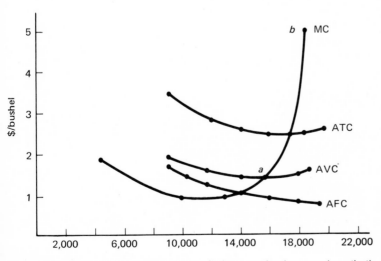

Figure 5-5 Average and variable costs of wheat production on a hypothetical farm.

Table 5-3   Costs of Wheat Production on a 500-acre Hypothetical Wheat Farm (Costs per Year)

Total fixed costs (TFC)	Total variable costs (TVC)	Total costs	Total wheat production (bushels)	Total revenue	AFC[a]	AVC[a]	ATC[a]	MC[a]
$15,000	.....	$15,000	.....	.....	.....	.....	.....	$1.944
15,000	$17,500	32,500	9,000	$42,000	$1.667	$1.944	$3.611	1.000
15,000	20,000	35,000	11,500	46,000	1.304	1.739	3.044	1.000
15,000	22,500	37,500	14,000	56,000	1.071	1.607	2.679	1.250
15,000	25,000	40,000	16,000	64,000	0.938	1.563	2.500	2.500
15,000	27,500	42,500	17,000	68,000	0.882	1.618	2.500	5.000
15,000	30,000	45,000	17,500	70,000	0.857	1.714	2.571	.....

[a]In dollars per bushel.

segment, but the relevant range for decision making is the rising segment. It is a kind of image of the MPP curve; its falling part is associated with increasing MPP and its rising part is associated with declining MPP.

The MC curve bears a specific relationship to the AVC and ATC curves. It intersects both from below at their minimum points, approximately $1.58 on the AVC curve and approximately $2.50 on the ATC curve. Regardless of the levels of average costs, the MC curve will intersect them from below and at their minimums as long as they are U-shaped.

The average and marginal costs permit us to determine not only the optimum level of output but also the profit per unit and the shutdown price. First, assume for the hypothesized farm that wheat is selling at $4 per bushel. If the farmer chooses to operate at 16,000 bushels of output, where the ATC is a minimum, total profit will be $24,000 ($1.50 × 16,000). But note that the additional costs of producing another bushel is $2.50, whereas it can be sold for $4. Total profit can be increased by $1.50 by expanding output by one bushel. Although the additional cost per bushel rises, the same rationale can be used for expanding output to somewhat in excess of 17,000 bushels. Beyond this point, additional costs of expanding output exceed the additional return (MR), which for the competitive market firm is the going price.

If the market price declines to $2.48, what output should be selected? If the farm continues to produce 17,000+ bushels, the farmer would lose about 2 cents on each bushel, the difference between price and average cost at that output level. Reducing output by one unit reduces cost by $3.25 and reduces total revenue by only $2.48. The output at which price (MR) just equals MC is 16,500 bushels. It is also the output of minimum average total cost, and at $2.48 per bushel the firm is just covering all fixed and variable costs.

For wheat prices below minimum average costs, it will be loss minimizing for the farmer to produce wheat in the short run as long as the price exceeds average variable costs of production. The reason it minimizes losses is that all variable costs are covered plus some contributions to fixed costs. Because fixed costs continue whether the farmer produces or not, any contribution to them by operating will reduce total loss.

Calculation of the optimum level of wheat production for profit maximization or loss minimization for any given price is at that output where price equals MC as long as MC exceeds minimum AVC. These points are on segment ab of the MC curve in Figure 5-5. It is also this firm's supply curve for that product—the amount of wheat produced at each alternative price.

MARKET SUPPLY

Horizontal summation of the individual firms' supply curves for wheat yields the market supply curve for wheat, disregarding stocks. If the hypothetical wheat farm is representative of 10,000 total wheat farms, then market supply for each price can be determined by multiplying the per farm output by 10,000. The market supply of wheat is shown in the following table.

Price ($/bushel)	Quantity (millions of bushels)
$1.56	160
2.48	165
4.00	170
5.00	172.5

If, as is characteristic of most industries, farms differ in size, then each farm may be characterized by a different MC relation. The horizontal sum still yields the market supply.

Market supply relationships for agriculture as well as for other industries are *ceterus paribus* relationships, that is, these are the quantities that will be offered at the alternative prices with all other factors affecting supply held constant. The factors are prices of inputs, prices of other products that can be produced with the same resources, technology, and the number of firms. The supply relationship, like the demand relationship discussed in Chapter 4, can be expressed by an implicit functional relation. For supply it is:

$$Q_s = f(P, P_i, P_o, T_e, N, E, C)$$

where Q_s = quantity supplied
f = function
P = price of commodity
P_i = price of inputs
P_0 = price of other possible outputs
T_e = technology
N = number of firms
E = expectations
C = capacity of the plant (number of acres)

Supply Shifters

What happens if one or more of the *ceterus paribus* conditions, such as the price of an input, change? Price of the variable input determines how much of it is used. At any given product price, an increase in an input price reduces the quantity used, consequently reducing output. A reduction in input price results in greater use and therefore greater output. Thus, increases in input prices shift the supply curve to the left, from S_1 to S_2 in Figure 5-6. A decrease in input price shifts the supply curve to the right, from S_1 to S_3.

Technological changes are embodied in new resource combinations or better resources that decrease total resource needs for producing any given level of output and, consequently, reduce total and average costs of production. The supply curve is therefore shifted to the right as technology is adopted. Technological improvements have been crucial in expanding U.S. and world food output. Improved seed varieties and increased fertilizer use have tremendously

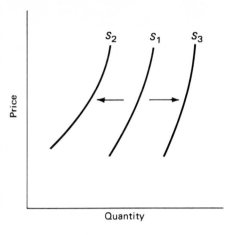

Figure 5-6 An increase in input prices shifts the supply curve from S_1 to S_2. A decrease in input prices shifts the curve from S_1 to S_3.

increased corn yields in the United States and wheat and rice yields throughout the world. Many other technical improvements are represented by new and improved machinery that permits better soil preparation, weed control, and harvesting. Chemical weed, insect, and disease control have been significant. All of these improvements have occurred primarily during the twentieth century, and they have resulted in tremendously increased production from a given quantity and labor resources.

Changes in prices of products that can be produced with the same resources will shift the supply curve. Thus, wheat supply on the Great Plains assumes a constant level of sorghum and cattle prices. An increase in sorghum price means that the land, labor, fertilizer, etc., used in sorghum production will now be more profitable than if used in wheat production. Wheat production will decline and no price change will be exhibited. Price increases for other products that can be produced with given inputs shift the wheat supply curve to the left; price decreases for the other products shift the curve to the right.

Supply relations have been estimated for numerous agricultural commodities. Empirical studies usually involve estimation of the response not only to its own price but also to input prices, prices of products competing for the same resources, and occasionally technology. These studies are used for predicting production of farm products as well as evaluating the consequences of alternative farm policies.

Supply relationships have been estimated using three different sources of data. These are (1) actual price, quantity, and shift variable observations, (2) accounting cost data provided by firms, and (3) "engineering" cost data.

Studies designed to estimate market supply curves for various agricultural commodities frequently use data obtained from survey observations of quantity changes made by producers as the price of the commodity, input prices, price of production substitutes, and variables that are proxies for technological change.

Accounting information provided by businesses that produce and sell farm inputs, farm products, or food products permits estimation of points on the firm's total fixed and total variable cost curves. As cost figures are collected over different levels of output and for different firms, additional points help "trace out" the short-run cost curves for the "average" firm. Aggregation of the derived marginal cost curves from these data permits an estimation of the market supply curve.

Where accounting data are unavailable, a "typical" firm's costs may be estimated from the hypothetical production costs developed by the "engineer" who designed the production process. The *number* of labor hours, *kilowatts* of electricity, and other *quantity* measures of production interrelationships are *valued* at present market prices. These cost values are then used to estimate fixed and variable costs and *marginal costs,* which are summed for all firms to obtain a market supply curve.

Of the three data sources and techniques, the two involving accounting and engineering costs are somewhat "normative" in character. This means that they do not show measurements of actual market supply responses, but indicate how a firm *should* respond *if* the costs recorded or engineered are reasonably correct.

ELASTICITY OF SUPPLY

Elasticity Formula

An explicit statement of the supply relationship in either algebraic or tabular form, although useful, is often meaningless to the lay person or even to other economists who are not familiar with actual price or quantity in the particular industry. Also, as with demand, comparisons from one industry to another are difficult. Thus, a standardized measure that can be used to compare response of quantity supplied to price changes between products is the *price elasticity of supply*. It is calculated in the same manner as demand elasticity and its interpretation is also similar. It is the percentage change in quantity supplied in response to a 1 percent change in price:

$$E_S = \frac{\text{percent } \Delta Q_s}{\text{percent } \Delta P} = \frac{(Q_1 - Q_2)/(Q_1 + Q_2)}{(P_1 - P_2)/(P_1 + P_2)}$$

The sign of the elasticity of supply is positive, indicating that the supply curve is upward sloping. It can be calculated at a point or at an average for an arc on the curve. Depending upon the position and shape of the supply curve, the elasticity of supply may be constant throughout the curve or continually changing. It is often reported as though it were constant. Since the price and quantity changes are often over a relatively small range, use of a constant elasticity may not be a serious problem.

Another important characteristic of supply relations is that the amount of adjustment to input price changes, technology, product price, or other factors may differ depending upon the time permitted for adjustment to take place. This is related to the characteristic of fixed and variable resources. As we extend the period in which adjustment can take place, the amount of adjustment increases.

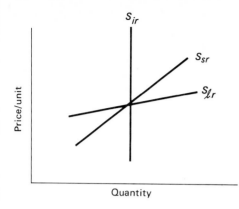

Figure 5-7 Immediate-run, short-run, and long-run supply curves.

To illustrate, consider the immediate run. It may be the marketing day or week for agricultural products. Nothing can be done to change supply. The quantity of tomatoes, for example, can be altered only by harvesting or not harvesting. As long as the price of tomatoes is above harvesting costs, it will either be profitable or loss minimizing to market the entire crop. Regardless of the price, nothing can be done to increase the size of the crop during the period. The supply curve for this situation is illustrated by the vertical supply curve S_i in Figure 5-7.

The other extreme is that situation where the time period is sufficiently long such that (1) the number of producers can change, (2) the size of the producing unit can be varied, and (3) each unit can vary all production inputs. These are the long-run supply conditions. Now, if all producers in total can purchase any quantity of each input at the going price (a completely elastic supply of inputs), then the long-run supply for the product will be infinitely elastic (horizontal). For a crop (such as tomatoes) that uses a relatively small part of each agricultural resource, the supply curve of inputs is likely to be highly elastic. Therefore, the long-run supply curve for tomatoes is likely to be quite elastic. Where the product uses a large portion of total agricultural resources (wheat, for example), then the supplies of each input are not likely to be completely elastic to wheat producers. The long-run supply curve will be considerably more elastic than for the immediate run, but it will not be completely elastic. Graphically, it may appear as curve S_{lr} in Figure 5-7.

Another decision period in which farmers find themselves is the short run, during which some of the inputs can be varied and some cannot. In this period the number of producing units remains fixed. Tomato producers can, during the production period, vary use of fertilizer, water, perhaps some land, labor, and various chemicals. But changes in the number of producers occurs more slowly and the shifting of new land into tomato production requires a longer period of time. Thus, the producers can vary more inputs than in the immediate run, but they are limited in adjusting the use of some. Further changes in numbers of producers are limited. The short-run supply curve S_{sr} lies between the immediate-run and long-run curve in Figure 5-7.

Table 5-4   Estimated Elasticities of Supply for Agricultural Products

	Elasticity of supply	
	Short run	Long run
Coffee (Brazil)[a]	0.117	0.625
Milk (U.S.)[b]	0.089	0.145
Soybeans[c]	0.840	. . . .

[a]R. G. Taylor, "Alternative Measures of Supply Elasticities: The Case of São Paulo Coffee," *American Journal of Agricultural Economics,* vol. 56, no. 1, Feb. 1974, p. 101.

[b]J. W. Hammond, "Regional Supply Analysis," Staff Paper 74-12, Department of Agricultural and Applied Economics, University of Minnesota, July 1974, p. 2.

[c]J. P. Houck and A. Subotnik, "The U.S. Supply of Soybeans: Regional Acreage Function," *Agricultural Economics Research,* vol. 21, no. 4, Oct. 1969, p. 106.

Elasticity of Agricultural Supply

Some measures of elasticity for agricultural products are presented in Table 5-4. For some of the crops, both long-run and short-run elasticities have been calculated. Both estimates indicate a low response of quantity supplied to price. Although the precise definition of elastic and inelastic does not apply as it does in demand analysis, it is generally considered that supply responses of less than 1 are inelastic. In Table 5-4 we have a value of 0.089 for milk, which means that a 10 percent increase in milk prices will bring about a quantity increase of 0.89 percent. Even in the long run, total milk production would increase only 1.45 percent. Soybeans are somewhat more responsive, showing a 10 percent increase in acreage in the following year. These elasticities, which are merely a few that have been estimated for agricultural commodities, indicate a highly inelastic supply for most agricultural commodities. They also indicate why the substantial price increases for agricultural commodities that have occurred since 1972 have generated very little supply response. In part, this happened because the other factors affecting supply have changed and in some cases have more than offset the impact of commodity price changes. Thus, in 1974, corn production, soybean production, and milk production were all down despite substantial price increases.

There are several causes for the extreme inelasticity of agricultural supply, particularly the short-run elasticities. Agricultural supply in the short run is highly inelastic because of the high proportion of fixed inputs, land, the farmer's own labor, buildings, and equipment. Some studies of agricultural costs show that fixed costs for many products account for 50–80 percent of total production costs. Thus, price can fall tremendously without driving producers out of business in the short run. In the situation of high and rising prices, new resources cannot be quickly brought into production.

The time necessary to bring some of the resources into production is quite long. Beef cattle production, for example, requires a buildup of the breeding herd. In fact, the immediate response to price increases may be additional reduction in supplies as heifers and cows are held back for breeding. Expansion of tree crop production is a several-year process. This causes short-run supply to be highly inelastic.

The limited alternatives for major farm resources cause total agricultural supply to be highly inelastic. This is particularly true of land, labor, and specialized equipment. Much of our prime agricultural land has very limited alternatives, even for recreation. Thus, crop and livestock prices would have to drop tremendously before the land is withdrawn from farming. Obviously, much of our cropland can be, and is, transferred from one agricultural enterprise to another. This implies that total agricultural supply is likely to be more inelastic than individual farm commodities. Professor Cochrane investigated this relation in the late 1950s and early 1960s. His conclusion was that total agricultural supply was essentially completely inelastic in the short run.[2]

Agricultural supply may also appear to be inelastic because of the close relationship between farm product prices and agricultural-input prices.[3] This is partly caused by the fact that many farm products are also farm inputs, such as feed for cattle. A general decline in the level of farm prices also brings about decline in feed prices. Another reason for this relationship is that the fixed resources, land and farm labor, are residual claimants on the income generated in production. As farm prices fall, the return to the fixed inputs (rent) declines. As farm prices rise, the return to fixed inputs rises. Thus, price changes may have a more important impact on these returns than upon bringing about large changes in variable resources and consequent production changes. This may be declining in importance with the increased share of nonfarm inputs in agriculture, but it is still important.

Evidence of this relationship is gained by comparing price changes for a recent rise in farm prices. Prices for feed grains, which make up a large part of agricultural output, increased by 128 percent from 1967 to October 1975. During the same period, all livestock and livestock product prices increased by 95 percent. Dairy product prices increased, but only by 83 percent.

The inelasticity of agricultural supply, both aggregate and for many individual commodities, is partially illustrated by the data in Table 5-5. Total annual farm output has changed by more than 5 percent in only 3 years since 1950. Output of livestock and livestock products has changed a maximum of 4 percent only twice since 1950. This reflects the long time period necessary to make adjustments in production and the large fixed-resource commitments during that period. All crop production changed by more than 5 percent four times during this period. However, individual crops did show considerably more variability. This reflects the greater ability of the agricultural sector to shift land from production of one crop to another from one year to the next. Some of the large changes that have

[2]Willard W. Cochrane, *Farm Prices, Myth and Reality,* University of Minnesota Press, Minneapolis, 1958.
[3]This is not really a cause of inelastic supply. Input prices change causing a shift of the supply curve.

Table 5-5 Farm Production: Indexes of Total Farm Output and Gross Production of Livestock and Crops by Groups, for 48 States, 1950–1974 (1967 = 100)

Year	Farm output[b]	Livestock and livestock products[a]				Crops									
		All[c]	Meat animals[d]	Dairy products[e]	Poultry and eggs[f]	All[g]	Feed grains[h]	Hay and forage[i]	Food grains[j]	Vege-tables[j]	Fruits and nuts[k]	Sugar crops[m]	Cotton[n]	Tobacco	Oil crops[o]
1950	73	75	74	93	56	76	65	77	64	85	87	68	135	103	41
1951	75	78	79	92	59	77	60	80	63	80	89	54	205	118	38
1952	78	78	79	92	59	81	64	78	81	81	86	55	205	114	37
1953	79	79	78	97	61	81	62	80	74	84	87	62	222	105	37
1954	79	82	81	98	63	79	66	80	66	83	88	69	188	114	41
1955	82	84	86	99	62	82	69	85	62	86	88	63	199	111	46
1956	82	84	83	101	68	82	69	81	65	91	92	63	180	110	54
1957	80	83	80	102	69	80	75	88	61	88	84	72	148	84	53
1958	86	85	82	101	73	89	82	88	90	90	91	70	154	88	65
1959	88	88	88	100	76	89	85	84	72	89	93	77	196	91	58
1960	90	87	85	101	75	92	88	89	86	91	87	75	192	99	61
1961	90	91	89	104	81	91	79	89	78	96	91	84	193	104	71
1962	91	92	90	105	81	92	80	92	73	94	92	86	200	117	72
1963	95	95	95	104	83	95	87	92	76	94	89	111	207	119	75
1964	94	97	98	105	87	93	76	93	84	90	90	113	206	113	75
1965	97	95	92	104	90	98	89	97	87	96	95	100	202	94	90
1966	96	97	96	101	96	95	89	96	87	97	97	100	129	95	96
1967	100	100	100	100	100	100	100	100	100	100	100	100	100	100	100
1968	102	100	102	99	98	103	95	100	105	103	93	116	148	87	112
1969	103	101	102	99	101	104	99	100	97	103	113	120	135	91	115
1970	102	105	108	100	106	100	90	99	91	101	107	119	137	97	117
1971	111	108	112	101	107	112	116	106	107	100	116	117	145	86	121
1972	110	108	110	102	109	113	112	105	102	101	104	128	187	88	131
1973	112	105	108	98	106	120	115	109	113	102	130	112	175	88	155
1974[p]	106	106	110	98	106	110	92	104	120	110	122	107	157	100	129

[a]Production of livestock products. Horses and mules excluded.

[b]The index number of farm output in some instances may be outside the range of the index number of all crops and the index number of all livestock production.

[c]Includes clipped wool, mohair, and for 1950 to date, honey and beeswax. These items are not included in the separate groups of livestock and products shown.

[d]Cattle and calves, sheep and lambs, and hogs.

[e]Butter, butterfat, wholesale milk, retail milk, and milk consumed on farms.

[f]Chickens and eggs, commercial broilers, and turkeys.

[g]Includes farm gardens, hay seeds, pasture seeds, cover-crop seeds, and some miscellaneous crop production not included in separate groups of crops shown.

[h]Corn for grain, oats, barley, and sorghum grain.

[i]All hay, sorghum forage, corn silage, and for 1950 to date, sorghum silage.

[j]All wheat, rye, buckwheat, and rice.

[k]Potatoes, sweet potatoes, dry edible beans, dry field peas, truck crops for processing, and truck crops for fresh market having value.

[l]Fruits, berries, and tree nuts having value. Citrus production is on year of harvest, 1960 to date. Earlier years on year of bloom.

[m]Sugarbeets, sugarcane for sugar and seed, sugarcane syrup, and maple syrup.

[n]Cotton lint and cottonseed.

[o]Soybeans, peanuts picked and threshed, peanuts hogged, flaxseed, and for 1950 to date, tungnuts.

[p]Preliminary.

Source: U.S. Department of Agriculture, *1975 Changes in Farm Production and Efficiency—A Summary Report,* Statistical Bulletin 548, Economic Research Service, Sept. 1975, p. 5.

occurred in individual crop production are the consequence of weather variability and major changes in farm programs between crop years. Cotton, feed grain, and tobacco have been under certain kinds of production control for much of the time since 1950. Major changes in the price support and associated production control programs can be associated with some of the major year-to-year production changes.

RESPONSE CURVES VERSUS SUPPLY CURVES

A number of researchers of agricultural supply relationships have observed a peculiar kind of adjustment to price changes. They have found that the quantity response for agricultural products to a given price change is larger for price increases than for price decreases, that is, a larger supply elasticity for price increases than for price decreases. Halvorson estimated that the supply elasticity for milk production during the period 1927–1957 was 0.268 for price increases and 0.197 for price decreases.[4]

The discrepancies between these results can be accounted for by distinguishing between two types of relations, the response curve and the supply curve. The short-run supply curve, as we have defined it, indirectly reflects the adjustment of quantity of resources in response to price change. In an actual situation of rising prices, farmers not only adjust the quantity of inputs, they adapt new and improved technologies. Rising farm prices result in increased income, cash flows, and availability of credit, which facilitates adoption of new technology. Once these changes have been made, falling prices do not cause farmers to drop the technology. Consequently, quantity supplied is reduced only by reduction of quantity of inputs. Supply adjustment to price rises is represented by curve *ab* in Figure 5-8. This is the response curve. Adjustment to a price decline is along curve *bc,* the new short-run supply curve. The response curve can also be considered as the shifting of the short-run supply curve.

The response curve implies some reservoir of output-increasing technology. Thus, the extent to which available technologies have been adopted should affect the slope of the response curve. Nevertheless, the possibility of more rapid technological adoption during periods of rising prices should be considered in evaluation of price policies or in projection of agricultural supply.

LONG-TERM CHANGES IN AGRICULTURAL PRODUCTION AND PRODUCTIVITY

The firm behavior patterns described in the earlier part of this chapter and technological changes imply alterations in agricultural output and changes in the way it is produced. A look at data relating to these dimensions of agricultural supply since 1910 indicates some major changes.

---

[4]H. Halvorson, "The Response of Milk Production to Price," *Journal of Farm Economics,* vol. 40, no. 5, pp. 1, 112, Dec. 1958.

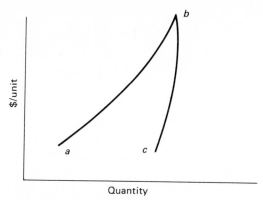

Figure 5-8 Response curve *ab* and supply curve *bc*.

Output Trends

There are two basic series that measure agricultural output: the *farm output index* and the *farm marketing and consumption index*. The two series differ primarily in how inventories are handled. The farm output index includes all production on farms regardless of whether it is sold or not. The farm marketing and consumption index includes the output that is sold regardless of the year of its production. It also excludes feeds. Over time, the behavior of the two indexes will be the same, while for any given year there can be substantial departures. The farm output index most accurately represents annual farm production.

The data in Table 5-6 are the 10-year indexes of agricultural output beginning in 1910. (All of the indexes in the section are calculated from the 1967 base period.) Output more than doubled since 1910 but the growth has been rather erratic. Output was essentially stable between 1920 and 1930. Largest decennial gains have been made since 1940. Although the long-term pattern has been erratic, it has been nonetheless strongly upward. It has kept pace with the

**Table 5-6   Indexes of Total Farm
Output, 1910–1970**
(1967 Base = 100)

Year	Index
1910	44
1920	51
1930	52
1940	60
1950	73
1960	90
1970	102

Source: U.S. Department of Agriculture,
*Changes in Farm Production Efficiency—Annual
Summary Reports*, Economic Research Service.

increased food demands and needs of a growing population, and it has maintained the United States as a major exporter of agricultural products.

Input Trends

How has the increase in total output experienced since 1910 been achieved? One could visualize a situation in which output increases were achieved by increasing the number of producing units, each of which continually combines the inputs in the same manner as in the past. But the way we produce has changed significantly. We have already reviewed the change that has taken place in number of farms. Farm numbers have declined continuously since 1910. Let us consider the three major classifications of inputs that are used.

The land resource base is essentially limited and expansion can be achieved by reclamation of wetlands or irrigation of irrigable land. Both produce only minor changes in cultivatable land. In spite of these possibilities for increasing cropland, we have actually reduced cropland use since 1910 (see Table 5-7). The high acreage occurred in 1930 and then fell about one-sixth by 1970.

Total cropland use is somewhat misleading regarding its use for salable farm products. During the early part of the century and well into the 1920s, a large share of the total cropland was needed to produce feeds for animal power. The almost complete switch to tractor power has enabled us to use almost all land for salable output or feeds that are marketed as livestock or livestock products. Excluding acres used to feed draft animals, the average picture is somewhat different, showing an increase of approximately 25 percent over the period. However, after allowing for these apparent deductions since 1940, land has remained a relatively stable input in agriculture. The 1930–1940 declines in acreages may have been due to the drought of the 1930s. The 1960 to 1970 decline has resulted from farm programs which removed land from production. It has been estimated that 60–70 million acres were removed as a result of the programs. With the removal of all acreage controls in 1974, we should see some increases in cropland in production.

The labor input in agriculture, measured in worker-hours of labor for farm

Table 5-7 Total Cropland Use in the United States, 1910–1970

Year	Millions of acres used for crops	Excluding acres used for feed or power
1910	325	237
1920	360	270
1930	369	304
1940	339	295
1950	345	326
1960	328	322
1970	293	

Source: U.S. Department of Agriculture, *Changes in Farm Production Efficiency—Annual Summary Reports*, Economic Research Service.

**Table 5-8 Index of Labor and
Input in Agriculture**
(1967 Base = 100)

Year	Index
1910	
1920	364
1930	293
1940	282
1950	208
1960	135
1970	90

Source: U.S. Department of Agriculture,
*Changes in Farm Production Efficiency—Annual
Summary Reports,* Economic Research Service.

work, has exhibited large decreases for the entire period and still appears to be declining (see Table 5-8). From 1940 to 1970, the index fell by two-thirds. Part of the decline in labor use is attributable to shorter working hours on farms, but most is due to outmigration.

Outmigration and reduced labor use in agriculture have been offset by substitution of other inputs. It is difficult to argue that agriculture has not made rapid labor adjustments when viewing outmigration figures. Farm population declined by one-third in the 1960s. Some argue that this net outmigration is now at an end. There are implications of this for the future of the farm sector and the way in which agriculture will adjust in the coming years.

Use of capital inputs has increased dramatically since 1910. Two of the more important items are listed in Table 5-9. Mechanical power and machinery use increased more than five times between 1910 and 1970, and fertilizer and lime use increased approximately 22 times. Mechanical power has substituted for manual labor and animal power. Fertilizer and lime have been substituted for land inputs.

Table 5-9 Indexes of Capital
(1967 Base = 100)

	Input use in agriculture	
Year	Index of mechanical power and machinery	Fertilizer and lime
1910	18	5
1920	29	8
1930	37	10
1940	39	14
1950	79	32
1960	91	54
1970	102	113

Source: U.S. Department of Agriculture, *Changes in Farm Production Efficiency—Annual Summary Reports,* Economic Research
Service.

**Table 5-10   Index of Total Input
Use in Agriculture**
(1967 Base = 100)

Year	Index
1910	82
1920	93
1930	97
1940	98
1950	101
1960	97
1970	102

Source: U.S. Department of Agriculture,
*Changes in Farm Production Efficiency—Annual
Summary Reports,* Economic Research Service.

This substitution has been the key to our expanded agricultural output. Its more recent and sometimes more planned and directed application and results in the less developed countries of the world are known as the "green revolution."

Thus, while total agricultural output has increased, the land input has remained rather stable, labor has decreased, and capital has increased. A composite measure of all inputs, the *total input index* (price weighted), calculated by the USDA is presented in Table 5-10. Assuming it is reasonably accurate, the index indicates that total input use has increased about 25 percent since 1910. Most of this occurred between 1910 and 1930. The index has increased only about 5 percent since 1930. The total bundle of inputs has increased slightly over time with a large change in the mix. It is this substitution of new and improved resources that has caused the farm supply curve to shift to the right.

Productivity

Many analysts of agricultural production speak of efficiency and gains in efficiency. Commonly used measures of productivity are output per acre, output per worker-hour, and output per farmworker. These measures show tremendous gains since 1910. Crop production per acre approximately doubled between 1910 and 1970 and output per worker-hour increased eightfold (see Table 5-11). The measure that politicians, deans of colleges, and economists are fond of quoting is the number of persons supplied with agricultural products by one farmworker—7.1 in 1910 and 47.1 in 1970. Obviously, these are strikingly distinct ratios, yet they may be somewhat misleading. Instead of using land to produce feed for power, the nonfarm sector is providing energy inputs. Thus, the total farm productivity index will probably more accurately reflect the increase in farm productivity. This is the ratio of the total output index to total input index in percentage terms. Presented in the last column of Table 5-6, it shows roughly a doubling of agricultural productivity since 1910.

There is not complete agreement, however, on the meaning of this index. There are those who argue that the index is basically correct and those who argue that it understates the productivity picture. The debate revolves around how

Table 5-11   Indexes of Agricultural Productivity

Year	Index of crops produced per acre	Index of output per worker-hour	Person supplied by one farmworker	Productivity index
1910	56	14	7.1	54
1920	61	15	8.3	55
1930	53	17	9.8	54
1940	62	21	10.7	61
1950	69	35	15.5	73
1960	88	67	25.8	93
1970	102	113	47.1	100

Source: U.S. Department of Agriculture, *Changes in Farm Production Efficiency—Annual Summary Reports,* Economic Research Service.

depreciation is calculated. Some say that the increase in production is primarily the result of the increased use of inputs. One way to consider the impact of technology is to assume that increased total input use will cause a proportional increase in production. Any additional increase in production will be the result of technological advance. Thus, from 1960 to 1970, total input use in agriculture increased approximately 5 percent. Total output increased by about 13 percent. Consequently, approximately 40 percent of the increase was the result of increased inputs and 60 percent was attributable to new technology. Economists are not always in agreement on the impact of the two factors. Some agricultural economists would ascribe 80 percent of the increased output to technological advance and 20 percent to increased input. Other economists would say that technology accounts for only about 40 percent of the increase in output and increased input accounts for the remaining 60 percent of the extra output. The difference in opinion comes from disagreement about what input costs are considered.

Regardless of the position taken, another important question is *what* has given rise to increasing technological advance. Technological advance is important in either case. It has been argued that the capital invested in the human agent (human capital) accounts for most of the increase in output not accounted for by increased inputs. *Technology* may be defined as the total flow of new knowledge into agriculture. Technological advance may also be embodied in operational advantages that provide greater output. For example, the average planting time for corn is limited to a few days per year. Introduction of machinery to do the job faster (six-row planters) allows greater plantings to take place in this limited time period.

SUMMARY

Although tradition plays a role, most farmers respond to the question of what, how much, and how to produce by deciding which is most profitable.

The single-variable resource problem treats the relationship between the production of a product (like milk) in terms of the amount of a single input (like feed grain) used in the production process. All other inputs are held constant. This relationship is called a *production function.*

The marginal product is the additional product realized from adding an incremental unit of input. The marginal product decreases as more and more units of input are added because of the law of diminishing marginal physical product. If we value the marginal product in terms of the price it will bring on the open market, we obtain the value of the marginal product (VMP), which is the firm's derived demand for the input.

The production function also can be valued in terms of the cost of the input(s). Where we have only one input (like feed) being varied, the cost of production includes variable costs (cost of feed) and fixed costs (cost of all other inputs). Combined, variable costs (VC) *plus* fixed costs (FC) equal total cost (TC). Costs can be viewed in total, average, or marginal terms. Average costs are simply total, fixed, or variable costs divided by the quantity of input; marginal costs are the incremental costs associated with each change in input usage.

A firm's marginal cost curve is also its supply curve. The decision of how much a farmer will produce depends upon whether the extra cost of more production is less than, equal to, or greater than the return which the farmer will receive for the extra product. If the marginal cost is less than marginal revenues, the farmer should produce more; but if MR is less than MC, then the farmer should reduce production. The farmer should produce that quantity where MC equals MR.

Market supply refers to the horizontal summation of all the individual producer supply (MC) curves for a product sold in the same market. The market supply relationship relates price and quantity—the quantity that would be provided at different price levels. The market supply curve (like the producer supply schedule), however, shifts to the left or right if the price of the inputs change, if the production function changes (due to technological developments), or if the price of the output varies.

Supply elasticity is a measure of the *relative* change in output quantity brought forth by a change in price. It is expressed in percentage terms:

$$E_s = \frac{\text{percent } \Delta Q_s}{\text{percent } \Delta P}$$

In the immediate run $E_s = 0$, meaning that it is perfectly inelastic. E_s takes on a positive value in the short run and long run, but short-run supply elasticity is always less than long-run supply elasticity.

The elasticity of supply for farm products varies by product, but individually and collectively the value is usually less than for nonfarm products because of the high fixed costs characteristic of farming.

U.S. agricultural output is measured by the USDA farm-output index. The index increased from 44 points in 1910 to 102 points in 1970. This doubling of agricultural production came about in face of a decrease in crop acreage and a substantial decline in farm labor. It is explained by strong increases in mechanical power, fertilizer and other farm chemicals, and improved inputs.

QUESTIONS

1 The supply relationships discussed in this chapter were applied to *farm* situations. But do the same production and cost theories apply to nonfarm businesses? Consider a processing firm that buys raw farm products and changes that commodity into a product ready for consumer purchase. Does the processing firm have the same kind of production decisions to make? Are its cost curves different?

2 Historically, farm prices have trended *downward* over a period of several decades. Nevertheless, farmers have continuously increased the quantity of production. Is this irrational behavior on the part of the farmers? Assuming farmers' rationality, how might we explain this phenomenon?

3 Certain inputs can be added to the production process in a continuous range of units. This was true in our feed and milk output example. We could add extra pounds (even ounces) of feed until we reached our optimum level of input usage.

For some inputs, however, we must add them in "lumpy" units. For example, under most labor contracts we usually cannot ask a laborer to work one-half hour per week or selectively permit him (her) to work 22 hours one week and 57 the next. Rather, we must offer 40 hours of employment per week. How would this affect the level of labor use if this is the only variable input? (Use a diagram like Figure 5-2 to illustrate the impact.) How might the "time-and-one-half" wage rule for labor hours exceeding 40 affect labor use?

4 Throughout this chapter we have assumed that input and product prices are determined in a purely competitive market situation. This means that more inputs could be purchased at the same price regardless of how many more inputs were bought. Also, additional product could be produced and sold at the same price.

Under imperfectly competitive conditions, increased input purchases would result in higher input prices paid for additional units. Also, increased product sales can be made only at reduced price. How would this affect the VMP curve? The MC, AVC, and AC curves?

BIBLIOGRAPHY

Cochrane, Willard W.: "Conceptualizing the Supply Relation in Agriculture," *Journal of Farm Economics*, vol. 37, no. 5, pp. 1, 171–172, 176, Dec. 1955.

———: *Farm Prices, Myth, and Reality,* University of Minnesota Press, Minneapolis, 1958.

Halvorson, H.: "The Response of Milk Production to Price," *Journal of Farm Economics,* vol. 40, no. 5, pp. 1, 112, Dec. 1958.

Heady, E. O., N. L. Jacobsen, J. P. Madden, and A. E. Freeman: *Milk Production Functions in Relation to Feed Inputs, Cow Characteristics and Environmental Conditions,* Research Bulletin 529, Agricultural Extension Station, Iowa State University, Ames, Iowa, July 1964.

U.S. Department of Agriculture: *Major Statistical Series of the U.S. Department of Agriculture,* vol. 2, *Agricultural Production and Efficiency,* Agricultural Handbook 365, 1970.

Tomek, William G., and Kenneth L. Robinson: *Agricultural Product Prices,* Cornell University Press, Ithaca, N.Y., 1972.

Chapter 6

Market Prices

INTRODUCTION

The process of market price determination and the roles and activities of individual firms in that process are the subject of this chapter. The basic competitive market model is used to illustrate market price and output determination, and adjustments to change and the roles of the individual firm in the adjustments. Next, the operation of supply and demand in farm markets is considered. Lastly, there is an examination of some of the operational methods which agricultural firms use to discover the point at which market supply just equals demand.

Price and output determination *under competitive conditions* means that certain market conditions are satisfied. These conditions include: (1) the presence of a large number of buyers and sellers; (2) the trading of a homogeneous product—the products of each firm in the market are indistinguishable in the eyes of the buyers; (3) the absence of barriers for firm exit from or entry into the market involved; and (4) the possession by both buyers and sellers of a substantial degree of information about prices and costs.

Although actual markets may depart from the perfectly competitive model, the model nevertheless provides a useful abstraction for explaining the operation of many markets. Furthermore, many agricultural markets probably more closely approximate competitive markets than any others in the economy. The model also provides a norm against which we can compare the behavior of other kinds of markets.

PRICE DETERMINATION AND ADJUSTMENT IN A COMPETITIVE MARKET

The intersection of the market supply curve with the market demand curve determines the market-clearing price in a competitive market. This point indicates that price at which the total quantity which consumers are willing to buy and all producers are willing to sell are just equal. If perfect competition exists in the market, other prices cannot be sustained. In the abstract theoretical model, this is an instantaneous adjustment with no other prices being possible. In actual market situations, adjustment to equilibrium prices can be observed when disequilibriums occur. Nonequilibrium price also may be due to imperfect information. In fact, disequilibriums are necessary to generate the time paths of prices that are observed in agricultural as well as other markets. Suppose a market had originally been in equilibrium at price P_1 in Figure 6-1, but demand decreased from D_1 to D_2 because of a fall in consumer income. At the original equilibrium price, the quantity offered Q_1 is now greater than that which consumers are willing to buy. Some or all producers will begin to offer their product at a lower price. The lower price discourages some production and encourages additional purchases and consumption. The process continues until price is lowered to the new market-clearing level P_2. The new equilibrium quantity is Q_2.

If demand had shifted in the other direction, the original price would have been below the market-clearing level. Some or all consumers would want to buy more product than producers are willing to supply at that price. Buyers or consumers will begin bidding up the price. The higher prices discourage some purchases and consumption but encourage producers to produce and sell more. The price will rise until the quantity offered just equals the quantity that consumers are willing to buy.

There is another dimension of the price-quantity adjustments for competitive markets. This is the long-run adjustment. The preceding model depicted a short-run adjustment—one that could occur from one crop season to another in agricultural markets. If some of the resources are fixed for a longer period of time, as they are in agriculture, the short-run price-quantity solution is not likely to be stable over time. The process of long-run adjustment can be illustrated by the use of Figure 6-2(a) and (b). Figure 6-2(a) illustrates the market supply and demand. Figure 6-2(b) illustrates the relevant cost curves of a representative firm in the market. The price axes are identical but the quantity scales for the market and for the firm differ. Recall that the sum of the marginal cost curves (MC) for the individual firm yields the total market supply.

Let us begin by considering the short-run supply-demand situation indicated by S_1 and D_1. The market equilibrium occurs at a price of P_1 and a quantity of

$/unit

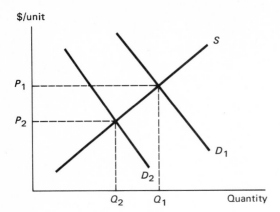

Figure 6-1 Achieving market price equilibrium.

Q_1. The profit-maximizing firm produces quantity q_1 at the market price. The firm is operating at point a, where price equals marginal cost. In this situation, it is also an output where price equals minimum average total cost (ATC) for the firm. The firm is just covering all costs with neither losses nor excess profits. It is assumed that ATC does include a normal profit which is the return on the owner's capital and entrepreneurship.

What will be the impact of a shift in demand on the firm in the short run and in the long run? Total demand for U.S. agricultural products is shifted for a variety of reasons. Foreign demand increases because of poor crops in other parts of the world, or it may be due to development programs in other countries

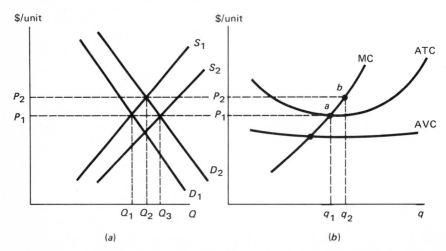

Figure 6-2 Process of long-run adjustment. (a) Market supply and demand; (b) relevant cost curves of a representative firm in the market.

that increase incomes and therefore increase demand for foods. Within the United States, demand increases because of increasing incomes, changing tastes and preferences for food, and expanding population. Suppose that any or all of these shifted demand for U.S. wheat from D_1 to D_2 in Figure 6-2. The short-run impact is to increase price from P_1 to P_2. Market supply and demand are equated at quantity Q_2. This is the sum of the output expansions by individual wheat-producing firms from q_1 to q_2. At the new price P_2, firms can now maximize profit at a larger output, indicated by the intersection of the new price level with the firms' MC curves at point b.

The firm is now obtaining an excess profit on each bushel of wheat equal to the difference between the price and ATC at output q_2. This is the distance ac in Figure 6-2(b). If the shift in demand persists, this short-run equilibrium is not stable. The excess profit ac attracts new firms into wheat production. Land and farms used on other crop or livestock production will be shifted into wheat production because the resources will earn more in wheat production than in other activities. This entry of new firms shifts the market supply curve for wheat to the right, which drives wheat prices down and begins to eliminate excess profits. The shift of supply continues until all excess profits are eliminated. If all inputs are available to wheat producers at constant prices, the new long-run equilibrium is at a market price of P_1, with total market quantity at Q_3. Each firm is again operating at output q_1, where price is just covering average total costs. Looked at another way, we can say that the long-run industry supply is completely elastic.

Industries that use a substantial portion of the total supplies of at least one input are not likely to find long-run industry supply to be completely elastic. As the firms use more and more inputs in expanding industry output, they drive up input prices. Consequently, the cost curves of the individual firms are shifted upward as industry output is increased. Thus, not only are excess profits eliminated as new firms enter, but also the upward shift of the cost curves is eliminating excess profits. The long-run market supply curve slopes upward as output increases.

The adjustment process, whether it be for a constant cost or an increasing cost situation, illustrates two basic characteristics of the competitively organized industry: the elimination of excess profits and the production of total output at lowest possible cost. This tendency exists regardless of the source of short-run profits, demand expansion, or technological change that reduces average and marginal costs of production.

The adjustment to adverse changes in demand or production costs can be traced in a similar manner. If price falls below the minimum average variable costs (AVC), firms will halt production immediately. If price falls below ATC but not below AVC, firms will minimize losses by operating where price just equals MC. In the long-run, firms will exit as the fixed resources are used up. The exit of firms shifts the market supply curve to the left, causing market price to rise. This process occurs until price just equals minimum ATC.

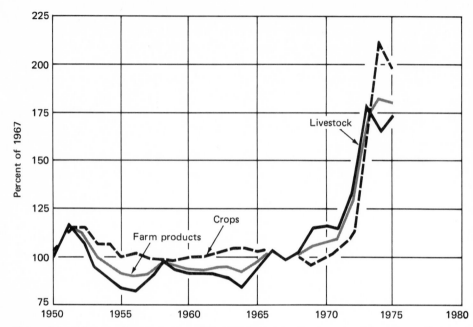

Figure 6-3   Prices received by farmers. The 1973 figures are the January–July average. *Source:* Economic Research Service, U.S. Department of Agriculture, NEG. ERS 7878-75(9).

OBSERVED PRICES IN AGRICULTURAL MARKETS

The forces of supply and demand operating in the manner described yield prices which are often reported on a daily, weekly, monthly, or annual basis for agricultural markets. Because the factors influencing food demand and supply are continuously changing, we would expect the time paths of agricultural prices to show variations regardless of the reporting periods used. Annual levels of farm prices since 1950 are plotted in Figures 6-3 and 6-4. Figure 6-3 is a composite index of prices received by farmers. Three major trends can be discerned for the period. From 1951 to 1955, farm prices declined as the Korean war wound down and the demands associated with it disappeared. From 1955 until 1964, all farm prices were relatively stable with minor year-to-year variation. Beginning in 1964, prices received by farmers began to rise, with a rapid acceleration noticeable in 1971. However, during the entire period since 1950, we have been experiencing inflation. Consequently, real farm prices, or the purchasing power of farm prices, declined, from 1950 to 1964. Evidence of this decline is indicated by comparing the index of prices received to the index of prices paid by farmers in the lower part of Figure 6-4. The prices-paid series increased throughout the entire period with the exception of 1953. Even after 1964 the series increased more rapidly than the level of prices received by farmers. It is only during the early 1970s that prices received by farmers increased more rapidly than prices paid by farmers.

Individual products show greater year-to-year price variability than all farm prices. For just the two groups of farm products, crops and livestock, we can see increased variation (see Figure 6-3). From 1951 to 1966, livestock prices were depressed relative to all farm prices. Crop prices, on the other hand, were above all farm prices. In 1966 the situation was reversed. The variation of individual products about average farm prices, when plotted, yields still greater year-to-year variation (see Figure 6-5). Each series of prices represents the results of the forces of supply and demand as they yield prices for the product. Although there is considerable deviation among product prices for a given year, or short-term period, the very long-term movements (not illustrated here) are similar for all products.

What are the major characteristics of supply and demand that have generated the behavior of agricultural prices? First, we have observed that both short-run supply and demand for farm products are highly inelastic. In fact, the elasticity of aggregate farm supply probably approaches zero. Thus, a small shift in supply or demand without a compensating shift in the other brings about a large price change relative to quantity changes. This situation is illustrated in Figure 6-6. Suppose that supply and demand for farm products shifts from S_1 to S_2 and from D_1 to D_2 over a 2-year period. Farm prices remain stable at P_1 with quantity increasing from Q_1 to Q_2. Assume that demand continued to shift to D_3 in the third year. Bad weather results in a stationary supply at S_2. Farm prices jump from P_1 to P_2 with relatively little change in the quantity Q_2 to Q_3. These erratic shifts in highly inelastic supply and demand caused by weather or domestic and foreign political developments can result in large year-to-year price changes.

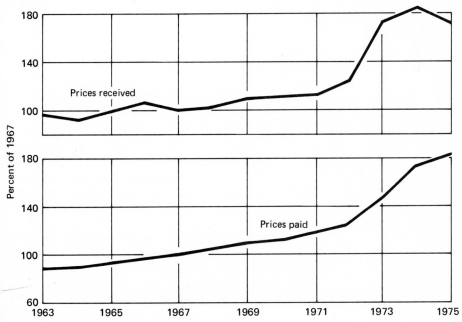

Figure 6-4 Farmers' prices, 1963–1975. Prices received are for all farm products; prices paid are for all items, including interest, taxes, and wage rates. *Source:* Economic Research Service, U.S. Department of Agriculture, NEG. ERS 8681-75(9).

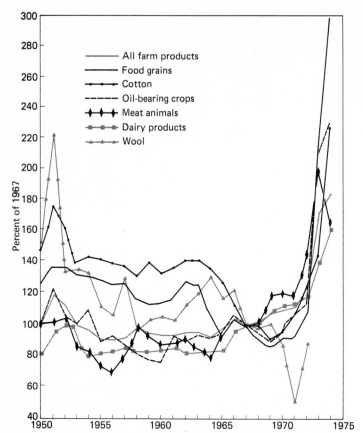

Figure 6-5 Prices received by farmers. *Source:* Statistical Reporting Service, U.S. Department of Agriculture, "Agricultural Prices," Annual Summaries.

Over longer periods of time, patterns of farm price behavior are explained by relative rates of expansion in aggregate supply and demand. Cochrane, in an analysis of farm prices, states that periods of falling prices are caused by supply outracing demand, and periods of rising prices are caused by demand outracing supply.[1] In *Farm Prices, Myth and Reality* and another book, Cochrane and his associates describe several kinds of shifts that yielded certain patterns of long-term price movements.[2] The period 1929–1932 was characterized by contracting demand and a fixed inelastic supply. Prices fell almost 50 percent but quantity decreased only 4 percent. From 1936 to 1941, supply and demand shifted to the right at approximately the same rate. Consequently, prices held rather steady. From 1941 to 1945, farm prices rose because of wartime demand expanding more rapidly than supply could be shifted. From 1951 to 1964, demand shifted outward

[1]Willard W. Cochrane, *Farm Prices, Myth and Reality,* University of Minnesota Press, Minneapolis, 1958, p. 59.
[2]W. W. Wilcox, W. W. Cochrane, and R. W. Herdt, *Economics of American Agriculture,* Prentice-Hall, Englewood Cliffs, N.J., 1974, pp. 248–250.

regularly because of increasing incomes and expanding population. Neverthe-less, technology shifted the supply curve outward at a more rapid rate. Prices fell approximately 20 percent over this period. This occurred even though major price support activities were in operation. Cochrane and his associates estimated that prices would have fallen by 50 percent without these programs.[3] Since 1965 aggregate demand has shifted outward more rapidly than supply, with accelera-tion of the demand shift in 1972, 1973, and 1974.

SEASONAL VARIATION IN AGRICULTURAL PRICES

The process of agricultural price determination has been considered to this point in terms of annual values. We find analysis of average annual prices useful for many policy and forecasting uses. A widespread drought, an early frost, a report of a large foreign sale of a farm product, the imposition of export quotas, or a major change in economic policy have immediate impacts on price. In addition to these rather unpredictable factors, prices of many farm products are characterized by well-defined seasonal patterns. For some products the seasonal variation is very pronounced, whereas for other products prices have practically no observable seasonal pattern. To the extent that farmers understand the seasonal price movement, they may be able to make more profitable production and marketing decisions. For economists, knowledge of the seasonal price movements is neces-sary in making short-term price projections.

[3]Ibid., p. 250.

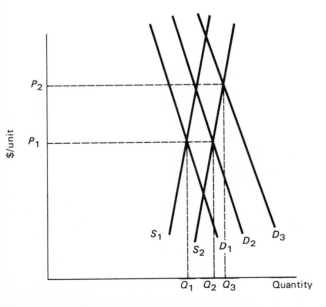

Figure 6-6   Shifts in aggregate demand and supply.

Seasonal price movements occur because of recurring seasonal patterns of demand and/or the biological nature of farm production which determines to a considerable extent the rate at which farmers market their products. An example of a highly seasonal demand is that for turkeys during the Thanksgiving and Christmas holidays. However, variations in the rates of marketing appear to be most important in seasonal price patterns for farm products. It has been reported that two-fifths of soybean production is marketed in October. One-half of the cotton crop is ginned in October and November.[4] In a number of areas, fresh vegetables are marketed only during a 1- or 2-month period. Even for products that are marketed throughout the year, such as livestock, livestock products, and some vegetables, a seasonal price pattern is very apparent.

For storable commodities, seasonal price variability should be related to the cost of storage. Low-cost storage items should have less variation than products costly to store. This assumption appears to be affirmed by the seasonal patterns illustrated in Figure 6-7(a) to (e).[5] The solid line in the graphs is the average pattern of seasonal variation over a period of years. Each month's price is calculated as a percentage of the average annual price. The shaded areas indicate the range within which 67 percent of each month's indexes fall. The crop indexes of average seasonal price variation show relatively low seasonal variation, and the patterns seem quite unstable. Because crops are easily storable, marketings can be easily changed with consequent changes in the timing of the high and low of seasonal prices.

The more perishable commodities exhibit greater relative seasonal price variation; see milk, egg, and steer and heifer prices in Figure 6-7(c), (d), and (e). Milk prices have the most stable seasonal price pattern as indicated by the very narrow band of irregularity.

Although the seasonal patterns of farm prices are similar from one year to the next, a pattern is seldom exactly repeated. The magnitude of variation is greater or less than other years. The points of maximum and minimum prices are seldom on the same day. Analysis of seasonal patterns of time often shows shifts in the seasonality and decreases or increases in the amount of variation. These changes occur because of changes in those factors that cause the seasonal price movements or because of changes in those other price determinants that bring about price changes.

CYCLICAL VARIATION IN FARM PRICES

Prices of some farm products have been observed to behave in a cyclical pattern over a period of years. Although the cycles vary in amplitude and duration, they are sufficiently repetitive to raise questions as to the nature of the system or

---

[4]Wayne Dexter, *What Makes Farmers' Prices*, U.S. Department of Agriculture, Agricultural Information Bulletin 204, Apr., 1959.

[5]These charts were prepared by Professor J. P. Houck, Department of Agricultural Economics, University of Minnesota.

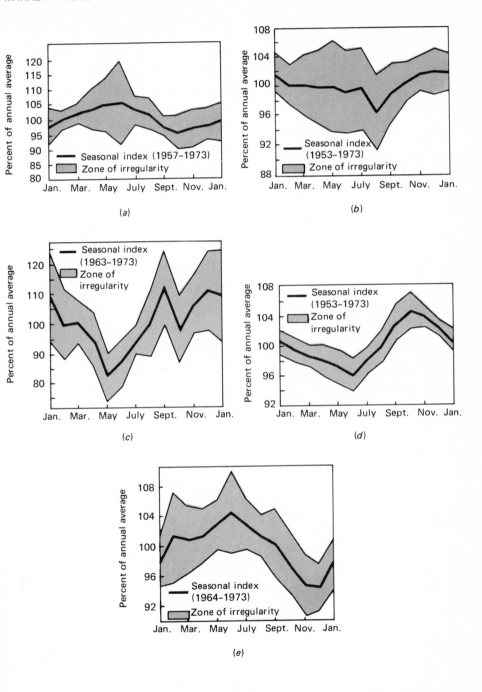

Figure 6-7 Seasonal behavior of Minnesota prices for (a) soybeans, (b) wheat, (c) eggs, (d) manufacturing milk, and (e) steers and heifers. *Source:* J. P. Houck, "Seasonal Variation in Minnesota Farm Prices," *Minnesota Agricultural Economist,* no. 561, Nov. 1974.

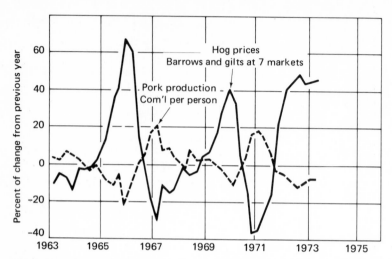

Figure 6-8 Changes in hog prices and pork production. The percentage change is from the previous year. *Source:* Economic Research Service, U.S. Department of Agriculture.

mechanism that generates the pattern. The cycles have been particularly apparent for hogs and cattle. The cycles occur in both prices and production—high prices are associated with lows in production and low prices are associated with highs in production. The hog cycle has occurred since at least 1861 with a fairly regular periodicity of about 4 years.[6] The characteristics of these cycles for hog prices and per capita pork production are illustrated in Figure 6-8 for the period 1963–1973. Two and one-half complete cycles occurred during that period. Cattle cycles have not been as consistent in duration as the hog cycles (Figure 6-9), but they nevertheless occur. McCoy reports that six cycles have occurred since 1896.[7] The cycles are characterized by two phases: (1) a build-up phase in cattle numbers that ranges from 6 to 8 years; and (2) the liquidation phase—reductions in cattle numbers exhibit considerably more variation than the build-up phase, varying from 8 to 10 years in the early cycles and from 2 to 3 years in later cycles.[8] The total cycle has varied from 8 to 16 years in duration.

The cyclical pattern of farm prices has been examined in detail by commodity analysts. A good knowledge of the cycle is necessary for reliable forecasting and economic analysis. Farmers should also be better able to make more profitable production and marketing decisions if they understand the cycle.

A widely used theory of the cycle is the "cobweb theorem."[9] The theory takes its name from the characteristic pattern of price-quantity adjustments on the supply-demand diagram of the cyclical model. The theory essentially involves a modification of some of the assumptions of the standard static supply-

---

[6]G. Shepherd, *Agricultural Prices,* Iowa State University Press, Ames, Iowa, 1961, p. 39.
[7]John McCoy, *Livestock and Meat Marketing,* Avi, Westport, Conn., 1972, p. 60.
[8]Ibid., p. 60.
[9]The theory is described by Mordecai Ezekiel, "The Cobweb Theorem," *Quarterly Journal of Economics,* vol. 52, no. 2, pp. 262–272, Feb. 1938.

demand model. In that model, recall that price and quantity are simultaneously determined at a market-clearing price. Given the algebraic form of the supply and demand relations:

Supply $Q_{st} = a + bP_t$
Demand $Q_{dt} = c - dP_t$

where t denotes time period t, the system can be solved for a unique price and quantity that holds as long as there are no shifts in either supply or demand. Graphically, the solution was illustrated in Figure 6-1.

In the cobweb model, the behavioral relations are changed so that price and quantity are no longer simultaneously determined. The change probably reflects more closely the price and quantity determination for many farm products. In the cobweb theorem, quantity supplied in a given period is not a function of that period's price. It is a function of last period's price or the prices of several past periods. Thus, the supply equation for period t is somewhat different; for example,

$$Q_{st} = e + fP_{t-1}$$

In period t, this quantity is marketed and it yields a price given the demand relation. Since quantity has already been determined, price is determined uniquely by the demand relation $P_t = g - hQ_t$. This price in period t generates another supply in the following period $t + 1$, which results in another price. Price and quantity determination is a sequential or recursive process rather than a simultaneous process. The system can be at a static stable position if this period's price generates the quantity in the next period that results in no price change. However, if it is moved out of equilibrium for some reason, then it will generate a cyclical pattern.

A graphic illustration of the cyclical adjustment is presented in Figure 6-10. Here, quantity Q_1 brings a price of P_1 in period 1. Producers base their production decisions for period 2 on this price, and they produce Q_2. Then the quantity marketed in period 2 yields a price of P_2. Production in period 3 falls to Q_3 as a result of this price. But it sells for P_3. Thus, we obtain prices and quantities oscillating in opposite directions through time. In this case, the system

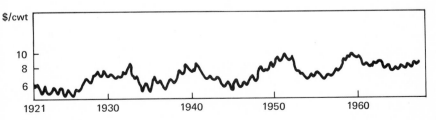

Figure 6-9 Number of cattle on U.S. farms, 1921–1967, and price received by farmers for cattle. *Source:* John McCoy, *Livestock and Meat Marketing*, Avi, Westport, Conn., 1972, p. 59.

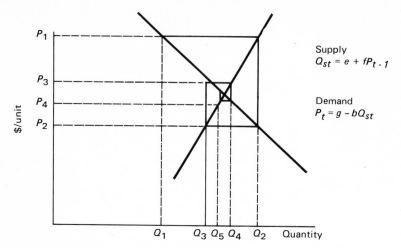

Figure 6-10 Cyclical adjustments in the cobweb model.

eventually converges to an equilibrium. The time path of the price-quantity adjustment for the converging cycle is depicted in Figure 6-11.

The cobweb model does not always generate a converging cycle. A continuous cycle on a diverging or exploding cycle can be generated. Whether or not the cycle is divergent, convergent, or continuous depends upon the relative absolute values of elasticities of supply and demand. If the supply elasticity exceeds the demand elasticity, the model is diverging. If the supply elasticity is less than the demand elasticity, the model is converging. If they are equal, the model will generate a continuous cycle of constant amplitude. A diverging cycle is generated by the demand and supply relations illustrated in Figure 6-12. The producers are still responding to last period's price, but the relative elasticities of supply and demand are different from the preceding sample. As a consequence, the cycle continues to expand in amplitude. Obviously, this cycle would continue to explode until price, production, or both falls to zero. This does not occur in observed cycles. Thus, in those cases in which supply may be more elastic than

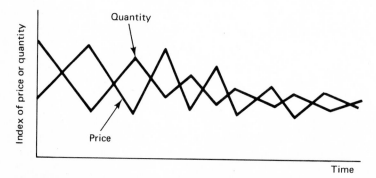

Figure 6-11 Time path of price-quantity adjustments for a converging cycle.

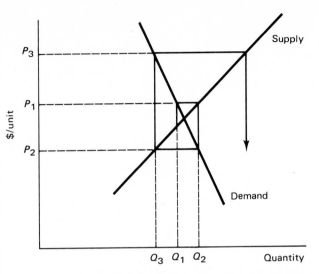

Figure 6-12 Diverging cycle generated by demand and supply relations.

demand, other factors must come into play that prevent the cycles from exploding.

The reader has perhaps already concluded that if the time periods used for an analysis were annual observations, then the model yields cycles of 2-year duration. This implies that the time periods to be considered must be related to the length of the production processes. For some livestock, several years are required for the process.

Other models of the recurring cycle have been developed, but the cobweb theorem is a plausible and easily comprehensible explanation of it. Mordecai Ezekiel listed three conditions for the theory to accurately explain the cyclical behavior of agricultural prices: (1) production is completely determined by the producer's response to a price that one expects to continue; (2) at least one full time period is needed for production once plans have been made; and (3) price is set by available supply.[10]

OPERATIONAL ASPECTS OF THE PRICING PROCESS

The way in which the forces of supply and demand generate price levels and output and how changes occur has been thoroughly researched by economists. Nevertheless, the abstractions of economic theory and research techniques leave one very important question largely unanswered. How are these forces actually translated into transactions and prices in real market situations? Various

[10]Ibid. Other explanations of the price cycle are modifications of the original. The most popular variations are those that employ concepts of immediate-run and short-run supply curves interacting with a static demand curve. Another explanation, called the *harmonic motion model,* is used more frequently to explain cycles of 4–15 years in duration.

techniques are used to price products in individual transactions or to discover the price which will clear the market. Tomek and Robinson have called these "mechanisms of price discovery" and they have listed five categories.[11] The following discussion involves a modification of their listing. Here we will consider (1) individual negotiations, (2) organized markets, (3) administered prices (both public and private administration), and (4) group negotiations. A consideration of pricing for a given product will usually show use of more than one mechanism or procedure. Nevertheless, the classification seems useful.

Individual Negotiation

As the name implies, *individual negotiation* is a simple bargaining process between individual buyers and sellers for each transaction. In its pure form, with equal market power and equal information for the participants, it is the implicit procedure of the competitive market model.[12] Formal rules are usually not in evidence. The seller tries to obtain the highest possible price and the buyer the lowest possible price. Used car sales are characterized by this kind of bargaining for durable goods. Many farm products are also priced and traded in this manner. Among the more important farm commodities are livestock, fruits, and vegetables.

Information on general supply-demand conditions for a product will influence the price outcome of the negotiations. Prices in previous transactions and judgments on supply and demand changes are likely to be explicitly or intuitively considered. To the extent that one participant is better informed on market conditions than the other, the price in a given transaction may be higher or lower than where both participants have sufficient information.

Individual negotiations as the sole means of pricing a widely traded product would probably be very costly. Each buyer and seller would want to obtain the best information on total supply and demand conditions, and yet each might find it advantageous to keep such information secret. Imagine the cost of pricing each milk delivery if each transaction were individually negotiated. The time and efforts would be extensive. Furthermore, monopolistic buyers or sellers are in the optimum environment to exploit the other participants.

In practice, sole reliance on individual negotiation to set prices in individual transactions is rare in agriculture. Even where sales appear to be individually negotiated, as for numerous livestock sales, the process is more likely the outcome of a rather organized and institutionalized pricing procedure. For livestock, the publication of central market quotations on average livestock prices by grade, type, and volume of trading probably provides the real basis for the country trading.

[11]William G. Tomek and Kenneth L. Robinson, *Agricultural Product Prices,* Cornell University Press, Ithaca, N.Y., 1972, pp. 215–232.

[12]O. D. Forker, *Price Determination Processes: Issues and Evaluation,* U.S. Department of Agriculture, FCS Information Bulletin 102, Sept. 1975.

Organized Markets

Organized markets have been more widely used for agricultural commodities than for any other industry. There are a number of reasons for this phenomenon. Numbers of transactions are so numerous that individual negotiations with no formalized rules are too cumbersome, time consuming, and costly. Thus, throughout the history of trade and in the more traditional and underdeveloped economies of the world, local markets and fairs have centralized and institutionalized exchange and pricing functions. As economies have advanced, more highly organized central and terminal livestock markets, commodity exchanges, and auction markets have developed.

Commodity exchanges have been important for the major grain crops, cotton, eggs, butter, and several internationally traded crops (cocoa, coffee, and sugar). The Chicago Board of Trade, the Chicago Mercantile Exchange, the Minneapolis Grain Exchange, and the New York Cotton Exchange are but a few of these organized markets. The exchanges provide a place for trading to take place under specified rules. Prices and transactions are immediately made known to all traders on the floor and reporting services document this information in the public news media. For some products, grains for example, samples may be displayed on the exchanges. Other products, such as butter, are traded by grade description only. In almost all cases, the product to be sold must be in an approved warehouse or in transit to be traded on the exchanges.

Some of the commodity exchanges provide for trading in contracts for future delivery of the commodity. On the Minneapolis Grain Exchange, for example, traders can buy or sell "cash wheat" for immediate delivery and receipt, or they can trade in standardized contracts for future delivery of wheat at specified months during the crop year. This latter activity, called *futures trading,* deals with the allocation of supplies of the commodity over time and the elimination of some of the risk associated with holding commodities. Futures trading will be considered in more detail in a later chapter.

Cash trading on the commodity exchanges often moves only a small proportion of the total trade for the commodity. Nevertheless, the prices arrived at on the exchanges are often the basis of most of the trading throughout the industry. For butter, a study by one of the authors indicated that less than one-tenth of 1 percent of total annual butter production moved through the commodity exchanges for butter. But approximately 99 percent of all butter sold at country creameries was priced at the exchange price, with adjustments for location, of course. Although the country point butter prices may seem to be established by individual negotiation, the central organized market is the place where prices are actually established.

For grains, larger proportions of the total production may be sold through the exchange, but again, country buyers of grain, whether they are local elevators or independent buyers, use the exchange price adjusted for transportation to determine their pay price for grains. Farmers have the choice of selling grain at these prices or holding in the expectation of a price increase. Changes in terminal market prices are usually immediately reflected in country buying prices for grain.

The commodity exchanges are a very efficient means for discovering market-clearing prices for some of our most important agricultural commodities. Costs of the pricing process are only a very small part of total marketing costs. Commodity exchanges are not used for pricing all farm crops. However, they seem to be most used where several conditions exist:

1 The number of transactions is large.
2 The product quality is easily identified by grades and standards.
3 The number of buyers and sellers is large and no single participant is able to manipulate prices.
4 Complete and unbiased information is available on supply and demand characteristics for the commodity.
5 The government is not the primary factor in determining price.

Terminal livestock exchanges were the focal points of livestock pricing in the United States for many years. The Chicago Union Stockyards was established in 1865 to facilitate trading in a rapidly growing industry. It was followed by establishment of terminal markets at Minneapolis, Kansas City, St. Louis, Omaha, and other cities. Terminal markets were all located at railway terminals.

Slaughtering and packing facilities were usually located adjacent to the terminal markets. They usually included some or all of the major packing companies, such as Swift, Wilson, Armour, and Cudahy. In fact, these firms had such a large share of the market and each firm's share was so stable over time that they were charged with monopolization and price fixing for livestock.

The procedures for selling through terminal livestock markets is essentially standard. Livestock producers consign their animals to a commission firm at the terminals. The commission agent searches out buyers for the livestock, negotiates the best possible price, collects payment, deducts yardage fees and commissions, and refunds the remainder to the seller. The prices at which transactions take place are reported by the exchange and the news media. The St. Paul Livestock Market provides for an alternative way of selling feeder cattle. Several times each week, an auction is held to market this type of animal.

The terminal market, although long the principal means of selling livestock, has been declining in importance. In 1930 more than 88 percent of all slaughter cattle were moved through terminal markets. Since that time, their share has dropped. Only 19 percent of all cattle moved through terminals in 1970 (see Table 6-1). The decline in volume of the Chicago Union Stockyards resulted in its closing in 1971.

The reasons for the decline of the terminal markets are several:

1 The development of truck transport and the interstate highway system has made direct movement of livestock or carcasses from production areas to consuming areas less costly.

Table 6-1 Packers' Livestock Purchases by Market Outlet for 1960, 1965, and 1970[a]

Market outlet and year	Cattle 1,000 head	Percent	Calves 1,000 head	Percent	Hogs 1,000 head	Percent	Sheep 1,000 head	Percent
Direct, country dealers, and others								
1960	8,420	39	2,572	43	47,104	61	7,654	54
1965	13,455	45	2,351	34	46,613	63	8,127	62
1970	21,014	65	1,332	34	55,398	69	6,986	73
Terminal markets								
1960	9,987	46	1,538	25	23,356	30	5,020	35
1965	10,162	34	1,127	17	17,375	23	3,321	26
1970	5,919	19	449	11	13,863	17	1,453	15
Auction markets								
1960	3,399	15	1,940	32	6,695	9	1,493	11
1965	6,235	21	3,373	49	10,151	14	1,571	12
1970	5,265	16	2,139	55	11,586	14	1,192	12
Total								
1960	21,806	100	6,050	100	77,155	100	14,167	100
1965	29,852	100	6,851	100	74,139	100	13,019	100
1970	32,198	100	3,920	100	80,846	100	9,631	100

[a]Includes data for all firms purchasing more than 1,000 head of cattle or 2,000 head of all livestock during reporting period.
Source: U.S. Department of Agriculture, *Packers and Stockyards Resume.*

2 Lower freight costs and improved refrigeration have resulted in shipment of slaughtered animals directly from the livestock production areas, which is often less costly than assembly at terminal markets.

3 Effective grading systems and market communication permit a more decentralized marketing system to efficiently price livestock.

Another type of organized market institution for trading livestock and other commodities is the auction market. It is quite extensively used in the trading of livestock, tobacco, and some fruits and vegetables. Auction markets appear to be most widely used where actual inspection of the product is desirable in order to determine its quality. The more traditional type of auction market is a publicly or privately owned facility where sellers bring their products. Progressive bidding for each transaction is made by public outcry. A number of variations of the traditional auction are now in effect. Telephone and teletype auctions are in effect for hogs in Canada and feeder pigs in the United States. Instead of buyers and sellers being physically present at a single location, teletype hookups and conference calls are used. Obviously, this requires the use of an acceptable grading system.

The Canadian auctions also use an alternative—the Dutch or Danish auction—to progressive bidding. In this system, offers are started at somewhat above the anticipated price. The offering price declines until someone accepts. The rationale behind this system is that the product is sold to the buyer at the maximum price which the buyer is willing to pay. Progressive bidding may result in the buyer paying the minimum price that the buyer is willing to pay.

During the 1940s and 1950s, auction markets expanded their share of total livestock markets. Since 1965 their share has stabilized even though there have been some changes for the different classes of animals. Packer purchases of slaughter cattle through auctions decreased from 21 to 16 percent in 1970 (see Table 6-1). However, the auction purchases of calves increased to more than one-half of their total purchases.

The increase in direct livestock sales by farmers to country buyers and on auctions has replaced the once dominant centralized terminal markets. Criticisms of this shift have been made by commission firms and terminal market authorities. The most common criticisms have been listed by Shepherd:

1 Direct buyers take the higher quality animals and thus prices for lower than average quality animals on the terminals are not representative of average livestock values.

2 Terminal markets are competitive regarding numbers of buyers and sellers whereas direct buying activities are not.

3 Direct buying reduced demand at terminal markets and therefore reduced prices.[13]

[13]G. S. Shepherd and G. A. Futrell, *Marketing Farm Products—Economic Analysis,* 5th ed., Iowa State University Press, Ames, Iowa, 1969, pp. 187–191.

None of the criticisms appear to be solidly based. First, if the livestock grading system works, one can easily determine if prices at various locations are out of line. Also, some very early work by the USDA showed no difference in grade proportions between terminal and direct markets.[14]

The second criticism implies that each organized exchange or individual transaction is a separate market demand-supply equilibrium. Actually, all transactions in the livestock industry regardless of location are part of a single market supply-demand system. This will be the situation as long as each participant has the opportunity to trade a product at any place in the market. All options represent competition even though they are not geographically centralized.

The last criticism—that demand is reduced by decentralization—implies the same market isolation for transactions and exchanges as the second criticism. The forces of supply and demand determine the price in competitive markets, not the mechanisms used to discover that price. This discovery can be achieved with only a limited amount of trading on the organized market. In fact, for butter, necessary adjustments on prices are often made by bids or offers with no trades occurring.

Administered Prices

Many agricultural products are sold under circumstances where central markets do not exist and where individual negotiation is impracticable and costly. This is particularly the case as farm products become more highly processed and more highly differentiated according to sellers. Fluid milk markets do not have open central markets and continual negotiation is found to be impracticable. In these situations, the individual sellers or an authorized agency of the United States or state government unilaterally establish the prices at which products will be sold. These procedures might be distinguished as public- and private-administered pricing schemes.

The reader may note that the administered pricing schemes often involve the use of formulas that tie market prices to other economic variables. Some analysts of price discovery processes distinguish between administered and formula pricing. However, they are so inextricably bound together that we have assumed the formula procedure to be merely a part of the administered pricing processes.

The price support program of the federal government for wheat, cotton, tobacco, milk, and feed grains is one of the most widely known government-administered price programs. It has been in effect since the 1930s. The price support program provides only a floor below which prices cannot fall but it has effectively established market prices in many years since the 1930s. The reasons for its application and the impact on quantities supplied and demanded will be the subject of a later chapter. The following paragraphs describe the mechanisms that established the support prices.

[14]U.S. Department of Agriculture, *The Direct Marketing of Hogs,* Miscellaneous Publication 222, 1935.

The 1973 Agricultural Act provided for farm price supports that relate directly to farm production costs. In the past, this support has been calculated to maintain a historic relationship between the price which farmers receive for their products and the prices which they pay for goods and services. The relationship has been defined as *parity*. Parity price is that price which maintains the same ratio between prices received and prices paid in agriculture as existed in the period 1910–1914. It means that any change in prices paid since that time must be matched by an equal change in prices received to achieve parity; for example, if 1974 prices paid by farmers are 300 percent of 1910–1914 prices (a quantity-weighted price index), then the parity price of wheat is 300 percent of the 1910–1914 wheat price.[15] Actual support prices have traditionally been set at some percentage of the parity price.

Another widely used administered price program of the government is the federal milk order program. It currently establishes the procedure for pricing milk in 55 fluid-milk marketing areas in the United States. The program establishes the prices which handlers must pay dairy farmers for milk. They are multiple-price programs which require handlers to pay one price for milk used in fluid products and another price for milk used in manufactured dairy products. Several different types of formulas have been and are being used to calculate these prices. Prices for fluid use milk (class I) are commonly calculated at a fixed margin over the prices paid for manufacturing grade milk sold in nonregulated milk producing areas. Another type of formula changes the price of milk according to movements in general economic indexes (per capita income, feed costs, and wholesale price indexes). Milk used in manufactured dairy products (classes II and III) in the regulated markets is often fixed at the same level as prices paid for manufacturing grade milk in nonregulated markets. Other types use a formula that ties the class II and III milk prices to the prices of products produced from milk and processing costs for milk. These administered price programs for milk are commonly known as *formula pricing*.

Many firms in the food industry—processors, wholesalers, and retailers—unilaterally set prices that they hope will sell their products and provide an acceptable level of profit. If there are few firms selling highly differentiated products, the firms may have a wide range of prices which they can charge for the product. Nevertheless, quantities sold are, as in perfectly competitive markets, a function of price. If the products of the different sellers are close substitutes, the firms may have to constantly review the price level and make adjustments to competition if they wish to sell their product.

Unilateral price decisions are usually not completely arbitrary. A number of procedures and guides may be used. The following are some that are used for food products as well as for other products and services.

The wholesale meat trade has been found to set their prices on the basis of quotations from the National Provisioner Daily Market and News Service report,

---

[15]In actual practice, the parity calculations have been altered to permit some adjustments in relative prices among farm commodities.

commonly known as the "Yellow Sheet."[16] This publication reports end-of-day carlot meat prices in Chicago. Wholesalers and meat dealers throughout the country use these prices plus or minus transportation adjustments in quoting prices to customers. One might argue that this is not formula pricing but merely a kind of central market indicator similar to that used by country buyers of grain and livestock.

Markup procedures are commonly used by individual firms. If no processing is involved, the procedure may involve adding either a fixed absolute or a percentage markup to the price at which the product was purchased. Markup pricing seems to be commonly used in the retail pricing of foods. Where firms are engaged in processing or manufacturing raw products, the markup formula may involve a number of elements or factors to account for costs of labor, materials, and capital. It may be a safe procedure, but it does have a major drawback for the individual firm. That is, it may not be the profit-maximizing price. A long-used traditional markup may have been originally calculated for a profit-maximizing price. But it is unlikely that a constant markup will continually result in a profit-maximizing price.

A formula procedure that includes both quantity and cost considerations in pricing is *break-even analysis*. With this procedure, one calculates the quantity of sales at which total costs will be just covered at an assumed price. The formula for the calculation is:[17]

$$\text{BEP (in quantity unit)} = \frac{\text{TFC}}{\text{FC contribution per unit}} = \frac{\text{TFC}}{\text{P} - \text{VC}}$$

where BEP = quantity at which all costs are just covered
    TFC = total fixed cost
      P = price
    VC = variable cost

In the formula, variable costs are constant per unit. If the calculation yields a volume that seems reasonable in view of the assumed price, then that price may be fixed for the product. If the estimated volume seems unduly high or low, then the formula may be used to calculate a new break-even price for some other price. Break-even analysis can be helpful in the firm's pricing decision, but it should not be misinterpreted as indicating what can be sold at the assumed price.

Food retailers are often observed to price one or several of their items either below the store cost of the item or at least substantially below store cost and any reasonable return for handling. This practice, denoted as *loss-leader pricing*, is

[16]National Commission on Food Marketing, *Organization and Competition in the Livestock and Meat Industry*, Technical Study 1, 1966, pp. 57–58.
[17]For a more detailed analysis of break-even analysis, see E. J. McCarthy, *Basic Marketing, A Managerial Approach*, Irwin, Homewood, Ill., 1968, pp. 532–534.

rational because the product is not being priced solely in regard to its own contribution to profit, but with regard to its impact on sales and profits on all other products in the consumer market basket. The loss leader is a strategy designed "to maximize attraction power of the store to customers and storewide profit."[18]

Collective Bargaining Approaches to Pricing

Dissatisfaction with prices determined in freely competitive markets has led farmers to form bargaining associations through which they can bargain for higher prices. Farmers have had varying degrees of success with this method. Collective bargaining is widely used in labor negotiations. This bargaining power of labor has been greatly increased by statutes requiring management to bargain with the authorized collective bargaining associates. Mandatory collective bargaining for buyers of farm products has not been achieved, but a number of bills have been introduced in the Congress to require it. Nevertheless, producers of some farm products have organized to the point that they have been able to collectively bargain with handlers of their product.

Some significant attempts to use collective bargaining for major farm commodities were made in the 1920s. Aaron Sapiro, a lawyer who had been successful in organizing such programs in California for fruits and vegetables, tried to establish similar programs for cash crops such as wheat and corn. Although many farmers and their cooperatives supported the schemes, many others refused to participate. The noncompliers made the prices and conditions agreed to in negotiations impossible to enforce. After a few years these programs were abandoned.

Since the 1960s, farmers and their cooperatives in fluid milk markets have been somewhat successful in bargaining for prices above the minimum established for fluid use milk by the federal orders. The National Farmers Organization has also undertaken and supported collective bargaining for the major farm products. But it also appears to be hampered in effectively bargaining for prices because of limited control of supply for the commodities.

A number of conditions that are necessary or permit effective collective bargaining have been listed by marketing specialists. First, the bargaining agency must have complete control over price so that outsiders are not offering the product at a lower price. In fact, it may be necessary for the bargaining association to require producers to cut back or restrict supply in order to obtain higher prices. Second, it is desirable that buyers are few in number in order to facilitate bargaining and so that buyers can readily see the advantages of settling or not settling a negotiation. An inelastic demand is desirable so that price can be raised without substantially reducing sales. Cutbacks in production, if small, will be easier to sell to farmers.

[18]Harold Briemyer, "The Economics of Agricultural Marketing, A Survey," *Review of Marketing,* 1974, p. 136.

SUMMARY

This chapter discusses price and output determination under competitive conditions. These conditions include a large number of buyers and sellers, trading of a standard product, the absence of barriers to exit or entry, and the possession of price and cost information by market participants. Market price is determined geometrically at the point where market supply intercepts market demand. At this price, the total quantity which consumers are willing to buy and producers are willing to sell is exactly equal. This price is called the *equilibrium* price, indicating that at any other price either the consumer or the producer would be dissatisfied in terms of the quantity transacted.

Market adjustments in competitive markets are of two types—short run and long run. In agricultural markets, short-run price adjustments are made from one cropping season to the next. However, longer periods of time permit the entry or exit of firms into or from the market environment as well as permit individual firms to expand their size. Whether firms are willing to enter or exit (and existing firms willing to change their size) depends upon the persistence of levels of *profit* that are above or below what these firms can earn in alternative market situations. In the long run, where profits exist, firms will enter a market until prices are driven down to a point where profits are equal to zero under competitive conditions.

Individual farm product prices show greater year-to-year variability than all farm prices taken together. And farm prices in aggregate tend to fluctuate more than nonfarm prices. The reasons for these fluctuations are due to the inelastic nature of the demand and supply for these products and the competitive structure of the farming industry.

Seasonal price movements (those within a year) occur because of the recurring seasonal patterns of demand and/or the biological nature of farm production. For storable commodities, the degree of seasonal price variability is related to the cost of storage.

Prices of some farm products also behave in a cyclical pattern over a period of years, apart from the seasonal pattern. These cycles have been explained by the so-called cobweb theorem. This theory explains the price variation by recognizing that individual farmers adjust to market prices in terms of their short-run planning curve. When prices are high they produce more. But by producing more they may in fact lower prices. When prices are lower they subsequently respond by producing less. This results in up and down price movement over time for a number of farm products. Depending upon the nature of demand and supply (and the respective slopes of these curves), prices may tend to fluctuate widely at first and less widely as time goes by. This is known as a converging cyclical pattern. A diverging cyclical pattern is one in which price variation begins with limited price movements over time and expands in its variability as time goes by.

Price determination in agricultural markets is made by several "mechanisms." Prices may be determined by individual negotiations, discovered on organized markets, obtained through administered pricing systems, or maybe found through group negotiations.

QUESTIONS

1 What has happened to the real purchasing power of prices received for farm products since 1950?
2 Increasing export demand for U.S. wheat and feed grains will result in new long-run levels of prices and quantities. Describe the adjustment process for individual firms to the new long-run equilibrium as a result of the increased demand.
3 What is the significance of demand and supply elasticities for the year-to-year variations that are observed in farm prices (in the absence of price support activities)?
4 What are the characteristics of supply and demand of some farm products (hogs and beef) that generate prices and quantity cycles over time? Do you see any shortcomings in the cobweb theorem as an explanation of these cycles?
5 A number of conditions are necessary for effective collective bargaining for farm commodity prices. What are these conditions and what mechanisms and/or regulations would be needed to obtain these conditions?

BIBLIOGRAPHY

Briemyer, Harold: "The Economics of Agricultural Marketing, A Survey," *Review of Marketing,* 1974, pp. 115–165.
Cochrane, Willard W.: *Farm Prices, Myth and Reality,* University of Minnesota Press, Minneapolis, 1958.
Dexter, Wayne: *What Makes Farmers' Prices,* U.S. Department of Agriculture, Agricultural Information Bulletin 204, Apr., 1959.
Ezekiel, Mordecai: "The Cobweb Theorem," *Quarterly Journal of Economics,* vol. 52, no. 2, Feb. 1938.
McCarthy, E. J.: *Basic Marketing, A Managerial Approach,* Irwin, Homewood, Ill., 1968.
McCoy, John: *Livestock and Meat Marketing,* Avi, Westport, Conn., 1972.
National Commission on Food Marketing: *Organization and Competition in the Livestock and Meat Industry,* Technical Study 1, 1966.
U.S. Department of Agriculture: *The Direct Marketing of Hogs,* Miscellaneous Publication 222, 1935.

Chapter 7

Marketing Margins

This chapter is devoted to "bridging the gap" between retail and farm levels in agricultural markets. It considers the problem of measuring margins, the concept of derived demand, the incidence of cost and demand changes at different levels of the marketing system, and the lags in price adjustment across different levels of the system.

DEFINITIONS

The *marketing margin* refers to the difference between prices at different levels of the marketing system.[1] The marketing margin is the difference between farm price P_f and retail price P_r. It is also represented as the vertical distance between the demand curves (or the supply curves) in Figure 7-1. The marketing margin refers only to the price difference and makes no statement about the quantity of product marketed.

The *value of the marketing margin* (VMM) is the difference in price at two levels of the marketing system multiplied by the quantity of product marketed. In

---

[1] The marketing margin is also referred to as the farm-retail *price spread*. This is especially true for U.S. Department of Agriculture statistics that present the retail and farm price differences. Another use of the term *marketing margin* is in reference to the description of the difference between cost and sales price. This latter usage is more common in accounting.

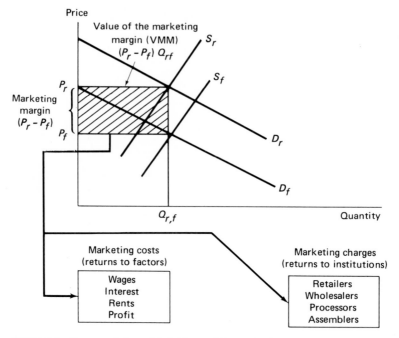

Figure 7-1 Representation of definitions of the marketing margin (MM), the value of the marketing margin (VMM), and marketing costs and charges.

Figure 7-1, the value of the marketing margin will be equal to $(P_r - P_f)Q_{r,f}$. Viewed in this manner, it is similar to the concept of *value added*. It is the value of the marketing margin that is measured by the marketing bill and the market basket statistics discussed in the next section.

The value of the marketing margin may be viewed as an aggregate or may be subdivided into different components. One way of subdividing the VMM is in terms of its returns to the factors of production used in providing the processing and marketing services rendered between the farmer and the consumer. These would include such things as wages, as a return to labor; interest, as a return to borrowed capital; rents, as a return to land and buildings; and profit, as a return to entrepreneurship and risk capital. This subdivision of the VMM is referred to as the *marketing costs*.

Another way of subdividing the value of the marketing margin is in categories of returns to the various agencies or institutions involved in the marketing of products, such as the return to retailers for their services, wholesalers for their activities, processors for their manufacturing activities, and assemblers for the work that they perform. This subdivision of the VMM is referred to as the *marketing charges*.

It should be recognized that in Figure 7-1 we used a marketing margin that was constant over all quantity ranges. This simply says that, regardless of the volume marketed, the *absolute* dollar difference between what is charged at the farm level and what is charged at retail levels remains fixed or constant. This is not necessarily characteristic of what actually occurs.

Marketing margins may be of absolute or percentage type. Furthermore, absolute marketing margins may be decreasing, constant, or increasing as quantity increases. Percentage margins also may be decreasing, constant, or increasing as quantity increases. Each of these types of marketing margins are represented geometrically in different ways. Notice the geometric representations of absolute marketing margins and percentage marketing margins in the Figures 7-2 and 7-3.

It is reasonably clear from earlier studies that many wholesalers use a constant percentage markup. That is, they add a fixed percentage margin to the cost of goods sold. On the other hand, retailers appear to make greater use of a fixed-absolute or dollar margin. While a constant-absolute margin seems to be most preferred, there is evidence of decreasing and increasing absolute margins in certain products.

The conclusion is that total marketing margins for agricultural products, as far as wholesaling and retailing are concerned, is a mixture of percentage and absolute margins. This means that margins are difficult to sort out in as meaningful a pattern as we would otherwise hope. Most of the margins used for purposes of discussion in this chapter will be the constant-absolute type.

MEASUREMENT

Where the product essentially retains its identity from the farm to consumer (for example, fluid milk, eggs, fresh fruits, and vegetables), the measurement of the margin is rather straightforward and easily understood. The major problem is converting from farm units to equivalent retail units. The greater the amount of transformation and the greater the number of farm foods in the final consumer

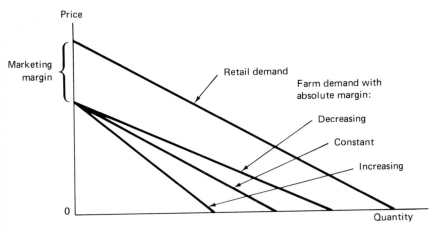

Figure 7-2 Geometric representation of *absolute* marketing margins that are decreasing, constant, and increasing over quantity.

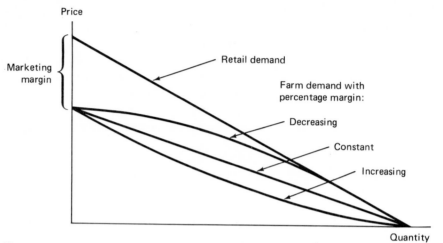

Figure 7-3 Geometric representation of *percentage* marketing margins that are decreasing, constant, and increasing over quantity.

product, the more difficult it becomes to identify and measure the margins for individual farm products. For example, white bread may include wheat flour, eggs, sugar, and vegetable oil. One can measure the farm value of all ingredients and determine the difference between this and retail prices. But how does one allocate the margin among the different farm ingredients? Furthermore, the highly processed products have so many types and variations that the margin calculation for one has little relevance to another.

Although there are difficulties in margin measurement and interpretation, the USDA calculates and publishes a continuing series on food costs and margins. Margins are calculated for individual foods and for several aggregations of foods on a monthly and annual basis. Furthermore, the marketing charges are broken down into their various components, either according to cost items or marketing functions. Two basic margin series are computed by the USDA: the *market basket series* and the *marketing bill*.

The Market Basket Series

The *farm-food market basket series* is a measure of the average cost of a fixed quantity of farm foods purchased by urban wage-earners and clerical-worker families and single persons living alone. It is the total cost of 65 domestic farm-originated products. It does not include foods consumed away from home, nonfarm-produced foods, or imported foods. The quantities are fixed at the average quantities purchased by the above groups. Total cost for any month or year is determined by multiplying these quantities by respective retail prices for each period. The series is compiled and published by the Economic Research Service (ERS) of the U.S. Department of Agriculture.

The quantities used in the series are the average quantities purchased by the above households for the period 1960–1961. Prior to that time, the quantity weights were fixed at the 1952 average quantities. The fixing of the quantities for the 65 foods permits comparison of the changing values of identical baskets of food purchases over time. Because the types and quantities of foods change over time, comparison of actual market basket purchases does not indicate changes in the quantity of marketing services over time. The farm-retail price spread has the property of the price indexes described in Chapter 3. Quality changes in either the basic farm product or in the marketing service may be involved in some of the changes, but they cannot be separated from the price changes.

The prices used in calculating the cost of the food market basket are those collected and reported by the Bureau of Labor Statistics (BLS). These prices represent average retail store prices for food in 56 cities.

The *farm value* of the market basket is calculated by multiplying the farm equivalents of each food included in the basket by the average price received by farmers for each food. Farm product equivalents are computed from standard conversion factors as reported in an ERS publication (*Conversion Factors and Weights and Measures,* Statistical Bulletin 362, June 1965). Prices received by farmers are collected and reported monthly by the Statistical Reporting Service of the U.S. Department of Agriculture.

The data series described above are used to calculate four components of the market basket series for individual foods, food product groups, and all 65 foods in the basket. The components are the "retail cost" to the consumer, the farm value, the farm-retail price spread, and the farmer's share of the consumer dollar. The annual indexes of these values of the market basket series for the period 1963–1975 are presented in Table 7-1 and plotted in Figure 7-4. The market basket series basically shows changes in the prices of farm products and changes in prices of marketing services.

Over the period 1963–1975, the farm value and the retail cost of the market

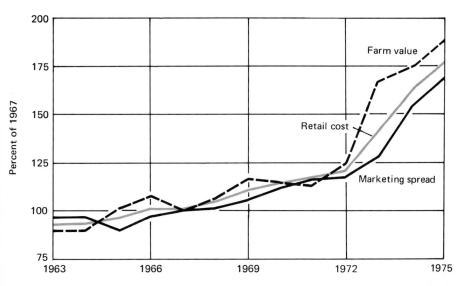

Figure 7-4 Retail cost, farm value, and marketing spread for a market basket of farm foods. *Source:* Economic Research Service, U.S. Department of Agriculture, NEG. ERS 76-75(9).

Table 7-1   The Farm-food Market Basket, 1963–1975[a]

Year	Retail cost (1967 = 100)	Farm value[b] (1967 = 100)	Farm-retail spread[c] (1967 = 100)	Share of retail cost, %	
				Farm[d]	Marketing[e]
1963	93	90	95	38	62
1964	93	90	96	37	63
1965	96	99	94	40	60
1966	101	106	98	41	59
1967	100	100	100	39	61
1968	104	105	102	39	61
1969	109	115	106	41	59
1970	114	114	113	39	61
1971	116	114	116	38	62
1972	121	125	119	40	60
1973	142	167	126	46	54
1974	162	178	152	43	57
1975[f]	176	190	166	42	58

[a]The market basket contains the average quantities of domestic farm-originated food products purchased annually per household in 1960–1961 by wage-earner and clerical-worker families and single persons living alone.
[b]Gross return to farmers for the fixed quantity of farm products equivalent to the foods in the market basket.
[c]Difference between the retail cost and farm value. It is an estimate of the charges made by marketing firms for assembly, processing, transportation, and distribution.
[d]Farm value as a percentage of retail cost.
[e]Farm-retail spread as a percentage of retail cost.
[f]Preliminary.
Source: U.S. Department of Agriculture, *1975 Handbook of Agricultural Charts,* no. 491, p. 28.

basket increased. There tended to be a parallel movement in both series, but farm values tended to be much more variable. As a consequence, the farmer's share of consumer food dollars varied from a low of 37 percent in 1964 to 46 percent in 1973. Between 1963 and 1975, the farmer's share trended slightly upward (see Figure 7-5). However, for individual food groups, the changes are not always consistent (see Figure 7-6). There also seems to be a tendency for the marketing share to decrease during the periods of rising farm prices and to increase when farm prices are falling. This phenomenon will be examined in greater detail in a later section.

The Marketing Bill

The *marketing bill* is an estimate of the total marketing costs of all domestically produced farm foods purchased by civilian consumers in the United States. Therefore, it excludes food consumed on farms where produced, food provided to members of the armed forces, and nonfarm foods. For the included foods, the measure is the difference between civilian expenditures for food and the farm values of these foods.

The marketing bill will change for the same reason that the farm-retail price spread changes from the ''Market Basket'' series, that is, changes in either farm prices or prices of marketing services. It will also change because of several other factors.

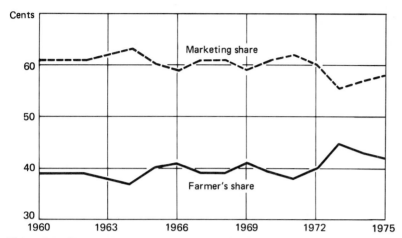

Figure 7-5 Shares of the market basket dollar that consumers spent in retail food stores for domestic farm-originated products. The 1975 figures are preliminary. *Source:* Economic Research Service, U.S. Department of Agriculture, NEG. ERS 303-75(9).

1 It will change because of a variation in the total quantity of food being marketed. This is a major factor in the changes that occurred through time, as indicated by the data in Table 7-2.

2 It will change because of greater quantities of marketing services associated with the foods. The greater importance of all foods consumed in eating establishments will be reflected in a higher marketing bill.

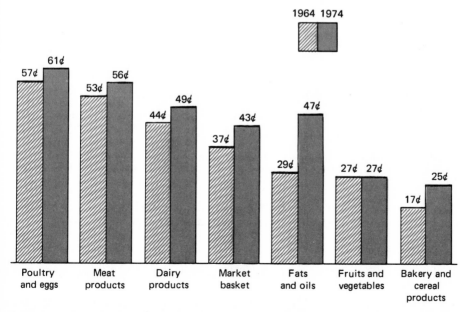

Figure 7-6 Farmers' share of the market basket dollar by food group. *Source:* Economic Research Service, U.S. Department of Agriculture, NEG. ERS 302-75(9).

Table 7-2 Marketing Bill, Farm Value, and Consumer Expenditures for Domestic Farm-food Products Bought by Civilians, 1947–1974

Year	Expenditures ($ billion)[a]	Marketing bill ($ billion)	Farm value[b]	Marketing bill as percent of food expenditure
1947	$ 41.9	$22.6	$19.3	53.9%
1948	44.8	24.9	19.9	54.9
1949	43.4	26.0	17.4	59.9
1950	44.0	26.0	18.0	59.1
1951	49.2	28.7	20.5	58.3
1952	50.9	30.5	20.4	59.9
1953	51.0	31.5	19.5	61.8
1954	51.1	32.3	18.8	63.2
1955	53.1	34.4	18.7	64.8
1956	55.5	36.3	19.2	65.4
1957	58.3	37.9	20.4	65.0
1958	61.0	39.6	21.4	64.9
1959	63.6	42.4	21.2	66.7
1960	66.9	44.6	22.3	66.7
1961	68.7	45.7	23.0	66.5
1962	71.3	47.6	23.7	66.8
1963	74.0	49.9	24.1	67.4
1964	77.5	52.6	24.9	67.9
1965	81.1	54.0	27.1	66.6
1966	86.9	57.1	29.8	65.7
1967	89.2	60.4	28.8	67.7
1968	93.9	63.5	30.4	67.6
1969	98.8	65.1	33.7	65.9
1970	106.0	71.2	34.8	67.2
1971	110.7	75.4	35.3	68.1
1972	117.1	78.4	38.7	67.0
1973	132.2	82.3	49.9	62.3
1974[c]	154.0	100.0	54.0	64.9

[a]Consumer expenditures for domestic farm-food products; excluded are expenditures for imported foods, fish, other foods not originating on U.S. farms, alcoholic beverages, food consumed on farms where produced, and military food purchases. Foods are valued at retail store prices except for foods sold in the form of meals and those sold at less than retail prices which are valued at the point of sale.
[b]The farm value is the gross return to farmers for products equivalent to those sold to consumers. Values of inedible byproducts, nonfood products, and exports are not included.
[c]Preliminary.
Note: Beginning with 1960, estimates are for 50 states.
Source: U.S. Department of Agriculture, *Marketing and Transportation Situation*, MTS-194, Aug. 1974, p. 16.

3 It will change because of a shift among foods that have greater or lesser quantities of marketing services embodied in them.

During the period 1947–1964, the marketing bill as a percentage of total retail expenditures increased rather steadily from 53.9 percent to 67.9 percent. With the surge in farm prices in 1973 relative to retail prices, the margin declined relatively. The change in the percentage during most of the period partially reflects an increase in the quantity of marketing services associated with food.

The marketing bill is also allocated to the various marketing agencies. The share of the bill for four agencies—processors, wholesalers, retailers, and eating places—are listed in Table 7-3 for the period 1958–1973. Three major trends in the share by agency are apparent. Processors now account for a much smaller part of marketing costs than in 1958. Between 1958 and 1973, the share declined from 44.8 percent to 34.1 percent. The wholesaler's share remained relatively constant. The retailer's share increased from 21.9 percent in 1958 to 29.8 percent in 1965 and has held rather stable since then. Although some variations occur, the share going to eating places increased from 20.1 percent in 1958 to 22.9 percent in 1973.

The individual cost components are also calculated for the food marketing bill. Eleven cost components are listed in Table 7-4. The relative importance of these items in 1973 is illustrated in Figure 7-7. The largest single item of marketing costs is labor, accounting annually for about 51 percent of total costs. The second single most important item is packaging materials, which account for about 12 percent of costs. Transportation costs make up 8 percent of the total; however, several important transportation components are not included in this figure. Intracity transport and air and water transport costs are not included.

Profits of food marketing firms do not appear to be expanding as a component of food marketing costs. The average profit rate before taxes for all firms varied from 4.7 to 6.0 percent of total marketing charges. These costs would have to be compared to returns on capital in other industries to determine if they are high or low.

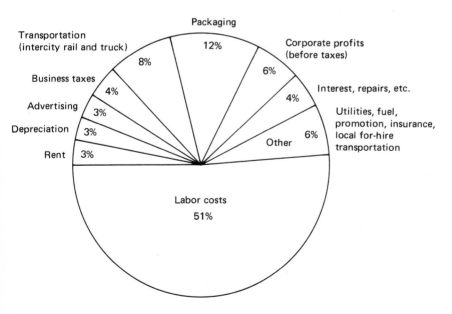

Figure 7-7 Components of bill for marketing farm foods, 1973 (preliminary data). *Source:* Economic Research Service, U.S. Department of Agriculture, NEG. ERS 8452-75(9).

Table 7-3   Share of Total Food Marketing Bill by Agency, 1958–1973

Year	Processors	Wholesalers	Retailers	Eating places
1958	44.8%	13.2%	21.9%	20.1%
1959	44.9	12.4	22.6	20.1
1960	43.1	12.4	24.6	19.9
1961	43.3	12.3	25.4	19.0
1962	41.7	12.6	26.2	19.5
1963	40.0	13.0	27.0	20.0
1964	40.2	12.3	29.0	18.5
1965	37.9	12.4	29.8	19.9
1966	36.7	12.9	29.8	20.6
1967	39.0	12.6	27.6	20.8
1968	38.5	12.8	27.8	20.9
1969	37.1	13.0	28.0	21.9
1970	35.5	12.6	29.1	22.8
1971	35.4	12.6	28.7	23.3
1972	35.6	13.1	28.6	22.6
1973	34.1	14.3	28.7	22.9

Source: U.S. Department of Agriculture, *Marketing and Transportation Situation,* MTS-194, Aug. 1974, p. 23.

A THEORY OF MARKETING MARGINS

Derived Demand

A useful concept of market analysis is the concept of derived demand. It explains how changes at one level of the market are reflected through to another level.

In a preceding chapter on supply, we described the derivation of the value of marginal product. The value of marginal product (VMP) curve describes the additional value of applying another unit of the variable input to a fixed resource for all levels of input use. The downward-sloping segment of this VMP curve was, for the individual firm, the short-run demand curve for that resource. It was calculated for a given final product price and a given technique of production. In very restricted adjustment situations, the horizontal summation of these curves for all firms would be the demand curve for the raw product. This demand for the input is a derived demand. It indicates the quantity of the input that should be used to maximize profits (or minimize losses) at each input price. A derived demand exists for each of the inputs used in the production of the final product. For any food product at retail, there is a derived demand for the basic farm product, labor, capital, transportation, credit, and any input used in producing and moving the farm product from farmer to ultimate consumer. The derivation of demands becomes more complicated if the final product prices vary as industry output adjusts when all firms adjust input use, but it still involves the procedures described above.

If competition exists in the purchase of the input and in the sales of the final product, the derived demand curve for the input will be below the primary consumer demand by the amount of the processing and distributing costs. This

Table 7-4   Cost Components of the Marketing Bill for Farm Foods in Billion Dollars, 1959–1974

Year	Labor[a]	Packaging materials	Rail and truck transportation[b]	Corporate profits Before taxes	Corporate profits After taxes	Business taxes[c]
1959	$18.8	$ 5.5	$4.0	$2.1	$1.0	$1.2
1960	19.7	5.4	4.1	2.1	0.9	1.3
1961	19.9	5.8	4.2	2.3	1.1	1.4
1962	20.8	6.1	4.1	2.3	1.1	1.6
1963	21.3	5.9	4.2	2.4	1.2	1.7
1964	22.1	6.0	4.3	2.8	1.4	1.8
1965	23.3	6.2	4.2	3.0	1.6	2.1
1966	24.6	6.8	4.2	3.4	1.8	2.2
1967	25.9	7.2	4.3	3.4	1.8	2.3
1968	28.0	7.8	4.5	3.6	1.8	2.6
1969	30.4	8.0	4.6	3.6	1.6	2.6
1970	32.3	8.5	5.2	3.6	1.6	2.9
1971	34.5	9.0	6.0	3.7	1.7	3.1
1972	37.6	9.4	6.1	3.5	1.7	3.2
1973	40.4	9.9	6.1	4.6	2.6	3.3
1974[d]	46.7	11.0	7.2	5.3	3.0	3.7

Year	Deprecia-tion	Rent (net)	Advertis-ing	Repairs, bad debts, and contributions	Interest (net)	Other[e]	Total
1959	$1.4	$1.1	$1.2	$0.7	$0.2	$6.2	$42.4
1960	1.5	1.1	1.3	0.7	0.2	7.2	44.6
1961	1.6	1.2	1.4	0.8	0.3	6.8	45.7
1962	1.8	1.4	1.6	0.8	0.3	6.8	47.6
1963	1.8	1.4	1.7	0.9	0.3	8.3	49.9
1964	1.9	1.5	1.7	1.0	0.3	9.2	52.6
1965	2.0	1.6	1.9	1.1	0.4	8.2	54.0
1966	2.2	1.8	2.0	1.1	0.4	8.4	57.1
1967	2.2	1.8	2.0	1.1	0.6	9.6	60.4
1968	2.1	2.0	1.8	1.2	0.8	9.1	63.5
1969	2.2	2.1	1.9	1.3	0.9	7.5	65.1
1970	2.5	2.3	2.0	1.5	1.1	9.3	71.2
1971	2.6	2.4	2.1	1.6	1.2	9.2	75.4
1972	2.8	2.5	2.2	1.7	1.2	8.2	78.4
1973	2.9	2.7	2.3	1.7	1.3	6.8	82.0
1974[d]	3.2	3.0	2.5	1.9	1.4	6.1	92.0

[a]Includes supplements to wages and salaries, such as social security taxes, unemployment insurance taxes, and health insurance premiums. Also includes imputed earnings of proprietors, partners, and family workers not receiving stated remuneration.

[b]Includes charges for heating and refrigeration; does not include local hauling charges.

[c]Includes property, social security, unemployment insurance, state income, and franchise taxes, license fees and other fees, but does not include federal income tax.

[d]Preliminary.

[e]Includes food service in schools, colleges, hospitals, other institutions, utilities, fuel, promotion, local for-hire transportation, water transportation, and insurance.

Source: U.S. Department of Agriculture, Marketing and Transportation Situation, MTS-194, Aug. 1974, p. 29.

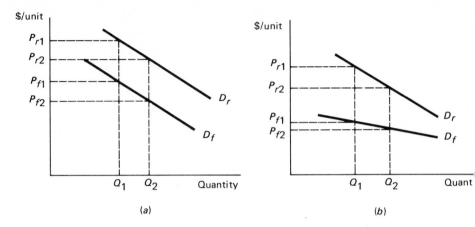

Figure 7-8 Two possible relationships between retail demand and farm demand for food products. (a) The processing-distributing industry for the farm product subject to constant cost; (b) the processing-distributing industry subject to decreasing costs.

assumes, of course, that the input and final product can be expressed in comparable quantity units. This can often be done for individual foods and the associated raw farm product.

In the long run, where no excess profits exist at any level of the market and the markets are competitive, three possible relationships could exist between primary (retail) demand and derived (farm) demand for food products. Two of these relationships are exhibited in Figure 7-8(a) and (b). Figure 7-8(a) illustrates a system in which the processing-distributing industry for the farm product is subject to constant cost; that is, the supply of marketing services is completely elastic. In this case, the marketing margins are constant regardless of the quantities marketed. The derived (farm) demand D_f lies below the retail demand D_r by a fixed-absolute amount.

Another possibility—one likely to exist in food marketing channels—is a processing-distribution industry subject to decreasing costs. In the long run, declining costs could result from external industry economies. In the short run, it could result because of fuller utilization of plant capacity. In food production, supply is often seasonal, thus contributing to large idle capacity during much of the year. With declining costs, the relation would appear as in Figure 7-8(b). The distance between primary demand D_r and derived demand D_f narrows with increasing volume. In the figure, the margin, although declining in absolute terms as quantity marketed increases, is an absolute percentage of retail price. Percentage margins are common in retailing and wholesaling.

If the processing-distributing industry for food products is characterized by increasing costs, the absolute distance between farm-level demand and retail demand would increase as quantity marketed increases. Empirical estimates of the relationship of farm-level prices and retail prices indicates that the margins for most foods vary between a fixed absolute and a fixed percentage of retail price.

The relationship between elasticities of demand at the different market levels has some analytical uses. As might be expected, the relationship depends upon the nature of the marketing margins. Let us compute the elasticities for the corresponding price-quantity changes with the kinds of margins illustrated in Figure 7-8(a) and (b). Recall that the general statement of demand elasticity is

$$E = \frac{\Delta Q}{\Delta P} \frac{P}{Q}$$

In Figure 7-8(a), the change in quantity (ΔQ) is the same at retail as at farm. Thus,

$$\Delta Q_r = \Delta Q_f = Q_1 - Q_2$$

The change in price at retail is

$$\Delta P_r = P_{r1} - P_{r2}$$

and the change in price at the farm is

$$\Delta P_f = P_{f1} - P_{f2}$$

Because both retail and farm demand curves have the same slopes with constant absolute margins,

$$\Delta P_r = \Delta P_f = P_{r1} - P_{r2} = P_{f1} - P_{f2}$$

Substituting the appropriate terms in the equations for elasticity, the elasticity demand at farm is

$$E_f = \frac{Q_1 - Q_2}{P_{f1} - P_{f2}} \frac{P_f}{Q}$$

The elasticity of demand at retail is

$$E_r = \frac{Q_1 - Q_2}{P_{r1} - P_{r2}} \frac{P_r}{Q}$$

The calculated ratio of E_r to E_f is

$$\frac{E_r}{E_f} = \frac{[(Q_1 - Q_2)/(P_{r1} - P_{r2})]\ (P_r/Q)}{[(Q_1 - Q_2)/(P_{f1} - P_{f2})]\ (P_f/Q)} = \frac{P_r}{P_f}$$

Thus, the ratio of the elasticities is equal to the ratio of prices.

Since retail prices always exceed farm price for the equivalent quantity, the absolute value of the elasticity of demand at retail will always exceed that at farm. Stated another way, farm-level demand is always more inelastic than retail demand if marketing margins are a constant-absolute amount. The reader may also deduce that the smaller the margin, the less the difference between elasticities at the two market levels.

The measurement in the preceding sections indicates that marketing margins for all foods tend to be a constant percentage of farm prices or, alternatively, retail price will be a constant percentage of farm price. If the retail price is k percent of farm price, then $P_r = kP_f$. This relationship holds for the example illustrated in Figure 7-8(b). In this situation, the elasticity of demand at retail for the indicated price-quantity range can be stated as:

$$E_r = \frac{Q_1 - Q_2}{P_{r1} - P_{r2}} \frac{P_r}{Q}$$

or alternatively as:

$$E_r = \frac{Q_1 - Q_2}{kP_{f1} - kP_{f2}} \frac{kP_f}{Q} = \frac{Q_1 - Q_2}{P_{f1} - P_{f2}} \frac{P_f}{Q} = E_f$$

Thus, with an absolute percentage markup, demand elasticities are identical at the two market levels.

Knowledge of the behavior of marketing margins and their implications for elasticity relations between market levels have been used to derive demand elasticities at other market levels given the elasticities at one level. George and King used these relations to estimate farm-level demand elasticities.[2] First they derived retail demand elasticities for a wide range of farm products at retail. Some of these elasticities are reproduced in Table 7-5. George and King then observed how retail-farm price relationships behaved as quantities changed. This provided information on margins that were used to calculate the farm-level demand elasticities listed in Table 7-5. Note that for all products, the farm-level demand is less elastic than retail demand.

Derived Supply

Just as farm-level demand can be derived for a given retail demand and a marketing cost schedule, the retail supply curve can be derived for a given farm supply and a marketing cost schedule. It can be estimated by adding marketing costs associated with each quantity of the commodity that could be produced to the farm-level supply curve. The relationship between the supply curve when the

[2]P. S. George and G. A. King, *Consumer Demand for Food Commodities in the United States with Projections for 1980,* Giannini Foundation Monograph 26, California Agricultural Experiment Station, Mar. 1971.

Table 7-5 Price Elasticities of Demand at Retail and Farm for Selected Food Products

	Price elasticity at:	
Product	Retail	Farm
Beef	−0.644	−0.416
Chicken	−0.777	−0.602
Eggs	−0.318	−0.225
Fresh milk	−0.346	−0.323
Apples	−0.720	−0.676
Wheat flour	−0.300	−0.244

Source: P. S. George and G. A. King, *Consumer Demand for Food Commodities in the United States with Projections for 1980,* Giannini Foundation Monograph 26, California Agricultural Experiment Station, Mar. 1971.

processing-distributing industry is characterized by constant cost is illustrated in Figure 7-9, where S_f is farm supply and S_r is retail supply. Note that in regard to supply, the primary relationship is the farm-level supply and the derived relationship is at retail.

A Dynamic System

Similar to so many other price-quantity relationships, observed margins, quantities, and prices at different market levels are the results of constantly changing supply-demand equilibriums, that is, intersections of short-run demands and supplies. The entire supply-demand relations are not directly observable. If they were, we might expect them to appear and shift through time as illustrated in Figure 7-10.

Both primary demand (retail) and primary supply (farm) shift to the right

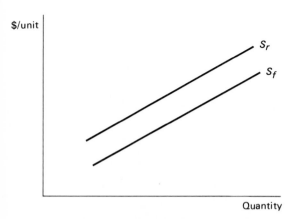

Figure 7-9 Relationship between farm supply S_f and retail supply S_r when the processing-distributing industry is characterized by constant cost.

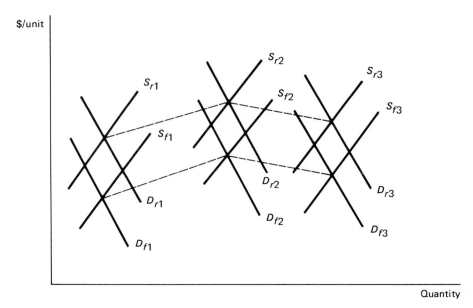

Figure 7-10 Supply-demand relations at farm and retail levels shifting through time.

through time. Primary demand shifts because of income and population growth. Primary supply shifts because of technological advance. Consequently, derived demand and supply are also shifted to the right. If marketing services are in completely elastic supply and the quantity of service demanded per unit of product is independent of the total quantity demanded or is independent of time, the derived relation will shift by the same amount as the primary relations. The upper dashed line in Figure 7-10, detailing the intersections of retail demand and retail supply, represents the movement of retail prices over time. The lower dashed line represents the movement of farm prices over time. Note that in the hypothetical example, both retail and farm prices shifted by exactly the same amount.

INCIDENCE OF CHANGES IN PRIMARY DEMAND, PRIMARY SUPPLY, AND MARKETING COSTS

We have described in an earlier chapter how changes in income, prices of substitutes, and tastes and preferences normally shift the primary demand for farm products. Likewise, the impact on primary supply of cost changes, technology, or prices of other products which can be produced with the same resources were examined. Now we will examine how these shifters of either supply or demand are reflected through different levels of the marketing system. Furthermore, we will examine the impact of changes in supply or demand for marketing services on market equilibrium at each level of the system.

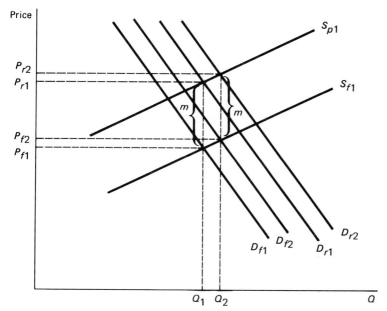

Figure 7-11 Incidence of price changes due to demand shifts.

First, let us trace the impact of a shift to the right of the primary demand for a food product. Assume an initial market equilibrium in Figure 7-11 illustrated by primary demand of D_{r1} and a primary (farm-level) supply at S_{f1}. Marketing costs are constant at m regardless of quantities marketed. Assuming also that stock-holding is not a significant part of demand at any point in the system and that the quantities can be expressed in equivalent units at farm and retail, derived demand and supply can be expressed directly on the same diagram. Derived demand at the farm (D_{f1}) lies below the primary demand by the amount of the marketing costs (m). The derived supply at retail (S_{r1}) lies above the primary supply by the amount of the marketing costs (m). The intersection of retail demand D_{r1} and retail supply S_{r1} at Q_1 determines the retail price of P_{r1}. The intersection of farm demand D_{f1} and farm supply S_{f1} is also at Q_1, but price at this level is P_{f1}. And the marketing margin is $m = P_{r1} - P_{f1}$.

Suppose now that increasing per capita income shifts primary consumer demand to the right to D_{r2}. Considering the retail level separately, the shift would increase the retail price to P_{r2} and the quantity to Q_2. But how is the change reflected at the farm level of the market? Since the marketing-processing industry is subject to constant costs and if competition is present, the derived demand at the farm level is shifted to the right by the same amount that retail demand is shifted. The new farm-level demand is D_{f2}. No other shifts in demand would occur and the supply relationships would not be altered. Farm price would rise to P_{f2} and quantity demanded and supplied at the farm is Q_2. The marketing margins determined by $P_{r2} - P_{f2}$ still equals m. Thus, the demand shift to the

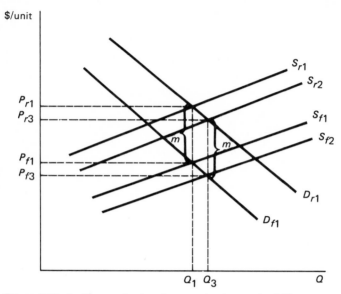

Figure 7-12 Incidence of price changes due to supply shifts.

right increased quantity and prices at both market levels. Marketing margins remained the same.

A common occurrence in agriculture is a supply shift. Over the long run, it shifts to the right because of technological change. Year-to-year changes are likely to occur because of weather changes, and year-to-year changes in demand are usually of smaller magnitudes. Let us examine the impact of a rightward shift in supply because of a major technological advance in farm production, for example, a new soybean variety that substantially increases yields. The impact can be illustrated by the use of Figure 7-12. Assume the initial equilibrium, as in the preceding example, at P_{r1}, P_{f1}, and Q_1. The technological advance shifts the primary supply relationship downward and to the right, from S_{f1} to S_{f2}. Because retail supply lies above farm-level cost by the amount of the marketing change m, the shift implies a movement in the retail-level supply from S_{r1} to S_{r2}. The new equilibrium results in a retail-level price of P_{r3}, a farm-level price of P_{f3}, and a quantity of Q_3. However, the marketing margin is still constant at m. Thus, the technological advance reduces both farm and retail prices while increasing the equilibrium quantity supplied and demanded.

The incidence of demand and supply shifts when the processing-distributing industry is subject to increasing or decreasing costs will add an additional dimension to the adjustments. With increasing costs, shifts of the primary demand or primary supply to the right will cause increased marketing margins. Shifts to the left will result in reduced marketing margins.

Changes in marketing costs will generally bring about price changes at all levels of the market as well as changes in the quantities moving through the marketing system. Analysis of the impact of changes in marketing cost may be somewhat more difficult than for changes in either primary demand or primary supply. Changes in marketing costs may occur because of increased promotion. The object of this activity is to shift the demand. If successful, primary demand will shift. Nevertheless, marketing margins will be wider at all possible quantities. Although increased costs by themselves will shift derived demand downward or to the left, the net effect of the promotion program may shift both primary and derived demand to the right.

The impact of a change in marketing cost that has no impact on primary demand is illustrated in Figure 7-13. Suppose that transportation rates increase. Because transportation is an important component of food marketing costs—approximately 8 percent for all foods and much greater for some products—it will mean that farm-level demand is shifted downward from D_{f1} to D_{f4} in Figure 7-13. This also means that the retail supply curve is shifted upward from S_{r1} to S_{r4} by the amount of increased transport cost. As long as increased transport costs do not result in increased farm costs, no shift will occur in farm-level supply. The increased marketing costs then cause retail prices to increase, farm prices to fall, and quantity of marketings to reduce. The new marketing margin n will be greater than old margin m by the amount of increased transport cost.

Note that both farm and retail prices changed by approximately the same amount in Figure 7-13. The relative incidence at the two market levels will depend upon the relative elasticities of supply and demand. The more inelastic supply is in relation to demand, the greater the impact on farm-level prices relative to retail prices. The more inelastic demand is in relation to supply, the greater the impact on retail prices. The two extremes of completely inelastic supply or completely inelastic demand indicate the maximum impact of changes

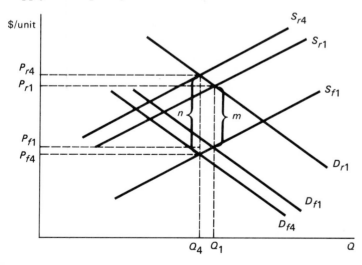

Figure 7-13 Incidence of price changes due to a change in the marketing margin.

in marketing costs. With completely inelastic demand, the entire impact is on retail price. With perfectly inelastic supply, the entire impact is on farm-level price.

OBSERVED PRICE VARIABILITY THROUGH THE FOOD MARKETING SYSTEM

The preceding section indicated an instantaneous and simultaneous adjustment in retail and farm prices. This is not likely to occur for a number of reasons. First, a certain amount of time is required between buying and selling for each market participant. Second, it may be possible that market participants may have enough market power to retain some of the returns from favorable supply or demand adjustments. Thus, in actual practice, one is likely to observe some differences in adjustments of prices at the different market levels. In some instances, price adjustments at retail appear to lag behind adjustments at the farm.

The lags that do occur are the target of criticisms by both consumers and farmers. Consumers allege that increasing farm prices are always translated into larger increases at retail, but declining farm prices are not passed on in the form of lower retail prices. Farmers and their representatives also tend to view the middleman as an exploiter. It is charged that marketing firms use rising farm prices to justify increases in marketing margins. They argue that middlemen are able to pass on any increase in farm prices merely by marking up their selling prices. Farmers as price takers are unable to pass on increasing costs by arbitrarily raising their prices. The argument is partially true. Farmers usually operate as perfect competitors in selling their product and are therefore price takers. Marketing firms operate in markets in which they have some discretionary authority in setting prices. However, this does not mean that they are immune from demand and supply conditions in the market.

How do these price movements at different market levels relate to one another? The data plotted in Figures 7-14 and 7-15 provide some answers to this question. Quarterly indexes of the retail and farm values of the consumer market basket are plotted in Figure 7-14 for the period 1970–1974. Monthly indexes of the same variables are plotted in Figure 7-15.

One can draw several conclusions from this series.

1 The same general movement throughout the entire period occurred in both series. Over the long term, farm and retail prices do move together. During most of the latter half of the period, farm prices moved out ahead of retail prices but narrowed again toward the very end of the period.

2 The variability in farm values is much greater relatively than at retail. This is apparent in both the monthly and quarterly figures. This observation is consistent with all other findings about price variability in farm and retail foods.

3 The leads and lags in prices, at least for the aggregate farm-food

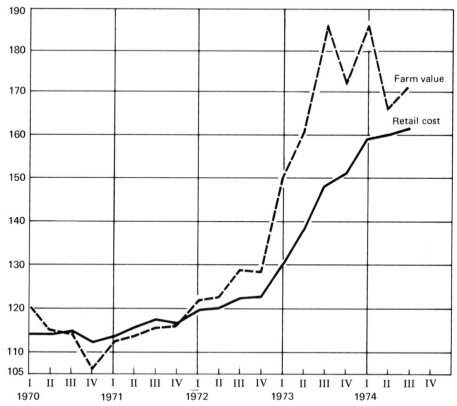

Figure 7-14 Quarterly market basket of farm food: retail cost and farm value by quarter, 1970–1974.

market basket, are not always consistent. Consider the period from May 1973 to September 1974 in Figure 7-15. Farm prices began to rise spectacularly in May 1973, but retail prices did not really take off until July. Both retail and farm prices then reached a peak in August. Retail prices fell for the following two months and then began to rise again, but this time farm prices lagged the reversal in retail prices by one month. In February 1974, farm prices began another decline while retail prices increased for another month. Farm prices rose again in June while the reversal in retail prices did not begin until the following month. The evidence therefore shows a somewhat greater tendency for farm price changes to precede retail prices, but it is not conclusive. Analysis for individual food products should provide additional insight into this relationship.

4 The monthly series plotted in Figure 7-15 indicates that some of the small month-to-month changes in farm prices are not reflected in retail prices. This, together with the above observations concerning the longer-term movements, would indicate that some price adjustments take more than a month to work themselves through the market system.

Figure 7-15 Monthly market basket of farm foods: retail cost and farm value by month, 1970–1974.

CAUSES OF CHANGING MARKETING MARGINS

Changes in food marketing margins have been investigated in several special studies by the Federal Trade Commission and congressional commissions. A rather comprehensive study was conducted by the National Commission on Food Marketing (NCFM) in the mid-1960s. The commission was established as a result of the kinds of charges cited earlier. The findings of the commission, published in a final report and 10 technical reports, is an excellent source of material on the U.S. food marketing system.[3]

Many of the findings regarding the food marketing system are still valid today. Those findings were summarized in a report of the University of Minnesota.[4] Four sets of factors were found to have had an impact on the monthly margins during the preceding 18 years. They were marketing input prices, increased food processing, the merchandising mix, and technological change.

[3]National Commission on Food Marketing, *Food from Source to Consumer,* July 1966, and Technical Studies 1–10.

[4]Jerome Hammond et al., "Why the Growing Farm-Retail Price Spread?" *Minnesota Farm Business Notes,* Oct. 1967.

Several marketing input prices have shown large increases over time. Labor rates exhibited a continual upward trend and they have continued to increase since that time. In fact, wage-rate increases have increased labor components of food marketing costs from 42 percent in 1965 to 48 percent in 1973. Power costs, a significantly increasing cost today, were increasing marketing costs between 1950 and 1964. Natural gas rates doubled during that era. Building and equipment costs rose somewhat during the pre-1965 period, and they have increased at an even faster rate since then.

Increased food processing is a reflection of increasing demand for food marketing service. Between 1940 and 1963, the marketing service associated with each unit of food increased by 23 percent.[5] These increased services are represented by more and improved packaging, greater use of processed fruits and vegetables rather than fresh vegetables, and increased use of ready-to-eat or ready-to-cook products.

The NCFM studies reported increasing emphasis on food distribution and merchandising rather than on food processing. This relative emphasis is indicated by the data in Table 7-5, which shows the share of total marketing costs accounted for by various agencies. The processor's share is decreasing and the retailer's share is increasing. The merchandising orientation of retailers may be reflected in increased promotional activities, larger and more expensive stores, air conditioning, music, and other services designed to attract customers into the store.

Increasing input costs for the food marketing system have been offset to some extent by technological improvements. Widespread adoption of pallets and fork trucks has increased handling efficiency at all levels of marketing. Use of computers for inventory control, ordering, and billing has reduced control problems. A recent development is the universal product code, which is an electromagnetic identification on each packaged product that permits the use of electronic sensing checkout equipment in retail stores. This permits continuous inventory control and sales records as well as reducing checkout time. Without technological improvements in food marketing, we could have expected much greater marketing costs, and hence greater retail prices, than have actually occurred.

SUMMARY

Retail prices, marketing spreads, and farm product prices are mutually arrived at in a continuous process of interaction and adjustment. Farm-level demand for each food product is derived from the final (primary) demand for each food purchased by consumers. Costs of providing the marketing service for each possible set of equivalent quantities determine the relation of farm-level demand to retail demand. The characteristics of these costs also determine the

---

[5]H. C. Trelogan and N. Townshend-Zellner, "On Benefits of Agricultural Marketing Research," *Journal of Farm Economics*, vol. 47, no. 1, Feb. 1965, p. 45.

relationship between elasticities of demand at the two market levels. Data generally show that demand for food is more inelastic at the farm level than at the retail level of the market.

Food marketing margins are regularly measured and reported in two major series of the U.S. Department of Agriculture. One series—the farm-retail price spread—is a measure of the cost of marketing a fixed quantity of foods purchased by urban wage-earner and blue-collar families. The other series—the marketing bill—is a measure of the total cost of marketing for all domestically produced farm products purchased by U.S. civilian consumers. The farm-retail price spread is a monthly series that provides an up-to-date view of absolute and relative changes in farm and retail prices. The marketing bill is reported only on an annual basis. Consequently, it does not provide an estimate of the very short-term movements in farm prices, retail prices, and marketing margins.

QUESTIONS

1 Since marketing services are *supplied* and supply relationships are of an immediate, short, and long-run character, would you expect the marketing margin to be constant in the immediate run and variable in the short run? Would you anticipate that the long-run marketing margin will increase by some trend pattern? Why? Why not?
2 Market basket statistics are frequently presented in percentage terms. For example, the percent of the market basket that represents returns to the farmer (farm value) is frequently used by politicians as a guide to the welfare status of farmers. The farmer's share has vacillated from a high of 47 percent in 1952 to a low of 38 percent in 1971 during the past 25 years. In what regard is this percentage measure (share of retail cost) a good indicator of farm welfare and to what extent is it a poor indicator of farm welfare?
3 If the marketing margin is not of a constant-absolute type, will the price elasticity of demand at retail always be greater than that at the farm level? Describe the nature of the elasticity relationships with a constant percentage margin.
4 Can you think of any situations in which the change in marketing cost results in a change in retail demand *and* has a price impact at the farm level of the system as well?

BIBLIOGRAPHY

George, P. S., and G. A. King: *Consumer Demand for Food Commodities in the United States with Projections for 1980,* Giannini Foundation Monograph 26, California Agricultural Experiment Station, Mar. 1971.
Hammond, Jerome, et al.: "Why the Growing Farm-Retail Price Spread?" *Minnesota Farm Business Notes,* Oct. 1967.
National Commission on Food Marketing: *Food from Source to Consumer,* July 1966; and Technical Studies 1–10.
Nicholls, William H.: *Imperfect Competition within Agricultural Industries,* Iowa State College Press, Ames, Iowa, 1941.

Shepherd, G. S., and G. A. Futrell: *Marketing Farm Products—Economic Analysis,* 5th
    ed., Iowa State University Press, Ames, Iowa, 1969.
Trelogan, H. C., and N. Townshend-Zellner: "On Benefits of Agricultural Marketing
    Research," *Journal of Farm Economics,* vol. 47, no. 1, Feb. 1965.
Waugh, Frederick V. (ed.): *Readings in Agricultural Marketing,* Iowa State College
    Press, Ames, Iowa, 1953.

Chapter 8

Markets over Space

INTRODUCTION

Prices vary from one place to another. We can expect the price of any agricultural product to differ geographically because of transportation costs, differences in supply or demand, legal and natural barriers to trade, and other factors.

It is the purpose of this chapter to consider the several aspects of the spatial dimension of the marketing system. First, the role of comparative advantage in determining where products are produced is reviewed. Second, the price structure within a market with a concentrated consuming center that is surrounded by a geographically dispersed supply area will be analyzed. Third, price structures in markets with multiple supply-demand areas will be considered. Fourth, a method for determining optimum market movements of a product will be reviewed. Finally, we will highlight the aggregate costs of moving food products in the United States.

LOCATIONS OF PRODUCTION

Why is U.S. agricultural production located where it is? Part of the answer rests on purely climatic or agronomic considerations. Date production in the United

States is undertaken in a few areas of the Southwest because the necessary climatic conditions are met only in these regions. Citrus fruit production is undertaken in only a few of the extreme southern regions of the country. Again, climatic requirements limit the production to these areas.

Other farm products are not so restricted by climatic requirements, and the reasons for the location of production are found in economic considerations. The Corn Belt region of the United States is endowed with climatic conditions and soil characteristics that make it very productive in a number of farm enterprises: wheat, corn, soybeans, cattle, hogs, milk, forage crops, and numerous others. All enterprises are undertaken but there is major specialization in corn, soybeans, and livestock feeding. Milk production is widely dispersed in the United States but it is highly concentrated in the Lake states. This occurs even though milk production per acre of cropland in the Corn Belt greatly exceeds that in the Lake states. Similarly, the Corn Belt yields considerably higher productivity of wheat per acre than the Great Plains, but the Plains states dominate wheat production.

The reason for the location of production and the specialization that occurs is explained by the *principle of comparative advantage*. This principle is commonly used to explain country specialization and the advantages of trade. It also explains regional specialization and the advantages of trade within countries.

To illustrate how comparative advantage determines regional specialization in agriculture, consider the hypothetical production possibilities per acre of cropland for corn and milk in the Corn Belt and the Lake states (see Table 8-1). We will assume that the total of all other production costs per acre, labor, and inputs are the same for either enterprise in both regions. (Obviously, this is at odds with actual facts, but it simplifies the example and does not change the results.) Table 8-1 shows several possible combinations of production per acre for each region. It shows that an acre devoted entirely to corn production is more productive in the Corn Belt than in the Lake states. Also, an acre devoted to milk production is more productive in the Corn Belt than in the Lake states. The Corn Belt has an *absolute advantage* in the production of both corn and milk.

In terms of what has to be given up in one region to produce a unit of the other product, Table 8-1 indicates a different situation. Another hundredweight

Table 8-1 Production Possibilities per Acre of Land in the Corn Belt and Lake States

Combination	Corn Belt		Lake states	
	Corn (bushel)	Milk (cwt)	Corn (bushel)	Milk (cwt)
A	120	0	40	0
B	80	10	20	10
C	40	20	10	15
D	0	30	0	20

of milk costs four bushels of corn in the Corn Belt. Another hundredweight of milk in the Lake states costs 2 bushels of corn. Thus, the Lake states have a *comparative advantage* in milk production. Measuring unit corn cost in terms of units of milk yields the opposite situation. The Corn Belt must give up only one-quarter hundredweight of milk to gain an additional bushel of corn. The Lake states must relinquish one-third of a hundredweight of milk for another bushel of corn. The Corn Belt has a *comparative advantage* in corn production.

In the classical international trade examples, the benefits of specialization in those products in which a country has a comparative advantage is illustrated by indicating how total production of both products may be increased by trade. For regions within a country, the same results can be shown. However, where the producing regions are not the consuming regions, what mechanism brings about specialization? The answer is the profit maximization objective operating through the price system.

Whether or not both products will be produced depends upon the relative prices of the two products. In Figure 8-1(a) and (b), the production possibilities for the two regions have been plotted. Assuming a given price relationship, isorevenue areas can be plotted. Thus, with corn and milk prices equal, I_1 and I_2 are those combinations of corn and milk that will yield constant income levels. There are an infinite number of isorevenue curves, all of which are parallel to I_1 and I_2. Isorevenue curves moving out from the origin represent successively higher levels of income. To maximize profit (with the assumption that cost of inputs other than land are equal), producers should use land at that combination of milk and corn production where the highest isorevenue curve (revenue) can be

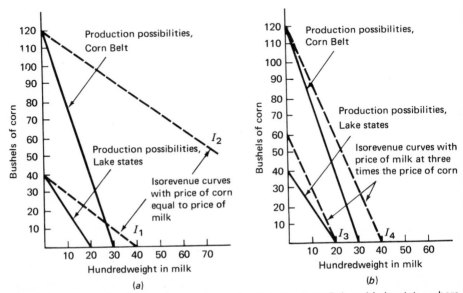

Figure 8-1 Production possibilities of corn and milk in the Corn Belt and Lake states where the price of (a) one bushel of corn equals 100 pounds of milk and (b) three bushels of corn equals 100 pounds of milk.

attained. In Figure 8-1(*a*), this occurs where only corn is produced in both regions. Relative milk prices are so low that corn production is most profitable in both areas.

Figure 8-1(*b*) illustrates a situation in which milk prices are three times the price of corn. Operating at a profit-maximizing level, the Corn Belt still devotes all land to corn production, but the Lake states now devote all land to milk production. Notice that the ratio of corn price to milk price, 1:3, is between the inverse of the marginal rates of substitution of corn for milk (1:2 and 1:4) on the production possibility curve for the two regions. For any price ratio between these two limits, the Corn Belt will specialize in corn and the Lake states will specialize in milk production.

The preceding example is a simplified explanation of regional specialization in farm production. Nevertheless, it should indicate that comparative advantage operates through the price system to cause specialization.

Comparative advantage is not stable, and shifts in production in U.S. agriculture have changed over time. The shift of cotton production from the South to the Southwest is a major change that has occurred during this century. Wilcox, Cochrane, and Herdt have listed the following reasons for changes in comparative advantages:

    1 Changes in natural resources, such as loss through soil erosion.
    2 Changes in biological factors, such as increased infestations of crops by pests and disease.
    3 Changes in input prices.
    4 Increased mechanization that is better adapted to level land free of stones than to hilly and stony land.
    5 Cheaper and more efficient transportation that decreases the disadvantages of areas most distant from markets.[1]

INTRAMARKET PRICE STRUCTURES

For a single consuming center for a farm product, observed prices at alternate locations in its supply area decrease with distance from the consuming market. These differentials reflect transportation costs for moving the product in either its raw form or its processed form, whichever is cheapest. Thus, for a given day, wheat prices at most any location in Minnesota, North Dakota, and South Dakota differ by the transportation cost differences for shipping wheat between the country location and Minneapolis. The pricing procedures by which country elevators set their buying prices to reflect this cost differential has been described in an earlier chapter.

This declining price structure with respect to distance from the consuming market is explicitly written into the federal orders which establish prices in fluid milk markets. These *zone differentials* based on the cost of transporting whole milk to the original Chicago Federal Order milk market are illustrated in Figure

[1]W. W. Wilcox, W. W. Cochrane, and R. W. Herdt, *Economics of American Agriculture,* 3d ed., Prentice-Hall, Englewood Cliffs, N.J., 1974, p. 21.

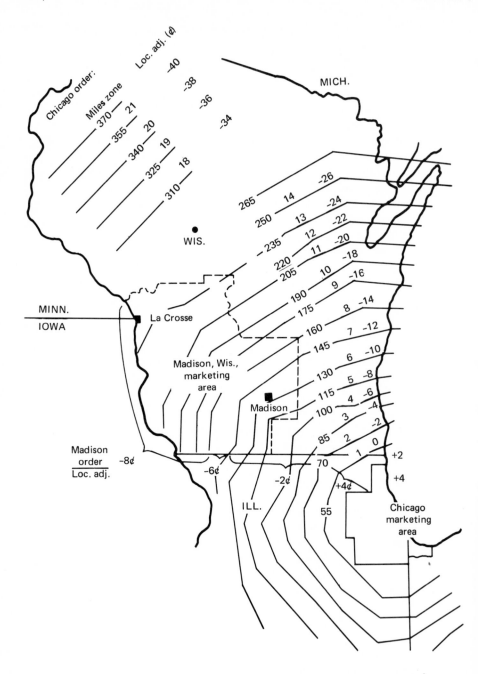

Figure 8-2 Pricing zones under Madison and Chicago orders. *Source:* R. E. Freeman and E. M. Babb, *Marketing Area and Related Issues in Federal Milk Orders,* Purdue University Agricultural Experiment Station, Research Bulletin 782, June 1964, p. 15.

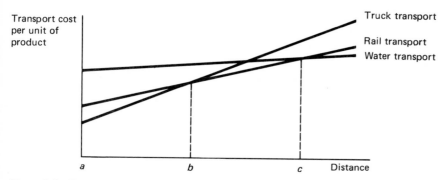

Figure 8-3   Transport costs per unit of product for three methods of transportation.

8-2. For each 15 miles from Chicago, required dealer-buying prices for milk declined by 2 cents per hundredweight.

The location differentials are determined by the lowest cost means of transportation in competitive markets with no barriers to movements of product. If truck transport is cheapest, it will determine location differentials. If rail costs are the least expensive, they will determine location differentials. For some products, the transportation rates may be such that trucks are cheapest for supply that is nearest the market, rail transport the least expensive for more distant supplies and where feasible, and barge transport possibly the cheapest for the most distant supplies. This categorization occurs because of the differences in fixed costs associated with each method of transport. High fixed costs mean that transport costs per unit of the commodity are high for short distances but increase very little as the length of the haul is increased. The impact of this on location differentials and the optimum transport method for each distance from a market is illustrated in Figure 8-3. In this figure, the rate structures are such that all three types of transportation are used. For locations within distance *ab* from market, truck transport is used, and prices within that area are the *at-market* price minus the trucking cost at each location. For distances *b* to *c* from the market, rail transport is least costly and rail costs determine the location differentials. For distances greater than *c*, water transport becomes the method of lowest cost.

Location differentials are not always determined by the lowest costs of transporting the raw farm product. Manufacturing-use milk location differentials are determined by the costs of transporting manufactured dairy products rather than the raw milk in purely competitive markets. The reason for this is that transport costs per hundredweight of raw-milk equivalent of the manufactured dairy products (butter, powder, cheese) are cheaper than for the raw milk. Not only is the location differential determined by transport costs for the processed products, but the location of the processing industry is determined by the transport cost. If it is cheaper to move the processed product, the processing is located in the raw-product supply area. Thus, manufactured dairy products are produced in the milk supply area.

Occasionally, trade barriers limit the effect of transport costs on the location of processing. The cost of transporting wheat to the consuming markets is less than the cost of shipping flour from the wheat-producing areas. Assuming that milling costs are the same in both areas, this would imply that the milling industry should be located in the major consuming markets. Various monopolistic practices and administered pricing systems have eliminated this cost advantage. This has partly accounted for the large amount of the flour-milling capacity of the United States being located in Minneapolis.[2]

The differential hauling rates for milk in its various processed forms tend to cause a distinct pattern of prices and processing zones. Although the high degree of price regulation and the many intermarket price relationships obscure the purely competitive intramarket price and processing structure, the following model is quite useful in explaining the location of the dairy processing industry.

The net price for milk in each of the possible uses at any distance from the consuming market is the at-market price in that use minus the cost of transporting milk in its processed form [see Figure 8-4(a)]. For the three milk products considered here, transport costs per hundredweight of raw-milk equivalent are highest for milk in fluid products, followed by milk in cream, and then milk in butter. This causes buying prices to decline more rapidly for uses which have high transport costs. Unless the at-market prices for milk in fluid products is higher than for the other products, no milk would be purchased for fluid uses. Demand for high-transport-cost products are usually high enough to generate at-market prices in excess of lower-transport-cost products. If at-market prices are ranked in this order, milk for fluid products is produced in the immediate supply area surrounding the consuming market. Transport costs reduce the net buying prices for more distant supply. The higher transport costs eventually reduce the net price below that for milk used in cream—at distance *oa* in Figure 8-4(a). Beyond this distance milk will be used in cream production. But transport costs per hundredweight of milk equivalent for cream exceed those for milk transported as butter. The net price to producers eventually falls below that for butter at distance *ob* in Figure 8-4(a).

The different at-market prices and the different transport costs for milk in each of the uses yield product zones surrounding the consuming market. The products with highest transport costs per hundredweight of milk equivalent are produced nearest the market. A mapping of the supply area yields a pattern similar to that depicted in Figure 8-4(b). This figure illustrates a static market. Changes in demands for any one of the products, changes in the total market supply of milk, or changes in transport costs will shift the product boundaries. Also, since milk production is highly seasonal, the boundaries will constantly shift in and out during the season.

The model of an isolated milk market is highly simplified, but it does conform to the geographic uses of milk in the United States. Milk producers near

---

[2]The mechanism for this has been the *in-transit* provision, which established the same rate for wheat that was shipped to Minneapolis, unloaded, milled into flour, and then shipped to consuming markets as for wheat shipped directly to the flour-consuming markets.

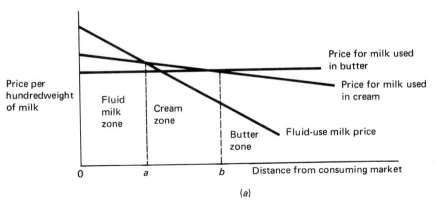

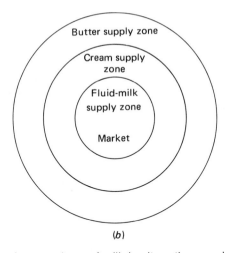

(b)

Figure 8-4 (a) Net prices for a producer of milk in alternative uses in relation to distance from the consuming market; (b) theoretical milk-product supply zones for an isolated consuming market.

the high population centers of the East produce primarily for the fluid uses. The heavy milk producing region of the Midwest has a lower population than the East and consequently produces the largest share of American manufactured dairy products.[3]

[3]For a more detailed analysis of the geographic structure of milk markets and prices, see J. M. Cassels, *A Study of Milk Prices,* Harvard Economic Studies, vol. 54, Harvard University Press, Cambridge, Mass., 1937.

INTERREGIONAL MARKET RELATIONSHIPS

Most markets for U.S. agricultural products are not characterized by a single consuming market with supply geographically dispersed around that location. Numerous consuming markets exist and a number of supply regions may be distinguished for most major farm products. The consuming markets for most food products might be divided into the major population centers of the United States plus the satellite markets in their areas. Numerous supply areas exist for many of the major farm products. These regions are likely to differ for each product. Consider citrus production. Three regions account for practically all production: Florida in the Southeast, Texas in the Southcentral, and California and Arizona in the Southwest. Heaviest wheat production is located in the Northwest and in the Plains states. Milk production is heavily concentrated in the Northeast, the Lake states, and the West Coast. Turkey production is heavily concentrated in the states of Minnesota, North Carolina, Missouri, and California.

The questions that we wish to deal with in this section are the determination and relationships of prices in markets with multiple consuming and supply regions and the determination of the movements of products between regions. The model that explains the behavior of price and product movement among submarkets for any market is the *trade model*. It indicates the relationships that we should expect to exist, or it explains those that do exist.

For the trade model, we will first assume that two supply-demand areas exist for the product. This could be, for example, the orange industry, where the area east of the Mississippi is one region with its supply centered in Florida. The other region is that area west of the Mississippi with its supply centered in California. The costs of moving oranges between the two regions are known and they can be reduced to an average cost per unit of product that moves between the two regions. The costs of product movements within each of the regions can be disregarded. Assume also that the oranges of the two regions are completely substitutable in all uses. Supply and demand for each of the regions are known and can be graphically illustrated as in Figure 8-5(a) and (c). What prices and product movements will occur?

Consider first the case where no trade is permitted. Each region is therefore an isolated market with supply and demand in each solely determining prices and quantities. Because no oranges can move into or out of the region, the supply-demand relations yield an equilibrium price of P_1 and a quantity of Q_{e1} for the eastern region. The supply-demand relations for the western region yield a price of P_2 and a quantity of Q_{w1}. As long as no trade can occur between the regions, prices in the two regions are completely independent. Demand or supply changes in one region vary prices and quantities in that region only.

Now consider the situation in which trade is permitted between the two regions. To facilitate the explanation we will first assume that the cost of transporting the product between the two regions is zero. Will trade occur, to what extent, and at what price? This can be determined by the use of the *excess*

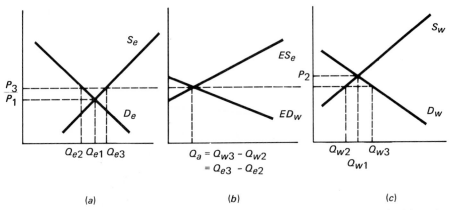

Figure 8-5 (a) Eastern region demand and supply; (b) excess demand and supply; (c) western region demand and supply.

demand and *excess supply* curves plotted in Figure 8-5(*b*). The excess demand of a region is that quantity by which quantity demanded in the region exceeds the quantity supplied in the region at each price level. For each price below the isolated equilibrium price P_1 in Figure 8-5(*c*), the excess demand is the horizontal difference between the supply curve and the demand curve. These horizontal distances are plotted in Figure 8-5(*b*) and noted as ED_w for the western region.

The excess supply of any region is the amount by which quantity supplied exceeds quantity demanded at each price. It is the amount by which a region's demand for oranges exceeds local production at each price. At the isolated equilibrium price, this is zero. At any price above the equilibrium price, it is the horizontal distance between the supply and demand curve at that price. These differences for the eastern region are plotted in Figure 8-5(*b*) and labeled ES_e. Excess supply for the west and excess demand for the east could also be calculated, but the higher pretrade price in the west indicates that these relations do not enter into the solution.

The higher pretrade price P_2 in the west attracts oranges from the east. This movement of oranges out of the east raises prices in that region and lowers prices in the west. With zero transport cost, this occurs until prices are just equal in the two markets. At any other price, it is not profitable for suppliers in the east to ship additional supplies to the west. At price P_3, total demand in the two regions just equals total supply in the two regions. This price is indicated by the intersection of the excess supply and excess demand curves. Quantity Q_{e3} is produced in the east. Quantity Q_{e2} is demanded in the east and the difference is exported to the west. These exports just equal the imports of the west. At equilibrium, the following conditions hold:

$$Q_{e3} - Q_{e2} = Q_t = Q_{w3} - Q_{w2}$$

exports from	imports from
the east	the east

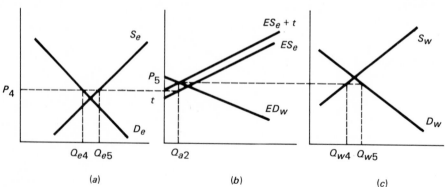

Figure 8-6 Equilibrium price determination for a two-region trading situation.

The introduction of positive transport cost between the two regions reduces the quantity of oranges shipped between them. In Figure 8-6(*b*), the excess supply curve and the excess demand curve are calculated as in the preceding example. However, the cost of transporting the product needs to be added to the price at which Florida oranges are made available to the west. Thus, the excess supply curve is shifted upward by the amount of the transport cost t. For this example, transport rates are the same regardless of the quantity transported between the regions.

The net movement of product between the two regions is determined by the intersection of the excess demand ED_w and the new excess supply curve $ES_e + t$. The quantity exported from the east to west is Q_{a2}. This quantity can be sold at a price of P_5 in the west, and the average price in the west is P_5. The net price for producers in the east for Q_a units sold in the west is $P_4 = P_5 - t$. At this price, quantity Q_{e5} is produced in the east and Q_{e4} units are demanded by local consumers. The remainder is exported to the west.

The prices in the two regions differ by exactly the amount of the transportation cost between the two regions. The intersection of the excess supply plus transportation and the excess demand curves determines the price in the importing region. To determine the net price in the exporting region, one merely reads the value on the original excess supply curve below this point. At these prices, the quantity that the eastern region is willing to export at price P_4 just equals the amount that the west will import at price P_5, or $P_4 + t$.

The impact of changing transport rates can readily be determined from the trade model. Assume that the transport rate per hundredweight of oranges increases from t to t_1 (Figure 8-7). This reduces the amount traded between the regions from Q_{a2} to Q_{a3}. Although not indicated, the new prices in each region can be read off these diagrams. The prices again differ by the cost of transport between the two regions. Now, assume that the transport cost rises to t_2. The excess supply plus transport cost no longer intersects the excess demand of the western region at any positive value. No trade takes place.

Prices in each of the markets are determined independently of one another, just as the isolated market situation was determined in the first example. Note, however, that the difference in the price determined in the isolated market situations can never exceed the transportation cost. If that situation arises, the markets are no longer independent and trade again occurs.

Two principles can be derived from the preceding analysis of interregional price relationships: (1) if trade occurs between two regions, the price differences between the two regions will just equal the cost of transportation; (2) if two supply and demand regions for a product do not trade with one another, the maximum price difference between the two regions for the product is the transport cost between regions. For these principles to hold, the markets need to possess some rather specific characteristics. The product must be completely homogeneous, competitive market structures must exist, and there can be no noneconomic barriers to trade between the regions.

The preceding principles may appear to be frequently violated in agriculture. Regional livestock, fruit and vegetables, milk, and other prices may sometimes vary by more than the cost of transport where no trade is, in fact, occurring. One or more departures from freely adjusting competitive markets may account for prices different than those indicated by the model:

1 The products may not be completely homogeneous. Florida oranges and California oranges are not always perfect substitutes in all cases.

2 Lack of information on the part of either buyers or sellers concerning alternative markets or supplies may permit departures.

3 Adjustments in dynamic market situations may occur with leads or

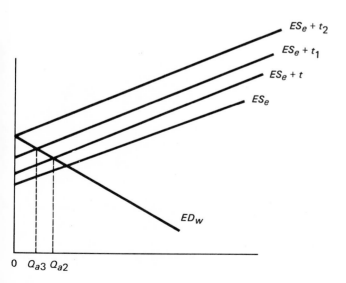

Figure 8-7 The effect of changing transport rates.

lags that obscure actual adjustments. For example, a reduction in freight rates, which would expand trade and reduce intermarket price differences, requires time for firms to expand markets and for price reductions in importing regions to occur.

4 Actual trading is often based on contractual arrangements that restrict market adjustment in prices and product movements until contracts have expired.

5 Barriers exist within countries that prevent or limit trade between regions. For years Madison, Wisconsin, had a health requirement which stated that all milk for fluid use in Madison must be pasteurized within a 5-mile radius of the city hall. Numerous states have applied special excise taxes to margarine. In some cases, the tax was levied on margarine produced from imported coconut oil. This tax was instituted by cotton producing states that did not want imported oils competing with domestically produced cottonseed oil. For many years Minnesota imposed a tax on all margarine because it competed with one of the state's important milk products. The barriers to movement of farm products have sometimes taken the form of discriminatory transportation regulations.

ALLOCATING SUPPLIES AMONG DEMANDS FOR SEVERAL REGIONS

The allocation of a product produced in a number of supply regions and marketed in several consuming regions is influenced by the factors described in the preceding section: relative costs of production, demands in each region, transportation costs, and institutional factors that limit the movement of product. From the aggregate economic point of view, the supplies should be allocated among the alternative market areas in such a way that aggregate costs are minimized. In an actual market situation, this requires determination not only of movements but also of the amounts produced in each supply area and the quantities demanded in each area together with prices throughout the market. This implies the simultaneous determination of a large number of variables in a rather complex system.

Using some simplifying assumptions about supply and demand, one method that solves for cost minimization for markets with multiple supply-demand regions is the *transportation model* of linear programming. The method has been used for a wide range of problems in interregional competition, as well as by individual firms that wish to determine the optimum assembly of raw products by multiple processing plants or the optimum distribution of products from several processing plants to multiple consuming markets.

The adaptation of linear programming to regional supply and regional demand areas can provide answers to several questions. First, it can determine the minimum cost of moving supplies to multiple consuming markets. It can also be used to determine the impact of changes in transportation rates or the opening of new ports, seaways, or transport methods on movements of products.[4]

4E. O. Heady and W. Candler, *Linear Programming Methods,* Iowa State University Press, Ames, Iowa, 1958, p. 332.

Table 8-2   Transport Rates for Potatoes (in Dollars per Ton) between Supply Regions and Consuming Regions

Destination or consuming region	Origin or supply region			
	A	B	C	D
1	$ 5	$ 6	$ 3	$ 6
2	3	6	6	5
3	5	7	4	4
4	6	7	5	3
5	6	3	5	2

The following example considers the problem of minimizing transport costs when both regional supplies and regional demands are fixed. More flexible linear programming models have been developed to approximate optimum marketing movements when supplies and demands are permitted to vary.

For our example, assume that the United States has four major producing areas for potatoes. Furthermore, the consuming areas of the United States can be divided into five regions. The total supply in all regions is fixed at 340,000 tons. For simplicity we assume that total demand in the five consuming regions is also 340,000 tons. The production of each of the supply areas is as follows:[5]

Region A	70,000 tons
Region B	110,000 tons
Region C	90,000 tons
Region D	70,000 tons
Total	340,000 tons

The total demand is distributed among the five consuming regions as follows:

Region 1	70,000 tons
Region 2	100,000 tons
Region 3	75,000 tons
Region 4	65,000 tons
Region 5	30,000 tons
Total	340,000 tons

The transport costs for shipping potatoes from each of the producing regions to each of the consuming regions is given in Table 8-2. The entries in column A indicate the costs of shipping potatoes from supply region *A* to each of the four consuming regions listed on the left-hand side of the table. Obviously, actual consuming regions or supply areas are each geographically dispersed so that transport costs will vary depending upon the precise origin and destination in the supply region and the consuming regions. The transport cost can, however, be considered as an average rate between any two areas.

[5]This example is adapted from one presented in R. S. Stockton, *Introduction to Linear Programming*, Allyn and Bacon, Boston, 1960, pp. 73–103.

Table 8-3 Hypothetical Regional Supply and Demand Characteristics for Potatoes in the United States

Consumption regions	Supply regions (origin)				Demands
	A	B	C	D	
1					70,000
2					100,000
3					75,000
4					65,000
5					30,000
Supplies	70,000	110,000	90,000	70,000	340,000

The problem can now be framed in such a manner that the transportation model can be applied to its solution. The problem is to allocate the supplies of the four producing regions to the five consuming regions so that the total cost of transporting potatoes is minimized. The restraints on the solution are: (1) the total shipment from each region just equals that region's supply; (2) total receipts in each consuming region are just equal to each region's demand; and (3) total supply from all supply regions just equals the total demand of all consuming regions. The restrictions on origin and destination are referred to as *rim conditions*. They are indicated in the last row and last column of Table 8-3. Note that the sum of supplies from each region equals the total demand of all consuming regions.

The first step in solving the problem is to find a feasible solution, that is, a solution that does not violate the restrictions listed above. There are a number of techniques which can be used for the first feasible solution, such as the northwest corner rule, the existing routing pattern if the market has already been allocating

Table 8-4 First Feasible Solution for Regional Allocation to Minimize Transport Costs and Evaluation of the Solution

Consumption regions	Supply regions (origin)				Demands
	A	B	C	D	
1	$5 +4	$6 0	$3 70,000	$6 +3	70,000
2	3 70,000	6 -2	6 +1	5 30,000	100,000
3	5 +3	7 15,000	4 20,000	4 40,000	75,000
4	6 +4	7 65,000	5 +1	3 -1	65,000
5	6 +8	3 30,000	5 +5	2 +2	30,000
Supplies	70,000	110,000	90,000	70,000	340,000

the supplies, or various inspection methods.[6] For the example, an inspection method will be used since it immediately brings an economic criteria into the procedure. The development of the first feasible solution can be illustrated by using Table 8-4. The values in the upper-left area of each grouping are the transport costs per ton of potatoes between origin and destination. They do not indicate allocation. Inspection of the table indicates that consuming region 1 can obtain potatoes from supply area C for the lowest transport cost. Its total requirements are 70,000 tons. Since supply area C produces 90,000 tons, all requirements of region 1 are met. For consuming region 2, lowest per-ton transport costs are from region A—$3 per ton. However, its total demand is 90,000 tons and region A supplies only 70,000 tons. The next lowest transport cost is from region D—$5 per ton. Region 2 takes 30,000 tons from supply area D. Lowest transport costs to region 3 are from supply regions C and D. However, only 20,000 tons are now available from C and 40,000 tons from D. Nothing is available from region A. Thus, we fill out its needs by importing 15,000 tons from B. All supplies of Regions A, C, and D are now allocated; therefore, consuming areas 4 and 5 must now obtain their supplies from region B, which has 95,000 tons to be allocated. Allocating 65,000 tons to 4 and 30,000 tons to 5 just meets their needs. Examination of Table 8-4 shows that none of the rim requirements have been violated and the allocation is feasible. Note that several cells are blank or inactive.

The total cost of shipping the product in the manner indicated can be calculated by multiplying each allocation by the respective transport cost. This is $1,460,000.

$$(3 \times 70,000) + (3 \times 70,000) + (5 \times 30,000) + (7 \times 15,000) + (4 \times 20,000) +$$
$$(4 \times 40,000) + (7 \times 65,000) + (3 \times 30,000) = 1,460,000$$

The next step in the procedure involves a search for better solutions. This search is an evaluation of alternative solutions. Considered another way, what is the economic effect of introducing an unused cell into the solution?

The effect of using any unused cell can be determined by assigning one unit (thousand tons) to an unused cell. Let us select cell 1D for this first assignment. By this assignment we can now observe that the constraints are violated for row 1 and column D. Row 1 totals to 71 and column D totals to 71. This initial imbalance can be corrected by subtracting 1,000 tons each from cells 1C and 3D, that is, reducing C's shipments to region 1 and D's shipment to region 4. Row 1 again totals to 70 and column 1 totals to 70, but an imbalance has been created in column C and row 3. This can be corrected by increasing cell 3C by one unit. Thus, one unit has been shifted to one unused cell and adjustments have been made so that none of the restrictions have been violated. These shifts would change the entries in the four cells as follows:

[6]E. O. Heady and W. Candler, *Linear Programming Methods,* Iowa State University Press, Ames, Iowa, 1958, pp. 332–377.

Row	Column	
	C	D
1	3 70 − 1	6 0 + 1
3	4 20 + 1	4 40 − 1

The impact on transport cost is the sum of the changes from the altered cells:

$$6(\text{cell 1D}) - 4(\text{cell 3D}) + 4(\text{cell 3C}) - 3(\text{cell 1C})$$

for a net change of $3 per ton, or a total of $3,000. The change causes an increase in cost, and therefore, it should not be undertaken.

The process by which we evaluated this inactive cell—and it is the process which will be used for evaluating all other inactive cells in the original solution—is called the *stepping-stone method*. It requires that for each inactive cell to be evaluated, readjustments to equilibrium or to rim requirements can be made only through active cells.

The net effect of activating each inactive cell is listed in the lower left-hand corner of each inactive cell in Table 8-4. Positive values mean that activation of that cell will increase total transport cost. Negative values mean that activation of that cell will decrease costs. Two cells 2B and 4D have negative values. Thus, reallocation of regional supplies in the manner indicated by the evaluation route for this cell will reduce total transport cost.

The quantities to reallocate among the regions should be the maximum amounts that are technically possible to transfer. This is determined by the smallest of that cell from which product is being subtracted. In this case to activate cell 2B product is being reduced in cells 2D and 3B. The maximum amount that can be reallocated is 15,000 tons. Fifteen units are added to cells 2B and 3D, and 15 units are deducted from cells 2D and 3B. The cost savings (in thousands) can be calculated by taking the difference between transport cost for the original allocation among the four cells and the new cost for the same four cells:

Original cost	$(5 \times 30) + (7 \times 15) + (4 \times 40) = 415$
New cost	$(6 \times 15) + (5 \times 15) + (4 \times 55) = 385$
Total savings	$ 30

It is common to employ computers as an aid in the evaluation of alternative feasible solutions. After several "tries" (called iterations), the optimum solution shown in Table 8-5 is obtained.

We have presented an example to show how supplies are allocated among supply and consuming regions to minimize total transport costs. The reader may have now surmised that if processing cost or prices at origins are also known, the model could be solved to minimize processing and transport costs or total cost at

Table 8-5 Optimal Solution for Allocating Potatoes of Four Supply Regions among Five Consuming Regions

Consumption regions	Supply regions (origin)				Demands
	A	B	C	D	
1	5 +2	6 0	3 70,000	6 +3	70,000
2	3 70,000	6 30,000	6 +3	5 +2	100,000
3	5 +1	7 50,000	4 20,000	4 5,000	75,000
4	6 +3	7 +1	5 +2	3 65,000	65,000
5	6 +6	3 30,000	5 +5	2 +2	30,000
Supplies	70,000	110,000	90,000	70,000	340,000

the receiving markets. Many variations of the transportation models have been developed and used to analyze the problem of interregional competition. Business firms make wide use of the transportation models in determining shipments from, or assembly at, plants.

Researchers for the U.S. Department of Agriculture recently applied the transportation model to the wheat, feed-grain, and soybean industries.[7] The objective was, in view of the expanding foreign demands for those products, to determine the optimum movement from production region to ports of exit. Four port regions were specified for the study: Lake ports, Atlantic ports, Gulf ports, and Pacific ports. The model included consideration of total foreign demands, domestic needs, and handling capacity at each port. The optimizing solution for each product and each port is listed in Table 8-6. In percentage terms, the solution indicated that 18 percent of total shipments be handled by Lake ports, 10 percent by Atlantic ports, 62 percent by Gulf ports, and 11 percent by Pacific ports. Almost 80 percent of the hard wheat would be exported through Gulf ports. The results of the analysis could be compared to actual shipments. Departures from the optimum may be indicative of transportation bottlenecks or institutional barriers to product movements.

COSTS OF FOOD TRANSPORTATION

The wide geographic distribution of farm production and consuming units, in addition to the long distances between raw farm products and the major consum-

[7]J. L. Driscoll and M. N. Leath, "Optimum Flour for Wheat, Feed Grain and Soybeans," *Marketing and Transportation Situation*, MTS-188, U.S. Department of Agriculture, Feb. 1973, pp. 23–28.

Table 8-6 Optimum Grain Exports (in Thousands of Bushels) by Type of Grain and Port Region, 1973

Port regions	Hard wheat	Soft wheat	Durum wheat	Soy-beans	Corn	Grain sorghum	Barley	Oats	Total
Lake ports									
Superior	44,599	—	20,000	55,645	104,756	—	20,000	—	245,000
Chicago	485	404	—	—	125,111	—	—	—	126,000
Toledo	—	4,596	—	24,355ᵃ	86,049	—	—	—	115,000
Total	45,084	5,000ᵃ	20,000ᵃ	80,000ᵃ	315,916	—	20,000	—	486,000
East ports									
Philadelphia	4,000	17,196	7,581	61,726	9,301	—	—	—	99,804
Norfolk	—	1,296	2,419	39,809	120,699	—	—	—	164,223
Total	4,000ᵃ	18,492	10,000ᵃ	101,535	130,000ᵃ	—	—	—	264,027
Gulf ports									
New Orleans	200,140	30,070	13,000	317,115	457,554	3,588	—	8,533	1,030,000
Houston	404,249	—	—	—	83,324	62,061	—	366	550,000
Corpus Christi	87,093	—	—	350	1,206	51,351	—	—	140,000
Total	691,482	30,070	13,000	317,465	542,084	117,000	—	8,899	1,720,000
West ports									
Los Angeles	—	5,971	—	—	—	—	—	—	5,971
San Francisco	45,025	8,821	—	—	—	3,000	—	1,101	57,947
Portland	94,409	133,646	2,000	—	—	—	—	—	230,055
Total	139,439	148,438	2,000ᵃ	—	—	3,000ᵃ	—	1,101	293,973
United States	880,000	202,000	45,000	499,000	988,000	120,000	20,000	10,000	2,764,000

ᵃThese volumes do not exceed the minimum coastal requirements specified in the model.

Source: J. L. Driscoll and M. N. Leath, "Optimum Flour for Wheat, Feed Grain and Soybeans," Marketing and Transportation Situation, MTS-188, U.S. Department of Agriculture, Feb. 1973, pp. 23–28.

ing markets and the multiple consuming markets, requires substantial transportation inputs in the marketing of farm products. Therefore, it is not surprising that
transport costs are an important part of the total food marketing bill. In 1973, rail
and truck transport charges of $6.1 billion for food products accounted for 7
percent of total food marketing costs.[8] In addition, there were costs of intracity,
air, and water transport for which statistics are not available. As the population
becomes more and more concentrated on the two coasts, transport costs should
become an even larger part of food marketing costs.

Although the costs of transport for food products are large because of the
wide geographic distribution of supply and demand, it should not be overlooked
that these costs are a significant determinant of where products are produced,
processed, and marketed and the interregional price differentials. New technology in transportation, development of alternative transportation systems, or
decisions by rate-making agencies (the ICC, for example) that change transport
costs will alter the entire system in the ways described earlier.

For the marketing participants, the changes in costs have an impact on the
quantities bought or sold and the prices paid or received. The consequences of
transport cost changes on the market participants has been traced by Dahl and
Hyslop for the wheat market.[9] They presented the following example of the
adjustment to freight-rate charges for wheat.

> Assume that on August 25th the price of wheat in Minneapolis is $2.00. The freight
> rate from some country point is $.30 per bushel. The price of wheat at that point is
> thus $1.70.
>
> On August 26th a new freight rate is $.35 per bushel. This increase does not
> affect the supply and demand factors at the central market, and the central market
> price remains at $2.00. Farmers cannot adjust immediately the quantities offered on
> this crop. Thus, the price of wheat at the country elevator is reduced to $1.65.
>
> That is the immediate effect. But over longer time periods (1, 2, or 3 crop years)
> farmers can adjust quantities in response to price changes. Over the longer period,
> the lower country price would probably reduce the quantities offered for sale.
>
> If all other supply and demand conditions at Minneapolis remained constant,
> consumers would bid higher prices for the reduced quantities. This would result in a
> Minneapolis price of something more than $2.00, say $2.01. Therefore, consumers
> also are affected by increased freight rates. They pay a higher price for a smaller
> quantity.
>
> After the central market price adjustment, the price in the country is still $.35
> less than at Minneapolis, of $1.66.
>
> Freight rates decline as well as increase. Immediately, farm prices rise by the
> full amount of the rate reduction. Over a longer time period, farmers can respond by
> increasing quantities offered. The increased quantities reduce prices to consumers.
> This is reflected back to the country and partially offsets the lower freight rate.

[8]U.S. Department of Agriculture, *Marketing and Transportation Situation,* MTS-194, Aug.
1974, pp. 24–25.

[9]J. Hyslop and R. Dahl, "The Farmers' Stake in Transportation," *Minnesota Farm Business
Notes,* no. 434, Agricultural Extension Service, University of Minnesota, St. Paul, Oct. 1961.

SUMMARY

U.S. agricultural production is located where the comparative advantage is greatest. Comparative advantage is determined by climatic and agronomic realities, relative factor prices, and transportation costs.

Prices of agricultural products vary geographically in relation to the transportation differential required to move commodities from one place to another. The means of transportation used depend upon the availability of trucks, railcars and lines, barges and waterways, air service, and the unit-distance rate for each mode.

Between regions that both produce and consume a product, trade will occur only if the equilibrium price in each region differs by more than the transportation cost. Two such regions will record equilibrium prices that exactly differ by the transportation cost. The solution is found by using excess demand and excess supply curves and the transportation cost.

Trade among several regions can be approximated by use of the transportation model. This model minimizes transport costs among regions and selects the cost-minimizing trade solution. The procedure is to first gain a feasible solution and then to improve upon it by selecting trade alternatives that reduce transportation costs until the lowest-cost trade solution is obtained.

The cost of food transportation in the United States is large. This is primarily caused by the fact that much of the food is produced in the Midwest states and must be shipped to the larger consuming centers on the East and West coasts. As transportation costs increase, farmers receive lower prices and consumers must pay more for their food.

QUESTIONS

1 During the past two decades, the production of chicken for slaughter has largely shifted from the Midwest to the southeastern and eastern parts of the United States. Why do you think this happened?

2 The production possibilities indicated in Figure 8-1 are *straight lines*. Is it realistic to depict these production alternatives with straight lines? If curved lines are better, how should they curve? Why?

3 "Equal-height" lines are drawn in topographical maps, and "equal-temperature" lines are prepared in maps showing climatic differences around the country. In a similar manner, "equal-price" lines can be prepared on a map to show how price surfaces vary (see Figure 8-2). What do low points and high points on these maps indicate?

4 Under what conditions do products *not* move from points or regions of surplus into regions of deficit for a commodity?

5 Compare the first feasible solution of allocating potatoes (Table 8-4) with the optimum solution (Table 8-4). What are the *exact* differences in the solutions? Could you have selected a first solution that would be closer to the optimum than that in Table 8-4? What selection rules would you suggest?

BIBLIOGRAPHY

Cassels, J. M.: *A Study of Milk Prices,* Harvard Economic Studies, vol. 54, Harvard University Press, Cambridge, Mass., 1937.

Driscoll, J. L., and M. N. Leath: "Optimum Flour for Wheat, Feed Grain and Soybeans," *Marketing and Transportation Situation,* MTS-188, U.S. Department of Agriculture, Feb., 1973.

Heady, E. O., and W. Candler: *Linear Programming Methods,* Iowa State University Press, Ames, Iowa, 1958.

Hyslop, J., and R. Dahl: "The Farmers' Stake in Transportation," *Minnesota Farm Business Notes,* no. 434, Agricultural Extension Service, University of Minnesota, St. Paul, Oct., 1961.

Stockton, R.S: *Introduction to Linear Programming,* Allyn and Bacon, Boston, 1960.

U.S. Department of Agriculture: *Marketing and Transportation Situation,* MTS-194, Aug. 1974.

Wilcox, W. W., W. W. Cochrane, and R. W. Herdt: *Economics of American Agriculture,* 3d ed., Prentice-Hall, Englewood Cliffs, N.J., 1974.

Markets over Time

INTRODUCTION

Most farm production and marketings are characterized by a high degree of seasonality. The period of harvest for crops encompasses periods of a few weeks to a few months at most. Even where production occurs continually throughout the year, varying degrees of seasonality are observed. On the other hand, demands for farm products tend to be rather stable throughout the year. This means that the marketing system for farm products must store or hold much of the annual production and allocate it throughout the year. Two kinds of costs are involved in this process: (1) the direct costs of providing the physical facilities for storage; and (2) the costs that are due to the risk of price changes which occur while the product is in storage. In this chapter we will examine part of the magnitude of storage for farm products, the nature of the risks involved in storage of commodities, and the major methods of eliminating or reducing risk.

STORAGE

Magnitudes of Storage for Farm Commodities

Farm products are stored to make them available the year around—to balance periods of plenty and periods of scarcity. All products are technically in storage during the interval between harvest and consumption. During that time, they may be moved from one place to another; be processed by canning, curing, and freezing; or subjected to various treatments, such as grading, sorting, and packing, any of which may change their form, shape, and taste so that a different product results.

Our major grain crops move into storage at harvest time in order to be utilized later. Annual U.S. wheat production varied from 1.1 to 1.7 billion bushels from 1962 to 1967. Carry-over stocks from one crop year to the next varied from 1.3 to 0.4 billion bushels, at times exceeding annual production.

Between 1962 and 1972, U.S. cotton production varied between 7.4 and 15.3 million bales annually. Carry-over stocks varied from 3.2 to 16.8 million bales. A crop of 15 million bales yields about 6 million tons of cottonseed, which also must be stored until use.

The tobacco industry usually keeps more than 2 years' production of tobacco in storage. As the new crop is harvested, stock in storage for 24 months may be brought into consumption.

Only a few of our fruits and vegetables can be stored in a fresh state for any length of time. Apples, potatoes, onions, and a few others are stored for several months in fresh form before final sale and consumption. Many fruits and vegetables are preserved by canning, pickling, freezing, and drying. Some 117 billion pounds of vegetables are consumed annually in the United States. Roughly 45 percent of this volume is consumed fresh, 45 percent canned, and 10 percent frozen.

We tend to consume meats at the rate that the live animals are marketed from farms. Reported storage stocks of fresh and cured meats at times reach a total of about 900 million pounds, but probably a larger volume is involved in the normal movement in marketing channels from slaughter through retail stores.

We may have on hand more than 100 million pounds of butter, 400 million pounds of cheese, and large amounts of canned and dried milk products in any year.

Storage Facilities

Each class of farm products has its own particular conditions under which it can be stored without much, if any, loss in quality. Some products, such as tobacco and cheese, go through a storage period (curing) to improve quality. A crop such as hay can be stored in stacks in the field without great loss in quality. Cotton can be stored with little protection without serious damage. But such products as whole milk, meats, green vegetables, and fresh fruits require exacting temperatures, humidities, and ventilation. Even then they may spoil so rapidly that they must be canned, frozen, or otherwise processed if their edible qualities are to be preserved. Because of these variations, storage requirements range from the one extreme of no structural facility to large cold-storage houses with elaborate equipment.

Grains are somewhat less exacting in regard to storage requirements; however, the moisture content of grain must be suitable for storage and must be kept at that level while the grain is in storage. Most of our facilities for storing grain are on farms in the form of corncribs, bins of wood and metal, and other containers into which bulk grains are stored after harvest. Farm structures and facilities were used to store about 8 billion bushels of harvested grain in 1973. Off-farm storage space in more than 15,000 grain elevators at country and terminal points is estimated to be sufficient to store about 2 billion bushels of bulk grain. Much of the storage space in grain elevators is used primarily to assist in the market movement of grains, with any given lot of grain remaining in such space for only a short period.

The total amount of refrigerated storage space reported in public, private, and semiprivate warehouses in 1953 was 711 million cubic feet; the amount surely exceeds 1 billion cubic feet today. The space was used mainly to store fruits and vegetables, meat products, poultry products, and fish. An enormous amount of storage space for canned and packaged foods and other dry groceries and provisions is maintained by manufacturers and processors, by wholesalers and retailers, and in pantries and kitchens in households.

Most types of tobacco are stored 1–3 years. Space in tobacco warehouses is estimated to be enough to store more than 3 billion pounds of tobacco. Numerous tobacco houses on farms and in auction warehouses, where the product is sold, provide additional storage space.

Large quantities of wheat are also stored in terminal elevators in ports like Galveston, New Orleans, and Baltimore in order to expedite export operations. Only sufficient volumes to permit shipload quantities that are reasonably certain to be moved through the particular terminal are stored there at any one time.

Substantial volumes of wheat also are stored at points of processing in large cities near or in the general areas of production or along the major flow route. Minneapolis, Kansas City, and Buffalo are examples. The purpose is to assure necessary supplies—working stocks—for stable blends and efficient operations.

Storage of apples in cold-storage plants at or near the orchard has become important because of the time, labor, and facilities required for proper sorting and packing. Refrigeration near the orchard relieves packers and shippers from the task of packing and shipping the fruit immediately after picking. Producers can protect their fruit while it awaits packing and they can employ crews of skilled sorters and packers for longer periods instead of having to mobilize large crews of inexperienced workers for a short time. Some varieties of apples can be stored 5–7 months. Producers who grow varieties that ripen at different periods can utilize storage houses efficiently for a large part of the year. However, quantities of apples are stored in public cold storages in large cities and in wholesale produce warehouses for the purpose of providing pipeline stocks in the distribution system and evening out fluctuations in supply and demand.

Late-crop potatoes are stored in relatively inexpensive "common" or air-cooled warehouses or underground pits and cellars. In Maine, New York, Idaho, and the Red River Valley, where most late potatoes are grown commercially, outside temperatures during harvesting and storing alike are such that natural storage is possible. Therefore, because of the climate in the area, the relatively long distances to markets, and the low value per pound, it is more economical to store most late-crop potatoes on farms or in potato-storage houses in the area of production until they are marketed.

The more complex the marketing system for a particular commodity and the greater the distance between the production and consumption areas, the greater is the need for quantities of the product to be stored at various points in the marketing channels. For example, large amounts of butter are stored in cities close to the area of production and in large consuming cities at great distances from where the butter is produced.

Many products that require expensive storage facilities are stored for relatively short periods. Those facilities may be utilized more efficiently if they are located so as to permit other surplus products to be stored in the same space at other periods of the year.

Butter, frozen cream, shell eggs, and similar commodities are therefore stored in public cold storages in cities near the producing areas, in transit at points along major flow routes from producing areas to consumption areas, and in large consuming centers.

Some products must be properly matured before they are put into storage. The length of storage life of most perishable commodities depends not only on how nearly proper temperature and humidity conditions are maintained in storage, but also on how promptly heat is removed from them immediately after harvest. With many perishable products, precooling—the prompt application of refrigeration prior to normal storage or transportation—is the key to successful storage.

Other products require controlled atmospheric conditions. For example, apples as they ripen in storage give off ethylene gas, which stimulates the ripening of other apples in the room, and other gases, which (if allowed to accumulate around the fruit) cause apple scald. By purifying the air to remove naturally evolved ethylene and scald gases, the fruit can be kept firmer and for longer periods.

RISKS IN COMMODITY MARKETING

Every agricultural marketing enterprise involves risk. Much of it is associated with the stored commodities, but it applies to any good or input purchased at one time for use in a production process or sale at a later date. The longer the time period between purchases and sales, the greater the risks. Two types of risks occur: risks of physical loss and risks of loss due to price changes. Those in business who are primarily engaged in processing or distributing commodities are usually anxious to reduce or eliminate these various risks which are necessary concomitants of their operations. They attempt either to avoid the risks or to reduce them to the point where the consequences may not have serious effects upon the business. This they do by shifting the risks to others who are willing and able to assume them—a service for which business people are willing to pay.

A number of kinds of physical losses of products in storage are possible.

There are losses from fire, theft, and natural disasters. These losses can be reduced to acceptable levels by the use of insurance. In most common practices, insurance involves a system whereby numerous persons make small, regular contributions to a pool of funds accumulated to compensate for specified contingent losses suffered by individual contributors. In many respects insurance is the simplest of risk-shifting devices. It is easily adaptable to cover such contingencies as fire, flood, hail, and windstorms because fairly accurate actuarial rates (predictions of loss) can be computed and business people can view fixed insurance premiums as predictable costs to take care of risks. A distinguishing feature of most insurance is that there is little, if any, chance for gain. The insured must forego this advantage when insurance is bought since it usually covers only losses from physical damage. Insurance is almost universally used by business people dealing with commodities.

Another type of physical loss of stored commodities is that caused by natural product deterioration over time and insect and pest damage. These risks can be eliminated or reduced by use of proper, well-operated storage facilities. Product deterioration might be reasonably well-predicted and standard among firms. Consequently, it may also be included as a normal cost of operation.

Inasmuch as prices are in a continuous state of flux, risks of losses in holding goods are inevitable. These risks are particularly great in the case of processors or dealers who have to accumulate stocks or retain title to goods over an extended period of time. In the absence of permanent changes in the supply or demand for particular goods, the gains and losses from price changes offset each other in the long run; however, the individual trader is seldom in a position to wait for the compensating changes to occur. That is to say, if a cotton manufacturer who is required to hold cotton for 3 months after the purchase time until it is ready for resale in finished goods bought the same quantity of cotton continually over a long period of years, the losses from declines in cotton prices occurring while the manufacturer held the cotton would be offset by corresponding gains from subsequent price increases. Cotton prices might decline for so long a time or so drastically that the manufacturer's capital resources would be depleted and operations curtailed or completely stopped from lack of capital before the losses could be recovered. When the trader varies the quantity of goods or time of holding, which is a common practice, gains and losses stand less chance of being equalized even over an extended period; and if the goods become damaged or obsolete during the holding period, losses would be permanent.

A price change at any given time represents a loss to some and a gain for others. That is, a price decline is deterimental to those who have goods to sell and beneficial to those who are buying goods. Similarly, a market price decline penalizes one who has a contract to accept goods at a predetermined fixed price and benefits one who is acquiring goods to sell on such a contract. Moreover, a person who stores goods stands to lose with a price decline, whereas a person who is buying for current processing or consumption is apt to gain. A market price increase, on the other hand, has just the opposite effect on the respective persons in each of these cases.

It should be recognized that the major function of marketing enterprises involves the assumption of some price risks based upon the expectation or forecasting of particular commodity price movements. Not infrequently, a processor or distributor will engage in a certain amount of intentional speculation in the commodity that is being handled by varying the volume of stocks. Business people of this type necessarily keep in close touch with market developments and attempt to profit by the information available to them. In fact, the buying and selling of stocks of goods in anticipation of certain price changes represents a significant form of competition among persons engaged in marketing agricultural products.

As with other risks, firms seek ways to reduce or eliminate price risks. However, losses resulting from price changes are less predictable and they strike more individuals simultaneously than do other hazards. Consequently, the problem of shifting price risks is much more difficult than in those cases where insurance is employed. One method of reducing price risks is to hedge the current transactions in futures markets, that is, the buying and selling of contracts for the future delivery of goods. The protective feature of futures trading is based on the assumption that changes in prices of spot goods (goods on hand for immediate delivery after sale) and the price of the futures contract for the product will be sufficiently similar that losses incurred from the purchase and sale of goods in the spot market can be largely offset by gains from an opposite transaction in the futures market. The protection afforded by futures trading is by no means complete. At best, hedging on a futures contract is only a means of reducing the possible gains or losses.

FUTURES TRADING

Organized trading of futures contracts has an important place in the marketing of agricultural commodities. Because of large stockholdings for long periods of time and the substantial price risks involved in marketing agricultural products, futures markets are considered indispensable, especially by marketing agencies operating on a large scale. In fact, futures market trading is so prevalent in agricultural marketing that a treatise on agricultural prices would be incomplete without discussion of the subject.

The Futures Contract

In organized futures markets, a *futures contract* is an agreement that is made subject to the rules of an organized exchange to buy or sell a stipulated amount of some commodity at a fixed price for delivery at a future date. Certain characteristics differentiate these contracts from ordinary agreements between buyers and sellers in transactions to be terminated or completed in the future. The provisions of the contract pertaining to all variables such as grades and time of delivery, except for those of quantity and price, are set forth in the rules of the exchange in which the transaction takes place. They are known to all participants in the market and need not be a matter of discussion at the time of entering the contract; hence, they facilitate speed in reaching an agreement.

Several features of these contract provisions are worthy of note.

1 The contract is made on the basis of a certain grade of the commodity to be delivered at the contracted price; the grade is known as the *contract* grade. Usually, however, there are other grades which are designated as *deliverable* grades at fixed premiums or discounts on the specified contract grade.

2 Futures involve transactions terminating in certain specified months of the year. For example, the favorite months for grain are May, July, September, and December. The seller has the option of delivery on any day within the month specified in the contract. Thus, the seller of a May future may deliver on the contract on any market day during the month of May.

3 There are provisions governing delivery of the commodity in fulfillment of the contract. Ordinarily, delivery is affected by transmitting warehouse receipts that assign to the purchaser of the contract the commodity which is stored in authorized warehouses where it has been weighed and graded by licensed inspectors.

4 Enforcement of the contract is ensured by a provision that a specified sum of money, or margin, be deposited with the clearinghouse by each of the contracting parties. The clearinghouse is an agency established by the exchange. In addition to the holding of margin requirements, the clearinghouse is an intermediary between all buyers and sellers. Once trade has been made between two parties, the clearinghouse assumes the position of buyer vis-à-vis the seller and seller vis-à-vis the buyer. This permits either the original buyer or seller to subsequently cancel the contract by an offsetting transaction without seeking out the original contractor. The provisions of the futures contract thus make it a highly standardized and easily traded agreement.

The individual who wishes to purchase or sell futures acts through a broker who is a member of the exchange. This broker deals with another broker who is also a member of the exchange. In this process, the two brokerage firms treat each other as principals despite the fact that each may be acting as an agent. As members of the exchange, brokers are responsible to the other members for completion of all contracts which they execute. As indicated previously, this completion on most markets is further guaranteed by deposit of a margin with a designated third party, which deposit is subject to the rules laid down by the exchange. Ordinarily, a margin deposit will be required of the customer as a protection for the broker since the broker is responsible for the completion of the contract. If the price moves against the customer so as to jeopardize the broker's position, additional margin funds are called for. Unless the customer meets these demands from the broker without delay, the buyer's account may be closed out at the broker's discretion. As far as the customer is concerned, the customer's responsibilities in the futures market are erased with a purchase or sale opposite to the original transaction and made through the same broker. Thus, if a customer buys May wheat in January, the customer may remove the obligation by the sale of May wheat at some other date, say in March. The clearing arrangements are set up by the exchanges so that the business between the brokers may be completed with a minimum of actual transactions.

Characteristics of Futures Trading in the United States

There are dealings in futures contracts for a number of commodities in the United States for both agricultural and nonagricultural commodities. Futures trading was being conducted for approximately 20 agricultural commodities in 1975. The futures trading in these commodities was supervised by the Commodity Exchange Authority in accordance with the requirements of the Commodity Exchange Act. Among the more important products are wheat, corn, oats, soybeans, cotton, eggs, potatoes, soybean oil, soybean meal, wool, orange juice, grain sorghums, live cattle, live hogs, and frozen pork bellies.

Although a number of exchanges may be designated to trade in a particular commodity, the bulk of trading ordinarily takes place on only a few of the exchanges. Trading in wheat futures, for example. is almost entirely done in the three largest markets. The Chicago Board of Trade, by far the most important, accounted for approximately 72 percent of all the trading, while the markets at Minneapolis and Kansas City together accounted for approximately 28 percent. In cotton, the principal market is the New York Cotton Exchange.

Soybeans, soybean oil, corn, frozen pork bellies, cattle, and wheat were traded in 1971–1972. These six commodities have accounted for approximately 95 percent of the estimated dollar value of trading in all commodities under the jurisdiction of the Commodity Exchange Authority. This percentage has declined somewhat in the past few years, however, owing to increased activity in several other commodities, notably soybeans and eggs. A substantial shift occurred in the 1960s in the relative importance of the commodities traded in the futures market (see Table 9-1). Two of the leading futures were not traded at the beginning of the period.

In a number of commodities, the volume of futures trading far exceeds production and marketing. This is especially true of wheat, where the ratio has been as great as 15:1, while futures trading in cotton has been nearly nine times as large as the average annual production. There is no necessary connection between the volume of trading and the size of the crops. Instead, the volume of trading varies largely in accordance with the speculative interest in the particular year. Since few who engage in futures trading desire to make or receive deliveries of grain on contracts, most of the trades are cleared before the specified delivery month. In fact, the peak of open commitments for each futures is reached several months before the delivery month. Consequently, actual deliveries of product made on futures contracts are small relative to the volume of trading in the grains and cotton. Usually less than 1 percent of all trades are completed by the delivery of warehouse receipts for the actual commodity. Very few traders depend upon the futures market as an outlet for their products or as a source of supplies.

Table 9-1 Estimated Value of Futures Trading, by Commodity, All Markets Combined, Fiscal Years 1962–1963 to 1971–1972

Commodity	1971–1972	1970–1971	1969–1970	1968–1969	1967–1968	1966–1967	1965–1966	1964–1965	1963–1964	1962–1963
Wheat	$5,510.9	$6,869.6	$5,162.7	$9,003.3	$13,818.5	$18,644.3	$9,958.9	$4,210.7	$10,643.3	$10,794.9
Corn	9,476.7	20,503.0	7,912.6	10,006.6	8,936.6	18,398.8	6,658.2	4,644.2	4,469.0	4,002.1
Oats	138.4	289.5	336.6	459.8	297.8	430.4	276.6	330.5	415.6	600.6
Rye	—	1.1	63.5	160.3	234.5	356.5	512.2	328.7	961.4	937.9
Barley	0	0	0	0	0	0	0	0.2	0.1	0.1
Flaxseed	0	0	0	0	0	0	0.1	0.2	2.7	21.0
Rice	0	0	0	0	0	0	0	0.1	0.2	0
Grain sorghums	24.7	18.5	4.9	11.5	13.4	70.6	0	0	1.1	0.3
Soybeans	$65,124.8	$40,172.4	$16,358.3	$12,126.7	$12,956.8	$28,637.6	$46,232.5	$56,042.9	$37,183.8	$21,274.4
Soybean meal	4,305.9	5,106.5	5,342.3	3,061.4	2,470.9	3,343.3	2,614.8	1,996.6	1,881.0	2,136.7
Soybean oil	9,947.5	10,669.1	10,350.4	2,045.5	1,397.1	2,917.7	3,741.1	3,666.4	2,215.8	2,077.0
Lard	—	—	—	—	—	—	—	—	—	2.0
Cottonseed oil	0	0.4	0	0.1	1.4	34.0	73.6	223.6	694.1	594.8
Cottonseed meal	0	0	0	0	0	0	0	0.2	0.2	0.3
Millfeeds	—	—	—	—	—	—	—	—	—	0.8
Cotton	$7,399.4	$2,295.3	$432.6	$2,235.6	$3,256.1	$10.7	$7.9	$32.2	$152.2	$486.4
Wool	15.5	15.7	33.0	55.3	107.8	184.2	367.2	162.6	298.5	249.1
Wool tops	—	0.3	0.3	0.6	1.2	1.5	1.4	1.9	4.7	7.4
Butter	$0	$0	$0.1	$0.3	$0.2	$116.8	$7.4	$0	—	$0
Eggs, shell	$2,358.8	$3,540.2	$5,166.9	$1,889.4	$252.5	$423.4	$486.9	$314.9	$695.9	$1,477.0
Eggs, frozen	0.2	a	0.7	19.9	10.1	27.2	158.1	52.2	472.7	443.2
Potatoes	228.8	338.1	834.6	995.5	580.5	1,236.2	753.0	1,490.6	273.3	194.5
Frozen concentrated orange juice	1,124.2	869.5	577.5	1,514.9	607.8	36.2	—	—	—	—
Cattle	$13,557.1	$7,510.5	$10,523.3	$6,524.9	$2,076.3	$1,747.4	$712.2	$73.3	—	—
Frozen boneless beef	—	—	—	—	—	—	—	—	—	—
Hides	22.5	13.7	22.2	3.1	14.1	37.4	85.7	22.0	48.7	23.9
Hogs, live	2,775.3	1,098.7	709.1	60.4	44.7	41.2	17.7	—	—	—
Frozen pork bellies	25,992.7	15,055.9	29,034.4	17,310.1	12,998.3	9,731.1	10,475.2	3,750.5	493.4	9.6
Frozen skinned hams	1.2	2.3	9.3	2.5	3.8	4.0	4.5	2.1	1.8	—
Total	$148,004.6	$114,370.3	$92,875.6	$67,487.7	$60,080.4	$86,430.5	$83,145.2	$77,446.4	$60,909.5	$45,334.0

aLess than $50,000.

Source: U.S. Department of Agriculture, Annual Summary of Commodity Futures Statistics, 1971–1972, Statistical Bulletin 5.16, Commodity Exchange Authority, Apr. 1973, p. 5.

Use of Futures in Hedging

Futures trading developed in response to several trading needs. It has been used to assure the seller of an outlet for a stored commodity, to assure the buyer of a supply of the commodity in the short production season, and to obtain operating capital. The need for this type of transaction was soundly illustrated in the development of time contracts—the precursors of futures trading—in eggs. During the latter part of the 1800s and the early 1900s, country storekeepers in the Midwest accumulated eggs obtained in trade with local farmers in the spring, during which production was at its peak. They placed the eggs in ice houses for sale in the fall and winter when fresh egg supplies were short. The sales were usually made to merchants in eastern cities who were unable to obtain enough fresh eggs to supply their customers. Such merchant-buyers were anxious to assure themselves of reliable supplies of storage eggs of dependable quality. They would seek country egg packers whom they could depend upon and contract for the stored eggs, usually at the time they were stored but sometimes even before the eggs were acquired for storage. Such a contract also provided the egg packer with funds to extend his operation on a larger scale.

The establishment of organized futures trading in eggs followed the introduction of mechanical refrigeration, which permitted more eggs to be concentrated in fewer hands in terminal warehouses and fewer eggs to be stored by country buyers at many outlying points. Under these circumstances, futures trading rapidly assumed the function of spreading the risks incurred by the relatively few companies that stored very large quantities of eggs. This function of transferring the dealer's risk gradually assumed major importance.

Today, one of the principal economic bases for the existence of organized futures trading is the opportunity it provides for hedging operations. A *hedging transaction* has been defined as a concurrent purchase and sale in two markets which are expected to behave in such a way that any loss realized in one market may be offset by an equivalent gain in the other. Hedges may be of two types: selling hedges and buying hedges. The selling hedge is illustrated by a country dealer, a terminal buyer, a miller, or an exporter who buys grain in the cash market and sells a similar quantity of futures as a protection against a fall in price while the grain is in his possession. The buying hedge is illustrated by an elevator who sells grain or a manufacturer who has sold his product ahead at a fixed price and buys a future as protection against a rise in the price of grain. Ordinarily, the hedging transaction involves a future in the same commodity as the cash transaction, but this is not necessary and is indeed impossible for commodities for which there is no futures market.

The following list may be taken as a typical illustration of a hedge by a country elevator of grain purchased under the assumption of equal price movements in the cash and futures markets.

October 1: Bought cash grain from farmer at $3.50; sold May future at $3.55.
October 30: Sold cash grain in central market at $3.35; bought May future at $3.40.
    Loss on cash grain, 15 cents   Gain on future, 15 cents

If cash and futures prices moved up and down together and by the same amount, all that would be necessary for a perfect hedge would be an equal but exactly opposite position in each market. However, identical price movements in these two markets are unusual. And while the cash and futures markets follow each other in the large price swings, there is considerable variation between them. Each time the cash-futures price relationship differs when concurrent transactions are made, the hedge is not completely effective and there is a profit or loss corresponding to the change in spread. In transactions which involve the sale of a future in putting on the hedge, a rise in cash relative to the future will result in a gain. Conversely, in transactions which involve the purchase of a future in putting the hedge into effect, a rise in the future relative to the cash will result in a gain.

Among the handlers of grain and cotton in the larger markets, hedging is a common practice. This is also true of the flour miller but is apparently not true of the mills buying cotton and selling cotton goods. Hedging by the country merchants in cotton is small, whereas in the grains it is a common but not a general practice. A survey by the U.S. Department of Agriculture with returns from over 1,200 elevators indicated that 44 percent never hedged and that half of the remaining 56 percent did not maintain a consistent policy with respect to hedging. Many of the country elevators shift their risk by selling promptly to terminal elevators. The latter accumulate storage stocks into large holdings, and they depend heavily upon the futures market.

Hedging involves more than just maintaining an even balance between cash and futures. Since the effectiveness of hedging in shifting risks varies between futures, between markets, and between types of product, proper hedging involves the selection of the particular future that will most nearly match the cash market risk involved. The future whose price will fluctuate most consistently with the cash is sought.

Speculative Traders in the Futures Markets

The two major groups of traders in futures markets are *speculators* and *hedgers*. Speculators on the grain exchanges include: (1) large and small position traders whose operations involve open accounts; (2) spreaders, a specialized group who trade on the basis of price differentials between contract months, markets, or commodities; and (3) scalpers of the pits, who usually close out each day, or in any event carry no open accounts of consequence. The hedgers use the market to offset risks from price movements while merchandising the commodity.

Spreaders in grain markets and their counterparts, *straddlers,* in cotton buy in one market and sell simultaneously in another in the belief that the one market is high relative to the other and that subsequently there will be a change in the existing relationships. They thus serve to keep the various markets in line. For example, the spreader may believe the price of wheat in Chicago is low relative to that in Minneapolis. In that event, the spreader buys wheat in Chicago and sells wheat in Minneapolis, thereby tending to raise Chicago prices and lower Minneapolis prices.

There is probably no phase of futures trading more precarious in nature than that of trading in spreads or straddles. It is not sufficient that one have a thorough knowledge of the usual factors affecting the price of futures. In addition, many problems of shipping costs, storage costs, the probable physical condition of deliverable supplies, exchange rules, and current problems must be estimated accurately.

Scalpers usually depend on the small everyday fluctuations of prices. At the close of the day they commonly leave the floor with no open contracts. The minor price fluctuations are occasioned by a variety of circumstances, and the scalper's skill lies in estimating these. Scalpers serve the purpose of providing a broad and continuous market. For example, if a hedger wished to sell a large quantity of wheat in the futures market, say, 1 million bushels, sufficient numbers of position traders willing to buy and hold this quantity would be difficult to find in a short time without greatly depressing the price. The scalpers, however, ordinarily stand ready to buy at only a slightly decreased price, expecting to be able to sell at various times later in the day when prices are higher because others wish to buy. Scalpers are generally specialized. They must quickly sense the ebb and flow of sentiment in the market and the current news and gossip likely to influence it. Scalpers are responsible for a large share of the volume of trading.

Orders which customers authorize a broker to execute are commonly of three types. These are the at-the-market order, the limited order, and the stop-loss order. The types of orders correspond with those used in the purchase and sale of stocks on a securities market. An at-the-market order instructs the broker to execute the instructions at once at the best price available. Thus, an order might read, "Buy 5 May corn, at the market." This order calls for the broker to buy contracts for 5 (units) of corn on the May futures as quickly as possible at the best price obtainable. A limited order instructs the broker to buy or sell at a specified price. Thus, "Buy 5 May corn at 72" instructs the broker to buy when and if the price reaches or goes below a price of 72 cents per bushel. The stop-loss order combines features of both the above types. Such an order might read, "Sell 5 May corn at 80, stop." In this case, the price of the May future would be above 80 cents when the order was issued, and the broker is instructed to sell 5 May corn if the price drops to 80 cents or lower. The stop-loss order is similar to a limited order in that it does not become effective until a certain price is reached; however, when this price is passed, it becomes a market order.

The fundamental purpose of a futures market is to provide for the shifting of risk through hedging, but this basic reason for the market is easily lost sight of. This is because its counterpart, speculation on the basis of price movements, is a major component of futures trading. Speculative trading of this sort, which is not concerned with basic commodity values, breeds manipulation. In fact, manipulative practices have occurred in futures markets for agricultural products. Because of the possibility of irresponsible trading in futures markets and the vital effect that such market prices have on producers, processors, and distributors of agricultural commodities, these markets are subjected to close governmental supervision and scrutiny. Nevertheless, as the preponderance of trading shifts more heavily in the direction of speculation, it is desirable for the hedger to understand, appraise, and anticipate characteristic price movements in the futures markets that are attributable to the actions and reactions of speculators under given sets of conditions.

The Pricing Function

Another basic function of an organized futures market is the determination of price. The futures markets are efficient arrangements for this purpose. In several ways, they mark the closest approach to conditions of pure competition because they involve a large number of traders dealing continuously with standard contracts, the provisions of which are widely known and understood by the trader. Transactions are consummated promptly with the prices transmitted quickly to all other traders.

The function of price determination is beneficial not only to participants in the futures market but also to those in related commodity markets. Since the contracts are standardized, the price quotations are simplified and can be readily disseminated by most means of communication to near or distant points. They assume the position of standards of comparison for traders in the physical goods. Furthermore, these prices, which represent a form of forward pricing, are virtually indispensable to persons engaged in storing commodities for future disposition. Such persons need the benefit of the best judgment available regarding prospective prices when they make decisions about when and how much should be stored and how long the stocks should be held. Futures prices represent the net judgment of many traders with many points of view. Persons relying upon these prices when they make business decisions need to understand the relationships between futures and cash prices.

Relationships of Cash and Futures Prices

Previous discussions of price changes over time and storage operations indicate the general nature of relationships which would be expected to exist between cash and futures prices and between the prices for various futures. The future price should not rise above the cash price by more than the amount of the carrying costs between the present and the delivery date for the futures contract since such a situation would provide a sure profit through the purchase and holding of the product together with a concurrent sale of a future. Similarly, a distant future could not rise above a near future by more than the carrying charges between the two delivery periods. There is no similar limitation on the amount to which a future contract price for a particular commodity may fall below the cash price for that commodity. Also, there is no limitation on the amount to which a distant future price may fall relative to near future price.

It would normally be expected that the cash price would be below the future price by the amount of carrying costs between the two periods and that successive futures within the crop year would likewise differ by the carrying cost between the near and distant futures delivery periods.

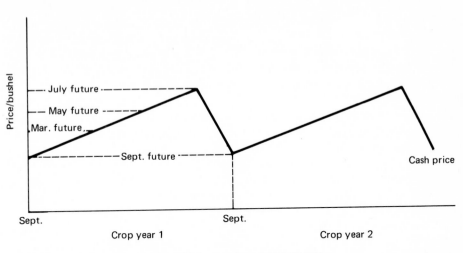

Figure 9-1   Relationship of cash and futures prices over seasons.

If it were not for uncertainties, the price of a given future might be expected to remain unchanged throughout the life of that future. The cash price would rise by the cost of storage and reach the futures price during the delivery month. This complete information situation is illustrated in Figure 9-1. The figure shows the more distant future price above the near future price and cash price. In a perfect market, this should be the cost of storage. The entry of new crops at harvest drives down both cash and future prices. During the next crop year, a similar cash-future price structure should develop. Changes in supply and/or demand through time prevent cash and futures prices from behaving in such a predictable pattern. Nevertheless, the price relationships are commonly observed to hold. The entire structure of price, cash, and futures move up and down in response to changing supply and demand for the commodity. The cash-futures differential (price of storage) will not behave in a perfectly predictable manner because it is also a price. Furthermore, it is a price which is determined by supply and demand, the *supply and demand for storage*. Since both supply and demand of storage are variable, the price of storage or the cash-futures differential will vary. One may compare the price of the future at various periods before the delivery month to the price of the future in the delivery month in order to observe the magnitudes and characters of these variations.

Cash and futures prices must and do follow one another in the broad fluctuations as long as there is the opportunity to deliver the product on a future contract. This is true because the buyer of a future has the opportunity to insist upon the conversion of the future contract into actual product if the price of futures fails to keep pace with a rise in cash prices. Conversely, the seller of a future has the opportunity to obtain the cash commodity on favorable terms and deliver upon the contract if the future price fails to decline with the cash price.

The future contract price will reflect the grade and class of a commodity deliverable on the contract. The seller will naturally deliver the poorest quality possible that meets delivery requirements in that class. The other grades, which are more expensive to deliver from the viewpoint of the seller, will not hold as close a cash price relationship to the futures as the grade and class of probable delivery. These will fluctuate relative to the future depending upon the current demand and supply situation for each. The prices for premium grades at times become considerable when isolated from the fluctuations in the futures market. These changes in relationships become extremely important in hedging operations because they may detract from the adequacy of the hedge.

Another feature to be noted is that the cash commodity customarily commands a premium over the future price at times just prior to or during the delivery month. Buyers prefer to purchase the commodity in the cash market rather than accept delivery of a "skin" grade. In some cases, there may also be costs connected with acceptance of the actual delivery of the commodity. The excess of the cash above the future is thus a premium paid for being able to select the type and quality of product sought by the buyer at the time that delivery is accepted or ownership is assumed.

SUMMARY

Food and fiber products are technically in storage from the moment they are produced until they are consumed. Accordingly, storage facilities exist at all levels of production-marketing-consumption systems. On-farm storage is most predominant for food and feed grains, with other raw farm products (except perishables) largely being held in warehousing facilities near the farm. Perishable products, of course, must be stored under refrigeration or conditions in which preservatives can be added. They must be kept in the refrigerated or preserved state through transport, handling, storage, distribution, and preconsumption storage activities.

Risk of loss by the marketing firms includes physical loss and risk of loss due to price change. Physical losses may occur because of fire, theft, or natural disasters. In these cases such losses can be covered by insurance. Physical loss can occur because of product deterioration. There is no way of shifting this risk; it must be assumed by management and it can be minimized only through good inventory control methods.

Risk of loss due to price change may be minimized by hedging on a futures market. A futures market is an organized facility and institution in which buyers and sellers engage in transaction for futures contracts. Futures contracts are promises to deliver specified products at some future time. The contracts are traded for both hedging and speculative purposes. A selling hedge is made by a person who wishes to avoid the possibility of price change and is accordingly willing to sell (promise) a delivery at some time in the future of the product that the person holds. Because futures and cash prices move together, a sale of a futures contract followed by a repurchase of the contract at a later date will generally minimize a loss due to price change. Speculators, on the other hand, wish to assume price risk in hopes of making financial gain through the purchase and sale of futures contracts. In effect, speculators assume the price risk that hedgers avoid.

QUESTIONS

1 In what respect does elimination or reduction of the risks of price change through hedging in futures markets differ from risk elimination for physical losses through insurance?
2 What is the relationship of the costs of storage to the price variation that would be expected throughout the marketing year for a storable commodity? For a nonstorable commodity?
3 Describe the process by which a grain exporter who has contracted for a foreign sale of 500,000 bushels of wheat to be exported in three months without holding the grain could hedge the transaction. Using actual market reports for wheat, determine the prices in the cash and the futures market on the current date. Hold the position for two weeks and then make the necessary cash and futures transactions to complete the trade and effect the hedge. Calculate the total gain or loss.
4 Describe the various types of trades that are made in futures markets.
5 Would you define commodity future markets as competitive or monopolistic? Why?

BIBLIOGRAPHY

Futures Trading Seminar, vols. I, II, and III, Mimir, Madison, Wis., 1964, 1965, 1966.
Hieronymus, Thomas A.: *Economics of Futures Trading, for Commercial and Personal Profit,* Commodity Research Bureau, New York, 1971.

Chapter 10

Quality Differences and Grades
for Farm Products

Public policymakers and consumers are concerned that the marketing system remains efficient and responsive. These performance aspects of marketing and pricing are generally referred to as *operational efficiency* and *pricing efficiency.*

Operational efficiency refers to the achievement of minimum costs in accomplishment of the basic marketing functions of assembly, processing, transportation, storage, distribution, and related physical and facilitative activities.

> Pricing efficiency refers to the ability of prices and price signals to allocate commodities among buyers and the returns for them among sellers, and thereby to give expression to consumer preferences as guides to the use of production resources in both primary production and marketing itself.[1]

Key to the achievement of both operational and pricing efficiency is the existence and transmission of complete and accurate market information.

---

[1]"Input-Output Relationship in Agricultural Marketing," Report of Marketing Research Workshop, Purdue University, July 1950; reproduced in F. V. Waugh, *Readings in Agricultural Marketing,* Iowa State College Press, Ames, Iowa, 1954, p. 239.

STANDARDS AND GRADES IN AGRICULTURE

There are at least two components of market information: (1) the delivery system by which it is delivered to users; and (2) classification schemes, grades and standards, which make the information readily comprehensible and amenable to comparison with other information. It is this last component of market information which will be examined in this chapter.

Weights and measures are crucial for meaningful information on all economic activity. Most countries establish a system of weights and measures for all internal trade. In the United States, the English system of measurement—inches, feet, yards, quarts, gallons, acres, etc.—are the basic units in most commercial transactions. A large part of the remainder of the world uses the metric system. Although there are standards for conversion from one system to another, the different units result in market information being more complicated and perhaps less meaningful than if all countries were to adhere to a single system. With increasing volumes of world trade, the need for a standard system becomes more urgent. Consequently, the United States is currently beginning the process of adopting the metric system of measurement.

Products can be standardized in dimensions other than quantity measures, that is, the quality dimension of the product. These dimensions include all those attributes of a product that make it more or less acceptable or usable by processors and/or consumers. For farm products, this may include such factors as weight per unit of volume, moisture, color, uniformity of size, taste, tenderness, foreign matter, age, texture, and numerous others. To the extent that differences in one or more of these characteristics make a given lot of product more valuable than another lot in specific uses or to different consumers, the information is relevant to marketing decisions.

Grading is the classification of units or lots of a product according to one or more of its quality attributes. Thus, cotton grading is classified according to length of the staple of individual fiber and its color. Beef is graded according to marbling and maturity, conformation and yield of carcass. The grade factors for wheat are market class (Hard Red Spring, Hard Red Winter, etc.), test weight per bushel, heat damage, foreign material, and shrunken or broken kernels. Although it does not enter into the official grade for wheat, protein content is also an important determinant of the value of wheat to millers. Tobacco is classified into 6 major classes with 24 types within these classes. Three of the classes are based on method of curing—flue curing, fire curing, or air curing—and three classes are based on use for which the tobacco is purchased—cigar filler, cigar binder, or cigar wrapper.[2]

Who establishes grades for farm products and who administers them? Although the U.S. government currently establishes grade specifications and may undertake the grading, the government need not be involved to develop and

[2]G. S. Shepherd and G. A. Futrell, *Marketing Farm Products*, 5th ed., Iowa State University Press, Ames, Iowa, 1970, pp. 201–216.

apply them. In fact, many grades and market classes of products were in existence before the government began to play a role. Sometimes, each terminal market where a commodity was traded developed its own grades. In other cases, the trade members developed grade terminology and specifications that facilitated marketing.

The role of the U.S. government in the grading of farm products began about the turn of the century.[3] In 1901 the U.S. Department of Agriculture began to investigate complaints about nonuniformity of grades in both domestic and foreign markets for grains. By 1908 a number of divisions of the USDA were investigating the relationship between quality characteristics and marketability for milk products, poultry, eggs, and fruits. Investigation and studies continued over a period of several years and culminated in several pieces of legislation. The Cotton Futures Act of 1914 provided for official grades for all cotton traded on futures markets. The Grain Standards Act of 1916 established mandatory grading for all grain traded in interstate commerce. Other legislation established USDA grade standards for other farm produce. The governmental role in grading was further expanded by the Agricultural Marketing Act of 1946.

Much of the cost of the government-sponsored program is assumed by users. In 1961, it was estimated that 80 percent of all the costs were paid by users.[4]

POTENTIAL GAIN OR IMPACTS OF UNIFORM PRODUCT GRADING

The potential gains or consequences of uniform grade standards have been enumerated in numerous studies of grades and in textbooks on agricultural marketing. The listing that follows is a combination of listings presented by Shepherd and Futrell and by Williams and Stout.[5] The gains or consequences are grouped according to whether they contribute to pricing efficiency or operational efficiency of markets as defined above or to other aspects of market activity.

Pricing Efficiency

Pricing efficiency in markets can be increased through a uniform grading system because:

1 It increases the meaningfulness of price quotations as reported in market news. The average daily market price for beef cattle currently ranges from $15 to $36 per hundredweight. This alone is hardly useful information to the livestock producer in regard to production or marketing decisions. Know-

[3]See G. L. Baker et al., *Century of Service, the First 100 Years of the U.S. Department of Agriculture,* U.S. Department of Agriculture, 1963, pp. 57–59.

[4]U.S. Department of Agriculture, *After a Hundred Years: The Yearbook of Agriculture 1962,* p. 491.

[5]Shepherd and Futrell, op. cit.; and Willard Williams and T. T. Stout, *Economics of the Livestock Meat Industry,* Macmillan, New York, 1964.

ing prices by market classes and knowing the approximate grade of one's animals within a system of grading can lead to more sound business decisions.

2 It increases the precision of the price formation process through greater knowledge. This knowledge increases and becomes more useful as products are grouped into classes with similar or homogeneous characteristics. There is less need for average market prices to reflect average values for the entire range of qualities represented in each product.

3 It may increase the level of competition in the market. Since an acceptable and meaningful system of grading reduces the need for direct inspection by buyers, the geographic limits of the market may be expanded. Thus, potential numbers of buyers and sellers in the market may be increased. In this respect, it has been argued that development of uniform grades has permitted smaller packers to compete more vigorously with the large national packers. The decreasing share of the total domestic meat sales controlled by the national packers tends to support this argument.

4 It permits a more systematic allocation of the available supplies of a commodity to the different demands in the market. Certain types and qualities of each of some fruits and vegetables are more preferable for canning than other types and qualities. Classifying into market classes and quality ranges within these classes facilitates allocation between fresh and canning uses.

5 It facilitates the collection of reliable information on demands, supplies, and prices. If wide ranges in quality exist for a product and there is no grading or classifying according to quality, there are still likely to be price differences according to the quality variations. Accurate price reporting would require judgment about prices for each quality type and the volume distribution according to quality. A standardized grading system eliminates much of the judgment required for market reports.

Operational Efficiency

Operational efficiency concerns the relationship of input to output. Anything that increases or achieves a given level of output for a reduced quantity of inputs means an increase in the operational efficiency of agricultural markets. Alternatively, it means that uniform grading can lead to reduced marketing costs. A standardized grading system may increase output-input ratios in marketing because:

1 It limits the time and expense of bargaining about quality as well as price for each transaction. This implies, of course, that the grade dimensions and standards reflect most of the economically relevant attributes of a commodity and that the grading scheme is universally accepted. Thus, farmers selling wheat to a country elevator generally accept the grade placed on their lots at the elevator. Only price is negotiable and even this may be readily agreed to be the central market wheat quotation for the grade less transport differentials.

2 It increases the ability and potential to buy and sell on descriptions alone rather than only after personal inspection. Large volumes of butter, cheese, eggs, grain, and cotton can be sold without buyers seeing the products. Buyers do not have to travel to the sellers' location or the product does not

have to be transported to central markets if grades accurately reflect quality. Transport of both people and product may be reduced. It reduces all costs that would be required where direct inspection is necessary. Buying can be done on a specification basis.

   3 It may encourage specialization of marketing functions. It may, for example, explain the increased specialization that has occurred in livestock slaughtering and processing operations since the introduction of beef grading in the early part of this century. However, increased specialization in beef slaughtering and processing has a number of other important advantages. Grading is useful to this specialization but is probably not the generating force.

   4 The enlarged marketing areas that may be caused by uniform grades can permit more optimum movements of farm products from farmers to consumers.

   5 It may reduce the amount of expensive advertising and promotion that is based upon unimportant or nonexistent quality characteristics. In the absence of grades, consumers or users may rely on a brand to be assured of consistent quality even though many small suppliers of the unbranded, slightly promoted product can meet the buyers' needs. A grading scheme on the relevant product characteristics can assure quality levels regardless of source of supply. At the same time that expensive product differentiation is reduced, competition in the market may be on the increase.

   6 It may increase the emphasis on technological innovations or other cost-reducing marketing practices through increased price competition. This consequence may be associated with the preceding one in that competition on the basis of highly differentiated products becomes less appealing if uniform grades are accepted and relied upon.

Other Consequences of Uniform Grade Standards

Some consequences of uniform grade standards do not fall neatly into the pricing and operational efficiency classifications. The following list delineates three consequences:

   1 Although uniform grades may reduce the advantage of highly differentiated production on a brand basis, some firms and industries have tied their promotional programs to the grading scheme. The original Land O'Lakes butter merchandising program in the 1920s was tied to the marketing of only grade AA under the Land O'Lakes brand. At that time, Land O'Lakes was the major source of graded sweet cream butter. If the graded product had been readily available from other suppliers of butter, its merchandising program may not have been so successful. Current industry promotion programs for Wisconsin cheese are tied to that state's cheese-grading program.

   2 Grade, size, and maturity characteristics of fruits and vegetables are a basis for regulating the total quantity marketed or at least regulating the flow of the product into different uses throughout the marketing season. Of the 90 federal and state marketing orders in effect for fruits and vegetables in 1966, 69 permitted this kind of control.[6] In some orders, marketing of a product that is

---

[6]National Commission on Food Marketing, *Organization and Competition in the Fruit and Vegetable Industry,* Technical Study 4, June 1966, p. 311.

below a certain grade, size, or maturity is restricted. One rationale for this is that the industry does not want product demand adversely affected by inferior products. In addition, limiting sales of fruits and vegetables to only the top grades may reduce spoilage during marketing. Another rationale may be overriding for most produce groups that use marketing orders. Demands for most food products are likely to be inelastic. Any method of reducing volume of sales will increase total industry revenue.

Allocation of product throughout the season according to grades or different uses or markets according to grades or classes may be undertaken because it increases total industry revenue by price discrimination. That is, product prices in each grade differ by more than cost difference. The objective of discriminating (which will be described in more detail in a later chapter) is to also increase total industry revenue from product marketing.

3 Grades may reduce unfair trade practices. Greater knowledge of relevant product quality characteristics through grading reduces the ability to misinform and misrepresent quality. This implies, of course, that grades are objectively applied.

ANALYZING THE IMPACT OF GRADING SCHEMES

Possible consequences of grading schemes, as indicated in the preceding section, are numerous, but the questions of concern to the economist are often more specific.

What is the impact of uniform grades on the average price received for the product?
What kind of price relationships will exist among grades?
What will be the impact on total demand?
What will be the impact on total supply?

In this section, we will describe some of the factors that need to be considered in responding to these questions. We will also present a framework that can be used to analyze the distribution of gains from applying or changing a grading system.[7]

A common misconception about grading is that grades can be ordinally ranked as best, second best, third best, etc. And furthermore, prices for each grade should progressively increase from the lowest-ranked grade to the highest. This conclusion may be valid for some commodities. However, ordinal ranking of grades is not always possible, and it is not necessary that prices among grades bear a constant relationship to one another. Grade meanings and grade-price relationships for a product depend upon certain characteristics of supply and demand.

What are the demand and supply characteristics that determine the impact of grades on market and price behavior? Whether demand is *homogeneous* or *heterogeneous* and whether supply is alterable or unalterable has a significant

---

[7]This section is based on J. P. Doll, V. J. Rhodes, and J. G. West, *The Economics of Agricultural Production, Markets, and Policy,* Irwin, Homewood, Ill., 1968, pp. 400–414; and Williams and Stout, op. cit., pp. 472–484.

bearing on consequences of grading. Homogeneous demand exists when all consumers or users agree on the ordinal ranking of quality variation for a product. The prices that consumers are willing to pay for each grade can also be ranked in the same order. It need not be the case that the price difference which each consumer is willing to pay be the same as long as the ordinal ranking of prices remains the same. Beef demand is probably a good example of homogeneous demand, at least for fresh meat consumption. Prime is preferred to choice, choice is preferred to good, and good is preferred to standard. Prices at both farm and retail reflect this ranking.

Demand is heterogeneous when consumers or users are not in agreement as to the same ordinal ranking for variations in quality. This can very often be the case for a product that has different uses. One type of tobacco is preferred by producers of cigarettes, another for cigars. One quality type of orange is preferred for processing into juice; another quality is preferred for sale in the fresh market. In these situations, there need be no consistent price relationship between the prices in the different uses. It might be concluded that with homogeneous demand the quality groups are reasonably good substitutes for one another. With heterogeneous demand, the quality groups are rather poor substitutes for one another.

Much of the quality variations in agricultural products are inherent in the biological nature of production and weather variations that significantly affect quality. For any given variety of wheat, cotton, corn, fruits, or vegetables, little can be done about variations observed in quality. This is natural variation and it is accepted. Weather changes may shift the quality distribution of supply from year to year, but the average distribution remains stable over the long run. Supply in this case is unalterable.

Supply of some animal and plant products can be altered through animal and plant selection and by greater control of such factors affecting agricultural production as disease, pests, water, and fertilizer. In these situations, supply may be adjusted or changed in the quality dimension in response to different demands of consumers and/or users. Supply in this case is alterable.

Grading can be beneficial in all four possible combinations of demand and supply, but different price relationships among quality classes and quality changes will occur with each combination. With homogeneous demand and unalterable supply, the grade distribution of supply according to the ordinal ranking of quality characteristics is likely to appear as in Figure 10-1. The average quality of the product represents the largest part of production. The very low and the very high qualities are not likely to be so numerous. A grading system facilitates the allocation of the total supply. The highest-quality product will be sold to those willing to pay the most for it. Those who are more concerned with price will purchase the lower qualities. This allocation may permit producers to increase their total returns from sale of the product.

If homogeneous demand is combined with alterable supply, a uniform grading system should change the quality distribution over time. Some uncontrollable quality variations are likely to remain, but the quality distribution of

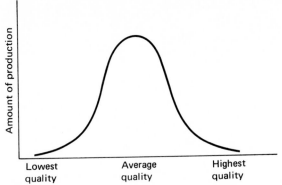

Figure 10-1 Distribution of quality for product *x* with unalterable supply and homogeneous demand.

supply would shift from one centered on low average quality to one centered on the highest or preferred quality. Additionally, the range of the new quality distribution may be narrowed. A necessary assumption for the occurrence of this change is that the price difference which consumers are willing to pay for the quality difference represented by the grades are less than the costs of altering the supply. This type of change is illustrated by the quality distribution shift t_1 to t_2 in Figure 10-2. This situation has probably been represented by the increasing proportion of beef cattle that have fallen into the choice and prime grades.

A consequence of grading a commodity with alterable supply may be the disappearance of certain grades from the market. In the dairy industry, the lowest grade of butter has become a smaller and smaller proportion of total volume.

The price difference for grades when demand is homogeneous will also depend upon whether supply is alterable or unalterable. With unalterable supply,

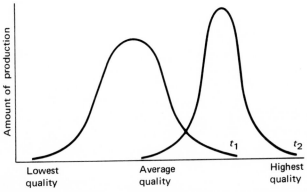

Figure 10-2 A shift in quality distribution of product *y* with homogeneous demand and alterable supply.

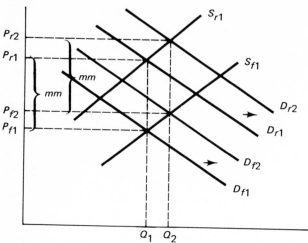

Figure 10-3 The impact of expanded demand through grading on market prices and quantities.

prices are likely to differ between grades. The relative quantities in each quality grouping due to natural or biological causes will cause the grade-price differentials to vary. If supply is alterable, then market forces of supply and demand for each grade should tend to equate price difference between grades with the cost difference associated with producing the different grades.

In the case of heterogeneous demand and unalterable supply, uniform grade can facilitate the allocation of supplies among the various uses. Since the grades are relatively poor substitutes for one another, grade prices need be neither higher or lower. Rankings of price will depend upon the relative supplies and demands for each grade. Changing relative supply for the grades can alter the price ranking.

Heterogeneous demand with alterable supply may be characteristic of quite a number of farm products, tobacco, fruits, and vegetables, and perhaps certain livestock. Unlike the situation with homogeneous demand and alterable supplies, none of the grades are likely to become empty sets. Each class or grade has uses in which it is preferred. Grading may assure optimum matching of demands with supplies. Quantities and prices of each grade should adjust according to the marginal conditions of resource allocation.

The possible incidence of grades on producer prices, consumer prices, and quantities marketed is illustrated in Figure 10-3. In this figure, assume that the product is originally marketed without grades. The total demand for the product at retail is illustrated by curve D_{r1}. The derived demand at the farm, which implies certain costs of marketing for each possible quantity, is illustrated by D_{f1}. Farm supply is S_{f1} and supply at retail is S_{r1}. The original price at retail is P_{r1} and at farm it is P_{f1}. The quantity moving through the market at the average price is Q_1. If the introduction of a uniform grading system permits a better matching of demand for the different qualities with the supply of each quality, we would anticipate a shift in the aggregate retail demand for the product from D_{r1} to D_{r2}. If the entire cost of the grading scheme is assumed by the government and the grades have no impact on marketing efficiency, marketing margins *(mm)* are the same after the imposition of grades as before. This implies that farm-level demand (derived demand) is shifted to the right by the same amount as retail demand. Neither farm supply nor retail supply is changed by the grading scheme. The final result of the grade is to increase the average price for the product at both retail and farm to P_{r2} and P_{f2}. The quantity produced and marketed is increased from Q_1 to Q_2.

As indicated by the listing of benefits in the preceding section, grades have the potential of reducing marketing costs as well as expanding demand. To the extent that the costs of grading are assumed by the industry, this will offset the reduced marketing costs. In net, however, marketing efficiency should increase and marketing costs should decrease. The impact of a grading scheme that both expands aggregate demand for the product and contributes to operational efficiency in marketing is illustrated in Figure 10-4. Again, we begin with the initial farm and retail prices of P_{f1} and P_{r1} and quantity of Q_1. Retail demand is shifted from D_{r1} to D_{r2}. Because marketing costs are reduced for any given level of retail demand, the derived farm demand shifts to the right by an even greater amount— from D_{f1} to D_{f3}—than retail demand has shifted. Furthermore, the retail supply is shifted downward or to the right because lower marketing costs are involved in moving any given quantity of farm supply from farm to consumer. This shift is from S_{r1} to S_{r2}. The new prices are P_{r3} at retail and P_{f3} at the farm. Farm prices

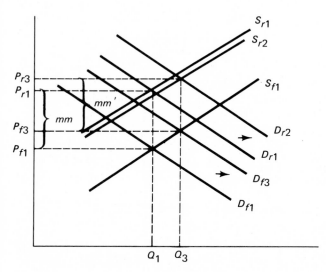

Figure 10-4 The impact of a grading system that both expands aggregate demand and reduces marketing costs.

increased by a greater amount than retail prices. In fact, large increases in marketing efficiency could reduce retail prices even though the grading system has shifted aggregate consumer demand to the right. In either case, the quantity moving through the market would increase. Here it increased from Q_1 to Q_3. The marketing margin has declined from mm to mm'.

The reader should note that the preceding situations were illustrated with demands and supplies that had approximately equal elasticities (in absolute terms) at the points of intersection. If the elasticities had been substantially different at these points of intersection, the relative impact of grading systems would have been substantially changed.

PROBLEMS OF DEVELOPING AND USING GRADES

The adaptation and implementation of grading schemes is not an easy task. They have an impact on all three major participants in the marketing system: consumers, farmers, and the food marketing firms. With each of these groups, there may not be complete agreement that grades should or should not be used. Between these groups, the areas of conflict on grades may even be greater. Assuming that all market participants agree on the need for uniform grade standards, what are the issues that need to be resolved?

Number of Classes or Grades

Presumably, the desirable number of grades should be such that each grade represents a completely homogeneous product with respect to the relevant grade characteristics. For many farm products, this would imply so many grades that it would be completely unworkable. One guide for number and limits for each grade is that each grade should include enough of the total industry supply to be meaningful in terms for price determination for the grade.

Grade Terminology

Grade terminology can be very misleading. For products with homogeneous demand, the terminology should connote something about the ordinal ranking of quality. Yet there seems to be little standardization in grading among products. Quality is denoted by numbers for some products. For example, grades 1, 2, 3, 4, and 5 denote qualities of Spring Wheat. Quality is denoted by letters for some products, for example, grades A, B, etc., for butter. Names are used for others, such as prime, choice, good, and standard for cattle. Name and number combinations denote the qualities for others, such as extra fancy, fancy, no. 1, no. 1 cooker, and no. 1 early for apples. Obviously, this seemingly limitless range of grade terminology can be confusing and, as a result, useless to consumers that buy all of these products. Is grade A the top quality for both eggs and butter? No, for both the top grade is AA. No. 1 is the top grade for many fruits and vegetables, but it is the third grade for apples. Extra fancy is the top grade. Although many benefits of grades have been cited, proliferation of grade terminology has detracted from the advantages.

For products with heterogeneous demands, the grade terminology may imply a ranking of demands when, in fact, the rankings differ among consumers or users.

Quality Deterioration

Natural deterioration of quality over time is common for many unprocessed farm products. Thus, products that meet top quality standards when they leave the farm or first handler can fail to do so when they are sold to the final consumer. One might argue that this can be solved by grading at a later point in the marketing channel. This raises the question of how producers of quality products can be rewarded and encouraged to continue quality production. Perhaps, the solution is a dual level of grading, with grading on the farm and regrading at or near the retail level of the market.

Relevant Quality Characteristics

Farm products have numerous quality dimensions that affect their acceptability by users and consumers. Actual grade is a composite of all the quality factors included in the grade. Both determination of relevant grade factors and measurements may be problem areas. Some of the quality characteristics are quite objective and can be easily measured—test weight per volume, moisture content, and product damage, to name a few. Others are more subjective, such as tenderness, flavor, and texture. For subjective quality traits, grades may be less than accurate measurements of quality.

Determination of the quality traits on which to grade the product is not readily apparent. Does egg color really make a difference to the consumer? Even if it may be a consideration for the consumer, is it important enough to use in grading?

SUMMARY

Uniform grades play an important role in the marketing of agricultural commodities. They can contribute to both operational and pricing efficiency in agricultural markets. Consequently, total returns to producers can be increased and marketing margins can be reduced.

The government plays an important role in establishing uniform grade standards for farm products. Industry and firms have implemented grading schemes themselves, but government participation has at least several advantages: (1) the government can more easily act as a disinterested third party in applying the grades; (2) grade proliferation may be reduced; and (3) grade terminology is likely to be less confusing.

Grading of farm products need not result in an ordinal ranking of qualities from best to worst, although this may often be the case. Qualities of some products may not be universally ranked the same by all consumers or users. If grades can be consistently ranked in order on a quality basis, demand is defined as homogeneous. If grades cannot be consistently ranked, demand is defined as heterogeneous. If the demands among grades are homogeneous, prices will bear a consistent ordinal relationship.

QUESTIONS

1 Frequently farm product processors will perform the quality grading function, judging the farmer's produce and allocating payment on the basis of grades. The obvious misunderstandings that could arise under this arrangement have been addressed by the use of third-party arbitration. How would you write a paragraph in a farmer-processor contract as to the selection and use of this arbitrator in settling any differences?
2 Does the term *pricing efficiency* imply *speed* of communication between producers and consumers? Should it?
3 In 1975 proposals were made to change the grade limits for U.S. choice beef so as to include more lower-quality beef under this grade label. What should be the price effects of this change in grade standards?

BIBLIOGRAPHY

Abbot, L.: *Quality and Competition,* Columbia University Press, New York, 1955.
Baker, G. L., et al.: *Century of Service, the First 100 Years of the U.S. Department of Agriculture,* U.S. Department of Agriculture, 1963.
Doll, J. P., V. J. Rhodes, and J. G. West: *The Economics of Agricultural Production, Markets, and Policy,* Irwin, Homewood, Ill., 1968.
Erdman, H. E.: "Problems of Establishing Grades for Farm Products," *Journal of Farm Economics,* vol. 32, no. 1, pp. 15–29, Feb. 1950.
Hyslop, J. D.: *Price-Quality Relationships in Spring Wheat,* Technical Bulletin 267, Agricultural Experiment Station, University of Minnesota, St. Paul, 1970.
Kohls, R. L., and D. Downey: *Marketing of Agricultural Products,* 4th ed., Macmillan, New York, 1970.
National Commission on Food Marketing: *Organization and Competition in the Fruit and Vegetable Industry,* Technical Study 4, June 1966.
Nelson, K. E., and Van Arsdall: "A Comparison of Present and Proposed Beef Grades," in supplement to U.S. Department of Agriculture, *Livestock and Meat Situation,* Dec. 1974.
Shepherd, G. S., and G. A. Futrell: *Marketing Farm Products,* 5th ed., Iowa State University Press, Ames, Iowa, 1970.
U.S. Department of Agriculture: *After a Hundred Years: The Yearbook of Agriculture 1962.*

Chapter 11

Market Information

Efficiently operating economic systems require information—information for rational consumer and producer decisions as well as for the planning decisions of the individual producing and marketing firms. Usually, information is desired but not necessarily used to the same extent by all market participants. It is provided by a number of government agencies, buyers and sellers themselves, commodity markets, specialized market information services, and the various news media. For agricultural products, a large amount of information is available from all of these services. For purposes of the following discussions, it is convenient to classify the market information into three types: (1) market news, (2) market outlook, and (3) advertising.

THE ECONOMICS OF INFORMATION

College students should not have to be reminded that information is a valuable resource. The fact that they are seeking degrees indicates that they know that knowledge is equated with power.

Prices vary in all markets and unless all sellers are located at one place, a buyer cannot know what all the selling prices are without undertaking a *search* for price information. What this means is that, at any given point in time, different prices exist for the same product purchased (or adjusted for) *under the same terms*. We all recognize the existence of price dispersion in retail grocery purchasing. Prices of identical items vary (sometimes by design, that is, "specials") from one store to the next.

> Price dispersion is a manifestation—and, indeed, it is the measure—of ignorance in the market. Dispersion is a biased measure of ignorance because there is never absolute homogeneity in the commodity if we include the terms of sale within the concept of the commodity. Thus, some automobile dealers might perform more service, or carry a larger range of varieties in stock, and a portion of the observed dispersion is presumably attributable to such differences. But it would be metaphysical, and fruitless, to assert that all dispersion is due to heterogeneity.[1]

At any one time a *frequency distribution* of price will exist for a product. A buyer has the option of purchasing at a price from the first seller encountered, or the buyer can "shop around" in an attempt to find lower price quotations. But shopping around is an activity that consumes time and other resources. Thus, there is a *cost of search*.

The important question for the buyer to answer is: *how much* shopping around should I do? The answer depends upon the nature of the price dispersion distribution, the value of the item to be purchased, the income of the purchaser, and the cost of search.

It should be intuitively clear that price dispersion is greater for some products than for others. One study has demonstrated that prices are more dispersed for farm inputs purchased by farmers than for farm products sold by farmers.[2] There seem to be some logical explanations for this. Inputs are usually purchased at a range of different geographic locations; farm products are sold at terminal markets. The government market news service provides daily quotations for farm products; such quotations are not available for farm inputs.

The existence of price dispersion is clearly more important to the buyer if the item priced is very valuable or of relatively great importance in the purchaser's budget. If the price of salt varies by 25 percent in the grocery stores in your vicinity, it is not important enough for you to spend considerable time or resources to learn of the dispersion or to take advantage of it. A 25 percent variation in meat prices, however, may call for a change in shopping patterns.

In addition to the *cost* of search, another variable of special interest to buyers is the *expected savings* that could accrue because of their search. The expected savings will be greater if prices are more dispersed and if the expenditure on the item is greater.

It should be clear that the rational buyer will expend time and other

---

[1]George Stigler, "The Economics of Information," *Journal of Political Economy,* vol. 69, no. 3, June 1961.

[2]Calvin L. Brints, "The Economics of Information in Purchasing Feed and Fertilizer in Minnesota," doctoral dissertation, University of Minnesota, 1973.

resources only up to the point where the additional (or marginal) costs of search are equal to the additional (marginal) expected savings realized from the search,

$$MC_S = MS_E$$

where MC_S is the marginal cost of search and MS_E is the marginal expected savings. The greatest purchasing problem is not in valuing the buyer's time (What are the opportunity costs?) or other resource expenditures. Rather, it is determining the extent and nature of the price dispersion.

Prices may be distributed "normally" or "uniformly" (see Figure 11-1). The nature of the price dispersion pattern will have to be ascertained by the buyer and a judgment made about how the observed price relates to the distribution. An example may be the purchase of a panel truck to be used in your retail food business. Once you have obtained one price quotation you should decide: (1) Is it likely that prices are dispersed? (2) Are the various prices dispersed uniformly or normally? (3) Where does the single quoted price for the truck fit into the distribution?

The attainment of $MC_S = MS_E$ is not an easy task. But it probably is well worth more time and resource investment on the part of consumers and farmers than has been allocated. The cost of search is greatly reduced by the existence of market news.

MARKET NEWS

The Need

Buyers and sellers must communicate to make transactions. This communication is not only oral and face-to-face but may take on a variety of other forms as well. For example, buyers and sellers may communicate by written word and may agree through use of written contract arrangements. It is very common in auction markets and fast-trading commodity futures markets to make complete use of sign language as well.

In communicating, buyers and sellers are interested in the price of the product in the transaction, the quantity and quality involved, the date and time of delivery, and the bearing of risk of loss or product deterioration during and immediately after the transaction. This information about market transactions is not always possessed, or is possessed in an unbiased form, by both members of the transaction process.

Different sellers may offer products to buyers at different prices and a buyer, unaware that price differences exist for identical products in a market situation, may pay an unnecessarily high price. If price differences do exist in a market situation, it may be advantageous for buyers to engage in a "search" of price information by going from one seller to another and obtaining price quotations, but such a search is economical only if the cost of search is less than

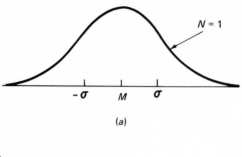

(a)

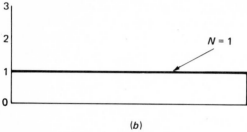

(b)

Figure 11-1 Hypothetical price distributions for a uniform product at a point in time under similar terms. (a) Normal distribution; (b) uniform distribution.

the price difference that can be gained by the search activity. Thus, it does not pay for a homemaker to travel 5 miles to buy a grocery item on special that would save 10 cents. The homemaker must consider not only the cost of operating an automobile to travel from one place to another but also the value of one's own time as well. Similarly, farmers should not travel from one terminal market to another looking for the "best price" unless the cost of searching for the best price is less than the price difference that might be realized.

Rather than requiring every individual buyer to incur the cost of search for price information, price information is made available by sellers through newspapers, television, and other communications media so that buyers and sellers might be able to take advantage of the best price without having to incur a considerable part of the cost of search. Knowledgeable, rational buyers also will make use of the telephone to contact various sellers and obtain price quotations without having to incur substantial costs, both in terms of transportation and time.

But price information is not always as clear as it should be when information is obtained from sellers. The price that may be quoted may not include a number of "extras" that may be added on after the individual buyer is ready to make the transaction. Or it may be that the product being purchased is not of adequate quality to meet the requirements of the buyer. Thus, a public news service, the Market News Service, has been developed in agriculture.

The Market News Service (Portions from Agricultural Handbook 118)

Primarily as an aid to farmers, a market news system was developed within the U.S. Department of Agriculture that collects detailed information on prices, supply, and market conditions and which disseminates this information to the public. The Market News Service covers the markets for a long list of agricultural commodities. It covers many fruits and vegetables, cotton, tobacco, livestock, meats, wool, dairy products, eggs and poultry products, grain, and other commodities, both at country points and at city terminals. It is a common occurrence in agricultural portions of the United States to listen to the "Farm Market News," which is the information gathered by the Market News Service.

The Market News Service has responsibility for collecting detailed information on prices, supply, and market conditions in a particular market place, for exchanging that information with other markets, and for disseminating it to the public. Information is distributed rapidly through a system of some 13,000 miles of leased wire, and by press, radio, and television. Frequently, several flash reports are issued during market trading sessions, as well as at the end or beginning of the day or week. The markets covered range from the large central markets for grain and livestock at Chicago and Kansas City to the large food distribution centers like Los Angeles, New York, and Boston, as well as production area markets at direct buying stations, local livestock auctions, assembly and shipping points, and increasingly at the farm, feedlots, ranch, and orchard.

Original data gathered by the Market News Service include prices, supply, local stocks, movement, receipts, weather conditions, and considerable general information regarding the situation prevailing during the market session. These original data relating to the particular market place, after serving their purpose in the current hour-to-hour or day-to-day marketing operations, become a part of the permanent record. They are valuable in many economic and marketing research studies and are used extensively as check information against estimates of total production and utilization. This part of the basic work of the Market News Service would be much more accurately described as *market reporting*.

The "news" aspect of this important market reporting activity actually becomes involved in some of the broader aspects of market news, as previously discussed. The report issued by a market reporter for any given market frequently includes, in addition to the data for that market, information derived from the current crop report, an outlook report, or a situation report, or any other information that may have a bearing on market trends or conditions.

History Sixty years ago, there was no federal Market News Service or state Market News Service. Some private concerns in large cities gathered and published data on receipts and prices of farm products, but these were limited in scope and adequacy.

This situation never really satisfied everybody; certainly, it did not satisfy farmers. Farmers often suspected that the information which they received was not trustworthy. For many decades, they sought means of getting more and better market news, and they were insistent that the information be unbiased, current, and reliable.

Food trades were not entirely satisfied with this situation either. While they had certain sources of information scattered around in strategic points, they could never be sure that the information received told the whole story. As the country grew and as the trade had to reach out farther and farther to obtain sources of supply, middlemen found that they also must have fuller, more accurate, and more timely information to make intelligent business decisions.

By World War I, the marketing of farm products had become highly specialized and integrated on a nationwide basis. This was largely the result of improvements in transportation, refrigeration, storage, and communication. Important technological breakthroughs for agricultural marketing were the telegraph and telephone. But neither the farmers nor the food trade could take full advantage of modern communication unless some impartial agent gathered price and supply information to communicate to them on a uniform and consistent basis.

The federal-state Market News Service grew out of these conditions. It has a long history of development and achievement, beginning in 1915 when the first market news report was issued by the U.S. Department of Agriculture. That report was a simple statement of prices and market conditions for strawberries at Hammond, Louisiana. Market conditions during and after World War I gave great stimulus to the news service as more and more information was needed in regard to the buying, selling, and availability of a rapidly growing volume and nationwide movement of farm products.

Soon after the strawberry market news service was begun, a small number of seasonal market news field stations were opened in various fruit and vegetable producing areas. Trained market news reporters also were assigned to cover the wholesale produce markets in large distribution centers, such as New York City, Chicago, St. Louis, Kansas City, Buffalo, and Baltimore. Arrangements were made with railroads to obtain daily information on shipments to market— including data on the number of cars arriving, unloaded, or diverted at principal markets. The popularity of the service was soon registered in Congress by requests from farmers and trade interests for its expansion and extension to other commodities.

Market news for meat and meat byproducts was initiated with the establishment of offices for that purpose at a few principal cities in 1917. One year later, daily reports on trading and prices for livestock at public markets in Chicago, Kansas City, and Omaha were begun.

Market news reporting on dairy and poultry products was then instituted at some of the principal markets for these commodities. Meanwhile, biweekly reports were being issued in a few Eastern states for wheat, corn, oats, and hay, showing stocks on hand, prevailing prices, probable receipts, and shipments. Market news for cotton was begun in 1919 under an amendment to the Cotton Futures Act.

The years 1915–1919 saw the small beginnings of what is now the world's most comprehensive public market news service for agricultural commodities. Authority for instituting or expanding market news services is contained in applicable agricultural appropriations acts and other congressional legislation, such as the Cotton Futures Act, the Smith-Doxey Act (cotton improvement), and the Tobacco Inspection Act.

Until 1951, appropriations for market news were usually made for specific projects requested by groups or individuals working directly with Congress. Such requests provided funds for additional reporting projects, but they made no provision for any increase in supervision or administration, which are necessary for nationwide uniformity. In 1951, Congress approved a program for development of federal-state Market News Services which have since served as a basis for a more unified approach.

Coverage and Organization   The Market News Service covers the markets for a long list of agricultural commodities. It covers many fruits and vegetables, cotton, tobacco, livestock, meats, wool, dairy products, egg and poultry products, grain, and other commodities at country points and city terminals. Country points and city terminals are almost entirely the places at which agricultural commodities are bought and sold in significant volumes.

The market news work is done principally by trained market reporters who record what they see and hear on the markets. Most market reporters are agricultural college graduates who majored in marketing, economics, animal husbandry, or in a field concerned with a special commodity area. Some employees of food or fiber processing and marketing firms are sometimes recruited for market reporting. Other employees were originally involved with the various grading, inspection, and other action program agencies of the federal and state governments that dealt with the marketing or classing of agricultural products. All reporters are given intensive on-the-job training in all phases of market reporting and field operations.

The organization for the collection and distribution of market news consists of over 200 field offices in important production areas and major assembly and terminal markets, as well as food distribution centers. Each local office is responsible for the accuracy of reports, the maintenance of working relationships with the trade, and the adjustment of collection and reporting methods to suit local conditions. For a quick exchange of information, most of these offices are connected by leased teletype lines.

Central headquarters for the Market News Service are located in Washington, D.C., and are in the immediate charge of Agricultural Marketing Service (AMS) branches within divisions organized for market news and other service work for groups of similar commodities. All of these divisions are under the supervision of divisions organized for market news and other service work for groups of like commodities. All of these divisions are under the supervision of division directors who in turn are under the direct supervision of an AMS deputy administrator for marketing services. This administrator is responsible for coordinating the work in the several commodity divisions into a unified market news service.

Dissemination

Every modern means of individual and mass communication is now used in the dissemination of market news. Major lifelines of the Market News Service are the leased teletype circuits into which most of the news gathered by the field stations is fed. This gives each office on a teletype circuit access to information on prices and conditions at all other markets for a commodity or group of commodities. Each office supplies the local market news and pertinent information received by leased wire from other markets to newspapers, press associations, radio stations, and television stations within its area.

With the nationwide leased wire system, market news is being dispatched throughout the United States by cooperating private and public agencies within minutes after it is collected. Literally thousands of daily and weekly newspapers and most trade journals print the news supplied by AMS and cooperating state departments of agriculture. In a 1958 survey of dissemination of market news by radio and television stations, 1,472 radio stations and 165 television stations scattered throughout the country reported that they feature market news on certain areas of their programs, mostly on a daily basis. Surveys indicate 1,400 newspapers daily carry some market news. Producers, shippers, distributors, and all other interested persons, wherever they may be, are kept informed as to what conditions prevail at any or all of the principal agricultural markets in the United States.

This complex system is very different from the simple beginnings of the Market News Service. The first reports between market news offices were dispatched in code over commercial wires and distributed by mail or telephone to individuals and newspapers. During World War I, wire circuits were leased 12 hours each day for the exclusive use of agencies administering government programs directed at increasing the production and rapid distribution of food. The top telegrapher's speed at that time was 50 words per minute, contrasted with 100-word-per-minute speeds of transmission today. More efficient ways of collecting market news were developed, and use was made of every available means of communication in disseminating the reports.

The first wireless market news report featuring information collected by government reporters was flashed from the radio station of the U.S. Bureau of Standards in Washington, D.C., in 1920. Ham operators relayed the news by posting the market quotations on local bulletin boards.

Market reports were first broadcast by radio telephone from the radio station of the University of Minnesota in February 1921, and the first regular schedule of reports was begun by station KDKA in East Pittsburgh, Pennsylvania, on May 29, 1921. In those days, the Bureau of Markets, with the cooperation of the Bureau of Standards, published instructions to farmers for the home construction of a simple radio receiver in the hope that this instrument would further more rapid dissemination of marketing information direct to farmers.

Mimeographed reports were accepted early as one sure way of disseminating market news to farmers and trade interests in the various industries. Anyone could get on the mailing list to receive daily, weekly, monthly, and annual reports that were issued free of charge by the various offices by simply making a request. Today, less emphasis is placed upon mimeographed mailed reports. Many mailed reports have been discontinued and are therefore no longer available to the public. But efforts are being made to increase dissemination by commercial media which, for the most part, can supply information faster.

How Market News Differs from Related Services

The Market News Service provides current information concerning prices, supplies, stocks, and market conditions in designated marketplaces, and movement in principal production areas, processing plants, terminal markets, and distribution centers. Trained market reporters gather information and report it promptly. Market reporters try to discover the biases that inevitably exist in the oral responses of interviewed buyers and sellers by cross-checking both buyers and sellers and spot-checking records.

By contrast, the monthly farm price report of the Agricultural Estimates Division of the AMS for states generally reflects the average of prices for all qualities and methods of sale.

The daily and weekly market news reports on supplies, stocks, and movements to market differ from the monthly AMS crop reports in that market news information is an observer's report on volume and prices at various selling levels for a market or movement for a given day or week, whereas crop reports are estimates or forecasts of total acreage, yields, and production volume for a given period. Crop reports do not cover current marketing of crops; they are not intended to do so.

Outlook and situation reports go beyond market news reports and crop estimates in two ways. First, they present a fuller explanation of reasons for recent and current trends; second, they point out some foreseeable trends. Market news reports comment on reasons for recent changes. For example, they may indicate that current supplies in some city markets are short and that prices have gone up because of a severe snowstorm that has disrupted transportation. However, the Market News Service does not generally undertake economic analyses or attempt to forecast future trends in supplies or prices. Statistics produced by the Agricultural Estimates Division are primarily useful in establishing longer-term marketing levels and production and marketing plans in making policy decisions. They are not generally adapted to hour-to-hour, day-to-day, or week-to-week use in making frequent and current marketing decisions.

Importance of Quality Standards to Market News

In addition to price information, it is important to transmit information regarding quality. In face-to-face buyer-seller confrontations, product quality can be determined by the buyer through inspection of the product to be purchased. However, this is a cumbersome and time-consuming activity in a fast-moving food and fiber system. Instead, many purchases are made based upon quality statements made by the seller in terms of the grades and the standards discussed in Chapter 10. In each industry subsegment of the U.S. food and fiber system, there has developed an elaborate system of designating the quantity and quality of information used in communications between buyers and sellers. Accordingly, it is very common for the purchaser to call a seller and to finalize a transaction on the basis of the price and the quantity and quality standards expressed in their agreement.

Although many food products have quantity and quality measurement specifications at the processor and wholesaler levels, these specifications are not always indicated at the consumer end of the food and fiber system. Final consumers must not only try to make price comparisons in the situation in which containers of products vary in quantity or volume size. Consumers must, except in a limited number of cases in which the quality specifications are in evidence, also purchase a product based upon their experience with it and decide whether or not it is of adequate quality to meet their taste and preference.

The information system that accompanies the marketing of agricultural and food and fiber products is not widely used at all levels of the marketing system. Again, technical or quality information about the inputs that farmers use in agricultural production processes are not always in evidence. Accordingly, farmers and consumers pay widely varying prices for products of widely varying quality, and they are frequently confused and misled in their purchasing activities. However, firms with market power throughout the rest of the food and fiber system generally have purchasing departments which utilize market information to the fullest extent.

MARKET OUTLOOK
The Need

Buyers and sellers not only engage in transactions but also have to make plans regarding future production and consumption activities. These plans depend upon estimates of the price at some time in the future. For example, farmers occasionally have to know what the best guess is for prices at some future point in time so that they may plan on the number of acres or animals which they wish to take on for growing purposes. Thus, it becomes necessary to make some type of forecast as to what the future economic situation will be for purposes of current planning.

Large companies may have marketing departments that are engaged in forecasting activities, but individual farmers and consumers are not in the position to make such forecasts. Accordingly, the U.S. Department of Agriculture, through its Economic Research Service (ERS), regularly surveys the situation in each of the several products to determine the likelihood of price increases or decreases at future points in time. The ERS then reports its conclusions so that individual farmers and agribusiness people can engage in planning activities. This information is found in a number of market situation outlook reports issued by the U.S. Department of Agriculture and modified and made available for state conditions by state Agricultural Extension Services throughout the country. This outlook of the U.S. Department of Agriculture and related agencies is the institutionalized procedure of forecasting economic variables that are useful or needed by farmers and the agribusiness sector.

Procedures Involved in the Preparation of Agricultural Outlook

Much of agricultural outlook is directed toward information on the probable price, production, and income for specific commodities. It may be short term (for the remainder of the season) or long term (for a period of a year or more). One might consider three components in this process: (1) obtaining data on relevant variables; (2) analyzing this information through use of economic and statistical models; and (3) dissemination of the information. The following paragraphs describe in somewhat more detail the procedures involved in "working-up" outlook.

Obtaining data on the relevant variables implies that the analyst has a good idea of the actual production and marketing activities for the product. It also implies that the analyst is familiar with the basic economic operation of the markets for the product. Knowledge of these two aspects of the product permit useful classification of the variables as well as determining if and when they are significant. Thus, last year's price of potatoes may be quite significant in determining production for this year before the crop is planted. Once planted, however, last year's price ceases to be of importance for determining this year's supply. In fact, the acres planted now become inputs or data for outlook work throughout the remainder of the season for the current crop.

The kinds of data used in outlook future supply and demand include all those factors previously described in the demand and supply chapters as well as a few that we have not explicitly considered.

Demand indicators include:

1 Domestic population
2 Level of consumer disposable income
3 Level of employment
4 Per capita consumption rates for specific commodities
5 Shifts in consumers' tastes and preferences for food and fiber products
6 Prices of competing products
7 Foreign demand [both commercial and government subsidized][3]

Factors to be considered in analyzing supply are:

1 Farmer intentions to produce
2 Expected product prices
3 Prices of competing commodities
4 Government production controls [if in effect]

[3]W. B. Sundquist and L. M. Day, "Problems in 'Working-Up' Outlook," *Minnesota Farm Business Notes,* no. 421, Agricultural Experiment Station, University of Minnesota, Sept. 1960, p. 2.

5 Expected yields
6 Acreages available for planting
7 Production costs
8 Livestock numbers on farms
9 Past marketings[4]

The above data are obtained from a wide variety of sources. Crop and Livestock Reporting Services of each state and the Statistical Reporting Service of the U.S. Department of Agriculture provide numerous series of data on the agricultural sector. The data and statistics on the general economy are available from various divisions of the U.S. Department of Commerce. Publications of the banking system and some private agencies may also be useful data sources. Depending upon the commodity, the analyst may still be unable to locate data on all variables relevant to the outlook preparation.

Making the Forecasts

The making of forecasts, given the preceding data and accurate measures of relationships among the variables in the agricultural sector, may at first glance appear to be a rather routine procedure. In fact, it would be somewhat similar to the procedure described for demand evaluation in Chapter 4. For a given change or expected change in per capita income, we can apply the income elasticity for a product to determine the impact on per capita consumption. Population growth rates can be applied to determine the growth in total demand. To the extent that other variables are measurable and the relationship to demand is known, further refinement in the forecast can be made.

Outlook does not always involve rigorous quantitative techniques. In many cases, data are not available and exact relationships are not known. In other cases, the analyst may have neither the time nor the expertise to undertake refined statistical and economic analysis. Consequently, the methods of forecasting differ in use of quantitative techniques. Thomsen and Foote grouped the forecasting methods according to the use of quantitative techniques:

1 The "hunch" method, which is more of an intuitive feel for market supply and/or demand changes
2 Mechanistic forecasting, which is the use of quantitative statistical measurements and measured relationships between supply and demand factors
3 A combination of mechanistic forecasting and personal judgment[5]

The hunch method of forecasting is widely used by market traders, farmers, and economists who prepare outlook materials. It may appear to be a guess, but it probably involves considerable intuitive feel for the markets. Although he or she may be unable to express clearly the reasons that lead to a particular

---

[4]Ibid.
[5]F. L. Thomsen and R. J. Foote, *Agricultural Prices,* 2d ed., McGraw-Hill, New York, 1952, p. 341.

forecast, the forecaster may observe that prices, production, or marketings will behave in a certain manner when certain conditions are present.

The mechanistic approach to forecasting requires that one have a knowledge of the supply and demand relationships for the product. These quantitative measures would have been obtained by the methods briefly described in Chapters 4 and 5 (demand and supply estimations). By inserting the values of the factors determining supply and demand, one can estimate the quantities and price for the period or periods in the future.

The reader may have already observed that mechanistic or formula forecasting requires forecasts of the determinants of the supply or demand. Unless the determinants are all lagged variables (that is, their values have been determined in past periods for which we have observations), the techniques are less precise than the quantitative procedures would imply.

Because of the preceding problem, most forecasts or outlooks involve a combination of the formula or mechanistic approach and judgment. The formula expression of the relationships permits one to express the relationships as they were in the past and to project into the future.

> It remains for the forecaster to determine by judgment the extent to which these relationships may change in the future and to allow for the influence of the many irregular or immeasurable factors which have not been taken into account in the statistical analysis.[6]

If one were to select a commodity—for example, hogs—forecasting prices and output by a formula approach with judgment might involve some of the following steps.[7]

1 List and analyze the relevant determining variables and their net relationships to the variables forecast—price and output. The net relationship of the relevant variables is often available from studies by academic and government economists.

2 Obtain values to the extent possible for the determining variables considered above. Sometimes these variables are lagged so that current values determine prices and outputs in the future. Values of other variables must be assumed or are forecast by other analysts.

3 Using the models indicated in 1 and the values of predetermined variables, make preliminary estimates of annual levels of output and price.

4 Analyze past trends and cycles in the price and output levels. Use these results to adjust forecasts for points in the cycle and trend movements.

5 Make adjustments for any unusual factors or conditions that may affect the results. This may require judgment for many of the factors that were not quantifiable. For example, "How is the sodium nitrate scare affecting demand for pork?" "What will be the impact of new trade agreements?"

---

[6]Thomsen and Foote, op. cit., pp. 343–344.
[7]Based on Thomsen and Foote, op. cit., pp. 344–346.

6 If available, check the results of the procedure with similar analyses for inconsistencies in techniques or results.

7 If price and marketing forecasts are being made for periods within the year, additional analysis is required. This will require analysis or knowledge of past or normal seasonal patterns in marketings and prices.

The above list is by no means a catalog of all steps that may be involved in preparing an outlook report. It does indicate some of the procedures that the U.S. Department of Agriculture and the state agricultural extension specialists use in preparing outlook materials.

Dissemination of Outlook

A key agency in the dissemination of much of the agricultural outlook is the state agricultural extension services. They use mailings of outlook reports, local meetings, radio, and television. Farm magazines, newspapers, and other media often pick up and report these forecasts. A major publication of the U.S. Department of Agriculture that provides short-term outlook on a wide variety of agricultural products, the agricultural sector, and related parts of the economy is *Agricultural Outlook,* which is published monthly.

ADVERTISING

As indicated earlier, market information may be obtained from sellers or independent governmental agencies with respect to prices, quantities, qualities, delivery date, and risk assumptions. Information provided by the seller is frequently in the form of advertising information. Firms marketing agricultural products advertise very actively. It was estimated in 1964 that corporate food organizations alone spent over $2 billion for advertising purposes. This type of advertising is of two forms.

First, there is advertising conducted by groups of firms that attempt to promote a particular line of product rather than individual products of specific firms. This is sometimes referred to as *generic advertising.* Examples of this type of advertising include efforts made by trade associations and proceeds from state checkoff legislation that attempt to promote greater use of milk, beef, lamb, and other broad categories of product. Checkoff legislation provided through state governmental agencies frequently promotes the products of particular states or regions as being somehow superior to those of other regions. The effort, of course, is an attempt to encourage an increase in demand for the broad categories of products (see Figure 11-2).

The second form that advertising takes is promotion of the products of individual firms. In this case, firms not only try to increase the demand for their product but also attempt to make the demand for their product more inelastic (see Figure 11-3). Through advertising persuasiveness, if individual consumers or buyers can be made to feel that the product of an individual firm is far superior for their needs than that of another firm, it will take a substantial

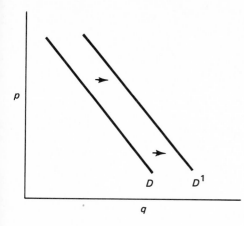

Figure 11-2 Nonbrand institutional advertising attempts to increase the demand for food products.

price differential to encourage the purchaser to shift allegiance to the product of the other firm.

Although promotion is used to a great extent by American enterprises, there is no unanimity of opinion as to its proper role in society and especially in agriculture. There are some who think that promotion will not be effective in increasing total consumption of agricultural products. This is based on the belief that cross elasticity of demand between food and nonfood products is low; therefore, it would be unlikely that promotion has the power to shift the complex relationship between two diverse families of products.

Proponents of food promotion think that total consumption can be increased because thousands of individuals and families have diets that do not provide adequate quantity or quality of food. It is possible to increase utilization of resources considerably without increasing the total pounds of food consumed per capita. An increase in consumption of foods which requires more resources in their production, such as red meats and poultry, would have this result. Six to seven times as much land is needed to produce a given number of food calories in the form of meats, eggs, milk, and dairy products as to produce the same number of calories in the form of wheat, vegetable fats, sugar, potatoes, and beans. Nutritionists indicate that there are limits to this direction too, but promotion can still be beneficial to many whose diets are currently deficient in animal products.

Probably the most widely held opinion by agricultural economists is that the advertising of food products is of limited or negative value. The opinion of these agricultural economists, however, apparently is not shared by farmers and by the agribusiness sector. Farmers themselves spend in excess of $200 million dollars each year for promotional purposes. These self-help efforts by farmers are designed to expand demand. Agriculturally oriented groups engaged in promotional activities may be broadly classified into two categories —commodity promotion groups and marketing cooperatives. One of the major characteristics of commodity groups is that promotion is usually their only function. Since they generally do not perform other marketing activities

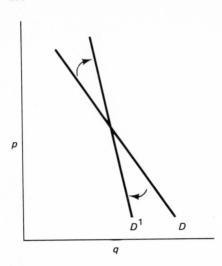

Figure 11-3 Brand advertising attempts to make the demand curve more inelastic.

involved in moving the product from producer to consumer, they have the advantage of specialization. But they are at a disadvantage in the task of integrating their activities with other important elements of marketing strategy, such as deciding on the price, quality, and supply which are related to the success of promotion. Nevertheless, industry groups have shown some benefits from these programs.[8]

One of the serious problems in developing new knowledge on promotion is devising a technique for measuring effectiveness of promotional activities. It is difficult to measure the net benefits gained from a specific promotional campaign because, at any given time, consumer and purchasing behavior is the result of many factors other than promotion. Availability and price of the product, competitive behavior of substitute products, seasonal factors, incomes, and that most elusive element, psychological "whims" of the consumer, are but a few of the factors influencing purchasing behavior. Many attempts have been made to measure the effects of promotion. These range from surveys of consumers' awareness and attitudes to various kinds of analyses of sales data. Consumer studies are usually designed to measure the number of people reached by the promotion, the degree of their awareness of the program, and the resulting changes in their attitudes. These studies help to improve the promotional approach, but they are limited in that very little is known about translating consumer awareness or attitude changes into sales and price response, which is the objective of promotion. Therefore, the trend has been to give more emphasis to various kinds of sales and price analyses.

The Federal Trade Commission (FTC) is a regulatory body that, among other trade practice regulations, focuses attention on advertising of all products.

---

[8]The United Dairy Industries Association and its predecessor associations have for years supported industrywide advertising of milk products. They have also attempted to measure the impact of various levels of advertising expenditures.

In more recent years, a number of regulatory laws have been passed that supplement the FTC's basic authority to permit it to be much more effective against misrepresentation of products by sellers. For example, if television or other media advertising provides misinformation to consumers and this is proven by the FTC through hearings, the FTC can now require the firm who issued the inaccurate information to spend an equal amount of money in the same advertising media to correct the erroneous information provided earlier. This has been a very effective technique and probably will be more fully utilized in the future. The FTC also regularly challenges the claims made by individual firms and has forced a degree of moderation into advertising verbiage, to the benefit of consumers.

SUMMARY

The rational buyer will engage in a *search* for price information prior to purchase in anticipation of realization of some savings. It is clear that the marginal costs of that search should become equal to the marginal expected savings before a purchase decision is made.

Market news is needed for the day-to-day buying and selling decisions of market participants. In agriculture, it is provided by private market news services, buyers or sellers themselves, commodity exchanges, and by the U.S. Department of Agriculture, Market News Service. This price and quantity information together with product grades that reflect value differences for each product is necessary for a well-functioning competitive market.

Economic outlook is the process of providing forecasts of future levels of any of a number of economic variables. In agriculture, much of the outlook is aimed at forecasts of farm prices, production, and demand. This kind of information is useful to those making both short-run and long-run production and marketing decisions. The agricultural extension services of the respective states have an important role in developing and disseminating agricultural outlook.

Advertising is a type of market information. It may provide buyers with useful information for making economic decisions, for example, weekly newspaper ads on best buys at local retail food stores. On the other hand, much advertising is aimed at persuading consumers that brand X is better than brand Y, often on the basis of some unsubstantiated claims. Farmers seem to be convinced that generic advertising, or industrywide advertising of a product, is of benefit since they annually expend large sums of money to support these programs. In spite of the necessity of advertising to individual firms or to individual industries, the net effect on all industries and firms is probably small.

QUESTIONS

1 It is sometimes difficult to assess whether price dispersion exists for a uniform product or whether we are dealing with a differentiated product. What is meant by the term *product differentiation?* Are some price differences justified? Why or why not?

2   Describe how a market for a product that you select would operate if there were no market information systems. Assume large numbers of buyers and sellers.

3   Distinguish market news from market outlook with respect to the use that will be made by farmers and processors of farm commodities.

4   What procedures are involved and what information is necessary for the preparation of outlook reports?

5   What are the differences in objectives and probable consequences of industrywide advertising programs and advertising programs of the individual firms?

6   What are the advantages and/or disadvantages of a government-operated market news service as opposed to private market news services?

BIBLIOGRAPHY

Collins, Norman: "Changing Role of Price in Agricultural Marketing," *Journal of Farm Economics,* vol. 41, no. 3, Aug. 1959.

Egertson, K. E., and L. J. Pickrel: "How Outlook Gets to You," *Minnesota Farm Business Notes,* no. 421, Agricultural Experiment Station, University of Minnesota, Sept. 1960.

Jensen, H. R., and K. H. Thomas: "Use of Outlook in Farm Decision Making," *Minnesota Farm Business Notes,* no. 421, Agricultural Eperiment Station, University of Minnesota, Sept. 1960.

Stigler, George: "The Economics of Information," *Journal of Political Economy,* vol. 69, no. 3, June 1961.

Sundquist, W. B., and L. M. Day: "Problems in 'Working-Up' Outlook," *Minnesota Farm Business Notes,* no. 421, Agricultural Experiment Station, University of Minnesota, Sept. 1960.

Thomsen, F. L., and R. J. Foote: *Agricultural Prices,* 2d ed., McGraw-Hill, New York, 1952.

U.S. Department of Agriculture, *Major Statistical Series of the U.S. Department of Agriculture, How They are Constructed and Used,* vol. 10, *Market News,* Agricultural Handbook 118, Agricultural Marketing Service, 1960.

Chapter 12

Market Structure Analysis

The prices charged by firms for their products, the nature and extent of their research and development activities, the type of product advertising, and the selling techniques that firms employ are all influenced by the *structure* of the markets in which they deal. This chapter defines the several types of market structure that exist in our economy and presents examples of each type as it is found in the food and fiber system.

INTRODUCTION

As indicated in Chapter 1, a market consists of one or more buyers and one or more sellers. Accordingly, there are two *sides* to the market—the buyer side and the seller side. The relationship among sellers and among buyers is called the *competitive relationship*. This refers to the ways in which firms interact and react to the actions of one another at the same level of the marketing system. All feed dealers, for example, interact with one another in trying to sell their individual products in greater quantity and at more favorable prices than other firms who offer similar products on the market. The relationship between feed sellers is referred to as a competitive relationship and may be characterized by price changes, advertising, and various types of selling strategies.

The relationship that exists between buyers and sellers is referred to as the *negotiative relationship*. This across-the-market relationship is characterized by the actions and interactions of buyers and sellers. For example, feed dealers have a relationship with farmers who purchase their product. This is a transaction relationship in which the forces of supply and demand are at work through the activities of the market participants. It is characterized by an exchange process whereby the farmer shows the intent to purchase a product and the seller expresses the offer to sell. Once there has been an initial contact, there may be subsequent offers and counteroffers until the "terms of trade" have been agreed upon by both parties. These terms of trade include the price at which the products are exchanged, the time and place of delivery, information about the nature of the product and whether or not product inspection needs to take place, as well as other items unique to the product and the transaction procedure.

Competitive and negotiative relationships may be viewed as individual in character (how firm *a* interacts with firm *b*) or aggregative across the whole market (how all firms interact). The factors that influence individual competitive or negotiative relationships are very numerous and difficult to categorize. The aggregative relationships among buyers and/or sellers are frequently referred to as *market conduct*. This refers to patterns of behavior that enterprises follow in relation to their markets. It includes the methods employed by groups of firms in determining price and output, sales promotion policies, policies that are directed at altering the nature of the product sold, and various selling tactics that are employed to achieve specific market results.

Market Structure Characteristics

The conduct of firms in a market environment is heavily influenced by certain features of that market. These features, or characteristics, are several and unique to the product and institution involved. But there are four market structure characteristics that are mutually important determinants of the type of conduct that prevails in all markets. These include: (1) number and size of firms; (2) nature of the product (as viewed by the buyers); (3) entry and exit conditions; and (4) status of knowledge about costs, prices, and market conditions among the participants.

It should be intuitively clear that the number of firms in the market will influence how the firms behave. The extreme example of a single seller versus a market environment where there are numerous sellers demonstrates this phenomenon. A single firm may conduct itself in such a manner as to maximize its total profits without concern about other firms trying to undercut that price. But where few firms exist in a market situation, each firm is striving to increase its share of the market and may use a number of sales tactics, including price cutting, to achieve this result. Accordingly, the market conduct of the two different situations is in contrast.

A second market structure characteristic of particular importance is the nature of the product in the eyes of the buyer. Some products are standardized (homogeneous). Most buyers feel that the products of one seller are virtually no different than those of another seller. For example, a farmer selling wheat will find it difficult to convince grain merchandizers that his or her wheat is any better than another farmer's wheat, except as would be measured by obvious grade differences. Wheat, when purchased at the farm level, is usually regarded as a standardized product.

The purchase by farmers of different feed formulations offers up an illustration where products are not regarded as standardized in a market situation. Various feed companies emphasize that their particular feed has unique nutritional characteristics and that the "quality" of the product is guaranteed by the brand name that they sell under. Much of this feed is physically different, most frequently in very modest ways. But it is also true that some branded formula feeds sold to farmers may not exhibit physical differences. However, the important consideration is not whether the feeds are in fact physically different. What is significant is that the feeds are *different in the eyes of the buyers*. As long as farmers think that the feeds are different, they are willing to pay different prices. When products and/or services are distinguished from one another in the eyes of the buyer through actual product variations or imagined differences, this is referred to as *product differentiation*. Where product differentiation exists, it is possible for firms selling differentiated products to act like small monopolies. The firms need not fear that an undercutting price will completely erode the market for their product. Thus, the nature of the product helps to determine the type of behavior that can be anticipated in market situations.

Entry and exit conditions and market information are closely related to the two characteristics indicated above. Entry and exit conditions refer to the ability of firms to enter or leave a market. There are definite barriers that might exist. For example, products that are patented cannot be produced and sold by firms other than the firm who holds the patent for a period of 17 years. In addition to patents, there may be other legal regulations that restrict firm entry (market order definitions) or encourage entry (the antitrust laws). Other factors that may influence entry and exit include absolute cost advantages held by existing firms, unique managerial or technical competence held by existing firms, or absolute entry costs that are prohibitive. An example of the latter is the capital requirements associated with substantial undertakings in the steel industry.

Market knowledge refers to information held by market participants (buyers and sellers) that permit them to make informed decisions in the market environment in which they operate. It is believed that buyers or sellers will make more rational decisions if they have useful information at their disposal. For example, industry employs specialists who are engaged in purchasing (purchasing agents). Their job is to be informed about the quality attributes as well as prices of a large number of raw material products used by the firms that hire them. Unfortunately, only larger businesses can afford to hire such specialists. Smaller firms and consumers usually have to make decisions with less than adequate information. This is particularly serious when we look at consumer market situations. Consumers entering the modern-day supermarket have to choose from among approximately 7,000 different items in making their choices of food products and

Table 12-1   Market Structures in the Food and Fiber Systems

Structural characteristic			
Number of firms	**Nature of product**	**Market structure**	
		Seller side	**Buyer side**
Many	Standardized	Pure competition	Pure competition
Many	Differentiated	Monopolistic competition	Monopsonistic competition
Few	Standardized	Pure oligopoly	Pure oligopsony
Few	Differentiated	Differentiated oligopoly	Differentiated oligopsony
One	Unique	Monopoly	Monopsony

services. It is obvious that no single person can be technically knowledgeable about all the products that could be purchased. This person is certainly not aware of the different prices that exist at this supermarket in comparison with other supermarkets in the near vicinity. While authorities disagree as to the amount of savings that could be achieved by greater information in the marketplace, it is clear that such savings do exist. But market knowledge extends beyond information concerning prices and technical product quality. It also includes knowledge of the actions that competitors and negotiative firms take, as well as reasonably informed judgments about future market conditions. It should be clear that as the number and size of firms vary, so does the market knowledge of firm participants.

Of the several characteristics listed previously, the two most important are the numbers of firms and the nature of the product. These two market structure characteristics can be used to delineate 10 important market structures that exist in the U.S. economy and in the food and fiber sector (see Table 12-1).

Market Structures

Where there are many firms on the seller side of the market that produce and sell a product which is standardized in the eyes of the buyers, we have a market situation which is referred to as *pure competition*. A purely competitive market is also characterized as one that has virtually no barriers to entry or exit. The level of market knowledge is used to distinguish between pure and perfect competition. Pure competition exists where the three characteristics noted above have been satisfied. Where full market knowledge (perfect knowledge) also exists, we have a condition of *perfect competition*. The same term—pure competition—is used on the buyers' side of the market where there are many buyers purchasing a standardized product. Pure competition is most closely illustrated by the farming sector. There exists a large number of farmers selling standardized products and there is a reasonable degree of freedom of entry and exit from the farming enterprise. Farmers also illustrate the buyers' side of the market in their purchase of certain standardized items, such as anhydrous ammonia, soybean meal, and so forth.

Where there are many firms selling differentiated products, we have a case of *monopolistic competition*. A number of farm-supply retail industries exemplify this type of market structure. The retail feed firm mentioned above is one example. There are many retail feed firms located throughout animal raising areas of the country that sell a differentiated product (in the eyes of the buyer) as branded formula feeds and feed supplements. The farmers on the buyers' side of the market offer up a good example of *monopsonistic competition* in their purchase of feed. There are many who buy a product that is slightly differentiated in their own eyes.

Where a few firms exist which sell a standardized product, we have the case of *pure oligopoly*. The most classic case of the pure oligopolists in agricultural markets may be the exporters of standardized agricultural products to various foreign markets. There are only a few exporting firms selling a homogeneous product. In most cases, the countries or companies purchasing from U.S. exporters represent an example of *pure oligopsony*.

Where there are a few firms selling differentiated products, we have the market situation referred to as *differentiated oligopoly*. The most common examples given for this type of structure in the U.S. food and fiber system are cigarette manufacturers. There are only a few such firms selling a highly differentiated product (cigarettes and other tobacco items). To the extent that these cigarette manufacturers sell directly to large chain stores, the chain stores represent an example of the *differentiated oligopsony* side of the market.

One firm selling a unique product is a *monopoly*. A monopoly is also characterized by completely blocked entry conditions and the continued efforts to keep the market to itself. An example of monopoly may best be characterized by the legalized monopoly power permitted under market order legislation. It is possible, for example, for a group of dairy producers to band together for purposes of fixing the prices at which their product is sold as if they were one large firm. To the extent that the market order which permits them to do this covers a specific geographic area, those firms or individuals purchasing milk in that area are dealing with a virtual monopolist. As we shall see later, monopoly is not necessarily always bad. Monopolies created under market orders, because they are regulated, may not achieve the high profits and inefficiencies normally associated with this type of market structure. *Monopsonies,* where one buyer exists for a product, is most common in the food and fiber sector on a smaller geographic level. There may be only one purchaser of farm products in certain highly dispersed farming areas. This one buyer thus has a negotiative edge over all those sellers with whom he or she deals. Again, the monopsonist can retain his or her position only by blocking the entry of other buyers in the market in which the monopsonist operates.

There are other market structures worthy of note in addition to the 10 indicated in Table 12-1. A very common market structure throughout the U.S. economy is a mixture of pure competition and pure oligopoly. It is common to have a market situation where there are a few very large firms on the selling or buying side of the market, but with the addition of many smaller firms who operate in the same markets as well. This type of market structure is sometimes referred to as an *oligopoly with competitive fringe*. In some cases, markets may exist where there are only two buyers or two sellers. In the case of two buyers, we refer to this as *duopsony;* the case of two sellers is referred to as a *duopoly*. It should be noted that the suffix "-poly" refers to the seller and "-sony" refers to the buyer. Similarly, the prefix "oli-" denotes few, "mono-" means one, and "duo-" refers to two. Where one seller faces one buyer in a negotiative relationship, this is referred to as *bilateral monopoly*.

MARKET STRUCTURE IN FOOD AND FIBER

The essence of the foregoing discussion is that two factors permit us to separate the several market structures that operate in reality. Each structure is different in that the conduct of firms in the market varies and the result of this behavior has social significance.

Let us now review the price equilibrium conditions for each of the several market structures discussed. In so doing, we will identify two *product performance* characteristics of these structures that will be further studied in a subsequent section.

Farmers, Consumers, and Pure Competition

For many products, farmers tend to represent the classic example of pure competition on the seller side of the market. They sell a standardized product (wheat is wheat) and there are many farmers who are engaged in producing and selling this product.

Given this market structure, let us examine the behavior of the "purely competitive" farmer in the production and selling activities. Farmers, like all firm managers, are faced with some basic costs in producing a product. As indicated in an earlier chapter, firms must pay *fixed* and *variable costs* in production, and the *average* and *marginal costs* involved help to determine the amount of product that will be produced.

The price at which purely competitive sellers transact their sales is constant regardless of the number of units sold. Farmers can sell 250 bushels of wheat at $3 per bushel or they can sell 25,000 bushels at the same price. The unique characteristic of pure competition is that the individual producer is unable to influence market price by his or her actions alone. For the farmer, the "price" represents the demand for his or her product, and it is constant over the range of the farmer's production possibilities.

This situation is depicted in Figure 12-1. The farmer's costs of production are represented by the average cost (AC) and marginal cost (MC) curves. The fact that the market price is the same as the demand curve is indicated by the $d = P = MR$ horizontal line. In this representation, the farmers would produce the quantity OQ_1, where marginal cost equals marginal revenue.

The example provided represents a long-run equilibrium for the purely competitive firm. If prices were higher than indicated, more firms would enter the industry until MC = MR = AC. If the market price were lower, firms would exit until this relationship held.

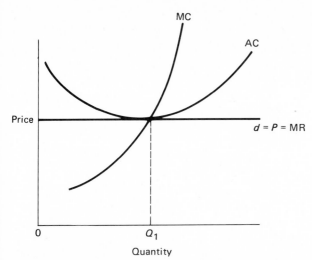

Figure 12-1   Long-run equilibrium for the purely competitive firm.

It should be noted that in such a market situation, the behavior of the pure competitor is restrained in producing and selling the product. Since the farmer has no influence in the market (lacks "market power"), the farmer can affect his or her income position *only* by reducing the costs of production. The selling behavior of the farmer is characterized as a *price taker*. The farmer simply accepts the price offered in the market.

It should also be noted that the purely competitive firm operates at the lowest point on the average cost curve. Thus, where the scale of operation suggests the existence of many firms, pure competition represents the most efficient market structure of the several presented in the earlier part of this chapter.

The consumer represents an example of pure competition on the *buyer side* of the market. There are many consumers and some of the commodities purchased are fairly standardized items. Many consumers, for example, recognize that graded milk is a standardized product regardless of the brand name. In its purchase any one consumer cannot influence the price of milk.

Farm-input Retailing and Monopolistic Competition

Products for the same use are *differentiated* if those who buy them consider the product of one firm different from the product of another firm. Products are differentiated by the variation of actual physical qualities. They are also differentiated in cases where buyers can be made to *believe* that they are different, even if they are not.

An example may be found in livestock feed. The feed concentrate sold by one firm may be physically different from that sold by another firm, but even if it is not the feed companies involved may encourage farmer-buyers to believe that some difference exists. To the extent that feed companies are successful, farmers are willing to pay different prices for feed offered by different companies.

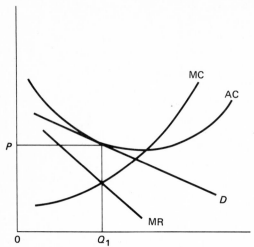

Figure 12-2   Long-run equilibrium and monopolistic competition.

Through differentiation, small firms may be able to operate like *monopolists*. They face the same AC and MC cost constraints as pure competitors. But because their product is different from other firms, they *each* face a downward-sloping demand curve. This means that they must accept lower prices for additional units offered in order to sell more product.

This situation for the feed dealer (monopolistic competition) is illustrated in Figure 12-2. AC and MC represent the traditional cost picture, but $D \neq P \neq MR$. The demand curve D is downward sloping, marginal revenue is below that, and price is determined by the intersection of MC and MR. The quantity produced by this individual monopolistic competitor is OQ_1.

It should be noted that the feed dealer's situation differs markedly from the pure competitor. The feed dealer *can* influence market price by changing products, advertising, or through sales promotion activities. Like the pure competitor, the feed dealer also tries to reduce costs. But to influence price the feed dealer must spend money to alter his or her product or to promote sales. Accordingly, there is a tradeoff involved. The monopolistic competitor expends extra costs in differentiating his or her product to the point where the extra returns from sales promotion and product development are equal.

Firms that "compete" in such a market will enter and exit the industry until the individual demand they face is tangent to the AC curve. At this point, profit is zero. But it should be noted that it is not the most efficient level of production; the lowest average cost is not achieved. Defenders of monopolistic competition argue that this inefficiency is offset by the tendency of firms to develop new products.

The farmer-buyer of differentiated feed products is subject to ranging prices; each feed is priced differently. Interestingly, the buyer in a monopolistically competitive market is usually uninformed about the technical qualities of the product purchased. In markets where purchasers are highly informed, monopolistic competition does not exist.

Market Orders and Monopoly

Monopoly, which is defined as a single firm selling a product in a market situation, exists because other firms are unable to *enter* the market. Barriers to entry are economic and legal. Economic barriers may include prohibitive production or selling costs or outright restraints of trade. Legal barriers may include patents or laws that permit certain firms (or firm groups) to behave as monopolists in an economic sense.

As discussed more fully in Chapter 13, farmers are permitted to join together to fix prices either directly or by adjusting quantities sold. These "conspiring" firms act as a single seller in an attempt to increase returns.

A monopolist, like the pure and monopolistic competitors, has costs like those depicted in Figure 12-3. And similar to the monopolistic competitor, the monopolist faces a downward-sloping demand curve. The amount of product produced, OQ_1, is determined where MC = MR.

This market structure, unlike the competitive models previously described, permits the earning of *profit*. The difference between P_1 and P_2 is pure economic profit. But it should also be noted that the monopolist is, for his or her scale, inefficient in that operation does not take place at the lowest point on the AC curve.

In light of excess profits, inefficiency, and restraint of trade, the government does not permit the existence of monopolies except where economies can be realized to the benefit of consumers or where the income position of industry members is socially inadequate.

Marketing orders, permitted by the Agricultural Marketing Act of 1937, allow farmers to join together to sell their product. Acting in this manner, farmers will tend to operate collectively as a monopolist. They will charge the price that

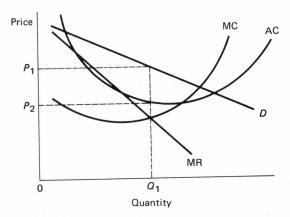

Figure 12-3 Long-run and short-run equilibrium for the monopolist.

will increase their returns even though they may not be able to maximize their profits as a single firm could.

Exporters and Oligopoly

In a market where there are few sellers, with each being able to influence market price by his or her sales, the individual oligopolist takes into account the action of other sellers in deciding upon production and selling activity. The kink in the demand curve means that each firm's competitors fail to follow the firm's price increase, but they always match its price decrease. This causes a discontinuity in the marginal revenue curve facing the individual firm (see Figure 12-4).

In the United States, exporters of grain exemplify the oligopolistic market structure. There are no more than 10 principal grain merchandisers selling in foreign markets, and they sell a highly standardized product. In much the same manner as other firms, these merchandisers face cost curves similar to those depicted in Figure 12-4.

The demand curve situation for the oligopolist, however, is different than for any other market structure situation. The oligopolist may choose among alternative strategies with regard to changing prices in a market environment. The oligopolist may choose to try to maintain his or her market share, or the oligopolist may choose to capture, or compete for, the market shares held by other oligopolists.

Given a downward-sloping demand curve for a product, the maintenance of a market share is represented by a demand curve that is parallel to the market demand curve but is leftward of it. The "share-maintenance" demand curve for individual oligopolists is represented by *dd* in Figure 12-4. It is one share of the *market* demand at each point as that curve slopes downward.

An oligopolist also can follow a competitive strategy. In this case, the oligopolist may choose to change prices, not anticipating any change in prices set by other oligopolists. Such a price change would alter the market shares held by the oligopolist. The "share-changing" demand curve for an oligopolist is represented by the demand curve DD in Figure 12-4. This curve indicates that the single-firm oligopolist would lose substantial amounts of its market share at prices above P_1. At prices below P_1, it would gain in market share.

The solid-line extension of DD above P_1 and the solid line extension of *dd* below P_1 represents the nature of the demand curve actually faced by the individual oligopolist in a market. The oligopolist who attempts to increase the price will lose his or her market shares as indicated by DD. But if the oligopolist lowers his or her price, other firms will follow the price decrease along *dd*.

This behavior pattern suggests that there is a tendency for prices to remain stable at P_1. Accordingly, prices tend to be fixed or constant over longer periods of time in oligopolistic situations than is true in other types of market structures. In the oligopolistic situation, the firm will usually produce OQ_1 and will charge OP_1. This oligopolist earns excess profits $[OP_1(OQ_1) - OP_2(OQ_1)]$. And oligopolists usually operate at volumes other than where average cost is at a minimum. Notice that OQ_1 is not at the minimum point on the AC curve.

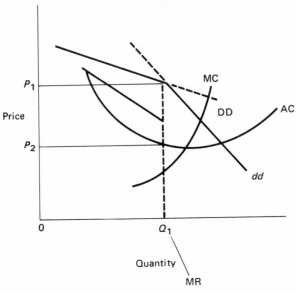

Figure 12-4   Long-run equilibrium for the oligopolist.

SUMMARY

Market structure analysis involves the study of how technical, motivational, institutional, and organizational factors influence the behavior of firms in the marketplace.

Industries have vertical and horizontal dimensions. The vertical dimension is characterized by an array of input-output-related production activities that are usually performed by different firms. The horizontal dimension refers to the total output at any level of the marketing system and the several firms that produce that product.

The number of firms and the nature of the product sold identify the market structure present. Pure competition exists where there are many firms and a standardized product. Monopolistic competition is characterized by many firms and a differentiated product. Oligopoly is characterized by the presence of a few firms. The nature of the product separates oligopoly into the pure and differentiated types. Monopoly exists when only one firm is present in a market. The suffix "-poly" denotes a seller, and the suffix "-sony" identifies the buyer side of market structures (monopsonistic competition, oligopsony, and monopsony).

In the long run, purely competitive and monopolistic competitive firms do not earn profits in the economic sense of the term. Monopolists and oligopolists can earn excess profits. Only the pure competitor operates at the lowest point on the average cost curve *by choice*. Through regulation, other firms may be made to operate more efficiently.

QUESTIONS

1 The competitive relationship is defined by the market conduct among firms that are at the same level of the marketing system. The negotiative relationship refers to the conduct of buyers with sellers and vice versa. In what way(s) is(are) the competitive and negotiative relationships similar? Different?

2 In defining the market structures of an industry, economists frequently discuss the local market separate from the national market for the same product and at the same level of the marketing system. What reasoning might underlie such a distinction?

3 Refer to Chapter 11 concerning market information. In what way(s) does(do) government policies encourage the existence of perfect knowledge in agricultural markets? What social benefits, if any, might justify this governmental expenditure?

4 The long-run equilibrium price and output solutions for the price-competitive firm and the pure oligopolist are presented in this chapter. What do you think the price would be (compared to the solutions in these models) in a market structure of oligopoly with a competitive fringe?

BIBLIOGRAPHY

Andrews, Richard: *A Study of the Sweet Corn Industry in the Midwest Farm Economy*, Technical Bulletin 232, Minnesota Agricultural Extension Station.

Blaich, O. P.: "The Theory of Vertical Structures with an Application to Hog Production," unpublished manuscript, University of Minnesota, 1961.

Chamberlin, Edward H.: *The Theory of Monopolistic Competition*, Harvard University Press, Cambridge, Mass., 1933.

Leontief, Wassily, et al.: *Studies in the Structure of the American Economy*, Oxford University Press, New York, 1953.

Nelson, Ralph: "The Nature of Competition among South Dakota Dairy Manufacturing Plants," unpublished doctoral dissertation, University of Minnesota, 1960.

Stigler, George: "The Division of Labor Is Limited by the Extent of the Market," *Journal of Farm Economics*, vol. 59, no. 3, June 1951.

Williams, Willard E.: "Structural Changes in the Meat Wholesaling Industry," *Journal of Farm Economics*, vol. 40, no. 2, May 1958.

Marketing and Pricing Institutions

INTRODUCTION

A number of institutions that are important in the pricing and marketing of agricultural products have been described and analyzed in preceding chapters. Commodity exchanges, futures markets, and grades and standards are some of the important ones that have dealt with price discovery and the time and form aspects of markets. There are two additional institutions that have particular relevance to the structure and performance of agricultural markets. They are farmer cooperatives and marketing orders. In the following sections, we will review the development of these institutions and analyze their impact on agricultural markets.

AGRICULTURAL COOPERATIVES

The Importance of Agricultural Cooperatives

Cooperatives and cooperative activity have gained wider acceptance in agriculture than in any other sector of the American economy. A few consumer cooperatives have succeeded in urban areas and consortiums for various functions are organized from time to time. But in the United States, cooperatives are most prevalent in agriculture. Agricultural cooperatives have been organized to perform several functions. Some are merely bargaining organizations which just bargain for price. Others are marketing and processing organizations where farmers jointly organize to market their product. Others provide for joint assembly and transportation to achieve lower cost in moving the product to the market. The marketing, processing, and service cooperatives have been organized to perform certain processing activities at cost to members.

Cooperatives have integrated into all levels of marketing; some cooperatives range all the way from the producer to the ultimate retailer or, in some cases, to the consumer. Dairy cooperatives such as Land O'Lakes Creameries of Minneapolis, Dairyman's League in New York State, and Challenge Creameries in the West are notable examples of complete or almost complete integration of all marketing functions.

Cooperative organization on the supply and service side of the market is also widespread. Supplies of all types are provided by these organizations to members. They include such items as farm machinery, chemicals, fertilizers, feeds, seeds, and products that are used to supply the farmer with various consumer goods and services. Electric cooperatives have been an important source of power for farmers. Cooperative credit associations have been useful in providing the farmer with funds for carrying on annual production operations. Mutual insurance companies provide farmers with fire, accident, and health insurance and casualty insurance for automobiles.

History of the Cooperative Movement

Cooperation and cooperative activity are probably as old as civilization. It is not difficult to envisage a situation in which groups of people joined together to provide themselves with some services that could not be provided by others or would not be provided by others. Perhaps by cooperation, these people or organizations provided the goods or services to themselves at lower cost than supplied by others. Records on cooperative activity in these early periods are difficult to find. Earliest records date from the Middle Ages. In London, there are some records of mutual fire insurance companies as early as 1530. The Amicable Society, a firm of this type, was organized in England in 1705. The Weavers Society in Fenwick, Scotland, began to jointly purchase goods in 1769. Many other purchasing cooperatives existed in Western Europe prior to 1800, but we have little information concerning them.[1]

One of the earliest pioneers in the cooperative movement was an Englishman, Robert Owen. He advocated the establishment of cooperative communities in which all resources were jointly owned and operated by the workers. The entire organization was based upon communal relationship and probably more closely resembles the cooperatives and collective farms in socialist countries today than anything we have in this country. Two of Owen's disciples, William King and William Bryan, established a cooperative on this basis in 1827—the

---

[1]This historical perspective is based on *Cooperation—Principles and Practices,* Circular 420, University of Wisconsin Extension Service, Madison, 1952.

Brighton Cooperative Benevolent Fund Association at Brighton, England. It was their plan that this society or trading society would gradually evolve into a communal type of organization. It disappeared in 1832. However, Dr. William King promoted the cooperative movement through a trade publication during the period of the cooperative's existence. This publication, in fact, reported the establishment of over 300 cooperatives from 1826 to 1830 in England.

Robert Owen was also closely associated with the English trade union movement, which was designed to improve the bargaining position of workers. However, the legal status of these trade unions came under attack by the courts, and hostility was directed toward the cooperative movement. This among other factors weakened the communal cooperatives and they passed out of existence in England.

Out of these earlier cooperative efforts, numerous organizations were founded. From one, we can trace the development of the modern cooperative system and philosophy. This cooperative was located in Rochdale, England. The original cooperative had failed, but its advocates, in looking over past performance, came up with a body of rules for cooperative organization and operation. Under the leadership of Howarth, these rules were used as the basis of organization for the Rochdale flannel weavers. These ideas form what we now know as the *Rochdale principles*. They are:

1 Democratic control—one member has one vote
2 Open membership—no limit on those who can enter the organization
3 A fixed limit on the return to capital
4 Distribution of returns on the basis of proportion of purchases
5 Trading on a cash basis
6 The sale of only pure and unadulterated goods
7 Providing of education to members in the cooperative way of doing business
8 Political and religious neutrality

Several of these criteria have been carried over into present-day cooperatives. It must be remembered that this organization was a purchasing organization in a less technically oriented system; therefore, principles which could easily be adhered to at that time require changes for a technologically advanced modern firm. The Rochdale cooperative rapidly became a success and similar organizations grew up in England and Scotland. Additional initiative was given to cooperative growth when Parliament passed special measures for their protection in 1846, 1852, and 1962.

The development and success of these consumer cooperatives then led to interest in wholesaling cooperatives. These were organizations designed to provide the local organizations with goods at lower costs than would be provided by others. The Rochdale pioneers took much of the leadership in organizing these wholesale firms. Because of legal limitations in what the cooperatives could do, their operations were severely limited. However, in 1862, Parliament granted to these purchasing organizations the right to federate into larger organizations. Following this, the famous Cooperative Wholesale Society Limited was formed.

The purchasing organizations were so successful that it did not take long until interest in production of the goods caught on. Cooperatives were formed for the purpose of handling perishable goods, for baking, milk pasteurization, tailoring, dressmaking, flour milling, furniture making, drug packing, leather work, tea blending, and so forth.

Cooperative credit caught on in Europe about the same time as the Rochdale pioneers were organizing their purchasing cooperative. At that time, Europe was undergoing a severe depression complicated by crop failures. Workers were unemployed, and they needed credit to buy goods and services. Crop failures were occurring in many countries. Northern Germany was particularly hard hit. In this area, F. W. Raiffeisen, the mayor of several small communities, organized loan societies to help the needy. This organization was designed to transfer assistance from those who could give it to those who were in need. The credit unions that we know today are based on the principles laid down by Raiffeisen.

Cooperation in the United States undoubtedly took many of the forms of development that it did in other countries. Most were informal types of organizations but records show that there were about 7,000 marketing cooperatives operating in 1848. The Grange sponsored many buying organizations for farmer supplies in this country during the 1870s when it was at its height. However, a favorable climate for cooperative organization did not occur until 1911 when enabling legislation was passed in California and Wisconsin. These acts became models for excluding cooperatives from restraint of trade violation. After 1911, the number of cooperatives multiplied rapidly, most of them in the Midwestern states and California.

Philosophy of Cooperation

The current philosophy of agricultural cooperation is largely based upon some of the early principles of the Rochdale pioneers. The four principles that are retained by most of our cooperatives are:

1 Democratic control of the organization (one vote per person).

2 Open membership. Many of our cooperatives still hold to the principle of open membership; however, this is being challenged in some areas, and in some cases we do have restricted membership.

3 Limited returns on invested capital. This is still a basic legal characteristic of all cooperatives. To benefit from income tax laws and to qualify as a cooperative under the Internal Revenue Act, the cooperative cannot pay a greater return than 8 percent on equity capital.

4 Distribution of returns on the basis of patronage. This principle seems to be consistently held to by cooperatives.

A number of the other characteristics of the original Rochdale cooperative have been modified. For example, the principle that all business must be done in cash is not held to by many cooperatives today. In fact, the volume of business done by each member is such that it is often impossible to do business on a cash basis alone. Furthermore, the member often needs credit in addition to goods or services, and the cooperative is an efficient way of providing the credit. That labor is provided by cooperative members is not held to today. Most of the labor in a successful cooperative is hired, and like other business organizations, it pays a comparable wage. Requiring labor to be provided by members was often one of the stumbling blocks that led to the downfall of cooperatives. This is because only a few members could or would provide labor, services, or management. Other members made no contribution to the cooperative. Thus, services of the cooperative were not supported on an equitable basis.

Other principles of agricultural cooperatives have been held to in a lesser or greater extent. The principle that requires the cooperative to use profits in fostering the cooperative movement has been generally held to. That of being politically and religiously neutral has been abused. In some cases, cooperatives take a very strong political role; in other cases, they are neutral. In regard to religion, cooperatives are generally neutral.

A few additional principles of cooperation have been developed from time to time. One principle states that dividends or returns of the business should be used to finance further expansion of the business. Many marketing cooperatives believe that they should avoid price wars, especially when they are competing among themselves. The holding of reserves for emergencies is held to by many cooperatives. There is a belief that cooperatives should merge whenever possible in order to gain efficiencies of processing or in order to achieve market power. Thus, we see some evolution of the fundamentals of agricultural cooperatives since the original principles laid down by the Rochdale pioneers.

Modifications of cooperative principles have occurred. It is probably safe to say that close adherence to the original principles has occasionally gotten many cooperatives into difficulty. The principle requiring limited return on capital has hampered cooperatives in obtaining adequate capital. This restraint is probably more important today than in the past. In the past, the main capital requirements were for land and a place to do business. At the present time, capital requirements are exceedingly high, running into the thousands and millions of dollars. The capital-labor ratio is very high, and thus the amount of financing required to keep these organizations going is tremendous. Contrast this with the situation in the early days when labor was provided by members and very little working capital was needed.

The open membership and free exit provisions for members have been a problem for cooperatives. Take the case of milk cooperatives and grain cooperatives who build facilities in order to process and market a given volume of commodity. Since they have no contract with members, the members are free to join or to leave the organization at will. This creates much uncertainty regarding the volume of the cooperative's business. As a result, many cooperatives find themselves in a situation of excess capacity. If they are extremely successful, new members will flock to them and their greater returns are dissipated among all the members.

Another way to look at cooperatives is to compare them with general business corporations. The following are the principle differences between the two types.

1 The purpose of the cooperative is to obtain a higher return for the product, to get better marketing services, or to obtain services at cost. All of these aims are sometimes combined in one cooperative. The general business corporation, on the other hand, has as its main purpose the achievement of the highest possible return on capital investment.

2 The basis of ownership differs. The cooperative is owned by those who use the services of the organization. Ownership of the corporation is not generally connected with the users but is vested in the common stockholders. It may be that some of the users of this corporation are also stockholders.

3 The control differs. In the cooperative, control is on a one-person one-vote basis—the democratic basis we have discussed earlier. In the general business corporation, control is based on the extent of ownership. The amount of capital stock determines the number of votes and therefore control of the organization. Also, in general business corporations, votes may be cast by proxy and by groups, whereas this type of activity is generally prohibited in the cooperative.

4 The distribution of returns differs. In the cooperatives, members profit on the basis of patronage with some limited control on the capital that they may own. In the general business corporation, the return is based on the amount of capital held.

5 In regard to prices and cost, cooperatives attempt to perform services on a cost basis. They attempt to make the marketing margin as narrow as possible. Inefficiencies in operation, mismanagement, or other factors can cause the margin to be no narrower than it is for the general business corporation. Nevertheless, the objective of a marketing cooperative is to obtain the highest possible price in the market for the product. The general business corporation attempts to operate on as wide a margin as possible, therefore returning a large profit to its owners. It also attempts to purchase a product from the farmer or the producer at the lowest possible cost. The supply and service cooperatives conversely try to provide service or supplies at the lowest possible price.

Business corporations and cooperatives also have similarities. The one that stands out most is that of limited liability. Limited liability means that the liability of cooperatives and corporations is not greater than the assets of the business. Creditors cannot generally go beyond the corporation in recovering debts. Both types of organizations are usually chartered by the secretary of state. Both are subject to the same laws of contract. They are subject to health and other regulations of the state or federal government; they are also subject to the fair trade and monopoly laws of the state and federal government. However, in certain instances, the ability of the cooperatives to join together and cooperate beyond the limitation of the antitrust laws is enhanced by special legislation. Furthermore, the success of cooperative organizations, like other organizations, depends upon good management striving to achieve efficiencies in operation and taking advantage of various market situations.

Legal Status of Agricultural Cooperatives

The ability of persons to organize into cooperatives in England was greatly enhanced in the 1850s by the enactment of special legislation. In this country, however, the legislation was much later in coming. In fact, passage of the Sherman Antitrust Act in 1890 made the legal status of the cooperative rather tenuous. After passage of the act, a 1,500-member farmer cooperative in Chicago was found to be in violation. Other cooperatives were subsequently charged with violation of this act. The Clayton Act in 1914 gave some exemptions to cooperatives. It exempted labor, horticultural, and agricultural associations. Courts subsequently restricted its exemptions to nonstock cooperatives. It was not until 1922, when the Capper-Volstead Act was passed, that cooperative organization was specifically exempted from antitrust violation by national legislation. However, there are limitations. One of the first major cases to clarify the positions of cooperatives regarding antitrust was the case of *United States v. Borden* (1939). Here, a labor union, a bottle exchange, a cooperative (Pure Milk Association), other distributors, and the Borden Company were found to have conspired to fix prices for milk. The cooperative claimed two statutes, the Capper-Volstead Act and the Agricultural Marketing Agreement Act of 1937, as a defense. The AMA Act allowed price fixing for milk by producers, distributors, and other interested parties in fluid milk markets if certain conditions were met. The defendants also claimed that the Capper-Volstead Act exempted them from prosecution for antitrust violation. The court decided, however, that the cooperative, though exempt, is not allowed to conspire with noncooperatives to undertake some of the activities that it did in this case. A similar decision was made more recently in the case of *Sunkist Growers v. Winkler-Smith* in 1960. These issues have been further discussed and interpreted in *Treasure Valley Potato Bargaining Association v. Ore-Ida Foods, Inc.* in 1974 and *Central California Lettuce Producers Cooperative* case in 1975. Here, the courts again stated that cooperatives could conspire among themselves to a certain extent, but that they could not conspire with noncooperatives.

There are several conditions that a cooperative must meet in order to be considered a cooperative, as defined by the Capper-Volstead Act: (1) such an association operates for the mutual benefit of members; (2) stock dividends cannot be more than 8 percent per annum; (3) no person can be allowed more than one vote; and (4) the cooperative cannot deal with nonmembers at more than 50 percent of the total volume of business of the cooperative.

Measures of Cooperative Activity

Since their initial development, cooperatives have grown to be an important part of our economy. They are important not only in numbers but in terms of the value of the commodity they handle and the services they perform. The data in Table 13-1 show that this volume continues to grow. For the period 1950–1951 to 1971–1972, the net volume of cooperative business, excluding intercooperative business, has grown to more than $13.5 billion. This represents an increase of 166 percent during that period. Even considering price increase, the cooperative volume of business has made significant advances.

The data in Table 13-1 also give the breakdown between types of cooperative business. There are three groups: farm products (also called marketing cooperatives), farm supply cooperatives, and related service cooperatives. The farm product cooperatives are by far the most important, accounting consistently for approximately three-fourths of all cooperative business. Farm supplies are next in importance, followed by related services which account for less than $1 billion of business.

Another way to measure farmer cooperative activity is the number of memberships (see Table 13-2). These data are also given for marketing, farm supply, and related service cooperatives, and are inversely related to growth in cooperative business. These numbers will vary directly with the number of farms and farmers. In terms of relative importance, marketing cooperatives are by far the most dominant. They accounted for 51 percent of total memberships for the marketing year 1971–1972. The supply cooperatives accounted for approximately 49 percent, and the related service organizations accounted for only 0.5 percent of cooperative memberships. Thus, we see that membership in supply cooperatives is much larger relative to business volume than for marketing cooperatives. As we can see, memberships in marketing cooperatives have shown about a 15 percent decline in recent years, mostly since 1965–1966. One thing to note is that memberships are much larger than the total number of farms in the country. This is because many farmers have memberships in several cooperatives. Thus, the data do not show the actual number of farmers that are members of cooperative organizations.

Data in Figures 13-1 and 13-2 indicate the relative importance of cooperatives by type of activity. Cooperatives in 1971–1972 handled 21.9 percent of the business of agricultural supply organizations.[2] The figure varies considerably from one commodity to another. By far the most important farm supply group is feed. In 1971–1972, 30 percent of all feed was purchased through cooperatives. Next in importance were petroleum products with 23 percent. For the farm marketing businesses, cooperatives were somewhat more important in total. Again, however, this varied from commodity to commodity. Cooperatives were most important in dairy marketing, accounting for 36 percent of all business. The grain soybean group is next with 23 percent, then livestock with 14 percent. Fruit and vegetables, cotton, livestock, poultry, and others had smaller percentages, although these were sizable in several instances.

[2]U.S. Department of Agriculture, *Statistics of Farmer Cooperatives, 1970–1971 and 1971–1972,* FCS Research Report 32, May 1976, p. 14.

Table 13-1 Estimated Gross and Net Volume (in Thousands of Dollars) of Business of Marketing, Farm Supply, and Related Service Cooperatives, and Percentage of Total, 1950–1951 to 1971–1972

	Gross volume (includes intercooperative business)				Net volume (excludes intercooperative business)			
Period[a]	Farm products	Farm supplies	Related services[b]	Total	Farm products	Farm supplies	Related services	Total
1950–1951	$ 7,984,777	$2,437,521	$ 99,958	$10,522,256	$ 6,361,766	$1,685,413	$ 99,958	$ 8,147,137
1955–1956	9,514,387	2,972,696	214,880	12,701,963	7,495,159	2,046,086	214,880	9,756,125
1960–1961	12,143,722	3,744,711	305,600	16,194,033	9,631,247	2,472,286	305,600	12,409,133
1965–1966	15,489,446	4,804,443	325,071	20,618,960	12,197,744	3,085,382	325,071	15,608,197
1970–1971[c]	20,118,015	6,748,989	414,299	27,281,303	15,801,872	4,339,529	414,299	20,555,700
1971–1972[c]	20,794,406	7,395,899	462,240	28,652,545	16,463,065	4,739,603	462,240	21,664,908

[a]For years prior to 1950–1951, see appendix table 7, FCS General Report 128. 1962–1963 in libraries. Data for prior years are not entirely comparable due to revisions in statistical procedures in 1950–1951.
[b]Services related to marketing or supply purchasing but not included in the volumes reported for these activities.
[c]Preliminary.
Source: U.S. Department of Agriculture, Statistics of Farmer Cooperatives, 1970–1971 and 1971–1972, FCS Research Report 32, May 1976, p. 10.

Table 13-2 Number and Percentage of Memberships in Marketing, Farm Supply, and Related Service Cooperatives, 1950–1951 to 1971–1972

Period[a]	Marketing		Farm supply		Related service		Total	
	Number	Percent	Number	Percent	Number	Percent	Number	Percent
1950–1951	4,117,950	58.1	2,878,890	40.6	94,280	1.3	7,091,120	100.0
1955–1956	4,223,260	54.6	3,443,610	44.6	64,865	0.8	7,731,735	100.0
1960–1961	3,473,425	48.2	3,679,675	51.1	49,795	0.7	7,202,895	100.0
1965–1966	3,635,605	53.3	3,154,490	46.2	36,180	0.5	6,826,275	100.0
1970–1971[b]	3,105,005	50.4	3,027,515	49.2	25,220	0.4	6,157,740	100.0
1971–1972[b]	3,133,505	51.0	2,991,240	48.7	21,805	0.3	6,146,550	100.0

[a]For years prior to 1950–1951, see appendix table 6, FCS General Report 128.
[b]Preliminary.
Source: U.S. Department of Agriculture, *Statistics of Farmer Cooperatives, 1970–1971 and 1971–1972*, FCS Research Report 32, May 1976, p. 9.

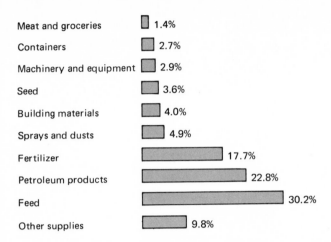

Meat and groceries   1.4%

Containers   2.7%

Machinery and equipment   2.9%

Seed   3.6%

Building materials   4.0%

Sprays and dusts   4.9%

Fertilizer   17.7%

Petroleum products   22.8%

Feed   30.2%

Other supplies   9.8%

Figure 13-1 Relative importance of major farm supplies handled by cooperatives, 1971–1972. *Source:* U.S. Department of Agriculture, *Statistics of Farmer Cooperatives, 1970–1971 and 1971–1972*, FCS Research Report 32, May 1976, p. 44.

A striking feature of the preceding data is the predominance of the cooperatives for dairy products. Why it is more important here than in other areas is not certain. One hypothesis considers that the proximity of the processing operation to milk production stimulated cooperative organization in this industry. In the past, most dairy products were processed in or near the area where the milk was produced. Producers could observe the processing firms operating in production areas and, in some cases, taking wider margins than necessary. As a result, the farmers decided that this was an area in which they should own and operate cooperative creameries, cheese factories, and other types of milk processing operations. This proximity of processing to farm production was much less for most other agricultural commodities.

The importance of cooperatives in milk marketing is not completely indicated by the above percentage for marketing cooperatives. Milk markets often have two types of cooperatives. One is a bargaining association that principally bargains for price. It may also assemble and ship the bulk milk, but it does not in any way process the milk. The second type is the handling association which actually processes the milk. It may package the fluid milk; it may process the manufactured products that are made from the surplus in this market; or it may do both. It has been estimated that cooperatives were involved in the marketing of 72 percent of the nation's milk supply in 1970. In a number of markets, we have cooperatives that are combinations of both the bargaining-type and handling-type associations. The importance of these cooperatives for 69 federal milk markets in 1962 is illustrated by the data in Table 13-3. In all of these markets, 83.7 percent of the milk was controlled by the cooperative. Bargaining cooperatives handled 32.4 percent of the milk in these markets for that year. These data show that a large part of the milk for the bargaining associations is assembled and shipped as bulk milk by the cooperative. There appears to be no consistent pattern

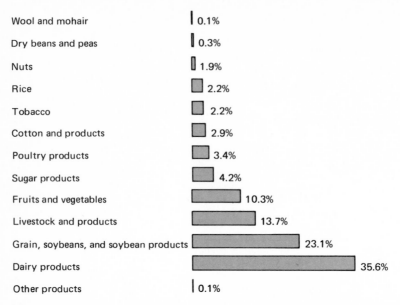

Figure 13-2 Relative importance of major farm supplies handled by cooperatives, 1971–1972. *Source:* U.S. Department of Agriculture, *Statistics of Farmer Cooperatives, 1970–1971 and 1971–1972*, FCS Research Report 32, May 1976, p. 13.

of relationships between the size of these markets and the proportion of milk handled by cooperatives. In all sizes of markets listed here, the average is roughly 80 percent of the market.

The above data, at first glance, indicate that farmer cooperatives are a predominant force in the marketing of farm products. However, another measure cited by Helmberger indicates that the actual marketing functions performed by cooperatives are rather small.[3] For 1954 and 1958, he observed that the value added by all cooperatives in food processing was 2.6 and 3.0 percent, respectively, of the value added by all food processing firms. These data, together with the other data that have been presented, suggest that farm cooperatives have made inroads in performing functions that are most closely related to the "farm gate."

Types of Agricultural Cooperatives

Cooperatives may be classified along several lines. We have already classified them as to consumer and farmer. Agricultural cooperatives have also been classified as supply, marketing, or service cooperatives. However, there are several other classifications and each may be important for analytical purposes.

Agricultural cooperatives are classified according to the following organizational characteristics.

[3]Peter Helmberger, "Future Roles for Agricultural Cooperatives," *Journal of Farm Economics,* vol. 48, no. 5, Dec. 1966, p. 1428.

Table 13-3 Percentage of Milk Deliveries by Specified Types of Cooperatives, by Size or Market, 69 Markets, 1962[a]

Size of market (million pounds)	Percentage of producer deliveries by									All cooperatives
	Bargaining associations			Handling associations			Bargaining and handling associations			
	Bargaining only	Assemble and ship bulk milk[b]	Manage surplus[c]	Package fluid milk	Process manufactured products	Fluid and manufactured	Package fluid milk	Process manufactured products	Fluid and manufactured	
Less than 8.0	17.2	26.6	12.5	4.1	—	5.0	—	17.8	1.5	84.7
8.0–15.9	17.0	39.0	0.3	0.1	2.9	10.7	3.5	8.4	—	81.5
16.0–15.9	12.5	19.0	0.8	2.6	—	6.1	0.9	33.5	9.4	84.6
24.0–59.9	8.0	21.4	0.2	0.2	2.9	5.2	1.0	25.1	23.9	87.6
60.0 or more	7.2	10.8	—	1.5	0.9	8.6	2.1	19.1	29.7	79.7
All markets	10.3	21.3	0.8	1.0	1.8	7.3	1.7	21.0	18.7	83.7

[a]Because some producers belong to two cooperatives, details may add to more than the total. Excludes Chicago and Rock River Valley for which data were not available.
[b]May or may not operate a plant.
[c]Does not operate a plant.

Source: U.S. Department of Agriculture, *Nature of Competition in Fluid Milk Markets; Market Organization and Concentration*, Agricultural Economic Report 67, Economic Research Service, Feb. 1965, p. 42.

Locals   These are usually single-unit organizations which are owned and controlled by members in the area in which the cooperative operates.

Federated cooperatives   This organization is a large multiple-unit organization which is made up of local cooperatives. Frequently, some services or goods are provided by a jointly owned facility. The control over this type of federated organization is exercised by the local members. In other words, the control is from the country plants to the centrally located facility. Savings in operations of this federated organization are then passed back to the member organizations, which in turn redistribute them to producer members.

Centralized cooperatives   This centralized organization is owned directly by producer members. It is usually a multiplant operation. The central organization manages the affairs and operates the local units. An example of this type of organization is Mid-America Dairies, which operates out of Springfield, Missouri. It has plants located in Minnesota, Wisconsin, and other Midwestern states.

Large multiple-plant cooperatives may be a mixed type of operation. That is, they contain characteristics of the federated and the centralized cooperative association. Land O'Lakes is a classic example of this type. It has many local organizations which are operated at the local country level by boards of directors. Directors from these organizations are directors of the operations in Minneapolis. On the other hand, Land O'Lakes owns and operates several processing and distribution centers at numerous locations in Minnesota and other states. This aspect of operation takes on the characteristics of a centralized organization.

A functional classification of agricultural cooperatives provides additional insight into cooperative activity. There are the electrical cooperatives which provide electricity for rural areas. There were 924 of these cooperatives in 1968. These had roughly 5 million members and the volume of business amounted to almost $1 billion.

Telephone cooperatives have become important in recent years. Like the electric cooperatives, they provide a service that has not been provided by the major companies. In 1968, there were 232 of these cooperatives. The membership, however, was not nearly as great as for the electric cooperatives. The volume of business was about $65 million.

The farm credit system is a unique type of cooperative organization. It is a government-sponsored cooperative system for providing credit to farmers and farmer-owned cooperatives. It is divided into three systems. There is a bank for cooperatives. This is an organization that is divided into 13 farm credit districts. The purpose of these organizations is to provide long-term capital financing for cooperative marketing and supply organizations. It is a major source of capital for many of our cooperative organizations.

A second division of the farm credit system is the Federal Land Bank, which provides long-term credit for farmers. It finances building purchases and major capital improvements.

The third type of farm credit system is the Federal Intermediate Credit Bank, which is composed of local production credit associations. These provide financing for productive activities and also for shorter-term activities than the federal land bank. Loans from these organizations are used to purchase livestock, feed, seed, chemicals, and fertilizer. The term of the loan is confined to a year or less.

The volume of business of the farm credit system is quite large. The volume of loans made for the year 1968 amounted to $8.4 billion.

The net assets of the farm credit system amounted to $2 billion in 1968. Most of the capital for this organization is provided by private sources. When it was originally established, government capital was the principal source of its financing. However, in 1967, only 6.5 percent of the capital structure was from government sources.

The Economics of the Agricultural Cooperative Firm

A well-established set of theories have been developed in regard to the operation of the classical business firm. The development essentially began with Adam Smith, was modified by Ricardo, Mill, and others, and was consolidated in the work of Alfred Marshall. This theory was basically one of competitive firms. Later work by Joan Robinson and Edward Chamberlin expanded this theory of the firm to imperfect markets. The question that arises here is whether the general theory of the firm, in either perfect or imperfect markets, applies to cooperative firms. Much of the early writings avoided the question. Cooperatives were analyzed from a socioeconomic basis rather than on a purely economic basis.

In terms of pure economics, one question that arose was whether the cooperative was a business entity apart from the firm or the persons which it serves. For example, one theory of farmer cooperatives is based on the assumption that the cooperative is a vertical extension of the farm firm. The farmer members of the cooperative consider their input-output decisions in light of the joint activity of their farm units and their cooperative.[4] It is probably well accepted at the present time that cooperatives, at least farm cooperatives, are entities apart from the farm production units. Various degrees of integration may occur, but, in general, input-output decisions for the two types of firms are made by different individuals with separate objectives.

If one accepts the proposition that the cooperative and the farm firm are separate entities, are the economic organization and decisions of the cooperatives similar to noncooperatives? Work by Peter Helmberger seems to provide the most solid basis for analyzing the differences and similarities between the two. The following discussion is based on his work.[5]

To consider the cooperative firm, let us first look at competitive equilibrium in terms of output and input prices. This allows us to consider how a cooperative

---

[4]Richard Phillips, "The Economic Nature of the Cooperative Association," *Journal of Farm Economics,* vol. 35, Feb. 1953, pp. 74–87. The input-output decisions for this joint firm are determined according to classical firm theory.

[5]See Peter Helmberger and Sidney Hoos, "Cooperative Enterprise and Organization Theory," *Journal of Farm Economics,* vol. 44, May 1962, pp. 275–290; and Peter Helmberger, "Cooperative Enterprise as a Structural Dimension of Farm Markets," *Journal of Farm Economics,* vol. 46, Aug. 1964, pp. 608–617.

might price a resource as opposed to a noncooperative. Let us begin by considering the application of a variable resource as it is applied to a fixed resource. As described in an earlier chapter, the output first increases over some range, reaches a maximum, and then decreases. These marginal increases in output to the variable input are known as the marginal physical productivity of the resource (MPP). This eventually declining marginal physical productivity occurs because of the principle of diminishing marginal productivity. If this increased product is sold in a competitive market (that is, the firm can have no effect on product prices), the value of the marginal product (VMP) is equal to the marginal physical productivity of the resource multiplied by the price of the product. In equation form, this may be written as

$$VMP_a = MPP_a \, (P_x)$$

It is obvious that for each level of the resource use, we have a different VMP. As with the marginal physical product, the law of diminishing productivity assures that the function eventually decreases at some level of production. This value of marginal product can be plotted graphically. Figure 13-3 shows the dollar value of output of successive unit increases in resource a. The firm will use resource a up to the point where its price is just equal to the value of marginal product VMP_a. Thus, at resource price P_1, Q_1 units of the resource will be used if the firm maximizes its profit. At price P_2, quantity Q_2 of the resource would be used. The VMP curve can also be considered to be the individual firm's demand for the resource in the short run.

Associated with any VMP curve are average revenue product curves (ARP) and net average revenue product curves (NARP). The NARP curve differs from the ARP curve only in that fixed costs are deducted from the total resource calculations. These functional relations become important in analyzing how the cooperatives operate relative to noncooperatives.

To analyze the economics of the cooperative firm, assume that the costs of production are the same for the two types of firms. Thus, they have the same VMP, ARP, and NARP curves. The firms differ in what they maximize. Instead of maximizing profits, the cooperative maximizes returns to its member producers.

With the above cost relations, suppose the competitive market price for resource a is P_1. Then the quantity taken by the noncooperative firm is Q_1. The cooperative will choose a different equilibrium point depending upon the supply curve it faces from its member producers. If the cooperative members are willing to supply the various amounts at alternative prices, as indicated by S_0 in Figure 13-3, then the cooperative can pay price P_3 for the resources and it will use quantity Q_3. This is the maximum price which can be paid and still cover all costs. The cooperative firm pays a higher price and it takes a larger quantity of the resource than the noncooperative firm. It may be that the cooperative will pay the competitive price during the marketing season and then pay the additional price as a patronage refund at the end of the year.

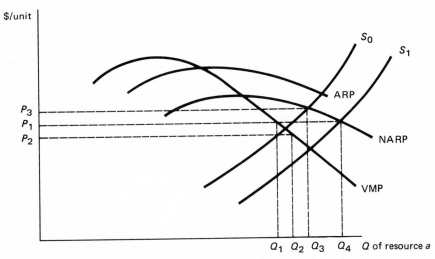

Figure 13-3 The cooperatives' revenue product and cost relationships.

The above price and quantity level is not, however, a stable equilibrium. Without some limit on the cooperative membership, producers will begin to join the cooperative. This will shift the supply curve facing the cooperative from S_0 to S_1. Consequently, the cooperative will be able to pay only the competitive price of P_1. Nevertheless, the quantity of the resource Q_4 purchased by the cooperative is considerably larger than that taken by the noncooperative at the same price.

Over part of the range of inputs, the cooperative firm and the noncooperative firm will arrive at the same price. Suppose that the market price for the resource is P_4 as in Figure 13-4. Although operating at a loss, the noncooperative will be minimizing losses by buying Q_5 units of the resource at this price. If the cooperative curve is S_2 and the cooperative attempts to cover all costs of production, it will pay less than the price of P_4. Its members will begin to leave to do business with the noncooperatives. This shifts the supply curve to the left of S_3. If the cooperative takes quantity Q_5 of the resource and pays the price of P_4, it will be making the greatest contribution to total cost at this point, and its losses will be minimized. Thus, at a competitive price (in excess of P_0 for resource a), the cooperative demand for the resource is the same as that for the noncooperative. In this case, at prices above P_0, the segment ab of the VMP curve is the cooperative's demand for the resource. Below price P_0, the NARP curve is the cooperative's demand for the resource. The noncooperative demand for the resources is that segment of the VMP curve indicated by abc.

The longer-run solution for resource price and quantity for this market for both cooperatives and noncooperatives is at a price of P_0 and a quantity of Q_0 for both types of firms. Maximum possible price for the resource will occur. Both firms will be paying the same price for the resource. In a dynamic situation, firms are seldom at equilibrium but are moving toward it. Although that equilibrium is

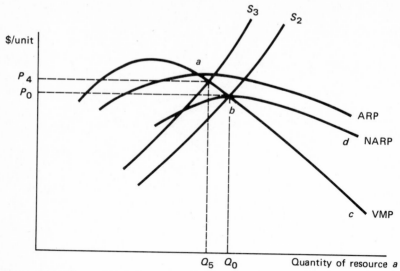

Figure 13-4 The cooperative in cost and revenue product equilibrium.

the same for cooperatives and noncooperatives, the paths they take in achieving it are different.

The previous example, though quite limited, illustrates that traditional concepts can be used to analyze the price and output behavior of cooperatives. For the processing cooperatives, short-run disequilibrium of positions can provide an incentive for cooperative organization. It offers a higher price for the resource than the noncooperative and it takes larger quantities of that resource. The demand of cooperatives for a resource is illustrated by segment *ab* of the VMP curve and segment *bd* of the NARP curve in Figure 13-4. Under very restricting assumptions, horizontal summation of these curves for all firms, cooperatives, and noncooperatives can yield industry demand curves for a given resource.

The implication of the above is that, in a dynamic setting, cooperatives can provide greater or equal returns to larger numbers of producers than noncooperative firms. In the long run, output and price decisions of the two will tend to be the same level. One may also conclude that the existence of cooperatives in the agricultural marketing and processing industries tends to assure more competitive performance than would otherwise occur. In the case of the processing cooperative, prices for purchased inputs would be higher than without the cooperative.

The theory indicates that there are no long-run differences in competitive markets between cooperatives and noncooperatives in regard to prices and outputs. The same does not apply to monopsonistic markets. Their excess profits persist even in the long run. Cooperative enterprise will result in higher producer prices as the cooperative pays these monopsonistic profits to producers. If membership is not restricted, output will also be greater and consumer prices at retail will also be lower.

MARKET ORDERS AND AGREEMENTS
Historical Background

Since the early 1930s, various state and federal statutes have authorized what might be termed as self-help programs for producers of specified agricultural commodities. These laws, unlike many other agricultural regulations, do not set up the program, but they allow the producers to set up orders and agreements which define terms and conditions under which a commodity may be sold and marketed.

Orders and agreements differ with respect to the applicability of provisions. Market orders are binding on all producers and handlers of the commodity for which the program is established. Market agreements are binding on only signers of the agreement. Thus, orders are usually necessary to make the program work. In most federal programs, an agreement and order are issued simultaneously. If the agreement is not signed by the market participants, and is therefore not binding on them, the order does bring them under its provision.

The basic federal regulation under which orders and agreements are authorized is the Agricultural Marketing Agreements Act of 1937 and its subsequent amendments. This act grew out of earlier attempts by the federal government to allow for a kind of self-help program. The first attempt was the Agricultural Adjustment Act of 1933, which allowed for a system of licenses and agreements. Under the program, the Secretary of Agriculture issued licenses to handlers and producer associations in metropolitan milk markets to control the conditions of milk marketing and to fix producer and retail milk prices. These licenses, like market orders, were binding on all handlers of milk in the market. Already, at this early stage, it was seen that the contract had to be binding on everyone in the particular market to be effective.

Problems arose soon after the application of agreements and licenses to fluid milk markets. The constitutionality of applying the provisions to nonsigners through automatic licenses was uncertain. Furthermore, fixing of prices at all levels of the market introduced rigidities that were deemed undesirable. How and who determined the marketing margin became a problem. As a matter of policy, the Agricultural Adjustment Administration dropped the resale pricing provision of the program early in 1934. Nevertheless, enforceability of the milk licenses under the Agricultural Adjustment Act of 1933 became tenuous during the remainder of 1934. The Justice Department refused to enforce certain provisions of the licenses. Violations then became widespread as handlers refused to pay prices which were established under the licenses. In addition to problems of administering the licenses, other features of the Agricultural Adjustment Act were emasculated. The processors' tax and the supply control provisions were declared unconstitutional in the famous Hoosac-Mills decision.[6]

Under the Agricultural Adjustment Act of 1933, marketing agreements and licenses were applied to fluid milk markets, evaporated milk, dry skim, peaches,

---

[6]*United States v. Butler et al.*, 297 U.S. 1 (1936).

other fruits, vegetables, nuts, and rice. Tobacco was included under the program in 1933 and 1934 but was eliminated by 1935. By the fall of 1935, 65 agreements had been put into effect, but many had been terminated.[7]

In 1937, the license and agreement provisions of the Agricultural Adjustment Administration program was reenacted in the Agricultural Marketing Agreements Act. Orders were substituted for licenses and the types of control were more clearly specified. The products which could be included under the program were listed. An amendment to the act in 1963 authorized the use of agreements and orders for any commodity other than those specifically excluded.

In general, the regulations do not provide for supply control at the farm, with the exception that the Agricultural Act of 1965 did authorize a limited form of supply control for milk. The supply control feature is not mandatory and it is utilized only after appropriate administrative procedures.

Many states authorize the use of marketing orders and agreements. In 1966, 25 states had programs similar to the federal order program for regulating the marketing of milk. These programs deal primarily with establishment of prices for milk. In many instances, the state and federal government jointly regulate the marketing of milk. The federal program, however, has the advantage that its authority extends across state lines. With milk supply areas for fluid markets often encompassing parts of several states, it can be seen that state regulations could be of limited usefulness.

Marketing orders and agreements for fruit and vegetables were provided for in the enabling legislation of 10 states as of 1965.[8] As would be expected, these states are principally those which are important in the production of these crops. California has long had an extension order program for its fruits and vegetables.

It should be pointed out that these regulatory programs are principally for the benefit of producers. The federal statute states in its preamble that the purpose is to ensure an orderly and adequate supply of the commodity. But in the absence of any control, supply will equal demand at some price. When is supply inadequate? Other than economic criteria are necessary for this decision. Furthermore, it should be recalled that the program was originally designed to deal with the problem of low and declining farm prices and incomes.

Extent of Regulation

The statutory authority for marketing agreements and orders is permissive, not mandatory. If producers decide that such a program would be in their interest, the type of regulation is proposed by producers. If the regulation is approved by the Secretary of Agriculture, it is put into effect. The regulation is thus decided upon by the producers, other interested parties, and the Secretary of Agriculture through administrative hearings and procedures.

[7]M. Benedict, *Farm Policies of the United States, 1790–1950,* Twentieth Century Fund, New York, 1953, p. 306.

[8]National Commission on Food Marketing, *Organization and Competition in the Fruit and Vegetable Industry,* Technical Study 4, June 1966, p. 287.

Table 13-4 Number of Markets and Volume of Milk Regulated by Federal Orders in the United States, Selected Years, 1947–1975

Year	Number of markets	Milk receipts in federal order markets (million lb)	Receipts as percentage of all milk sold to plants and dealers in United States
1947	29	14,980	21
1950	39	18,660	25
1955	63	28,948	32
1960	80	44,812	43
1965	73	54,444	48
1970	62	65,104	59
1975	56	69,251	63

Source: U.S. Department of Agriculture, *Federal Milk Order Market Statistics, Annual Summary, 1975,* Statistical Bulletin 554, Agricultural Marketing Service, June 1976, p. 9.

In no area has the application of order programs been greater than in fluid milk markets. Under the Agricultural Adjustment Administration program, 15 agreements and licenses were issued for some of the major fluid milk markets of the country. By 1947, the number had only doubled to 29 (see Table 13-4). Approximately 15 billion pounds of milk were under the federal legislation, representing approximately 21 percent of all milk sold to plants and dealers. The dairy program has shown a continued expansion since that time. The number of orders reached a peak of 83 in 1962. Consolidation of order areas has resulted in the reduction of the number of orders to 56 in 1975. Nevertheless, the volume of milk under regulation has increased to about 63 percent of total U.S. milk production.

The number of states active in regulation of their dairy industries through marketing orders is quite large. In 1966, 23 states had programs for establishing prices to be paid to producers. A total of 25 states authorized establishment of prices at one or more of the market levels (see Table 13-5). In most cases, the pricing regulation applies only to fluid eligible milk. Some states have almost complete control. California, for example, regulates the prices on approximately 98 percent of the milk produced within the state.

The extent of regulation under federal and state agreements and orders is large. It has been estimated that 90 percent of the milk that meets quality requirements for fluid use is regulated under either federal or state orders or both.[9] Furthermore, fluid milk not directly regulated is likely to be strongly influenced by milk which is regulated.

Orders and agreements are widely applied to fruit and vegetable marketing. As of 1966, 90 orders were in effect which regulated marketing of these commodities. Forty-seven have been established under the federal statute, and 43 have been established under state laws. The states in which these orders operate are

[9]U.S. Department of Agriculture, *Dairy Situation,* Economic Research Service, May 1965, p. 39.

Table 13-5   Price Regulation in the Dairy Industry by States, 1966

Price-fixing regulation					
Producer		**Wholesaler**		**Retailer**	
Ala.	N.J.	Ala.	N.J.	Ala.	N.J.
Alaska	N.Y.				
Calif.	N.C.	Calif.	N.C.	Calif.	N.C.
Conn.	Oreg.				
Fla.	Pa.	Fla.	Pa.	Fla.	Pa.
Ga.		Ga.	R.I.	Ga.	R.I.
La.	S.C.	La.	S.C.	La.	
Maine		Maine	S.Dak.	Maine	
Mass.	Utah	Mass.		Mass.	
Miss.	Vt.	Miss.	Vt.	Miss.	Vt.
Mont.	Va.	Mont.	Va.	Mont.	Va.
Nev.	Wyo.	Nev.	Wyo.	Nev.	Wyo.
N.H.		N.H.		N.H.	

Source: R. D. Knutson, J. W. Hammond, and E. F. Koller, *Price and Trade Regulation in the Dairy Industry*, Minnesota Farm Business Notes, no. 487, Sept. 1966.

listed in Table 13-6. California leads all states with 44 separate orders in effect, 29 under its own law and 15 under federal legislation.

A large number of orders have been put into effect since 1950. Of the 90 orders in effect in 1966, 56 were put into effect since 1953 (see Table 13-7). Only 10 were in effect prior to 1940.

Numerous types of fruits, vegetables, and nuts are covered, but regulations under the federal program are not applied to processed fruits, vegetables, and nuts. Several of the state laws allow application to products for canning and freezing.

State orders for fruits and vegetables differ from federal orders in another respect. Control of *farm production* or *total marketing* with federal orders is not possible. Some state programs allow for quotas which specify the amount that each producer can market. The ability of the state to make such a restriction beneficial to producers depends upon the characteristics of supply of the commodity. If the entire production emanates from one state, price and income increases may result from the program. If other states are important in the total supply situation, the limitations on marketings may have little or no impact on prices and income.

The Nature of Regulation under Orders and Agreements

The purpose of marketing orders and agreements is, very broadly, to increase returns to producers by regulating the marketing of specified commodities. State and federal statutes generally authorize the methods that can be used to increase returns. Not all will be used in each order, nor do all state laws or the federal act allow all methods.

The following lists the methods which are used and authorized under the Agricultural Marketing Agreements Act and most state enabling acts:

1 The establishment and enforcement of minimum standards of grade, size, maturity or other attributes of quality in marketing of an agricultural commodity.

2 Limitation of the quantity of the commodity marketed in total or by grade, size, maturity, or other attributes of quality during a specified time period. Such limitations may differ among markets for the commodity by time, space, or farm.

3 Regulation of the characteristics of pack or container applicable in marketing the commodity.

4 Specification and prohibition of trading practices deemed to be unfair.

5 Price posting and reporting.

6 Research.[10]

In addition to the above, the federal act allows for:

7 Establishing of minimum *prices to be paid producers for milk only*. State laws provide for establishing producer milk prices and in many cases, for establishing resale milk prices.

8 Limited control over the total marketing of milk where authorized through market orders by the 1963 Agricultural Act.

9 Product promotion activities are allowed under some of the state orders and for certain commodities under the federal program.[11]

[10]National Commission on Food Marketing, op. cit., p. 294.
[11]Ibid.

Table 13-6 Number of Marketing Orders Applicable to Fruits and Vegetables by State, January 1966

	Number orders under authority of	
State[a]	Federal legislation	State legislation
Arizona	4	—
California	15	29
Colorado	3	2
Connecticut	2	—
Florida	7	2
Georgia	1	3
Massachusetts	2	—
New York	1	2
Oregon	10	—
Rhode Island	2	—
Texas	5	—
Washington	9	3
Wisconsin	1	2

[a]States in which two or more orders are effective. Several federal orders apply to more than one state. In addition, one federal order applies in each of the following states: Michigan, New Jersey, Minnesota, Virginia, North Carolina, Maine, South Dakota, New Hampshire, Vermont, and Utah.

Source: National Commission on Food Marketing, *Organization and Competition in the Fruit and Vegetable Industry,* Technical Study 4, June 1966, p. 296.

Table 13-7   Age of Currently Effective Marketing Orders for Fruits and Vegetables, United States, 1966

Type of commodity and order	Number of orders effective for					
	5 yr or less	6–10 yr	11–15 yr	16–20 yr	21–25 yr	26 yr or over
Citrus						
Federal	2	1	3	0	2	1
State	0	0	0	0	1	0
Deciduous tree fruit						
Federal	1	6	0	1	1	2
State	7	5	0	4	1	2
Semitropical tree fruit						
Federal	1	0	2	0	0	0
State	2	1	0	0	1	0
Berries						
Federal	1	0	0	0	0	0
State	1	2	2	0	0	0
Grapes and grape products						
Federal	0	0	0	1	0	1
State	0	0	0	1	0	1
Edible tree nuts						
Federal	0	0	0	3	0	0
State	0	0	0	0	0	0
Potatoes						
Federal	0	0	1	4	3	0
State	1	3	0	0	0	0
Other vegetables						
Federal	2	4	1	0	0	1
State	4	2	1	0	1	0
All commodities						
Federal	7	11	7	9	6	7
State	15	13	3	5	4	3
Total	22	24	10	14	10	10

Source: National Commission on Food Marketing, *Organization and Competition in the Fruit and Vegetable Industry,* Technical Study 4, June 1966, p. 298.

Inspection of these techniques indicates that improved income may not be the only goal, but orderly and more efficient marketing appears to be the objective. The following section deals with these types of activities with respect to objectives and rationale of control.

Price and Quantity Controls   For milk only, under the federal order program and in some of the state programs, administered pricing is permitted under the orders. These programs set up procedures for determining and fixing milk prices according to the use made of the milk. However, the quantities of milk that buyers take at these prices are determined by the competitive forces. Although the quantity control or price control features of the program are not complete, they do allow enough manipulation that producer prices, and hence gross returns, may be increased.

For other products, fruits, vegetables, and nuts, prices are not set by administrative procedures, but the quantities allocated to different uses are controlled. Or the amount sold during any one marketing period is determined by the regulating agency. Limitation on total marketings is achieved in some areas by the setting of minimum quality attributes. Only products meeting the specified standards may be marketed in certain areas. Thus, prices and incomes may be affected through marketing orders and agreements by direct setting of prices, allocation of available supplies to various markets in such a way as to maximize or increase revenue, or to some extent by quality control.

The Theory of Price Discrimination

The theory behind these price or quantity programs is that of price discrimination. The supply control provision by itself is not based on price discrimination, but it may be used in conjunction with discrimination. To obtain some idea of how these programs work, let us first look at a simple price discrimination model of a monopolist. Suppose the total demand for a product (say, peaches) can be divided on some workable basis—the demand for fresh peaches and the demand for use by canners. The demands in each use are known and are depicted graphically as in Figure 13-5. D_f represents the demand for fresh peaches, and D_c represents the demand for fresh peaches by canners. At any given price, demand for fresh peaches is less elastic than the demand for canning peaches. There is only one seller who is willing to offer the various quantities at alternative

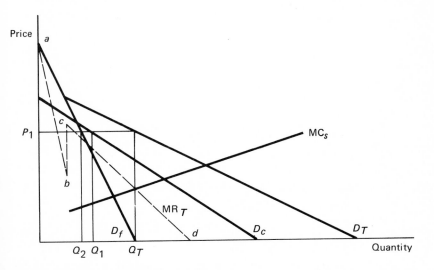

Figure 13-5 The price discrimination model.

prices, as depicted by MC_s in Figure 13-5. Now, what quantity would this individual sell in each market to maximize profit if a *single price* is to be established for both uses? First, add the total quantities that would be demanded at any given price. The heavy line D_T is the total demand in both uses. Basic economic analysis tells us how to plot the marginal revenue course to this demand, which is depicted by the dashed line *abcd* in Figure 13-5. It is to be noted that this is a discontinuous function. To maximize profit, the seller would sell that quantity where $MR_T = MC$, which is at quantity Q_T in Figure 13-5. This quantity would be sold at price P_1 in both markets. At this price, fresh peach buyers would take Q_2 units and canners would take Q_1 units. These two sum to Q_T.

Now assume that the seller is able to discriminate, that is, sell and maintain different prices in each market. With the demand and cost functions as depicted in Figure 13-5, it would be profitable for the seller to discriminate. But what are the prices that the seller would charge in each market and how much would he or she sell in each market? By the use of Figures 13-6 and 13-7, it can be readily shown that price discrimination is profitable. The cost and demand curves are the same as in the last example. In this model, however, the marginal revenue curves for each of the separate markets are constructed—MR_f for the fresh market and MR_c for the canner's market. Assume that the original position is a single price P_1 with Q_1 allocated to the fresh market and quantity Q_2 allocated to the canner's market. Figure 13-6 shows that MR_c exceeds MR_f at this solution. This means that an additional unit of peaches allocated to the canned market would add more to profit and revenue than the decrease in profit and revenue wrought by removing it from the fresh market. That is, by reducing peaches in the fresh market by one unit, the seller would reduce revenue by an amount equal to Q_2e.

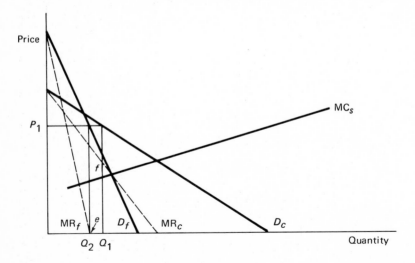

Figure 13-6 A possible price discrimination solution.

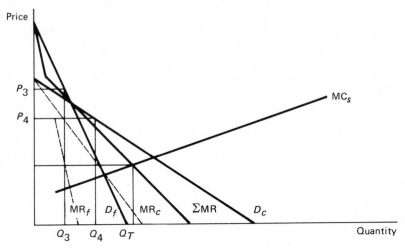

Figure 13-7 The optimum price discrimination solution.

If the unit is sold in the canner's market, it would increase total revenue by Q_1f. (Note the definition of marginal revenue.) The only point at which profit and revenue cannot be increased by shifting the product between markets is where marginal revenues in the two markets are equal, that is, $MR_f = MR_e$.

Determination of the optimum price discrimination solution is illustrated graphically in Figure 13-7. The respective marginal revenue curves are the same as in Figure 13-6 for each market. These marginal revenue curves are summed horizontally, which gives ΣMR as indicated by the heavy line in Figure 13-7. At Q_T, $MC_S = \Sigma MR = MR_f = MR_c$. A price of P_3 will be charged for fresh peaches and a price of P_4 will be charged for peaches used in canning. These prices can be found by moving upward from the points of equal marginal revenue to the appropriate demand curves. In this case the highest price is charged in the market with the most inelastic demand. Also, in this illustration, the total quantity with discrimination is greater than without discrimination. The actual amount of profits have not been illustrated in the above discussion. Average cost curves could be incorporated to show that profit will be increased through discrimination.

Several conditions must exist before price discrimination can and should be practiced.

1 Two or more markets with different-sloping demands must exist.
2 It must not be possible for buyers to transfer products from one market to another. If this is not the case, the product will be bought at the lower price and transferred to the other use.
3 The seller must possess almost complete control over the supply of the product.

The above concepts illustrate the rationale behind discriminatory price programs for agricultural commodities. However, in most situations, application does not yield the optimum results as indicated by theory. Total revenue and profits are increased for the industry although they will not be maximized. A number of reasons cause this.

1   The legislative authority may not permit maximization.
2   Marginal cost and revenue curves are not known with sufficient accuracy to permit determination of the maximizing volumes.
3   Sellers are producers who are only loosely organized in their marketing activities. In production decisions, sellers act as if they were in a competitive market; thus, their aggregate decisions do not permit profit maximization.

The application of this concept to farm products takes one of two forms. For fruits, vegetables, and others, the administrative agency allocates *quantities* to the various markets in such a manner as to maximize or increase revenue. If sufficient knowledge of demand and supply characteristics is available, revenue maximization could be undertaken (or indicated as in Figure 13-8). Assume that growers produce Q_T units of walnuts during the season. Demand for walnuts in shells is indicated by D_s and demand for shelled walnuts is indicated by D_c. Since supply cannot be changed, the MC is identical with the vertical line S_T. Using the method described earlier, total profits will be maximized by selling Q_s units in the shell market and Q_c in the shelled market. Given these demands, buyers will pay P_s and P_c for these quantities in the respective uses.

Since numerous producers of the product are involved, total returns from all

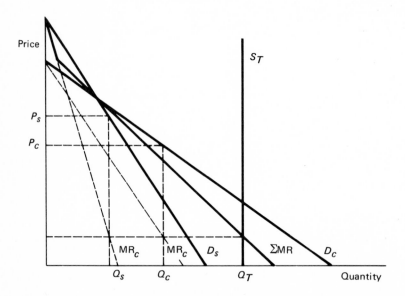

Figure 13-8   Maximizing resources in two markets under fixed supply conditions.

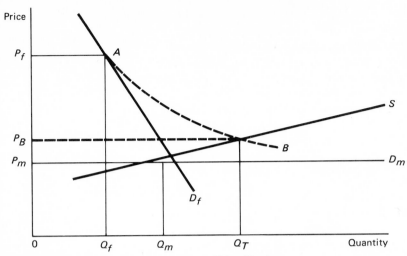

Figure 13-9 Price discrimination and the "blend" price.

uses are pooled by an administrative agency, the costs of handling and administration are deducted, and the total returns are prorated back to producers on the basis of marketings.

Orders and agreements when applied to milk are used to establish *prices,* not the quantities, sold in each use. There are two broad uses of milk: fluid products (fluid whole, skim, low fat, and cream products) and manufactured products (cheese, butter, dry milk, evaporated milk, ice cream, and so forth). Demands differ in each use. The market for fluid milk is usually quite local, generally a metropolitan area. Milk is supplied from the immediate surrounding area. The fluid demand facing these producers is usually highly inelastic, as shown by D_f in Figure 13-9. The market for manufactured dairy products is a national market. Products from the local market can be sold anywhere in the nation. Although the national demand for manufactured products may be very inelastic, the producers in the local fluid market area represent such a small part of the total supplies that the demand for milk in manufactured products is almost completely elastic, as shown by D_m in Figure 13-9. In actual practice, the milk used in manufactured products is generally priced at the U.S. average price for manufacturing grade milk. According to the statute, the fluid price is established at a level which will ensure an adequate supply of milk and bring about parity of income. These prices, once established, are the prices which must be paid by handlers to producers for milk in each use.

Because milk sellers (producers) are not a complete monopoly, some method for distributing returns has to be devised. In order programs, this is the pooling procedure. Two types have been used in federal order marketing—the *individual handler* pool and the *marketwide* pool. Under an individual handler pool, the producers are paid a price which is based on the utilization of milk of the processor or buyer to whom they sell. If the buyer uses most of the milk in manufactured dairy products, then the producer price will be very near the price for manufacturing grade milk. If most of the milk is used in fluid products, the producer price will be near the administered price for fluid use milk. Under the marketwide pool, returns to a producer depend upon the utilization for the entire market, not on the utilization of the buyer of his or her milk.

The following example illustrates payment for milk under a federal order program for a metropolitan area. Assume that:

Class I (fluid) milk price = $5.00
Class II (manufacturing) milk price = $4.00
All milk tests 3.5 percent butterfat
Total market supply for the period is 5,000 hundredweight

The milk is used in the following way by these processors:

	Class I	Class II	Total
Processor 1	1,000 cwt	0	1,000 cwt
Processor 2	1,000 cwt	1,000 cwt	2,000 cwt
Processor 3	500 cwt	1,500 cwt	2,000 cwt
Total	2,500 cwt	2,500 cwt	5,000 cwt

The total payment for milk by these processors is as follows:

	Class I	Class II	Total
Processor 1	1,000 × 5 = $5,000	0	$5,000
Processor 2	1,000 × 5 = $5,000	1,000 × 4 = $4,000	$9,000
Processor 3	500 × 5 = $2,500	1,500 × 4 = $6,000	$8,500
Total	$12,500	$10,000	$22,500

With an individual handler pool, producers selling to processor 1 would receive $5,000/1,000 = $5.00 per hundredweight for milk; producers selling to processor 2 would receive $9,000/2,000 = $4.50 per hundredweight; producers selling to processor 3 would receive $8,500/2,000 = $4.25 per hundredweight. Under a marketwide pool, all returns for the market are pooled and redistributed equally.[12] In this situation, each producer would receive $22,500/5000 = $4.50 per hundredweight, which is known as the *uniform producer blend price*. This procedure is the most popular method of payment under federal orders.

It can readily be seen that classified milk pricing does not follow the same procedure as pure monopolistic price discrimination. Additional examination of Figure 13-9 will indicate some differences. Let curve S represent the quantity of milk that producers are willing to supply at various prices. With the Class I (fluid) price set by administrative procedures at P_f and the Class II (manufacturing use)

---

[12]Location differentials are applied to each plant to cover costs of moving milk into the market.

price set at P_m, curve $P_f AB$ traces our producer prices for each quantity of milk supplied to the market. With this structure of prices and costs, the market will be in equilibrium when the blend price is at P_B. Quantity Q_T will be supplied to the market. These producers will consider the blend prices as their marginal revenue.

The total supply of milk will be allocated between the two markets. At price P_f, fluid processors will take quantity Q_f. The remaining quantity Q_m will be sold to manufacturing milk processors at price P_m. According to this illustration, processors are willing to take any quantity of milk that is offered at price P_m.

Thus, the price and quantity results are different from those under pure monopolistic price discrimination. The differences could be shown graphically, but they will only be listed here.

1 The revenue curves facing the producer are different in the two situations.
2 The quantity of milk supplied at equilibrium will always be larger under the federal order programs.
3 Allocation of supplies to the various markets is determined by the buyer rather than the seller.
4 The system outlined here would still result, in the long run, in complete elimination of excess profits from producer returns. If the supply curve is upward sloping, discrimination will lead to a higher level of prices. The excess profits will be eliminated at a higher price either through capitalization into land values or increased returns to labor. If the long-run supply is completely elastic, there is no long-run benefit to either land or labor. This last characteristic has important implications for administration of this program. This potential also leads to political pressure by producers' groups to imposed production or marketing controls.

Grade, Size, and Maturity Regulations   Regulation of grade, size, and maturity is undertaken for a large number of products other than milk. For milk, the grade and quality requirements are established by the local or state health agency. Nothing in the order determines the quality requirements. Of the 90 fruit and vegetable orders in effect in 1966, 69 regulated some aspect of grade, size, maturity, or other quality characteristic.[13] This type of regulation also relates to economic consideration. If distinct separable demands exist for each grade, size, or maturity level, then the allocation along the discriminatory lines previously discussed can be practiced. In fact, the ability to control quantities in alternative uses often depends upon the classification of products according to some quality attribute.

Quality regulations have been grouped into three types:

1   Establishment of minimum product standards in order for the product to be marketed.

---

[13]National Commission on Food Marketing, op. cit., p. 311.

    2 Restriction of the sale of the entire supply or a certain size or grade from sale during certain periods.
    3 Restriction of a certain proportion of each grade or size from sale.[14]

Enforcement of the first type of regulation may benefit both consumers and producers. Producers will be stimulated to produce only a high-quality product and consumers are assured of high quality. Losses from deterioration or spoilage may be eliminated or reduced.

    Regulations of the second and third types are merely regulations of the total marketings of the commodity. As such, they are a form of supply control. Whether they increase or decrease total revenue and/or profits depends upon costs and demand elasticities. If a product has an elastic demand, such restriction can decrease total revenue.

    Pack and Container Regulations   The purpose of this regulation is to ensure uniformity among packages and containers so as to increase efficiency in handling. Numerous size containers and methods of packing can cause inefficiencies. Greater mechanization of handling can be ensured by this method.

    It seems questionable whether such regulation is necessary. Where it is not in effect, uniformity often occurs. Sometimes it is ensured by the buyer providing the container. Refusing to accept any but a standard container would likely ensure compliance with standardization.

    Prohibiting Unfair Trade Practices   Most states have general and some specific laws prohibiting unfair trade practices. In addition, federal orders for products other than milk and state order programs allow for prohibition of other trade practices that are deemed unfair. The California cling-peach order prohibits contracting for cling peaches other than those that meet the grade requirements of the order. Some federal orders prohibit handlers from selling below cost of acquisition.[15]

    Although a feature of several orders and authorized in both state and federal enabling legislation, other state and federal programs may be a more effective method of dealing with unfair trade practices. Many states have general laws which prohibit selling below cost. In some cases, minimum wholesale and retail markups are required. Furthermore, duplication of administrative agencies may be costly and unnecessary.

    Price Posting and Reporting   Price posting, in addition to being an information device, is probably related to the desire to regulate unfair competition practices. A number of orders require that handlers of the product post the prices which they are receiving or paying for the regulated commodity. Also, any change in these posted prices is to be reported within a certain period of time.

[14]Ibid.
[15]Ibid., p. 313.

Accurate posting and reporting of information on prices is necessary if the programs are to operate. For milk, where the order establishes minimum prices to be paid by processors, reporting of prices is absolutely essential to administration of the program. Monthly reports are required of all prices and quantities. The agency ensures accuracy and honest reporting by regular audits of the handlers.

Research Some orders and agreements allow for funding of research and development projects under the order provisions. The order specifies deductions from the receipts of producers and/or handlers to be used in research.

The purposes of these research projects are to expand the uses of the products, improve the market efficiency, and in some instances to study the provisions of the order. The benefits of increased efficiency of marketing may not, however, be passed back to the producer. In the extreme case of completely elastic demand, all benefits will be passed back to the producer. In the extreme case of completely inelastic demand, all benefits will be passed on to the consumer. The situation does not normally exist in the real world, and therefore both consumers and producers benefit.

The National Commission on Food Marketing has reported that several California orders have contributed funds to research designed to forecast crop production.[16] Other projects have been designed to study methods of disease control, methods of harvesting, insect control, and market potential for the commodity. A study of the date order reported the following studies which have been encouraged and supported through the order:

1 New ways of using dates.
2 The safety of certain mold inhibitors for use in dates.
3 The value of cull dates for livestock feed.
4 Ways of preparing cull dates to simplify handling and encourage their use in livestock feed.
5 Mechanical harvesting methods and devices to reduce the need for specialized hand labor.
6 Changes in quality and chemical composition that affect the shelf life of dates.
7 The new processing methods that may improve the quality of packed dates.
8 Handling methods to insure that the consumer receives high-quality dates.
9 Electronic sorters to decrease the amount of hand sorting required.
10 Costs and efficiency of currently used work methods and equipment in packing houses.
11 The effectiveness of various methods of in-store merchandising.
12 Attitudes and opinions of homemakers concerning dates.
13 Development of objective means of estimating crop size several months before harvest.[17]

---

[16]Ibid.
[17]Dennis Carleton, *The Federal Date Order,* U.S. Department of Agriculture, ERS-214, Feb. 1965, p. 8.

Inspection and Certification   These activities are usually a corollary of regulations on grades, size, and maturity. Authority to inspect and certify these characteristics is necessary to ensure compliance with the terms of many orders. Certification of a grade or standard may also improve the efficiency of the marketing system if some other program is not available.

Product Promotion   Promotion and advertising funds may be collected under some state orders and for certain commodities under the federal act. These deductions are established at a fixed amount per unit of the commodity delivered to handlers. The appeal of this type of activity under orders seems to be gaining momentum at this time. This has occurred despite the fact that our knowledge of response to industrywide advertising is largely unknown for many commodities. Here also, the impact depends upon the elasticities of supply and demand and whether advertising can change the demand.

Formulation of Marketing Orders and Agreements

Although development of an order under state enabling legislation may differ in many details from one state to another and from federal orders, the procedure is essentially as follows:

1   Interested producers (handlers may also be involved) propose a plan of regulation for the commodity. Very often, this is proposed by a cooperative or the cooperative handlers of the product. This proposal, together with a request for a public hearing on the proposal, is submitted to the Secretary of Agriculture.
2   If the Secretary of Agriculture decides favorably on the request, a public hearing is called for a specific date and place. Usually the hearing is held somewhere in the area where the commodity is produced. At this hearing, evidence may be received from all parties which will be affected by the proposed order. The evidence may be in support or opposition to the entire proposal or merely to certain features. Written briefs on issues discussed in the hearing may also be filed after the hearing.
3   A recommended decision is then published by the Secretary of Agriculture together with the exact terms of the order. This decision and order is based on the evidence presented at the hearing. It is written by specialists in the Department of Agriculture. Interested parties, following the publication, may submit exceptions to the recommended decision and order.
4   A final decision is written, either accepting or rejecting the exceptions, and then published. Dates are established for a producer referendum on accepting or rejecting the order program.
5   To be put into effect, producers of two-thirds of the commodity or two-thirds of producers must favor the order. California citrus fruit orders and individual-handler-pool milk orders require approval of three-fourths of the affected producers for the order to become effective.

Administration of Orders

For products other than milk, administration of the terms of the order are handled by a board of producers and handlers. They are selected by the Secretary of Agriculture for federal orders. The board may select a staff to carry out routine administration.

Certain powers are vested in the boards. They can make administrative rules, require records to be kept, and make investigations. The boards are also required to keep records, audit records, analyze growing conditions, and make recommendations to the Secretary regarding the regulatory program.[18]

Administration of milk orders is somewhat different. Here, the Secretary of Agriculture appoints a market administrator whose functions are defined in the order. They are those functions necessary to administer the terms of the order. They include such things as monthly computation and announcement of class prices, blend prices, and appropriate butterfat differentials. The market administrator audits books and records of handlers to determine compliance with terms of the order. He or she publishes statistical data relevant to the order. Decisions regarding to whom the order applies and in what manner it is to be applied are made by the market administrator. Also, the market administrator hires a staff for carrying out the terms of the order.

Costs of administering all types of orders are defrayed by assessments on handlers and producers. They are based on the cost of administration; excesses are returned to producers.

Effects of Market Orders and Agreements

It is impossible to determine the exact impact of these programs on any industry. A list of achievements would probably include the following:

1 The programs have contributed to more orderly marketing.

2 Prices and incomes have been increased moderately with greater stability in returns. Since rigid production control on producers is not possible, the price- and income-enhancing effects are limited.

3 Some market power has been transferred from handlers to producers (orders have probably accelerated the decline of small handlers).

4 The amount of market information has been increased.

5 The programs have contributed to increased market efficiency for some commodities.

6 Except for the uncertain impact of marketing efficiency gains, the programs have probably done little for consumers.

SUMMARY

This chapter describes and analyzes two major institutions that influence the marketing of farm inputs and farm products—farmer cooperatives and marketing orders and agreements. Farmer cooperatives account for a major share of all sales to farmers of fertilizer, feeds, and petroleum products. In 1971–1972, 30 percent of all feed sold to farmers was purchased from cooperatives. Many of the products are actually produced in cooperative-owned plants. In the marketing of

---

[18]U.S. Department of Agriculture, *Self-Help Stabilization Programs with Use of Marketing Agreement and Orders,* PA-479, Nov., 1961.

farm products, cooperatives are most important in dairy processing. Cooperatives processed 36 percent of all dairy products in 1971–1972. Additionally, large amounts of milk used by fluid processors were assembled and delivered to plants by cooperatives.

Farmer cooperatives in the United States trace many of their operating principles to a cooperative flannel weavers' association at Rochdale, England, in the 1830s. Several of these principles are now embodied in the statutory definition of farmer cooperatives of the Capper-Volstead Act. They are (1) one member, one vote, (2) a fixed return on capital, and (3) distribution of returns on the basis of membership.

Cooperatives have some similarities to, and several important differences from, the general business corporation. Cooperatives and corporations are generally franchised to do business under the business incorporation laws of the state. Both enjoy the advantage of limited liability for the debts and actions of the business. Regarding differences, cooperative voting is limited to one vote per member. Corporation voting is proportionate to stock ownership. Cooperatives distribute returns primarily on the basis of patronage. Corporations distribute returns according to share of ownership. The objective of cooperatives is business at cost, whereas corporations operate to obtain highest returns on investment. Ownership of cooperatives is by member patrons. Corporations are not generally owned by those receiving goods or services from the corporation. Price and output decisions of cooperatives are on a cost basis. This often permits the cooperative to pay higher prices for products than the corporation.

Marketing orders and agreements are state and/or federal regulations that specify some of the conditions under which farm products are marketed. For milk, they establish procedures for setting prices at which milk will be sold. About 57 percent of all milk produced in the United States is priced under federal orders. For fruits, vegetables, and other products, federal orders provide for allocation of supplies among different uses, grading and packing standards, and promotional and research programs.

Marketing orders are often used to practice price discrimination in the sale of products produced by farmers. By setting different prices that processors and assemblers must pay according to the use of the products or by allocating available supplies such that different prices prevail in each market, total returns from sales can be increased over what they would be if a single price prevailed in all markets for each product. In milk markets, highest prices are set for milk used in fluid products and a lower price is set for milk used in manufactured dairy products. For fruits and vegetables, product is allocated into the fresh and processed uses such that higher prices generally prevail for products sold in fresh uses. In some respects, price discrimination as practiced under orders corresponds to that practiced by the pure discriminating monopolist.

Because producers of farm products are numerous, orders must provide for a method of distribution of returns from the sales of the product. In milk markets, a common method is to pool the returns from the sales of all products in all uses and to calculate a blend price which is a weighted-average price. Each producer receives the weighted-average or blend price for each unit of product sold regardless of the use allocation for his or her production.

QUESTIONS

1 How does a cooperative firm differ from a general business corporation in terms of its organization and legal characteristics?
2 A cooperative firm under the condition of perfect competition will operate at the same price and output level as a noncooperative firm. Do you agree or disagree? Why?
3 Select an agricultural product other than milk for which a marketing order is in effect. Describe the programs carried on under the order for that product.
4 How does price discrimination under federal orders differ from pure-monopoly price discrimination?
5 As a farmer, why would you support or oppose a marketing order for a product which you produce?

BIBLIOGRAPHY

Benedict, M.: *Farm Policies of the United States, 1790–1950,* Twentieth Century Fund, New York, 1953.

Carleton, Dennis: *The Federal Date Order,* U.S. Department of Agriculture, ERS-214, Feb. 1965.

Cooperation—Principles and Practices, Circular 420, University of Wisconsin Extension Service, Madison, 1952.

Helmberger, Peter: "Cooperative Enterprise as a Structural Dimension of Farm Markets," *Journal of Farm Economics,* vol. 46, pp. 608–617, Aug. 1964.

National Commission on Food Marketing: *Organization and Competition in the Fruit and Vegetable Industry,* Technical Study 4, June 1966.

Phillips, Richard: "The Economic Nature of the Cooperative Association," *Journal of Farm Economics,* vol. 35, pp. 74–87, Feb. 1953.

U.S. Department of Agriculture: *Self-Help Stabilization Programs with Use of Marketing Agreement and Orders,* PA-479, Nov. 1961.

——: *Statistics of Farmer Cooperatives, 1969–1970,* FCS Research Report 22, July 1972.

——: *The Dairy Situation,* Economic Research Service, May 1965.

United States v. Butler et al., 297 U.S. 1 (1936).

Market and
Price Policy

INTRODUCTION

Economic theory to this point has been used primarily to describe and analyze agricultural markets. For descriptive purposes, the perfectly competitive model of economic theory has been used as a framework for empirical data, describing how the marketing system would operate *if* perfectly competitive conditions prevailed throughout the marketing system. The analysis accompanying this method of description is an attempt to explain why *real* marketing activity differs from this theoretical norm.

Statisticians and econometricians have been partially successful in testing various aspects of economic theory through empirical research involving the use of sophisticated mathematical tools. Such researchers are currently specifying supply and demand relationships at various levels of the marketing system, and they are also considering locational aspects of the marketing of farm products by employment of combined transportation and input-output analysis.

Departure from the norm of perfect competition has led to the study of the marketing system by investigating those elements peculiar to the "structure" of the market as well as explaining how those markets that depart from perfect competition operate with respect to price and outputs.

Regardless of the type of market structures that prevail, firms operate in two markets: as demanders of inputs and as suppliers of outputs. In each of these markets the firm deals with other firms in two dimensions: (1) vertically, by dealing with other firms "across the market"; and (2) horizontally, by considering the actions or reactions of "like firms" in terms of outputs sold or inputs procured. These vertical and horizontal relationships among firms—called the exchange (negotiative) and competitive relationships, respectively—largely explain why firms or groups of firms behave as they do.

The essence of governmental marketing policy is to exert control over these relationships through the regulation of market practices, commodities sold and their prices, the number and size of firms at various marketing levels, and the direct or indirect regulation of other market conditions. Broadly speaking, the government attempts to influence business activity in three ways.

1 Federal and state legislation directly aids industries by guaranteeing price supports, restricting competitive imports, providing new technology through governmental research and dissemination activities, and by financing the education, training, and capital needs of firms and individuals. It is interesting to note that the government may become a large marketing firm itself through its support of farm prices.

2 The government influences business activity by regulating or prohibiting monopolies and the use of monopoly power or by sanctioning the evolution of countervailing monopolies and monopoly power.

3 Legislation is aimed at *maintaining competition* by regulating the nature of the product and degree of entry, reducing uncertainty and lack of knowledge, reducing locational disadvantages, and specifying trading "rules" that foster competitive market practices.

This chapter discusses public policies of all three types. It is by no means exhaustive of all government programs that regulate agricultural markets, but it does examine some of the major programs that have developed. The goals of agricultural marketing policy will be examined first.

GOALS OF AGRICULTURAL MARKETING POLICY

Fundamental to policy formulation and execution are the goals toward which such programs are directed. All purposeful actions, both economic and noneconomic, are characterized by the explicit or implicit expression of certain objectives or goals. These goals derive from beliefs and valuations.

Beliefs

Beliefs are a combination of our observations of existing phenomena and our understanding of *why* these phenomena exist and behave as they do. The descriptive method in agricultural marketing provides one way of classifying observable phenomena. Agricultural marketing analysis attempts to explain why such phenomena prevail. Our beliefs concerning agricultural marketing are thus conditioned by how marketing activity is described and how it is analyzed. Where both the descriptive system and analytical techniques are agreed upon by those interested, fundamental agreement is usually easier to achieve regarding the beliefs held.

Where disagreement concerning methodology exists, as it does in agricultural marketing, fundamental beliefs about the marketing system show variation. To illustrate, the market phenomenon of vertical integration caused a host of beliefs to be formed, not only in terms of describing what vertical integration is, but more so as to why it prevailed. The continued development, use, and acceptance of economic theory in the analysis of such phenomena will tend to dispel such disagreements.

Opposing beliefs in agricultural marketing are not solely the result of conflicting methodology. Many forces prevail simultaneously in any market situation in varying degrees of intensity. All of these forces must be considered in an adequate explanation of market conduct. In any decision-making process, it is necessary to "hold other things constant" while analyzing the changes in one or two variables.

Values

Values are expressions of certain fundamental norms or standards of behavior. These behavioral norms are formulated fundamentally by ethical teachings that are related to the behavior of individuals. The individual must deal with his or her environment, other persons and one's self. Ethical teachings provide behavioral standards for individuals in each of the aspects of their lives.

These behavioral standards extend to economic activity through the individual as a policymaker. *How the individual should behave* with respect to other people is recast in terms of how firms should behave in regard to other firms. Behavioral relationships between firms are manifested in the market through their negotiative and competitive relationships.

Output decisions and the negotiative and competitive conduct of firms in the market, viewed in terms of public welfare, provide dimensions of *market performance*. Just as the performance of an entire economy or economic system is judged through the standard of living it provides, its efficiency of production, pattern of income distribution, progressiveness, and stability are judged and measured by similar criteria.

Moving from market structure and conduct to market performance involves the insertion of social value judgments into the analysis of agricultural marketing.

Beginning texts and courses in agricultural marketing frequently set out to solve "the marketing problem" or a set of problems in the distribution of farm products. Such treatments implicitly analyze marketing activity in terms of "desirable" states of affairs. The most common performance dimension used is efficiency.

Marketing efficiency, like other performance dimensions, is difficult to relate to individual valuations. Certainly it suggests that resources *should be* allocated in such a way that maximum satisfaction will be gained by a group of consumers without worsening the condition of the group of resource owners and users. However, the tracing of this optimality criteria to ethical teachings involves considerable speculation. Perhaps some of the iterations of the 10 biblical commandments apply; perhaps some elements of the democratic political creed are pertinent.

Such speculations need not concern us here. It is sufficient for our purpose to suggest that the performance dimension of agricultural marketing is derived from more fundamental value judgments.

Goals

Goals are the expressed objectives of action programs. They differ from performance dimensions only in the sense that, in addition to judging and measuring the conduct of firms engaged in agricultural processing and distribution by some desirable standard, they are set forth in terms of some proposal designed to "bridge the gap" between what is and what ought to be.

Using marketing efficiency as an example, a marketing system may be measured and judged as inefficient in the context of market performance. This performance dimension becomes a *goal* when action proposals are made with the objective of reducing marketing inefficiency.

In economic policy discussions, goals are generally treated as variables that are influenced by *instrument* or *policy* variables. For example, the goal of full employment may be reached by using the instrumentalities of government spending (fiscal policy) or changing of the money supply (monetary policy).

The goal variables in agricultural marketing policy are obtained from the performance dimensions of the market. The instrument variables may be market structure elements and market conduct. This is to say that market performance is influenced by the government through the prohibition, regulation, or advocation of certain market structures and/or conduct. The government may encourage the standardization of a product (structural element) or may prohibit certain trade practices (market conduct) so as to gain a "socially desirable" market performance.

What is considered socially desirable performance in marketing, and in economics generally, commenced with the work of Adam Smith during the Enlightenment period.

Value Setting for Economic Policy

The Wealth of Nations was both an ethical attack on the government regulation of business activity and a logical construct of an economic system of free enterprise. This analysis of a self-operating economy rested upon a number of restrictive market conditions, but it revealed the workings of the "invisible hand of the marketplace" that matched the desires of consumers to a group of selfish, profit-seeking entrepreneurs in such a way that only "normal profits" prevailed while a high-quality product was made available at the lowest possible cost.

This explanation netted Smith not only the admiration of fellow economists but the wholehearted support of the people of his time. That the economy would operate not only *as well* as if government directed its workings, but that it would be even *more* efficient when people individually sought their own selfish ends, was an analysis consistent with the philosophical developments during this period of Enlightenment.

Brewster has derived from this philosophical movement a set of value judgments that are both basic to and consistent with the analysis of Adam Smith. The political and religious order of Smith's era had shifted the concept of God's work from religious to secular occupations, which, in turn, clashed with the politically dominated economy of early feudalism. It came to be thought that, politically, each serf was his own lord and that all individuals were of equal worth and dignity, with no one allowed arbitrary power over another.

Under such a political philosophy, each individual should have a castle in the form of a plot of land. By natural restraints, farm firms would be held small in size by the limitations imposed by family labor and management. The rewards reaped from such productive effort would be equivalent to one's contributions, yet the individual would have opportunity equal to that of his neighbor. With the farm thus tied to the owner-worker-manager, any interference by an "outside" power would rob proprietors of their natural freedom.

The analysis of what came to be called a *perfectly competitive* economy by Smith fitted in and gave strength to these valuations by showing that the laissez-faire economic system not only allowed the individualism advocated by political and religious change, but that the economy would be in better condition with such valuations as a guiding force rather than with governmental regulation.

Coupling these developments with the opportunities found in America, Brewster states:

> This enabled classical economic theory here to become a far more formidable system of judgments than the Old World ever shared concerning what ought and ought not be done for the good of all. Here, as nowhere else, anyone who advocated departure from the sound economic doctrine could be annihilated with the retort that he was putting a ceiling on the American Dream.
>
> Thus, the analysis of a perfectly competitive economy agrees with, and expounds through its assumptions, the value setting of the free enterprise, democratic nature of the American people. That perfect competition be advocated as a method of describing and analyzing economic activity is no more surprising than it being advocated as a behavioral "norm" for economic activity. Applied to agricultural marketing this norm is the "perfect market concept."[1]

The Perfect Market Concept

The idealized economic system presented by Adam Smith spurred subsequent economists to refine and modify his analysis in such a way that a rigorous network of economic logic developed. Much of this study was aimed at specifying *exactly* what kinds of conditions needed to prevail so that the automatic nature of the "invisible hand" would work toward the attainment of that economic performance consistent with the philosophy of individualism.

---

[1]John M. Brewster, *A Philosopher among Economists*, J. T. Murphy, Philadelphia, 1970.

Study and reflection revealed that the invisible hand of the market could replace the iron hand of government if *perfect competition* prevailed. Perfect competition is a market situation in which a number of *conditions* exist. If these conditions are met and costs and demands are known, it then becomes possible to predict the output and price decisions of the firms in the market. It is also possible to predict the market performance that such a market would generate.

The conditions that must exist for perfect competition are numerous. The following list provides a summary of some of these conditions, which, of course, also serve as assumptions to any analysis of such a market situation.

1   The size of the firm's output is sufficiently small relative to industry output to guarantee that each firm's output actions cannot perceptively affect the behavior of the market price prevailing for the industry. (This is referred to as the *atomistic assumption,* and it essentially eliminates from analysis the existence of power relationships between firms either horizontally or vertically.)

2   The commodity output of the firm is homogenous with respect to the output of firms on the same level of the marketing spectrum. (Although this element of homogeneity is frequently discussed in terms of the physical characteristics of the product, Chamberlin and Triffin specified the definition of homogeneity of product in terms of ultimate consumer demand, not its physical attributes.)

3   The market transactions are spatially oriented to a single point, geographically a marketplace. (This assumption disallowed any locational advantage or disadvantage in the market. By assuming equal transport rates, this assumption can be replaced by a more realistic spatial market—but only by such a new assumption.)

4   The firm is unable to establish any artificial restrictions in buying inputs or selling its output. (Discriminatory pricing and the possibility of holding monopoly rights, such as patents, is ruled out by this assumption. This condition further excludes the possibility of any form of market power by the firm.)

5   The complete freedom of entry into and exit from the industry is allowed, which ultimately serves as a necessary long-run equilibrium condition for industry price and output solutions. (This condition of entry is normally discussed in terms of an economic barrier—where little capital is needed to produce the product. But entry restrictions provided by laws and pure market power also are eliminated by this assumption.)

6   Perfect or equal knowledge by all firms regarding present and future prices in both the input and output markets provides a further limitation to the possibility of price discrimination or power relationships, but it also avoids the possibility of uncertainty entering the "best available technologies." (This assures an optimum allocation of resources and the long-run efficiency by both the firm and industry.)

It becomes apparent that some of the conditions could be influenced by the government through legislation. If a large number of firms are desired in an industry, the government could *prohibit* single firms from producing the entire industry output, making the firm "split" and sell part of its plants to other firms. Or the government could *encourage* the development of new firms by providing credit, lessening the tax burden upon them, or briefly creating a competing operation of its own and later selling this to a new firm. Similarly, the government could take measures with respect to the other conditions.

If the conditions of perfect competition are believed to lead to market performance that is considered socially desirable, governmental policy can be aimed at trying to establish these conditions in economic reality.

Adam Smith and others have successfully argued that such market performance is desirable and that it conforms to an accepted national, religious, and political philosophy basic to the American Dream. That the perfectly competitive model serves as a grand accumulation of goals as a normative standard for business behavior should not be surprising. Legislation aimed at prohibiting monopolies and maintaining competition is the resulting evidence of this ethical norm for American business.

The Concept of Countervailing Power

The realities of the economic world of American business, including the agribusiness sector, has demonstrated that perfect competition is not a sustaining market structure over time even though it may be socially desirable. The development of large firms with a capacity to dominate vast industrial sectors, to reap great profits, and to restrict their would-be competitors has forced the government to *countervail* this power by legislation.

The Sherman Antitrust Act and subsequent amendments were aimed at dissipating the economic power of such giant corporations by *prohibitions* against conspiracies in the restraint of trade or unfair practices. Additional legislation also was enacted in an attempt to re-create the conditions of a perfectly competitive economy to maintain competition.

This legislation accomplished one other thing. In addition to letting the government countervail the corporate giants by prohibiting certain market conduct, one amendment excused certain business groups from antitrust enforcement and subsequently encouraged these groups to form and merge in such a way that these firms could themselves countervail the power of vertically related industries. These were the labor union and agricultural cooperative exemptions from antitrust legislation provided for in the Clayton Act of 1914.

In addition to allowing certain firms to form and merge so as to countervail other firms, it was implicitly recognized that uncontrolled competition would not necessarily result in desirable performance. The most particular case in point is that of agriculture. Because of the nature of the demand for farm products and the nature of the farming industry, this nearest equivalent to perfect competition on the American scene demonstrated low labor and enterprise earnings relative to other industries. So low were these earnings that it became necessary to protect these *competitors* by restricting their *competition*. In addition to encouraging the cooperation of farmers to jointly market their outputs and purchase their inputs, governmental policy also encouraged the "fixing" of market prices by formal agreement.

These policies to restrain competition among farmers can be directed to either of two goals. The peculiarities of the agricultural sector (the demand faced, the technologically driven treadmill *increase* in average cost, and so forth) require that government aid this industry in many ways because it is a victim of its own market structure. The form that aid takes includes the marketing of their product. Certainly, it is argued, farmers should receive a "fair" price for their product and *anti*-antitrust measures should be used to attain this parity price and income.

Another approach and another goal is to argue that the businesses surrounding agriculture are structured such that they inherently possess greater bargaining power than the farmer. Therefore, it is only logical that the farmer, given the privilege of combining or using pricing practices, will effectively restrain or countervail the nonfarm agribusinesses.

Regardless of whether the *parity income* or *parity power* argument is used, it is a fact that protective or countervailing policies have arisen that are of extreme importance in agricultural marketing.

Conflict of Goals

It becomes clear that the goal of attaining a perfectly competitive situation seriously conflicts with the goal of countervailing the power of imperfectly competitive firms by encouraging monopoly and monopoly practices. Such goals would not conflict if they were considered in a short-term sense. If farmers were given temporary marketing powers while those with whom they negotiate were forced toward a perfectly competitive market structure, the policies would not conflict but would serve as a two-pronged attack against monopolization. But this has not been the case. Both goals have served as the basis for continued long-term policy programs.

AGRICULTURAL MARKET POLICIES

The conditions necessary for perfect competition also specify certain market structure elements that serve as instrument variables in policy formation. Given that certain performance norms are desirable to society in general and that such performance automatically results under perfectly competitive conditions, it follows that market conditions should be made as "perfect" as possible.[2]

Perfect Market Policies

The market structure elements that serve as instrument variables in perfect market policies can be derived from the conditions necessary for perfect competition. Each of these elements significantly influences the supply or demand relationships present. If they should change, such changes, in turn, influence market conduct and performance. Certain conduct conditions are also listed for

---

[2]For a critical appraisal of this syllogism, see Jesse W. Markham, "Changing Structure of the American Economy: Its Implications for Performance of Industrial Markets," *Journal of Farm Economics,* vol. 41, no. 2, pp. 389–400, May 1959.

perfect competition, and where these can be regulated directly, they also become part of those policies aimed at creating a perfect market.

The following brief review of existing perfect market policies is cast in terms of those perfectly competitive market conditions previously listed.

Atomisticity of Power   *The size of the firm's output should be sufficiently small relative to industry output in order to guarantee that each firm's actions cannot perceptively affect price.* This condition implies that both the *number* of firms and the size of individual market shares are important structural elements. To influence industries so that the number of firms will be large, and so that each will possess a small market share, is to make the industry more perfectly competitive. The number of firms and their market shares serve in market structure analysis as basic data in the computation of *concentration ratios.* The percent of total industry sales by the largest eight, six, or four firms in the industry is computed; the percentage serves as a comparative device for business concentration in several industries.[3]

One method to achieve many firms of small size is to simply prohibit the existence of monopolies or near-monopolies in any industry. This was the first major step in marketing policy enacted by the federal government through the Sherman Antitrust Act.

The wording of the Sherman Act of 1890 did not specifically state that the size of firms was the determinant of whether monopoly existed, but the courts interpreted the act in this way until 1944.[4] Condemning evidence in support of previous prosecutions was concentration ratios showing that a firm was too large in terms of total industry sales.

How big is "too big" is an arbitrary question unless it can be tied to market conduct and performance. While it is presumed true that large firms possess great market power, it does not necessarily follow that such power will be used to restrain trade. The conclusion of the Hartford case of 1944 vividly demonstrated that to merely manipulate market size alone is not enough to ensure certain market conduct or performance. To suggest that market power *exists* by measurements of number and market share is one assumption; to suggest that the possession of market power is bad because it leads to poor market performance is quite another assumption.[5]

---

[3]For an excellent discussion of concentration ratios, their construction and use in analysis, see Joe S. Bain, *Industrial Organization,* Wiley, New York, 1959 (especially chap. 4).

[4]An interesting review of court interpretations of antitrust legislation over time is presented in Dykstra, *Cases on Government and Business,* Callaghan, Chicago, 1948. The 1944 case that finally reversed the decision that size alone does not constitute restraint of trade was *United States v. Hartford Empire Company,* 323 U.S. 386 (1945). This issue was also discussed in *United States v. United States Steel Corporation,* 251 U.S. 417 (1920), but it was still unsettled there.

[5]This very argument is the unfortunate crux of a recent journal article that deserves reading merely to see the unjustified assertions that can lead from otherwise sound analysis. See Robert F. Lanzillotti, "The Superior Market Power of Food Processing and Agricultural Supply Firms—Its Relation to the Farm Problem," *Journal of Farm Economics,* vol. 42, no. 5, pp. 1228–1247, Dec. 1960.

However, even to prohibit monopoly-size businesses does not ensure atomisticity. Such action only places an upper limit on the size of the firms. The
famous Aloca case and subsequent governmental actions demonstrate another
method that can be used to attain atomisticity.[6] Although "cease and desist"
orders resulted from finding of monopolization in aluminum by a single firm, the
efforts of World War II required the development of competing aluminum operations by the federal government. Following the war, these operations were sold to
firms that would compete with Alcoa. Although it can be effectively argued that
such actions were not antitrust in nature, this example does demonstrate another
way in which government can dissipate the size of large firms.

Still other methods are available under the taxing and aid programs of the
government. Large concentrated businesses can be taxed heavily, thus creating
competitive disadvantages, or small business developments can be encouraged
by provision of credit. But these methods have either been used in a limited way
or are normally justified on other grounds.

The feature policy program directed at the atomisticity condition has been
antitrust legislation. As noted previously, it serves only as a restraint to very
large size and does not create the condition of many firms of small size in a
perfectly competitive industry.

Homogeneity of Product   Real or fancied differentiation of the product by
firms (a market practice) diminishes the competitive nature of markets by reducing
the substitutability among similar products of competing firms. To make products
less differentiated or more homogeneous in the minds of consumers is the general
aim of legislation concerning grades and standards, and, to a lesser extent, sanitation requirements.

Most of the federal grades for farm products have resulted from a series of
separate pieces of legislation concerning specific commodities.[7] The goals or
purposes of grading are normally given in terms of production and marketing
efficiency and intelligent consumer decision making. These goals are performance dimensions of the perfect market and serve separately to justify grading
regulations.

To interpret grading as a marketing policy requires recognition of an explicit
and perhaps overriding goal in such policy programs—to encourage a *high-
quality* product. This implies that a high-quality product would not be forthcom-
ing otherwise under existing market conditions and that such a policy action is
needed to ensure quality.

The perfect market by its assumptions ensures a homogeneous product, and
by its structure it ensures a high-quality output. Quality is a performance

---

[6]*United States v. Aluminum Company of America,* 148 F. 2d 416 (1945).

[7]For a survey of the acts from which these grades arise, see U.S. Department of Agriculture,
Compilation of Statutes Relating to Marketing Activities of the AMS, Agricultural Handbook 130,
Jan. 1958. For a detailed breakdown of current grading standards, see U.S. Department of Agriculture, *Grade Names Used in U.S. Standards for Farm Products,* Agricultural Handbook 157, Feb.
1960.

dimension. Grading serves as an instrument variable to homogenize the product.[8]

Standards can be interpreted in two ways. First, an accepted grading system can become a standard for quality. This is a frequent interpretation of the term when used jointly as "grades and standards." Second, standards are accepted units of measurement (bushels, hundredweights, etc.) and even extend to retail packaging. In this second context, product differentiation is disallowed by variation in the measurements of the product. The "economy-size" package is frequently a misnomer of its actual content.[9] By requiring standardized measurements of packages, the market is being made more perfect in terms of the homogeneity condition.

Homogeneous products are also a side effect of governmentally imposed sanitation and purity requirements. A lower quality limit on product variation is set by demanding purity within narrow tolerance limits. Seed certification programs, for example, help homogenize products by purity standards for producers using seed. Meat inspection programs provide a sanitary, disease-free product to consumers but also place a limit on product variation in livestock products.

These product standardization policies do not completely disallow product heterogeneity. *Real* product variation in quality continues to occur despite long-run tendencies toward more standardized products. It can be argued that such variation is good on the grounds that more consumers are satisfied by the existence of greater product variety. *Fancified* product variation, the promulgation of ignorance rather than knowledge, is lessened by those policies if they are made effective through enforcement and education.

Locational Equalization Locational disadvantage to farmers has three important legislative aspects. The first of these relates to the Interstate Commerce Act of 1887. All interstate commerce became subject to federal regulation under this bill, which was upheld in later Supreme Court decisions.[10] While this legislation applied to all business, there was a single exception—the shipment of agricultural products.

The agricultural exemption in interstate trucking of farm commodities and "unmanufactured items thereof" has received considerable written treatment and serves as testimony of agricultural favoritism in current economic policy. This exemption now means that the Interstate Commerce Commission (ICC) has no control over who enters the business of trucking these commodities, the routes traveled, the areas served, and the rates charged.

The apparent original intention of the exemption was to aid the farmer by

---

[8]To differentiate by quality attributes is only to differentiate. But as grades and prices become related, the effect is to homogenize.

[9]The September 1960 issue of *Consumer Report* investigates some deceptive packaging practices. Current congressional hearings are also being held in this field.

[10]The earlier case of *Gibbons v. Ogden*, 9 Wheat, 1(1824), set the stage for this act. Commerce powers were greatly (and peculiarly) extended in the case *National Labor Relations Board v. Jones and Laughlin Steel Corporation*, 301 U.S. 1 (1937). This latter case allowed government regulation of those businesses dealing only *interstate* by the precarious logic that *if* such a business did not exist in the state, its product would have to be shipped in. Thus, the business is under federal control.

withholding restraints on the shipments of products to the *first point* of transfer. Since farmers normally handled this transportation, the law was aimed at providing special aid to a geographically dispersed and disadvantaged farm community. However, the scope of this original legislation extended to all nonmanufactured farm products and created a special advantage to transportation until enactment of the Transportation Act of 1958, which limited the exempt commodities somewhat.[11]

The exemption provision of the Interstate Commerce Act served as a means of attaining more-perfect locational competition for the farmer and later for those businesses that assumed this task.

Another locational policy has already been briefly summarized in the Sherman Antitrust and Interstate Commerce Acts by their subsequent regulation of rail transportation. The charge of rate profiteering at the expense of farmers who had no other way to reach their markets was an important influence in the adoption of these acts. To regulate rail rates was to again lessen the locational disadvantage of farmers.

A further method to lessen or strengthen locational misfortunes of businesses are a group of state laws that serve as barriers to trade between states. An early compilation of these laws shows a forbidding array of such state legislation that remain current law.[12] The direct prohibition or taxing of imports across state lines may either serve to encourage or discourage a perfect market, but many of these laws serve to protect the farmer from out-of-state competition.

Nondiscriminatory Pricing   The battle against discrimination and restraint of trade is, of course, the essential feature of the Sherman Antitrust Act of 1890. Courts later interpreted this act to mean that *monopolization,* not *monopoly,* was a violation of the law; the assumed difference was that monopoly indicated only size while monopolization indicated monopolistic practices. The Sherman Act simply declared such actions illegal.

The Clayton Act (1914) and Federal Trade Commission Act (1914) went further than the Sherman Law by specifying how firms should and should not compete. These pieces of legislation, frequently termed *amendments* to the original antitrust act, were aimed directly at controlling market conduct.

Several legislative enactments following these were also aimed at controlling market practices *directly.* The legislation includes the Robinson-Patman Act of 1936 (establishing rules against price discrimination) and the Miller-Tydings Act of 1937 (making state fair-trade laws legal in interstate commerce). After a Supreme Court ruling decreed that the Miller-Tydings Act was illegal, resale price maintenance was restored by the McGuire Act of 1952 until recently.[13]

---

[11]For a discussion of the agricultural exemption in interstate trucking, see U.S. Department of Agriculture, Marketing Research Report 188 (a legislative and judicial history), July 1957; see also Market Research Report 352 (developments in 1957–1958), July 1959.

[12]Works Projects Administration, *Comparative Charts of State Statutes Illustrating Barriers to Trade between States,* Marketing Laws Survey, May 1939.

[13]A review of this legislation is given in Marshall Dismark, *Business and Government,* Holt, New York, 1953, chap. 8.

The direct control of market practices was also enacted by agricultural commodity groups. These laws, familiar to agriculturalists, include the Commodity Exchange Act, Packers and Stockyards Act, United States Warehouse Act, Produce Agency Act, and Perishable Agricultural Commodities Act.[14]

While some portions of these acts deal with grades and standards, much of their content is aimed at directly regulating the conduct of firms in the marketplace for these products. The general form of this regulation is directed toward the prohibition of monopolistic practices and the encouragement of more competitive conditions in the market.

It should also be noted that the Agricultural Marketing Agreement Act permits producers of farm commodities to set up, within limits, discriminatory pricing schemes. This program was described in the preceding chapter on marketing institutions.

Free Entry and Exit   The *economic* aspects of entry conditions in the market are regulated by the government through antitrust legislation, and they are influenced by the provision of credit and education to firms and laborers. For agriculture, these latter policy programs are evidenced by the vast farm credit system set up by law to aid agriculture and by the educational and extension programs to "help the young people get started in farming."

The *legal* aspects of entry deserve brief comment. The patent laws providing monopoly rights to inventories and public utility franchises, and allowing monopoly under the strict control of government, provide interesting examples of nonperfect conditions promulgated by the federal government. These examples demonstrate some of the conflict in agricultural marketing goals that will be pursued later in greater detail.

Generally speaking, however, unrestricted entry and exit is the primary target of federal policy aimed at the regulation of marketing activity.[15]

Perfect Knowledge and Certainty   Lack of adequate information by farmers concerning market prices led to the formation of government agencies that collect information on prices and quantities of farm products sold. The government agencies disseminate these data to farmers (market news) and use it to predict future prices (market outlook). These marketing services tend to dispel lack of knowledge and uncertainty in marketing farm products and tend to make such marketing more perfect (see Chapter 10).[16]

Several programs already discussed can also be related to this condition. Grading, standards, and sanitation requirements, if made effective by educa-

---

[14]Reference to these laws are compiled in *Abridged List of Federal Laws Applicable to Agriculture,* Office of Information, Mimeograph 2, 1950.

[15]Enactments and administrative rulings concerning the entry conditions are discussed in Bain, op. cit., pp. 237–264.

[16]A comprehensive historical survey of the market news and outlook services provided by the federal government is contained in H. C. Taylor and A. D. Taylor, *The Story of Agricultural Economics in the United States,* Iowa State College Press, Ames, 1952, chap. 12, 13, and 17.

tional programs, also serve to improve market information. The research and extension services of the federal government also provide examples of programs that lessen the lack of knowledge and uncertainty in the market. Uncertainty, of course, is reduced by credit provisions involving insurance and price supports.

This brief overview of agricultural marketing policies suggests their dependency on the concept of the perfect market. It also suggests that, despite the magnitude of the complex of regulatory activity, a perfect market is actually unattainable by policy action under our political philosophy. Most of this policy either prohibits *extreme* variation from the conditions of perfect competition or *encourages* perfectly competitive behavior.

In the words of Sosnick,

> The set of market structure and conduct attributes which define "perfect competition" constitute individually and collectively neither a normative ideal nor a satisfactory basis for appraising actual market conditions. . . . The extremes which define atomistic and otherwise perfect competition tell us nothing about desirable gradations in even the few dimensions to which they refer.[17]

While perfect competition is unattainable, it is necessary that some consideration be given to what is a *workable* goal toward which policy can be directed. It is under the guidance of workable competition that it is possible to justify countervailing power policies in agricultural marketing.

Countervailing Power Policies

When businesses combine, merge, and grow in size in one industry while those in a vertically related industry do not, the balance of bargaining power in the market becomes one-sided. This has been the historical experience in farming and agricultural marketing.

This lack of bargaining power on the part of the farmer was recognized in antitrust legislation by exempting the agricultural industry from prosecutions under the Clayton Act. The exemption of excused marketing and supply cooperatives and cooperative mergers from antitrust action gave countervailing power privileges to the farmer.[18]

The Capper-Volstead Act, of course, followed the Clayton Act exemption in giving special encouragement to the formation of agricultural cooperatives. The act also specified the criteria for cooperative organizations to exempt them from paying business income taxes. Succeeding legislation and the formation of special agencies in the government prompted and encouraged the growth of agricultural cooperatives to a size and extent in some markets that today exceeds most of their marketing competitors.

---

[17]Stephen A. Sosnick, "A Critic of Concepts of Workable Competition," *Quarterly Journal of Economics,* Aug. 1958, pp. 383–384.

[18]A discussion of "types" of bargaining power available to farmers is found in Robert Clodius, *Opportunities and Limitations in Improving the Bargaining Power of Farmers,* Agricultural Adjustment Center, Iowa State College, Ames, Oct. 1958.

But to countervail power in the marketplace by encouraging changes in size and concentration was deemed insufficient. The Agricultural Marketing Act of 1937 allowed farmers and their negotiating parties to "fix" prices and restrict entry by formal agreement. A host of marketing orders and agreements have arisen for various farm products that aim at protecting the farmer from the disadvantages that perfect competition imposes. While general antitrust policy prohibited collusion on pricing and restraint of trade, the Agricultural Marketing Act allowed and encouraged such marketing conduct.

This rather astounding conflict in policy programs has been treated passively as a simple exception that does not seriously affect the operational performance of American business in general. Contrary to this feeling, Bain states:

> In consequence of the scope and character of the treatment of the "exceptional" cases, it is no longer possible to regard the various anti-competitive policies as merely an assortment of unusual and special departures from the general pro-competitive policy. Rather, all must recognize that these exceptional policies as a group embody a second orientation or line of emphasis in American public policy toward business, *which an important part is potentially in conflict with and inconsistent with the general pro-competitive policy.*[19]

PRICE AND INCOME POLICY

Historically, the price and income policies for agriculture in the United States have been directed at the resolution of two important economic welfare problems. The first problem is that of price and income instability, brought about by the existence of severely inelastic aggregate demand and supply relationships for food in the United States along with a lack of farm bargaining organization and the vagaries of weather. Left uncontrolled, agricultural prices would fluctuate severely from one year to the next depending mostly upon supply factors beyond the control of the individual farmer. An important focus of some U.S. agricultural policy is to help reduce severe fluctuations in agricultural prices and income for the welfare benefit of the farmers in this country. Severe price fluctuations also serve as poor allocative indicators within agriculture and between agriculture and the remainder of the economy.

The second major concern of U.S. agricultural policy has been to bolster sagging farm prices which have, in real terms, diminished gradually over a substantial period of time. The cause of this decline is the technology treadmill and the behavioral limitations imposed on farmers by the market structure characteristics that make the farmers "price takers" in both product and input markets. Thus, the price support programs of the federal government have also been directed to the resolution of low-income problems, at least up to more recent times.

The first major entrance of the U.S. government into price stabilization and

---

[19]Bain, op. cit., p. 541. The italics have been added.

support for farm commodities began with the Agricultural Marketing Act of 1929. This act created the Federal Farm Board to administer a program to stabilize farm prices. It was funded with $500 million which was to be used through national commodity cooperatives to buy farm commodities when prices were depressed and to release commodities when prices rose. It was the assumption of the program that the major farm problem was instability in farm prices and incomes. The cooperative began to buy products to bolster low prices, but prices never reached a point where products could be released. The cooperatives were soon bankrupt. But this does not mean that the objective is unattainable. Prices could be stabilized through such a program with sufficient knowledge about price variability. However, prices have to be stabilized around an average of the free market price. The Federal Farm Board attempted to stabilize around a price above this level.

As a result of this experience and because of deepening depression, the government enacted new price support legislation—the Agricultural Adjustment Act of 1933. Under this program, farmers were paid to reduce production. Thus, prices would rise because of reduced marketing and income would be further supplemented by payment. Payments were to be made from funds collected from a processing tax on the commodities where the programs were to be undertaken. Provisions of the act were declared unconstitutional in 1936. In the same year, a new AAA was passed which used governmental grants to pay farmers to shift from cash crops to soil-conserving uses. Furthermore, the act provided for support of price at above-market levels through nonrecourse loans. Since that time, price support provisions have been reenacted to provide for continuous authority for price support. The most recent piece of legislation is the Agriculture and Consumer Protection Act of 1973. Procedures of each price support have been modified to reduce costs and to reflect changing economic conditions. However, the basic objective of all has been to prevent farm prices from falling below specified levels.

Several different procedures can be used to support prices above free market levels. All procedures have been and are used singly or in combination in domestic U.S. farm price programs. These are:

   1   Import controls to maintain prices above world market levels where we are deficient in meeting our own needs (sugar).
   2   Deficiency payments, which are payments by the government to farmers for the difference between the excess of the support price over the market price, thus clearing the market of total production (wool).
   3   Purchases of supported commodities by the government sufficient to raise market prices to the support levels (for grains and dairy products).
   4   Production and/or marketing controls that limit the supplies that would come on the market in the absence of the controls (grains, tobacco, and cotton).
   5   Demand expansion programs for food products (the Food Stamp, School Lunch, and domestic-feeding programs).

Let us consider some economic aspects of each of these programs. First, for products in which a nation is a deficit producer in terms of domestic use at the world price, import controls are a means of supporting price above the world price. Either quotas or tariffs on imports can achieve the same impact on domestic prices. If we assume that the world price is fixed to the importing country, then Figure 14-1 illustrates the impact of using import controls. Domestic demand and domestic supply are indicated by the usual downsloping and upsloping curves. Their point of intersection indicates the price and quantity if no trade is permitted. With a world price of P_w, quantity Q_1 is demanded in the domestic market and quantity Q_2 is supplied by domestic producers. The difference $Q_1 - Q_2$ is imported. If the government decides that it wants to raise the price to domestic producers in order to encourage self-sufficiency for the product, it can do so by imposing a tariff. If the goal is to support price at level P_s, the government can institute a tariff on all imports equal to the difference between P_s and P_w. This will encourage domestic producers to expand production from Q_2 to Q_4. Domestic consumption will decline from Q_1 to Q_3 and imports will decline from $Q_1 - Q_2$ to $Q_3 - Q_4$. Tariff revenue generated by the program will equal $(P_s - P_w) \times (Q_3 - Q_4)$.

The same reduction in imports and rise in domestic price can be achieved through an import quota set at $Q_3 - Q_4$. Quotas, however, yield no revenue to the government, and increased returns are obtained either by the exporting countries or by the importers who are fortunate enough to obtain the authorization to import.

The import program was used in the U.S. domestic sugar industry until 1975

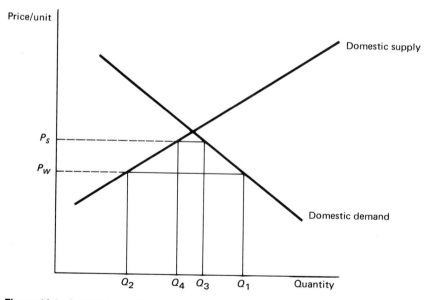

Figure 14-1 Impact of tariffs or quota on domestic production and consumption.

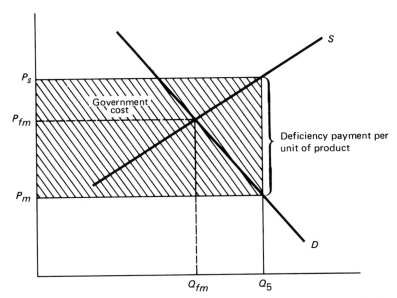

Figure 14-2   The use of deficiency payments to support the price above the free market level.

when it was permitted to expire. It has been estimated that domestic sugar production would have been only about 25 percent of domestic use instead of 80 percent had it not been for the sugar program.

The deficiency payment method of price support makes payments to producers equal to the difference between the support price and the market price for total production. Here, if the free market price falls below the support price, we have the situation illustrated in Figure 14-2. P_{fm} is the free market price. Quantity Q_{fm} will be produced and marketed at that price. However, the support price P_s generates production of Q_5. This quantity of production will clear the market only at a price of P_m, which is indicated by the height of the demand curve for quantity Q_1. To bring producer price up to P_s, a payment equal to the difference between P_s and P_m is made to producers. The government cost of this program is the deficiency payment multiplied by the quantity produced: $(P_s - P_m) \times Q_5$. It is illustrated by the shaded area in Figure 14-2.

The deficiency payment approach bas been used for wool price supports in the United States. A price support level is established at the beginning of the marketing year. All wool is sold in commercial markets at a market-clearing price. If the average of this price for all producers is below the support price, each producer receives the difference between the support price and the average U.S. market price for wool for each pound of wool that is marketed. Since quality variations still exist for wool, this method of payment still results in price differences among producers for the quality differences.

Governmental purchases of farm products as a means of price support involves the government as one of the buyers in the market. Let us assume the

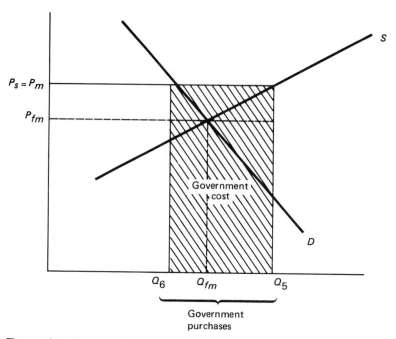

Figure 14-3 The use of government purchases to support the price above the free market level.

same demand, supply, and level of price support as was used for the deficiency payment example. The uncontrolled market price and quantity would again be P_{fm} and Q_{fm}, respectively, as shown in Figure 14-3. With a support price of P_s, farmers would still produce quantity Q_5. Since the program is designed to maintain market price at P_s with $P_m = P_s$, commercial buyers of the product will buy quantity Q_6 at that price. The difference between production and commercial purchases $Q_5 - Q_6$ will be purchased by the government at the support price. The total cost to the government of this program is the shaded rectangle in Figure 14-3. Note that consumers obtain only Q_6 units of the product with this program, whereas with deficiency payments consumers obtain quantity Q_5. Furthermore, governmental purchases must be disposed of in noncompeting commercial uses, destroyed, or perhaps exported.

   Purchases of farm products for price support in the United States are made by two different procedures: direct purchases or nonrecourse loans. Direct purchases have been widely used to support milk prices. The government purchasing agency, the Commodity Credit Corporation, stands ready to purchase butter, nonfat dry milk, and cheese at prices calculated to permit milk processors to pay milk producers the support price. Commercial prices for these products cannot fall below these levels and, except for minor deviations, neither can farm milk prices fall below the support price. The nonrecourse loan has been widely applied to grains. A producer can obtain a loan equal to the support price on each unit of grain produced and held in storage if the market price for grain is below the support price. This assumes that the producer meets other requirements for participation in the program. If the market price rises above the support price during the marketing year, the producer can sell the grain for the market price and pay off the loan at the support price. If market price fails to rise above the support price, the producer merely allows the government to take title to the grain.

The relative governmental costs of the programs of deficiency payments or purchases depend upon the elasticities of supply and demand. Given a fixed supply curve as in Figures 14-2 and 14-3, deficiency payments become less costly and purchase programs become more costly as demand becomes more elastic. As demand becomes inelastic, purchase programs become less costly and deficiency payments become more costly. Because demands for most farm products are highly inelastic, as described in earlier chapters, purchase programs are the least costly (not considering administrative and storage costs) of the two methods of price support.

Production and/or marketing controls either by themselves or in conjunction with other programs can raise the average level of farm prices. Thus, with demand, supply, and support price P_s in either Figure 14-2 or 14-3, restriction of supply to less than Q_5 will reduce governmental costs. This will mean a higher market price than P_m in Figure 14-2. Governmental costs are reduced because of a smaller quantity on which to pay deficiency payments, or the deficiency payment per unit of product is reduced. If production control is combined with a purchase program, it does not change the market price of the commodity, which still equals the support price, but it reduces the amount of product to be removed from the market to achieve price level P_s.

Demand-expansion program approaches can assist in achieving support-level prices for farm products. The School Lunch program, the Child Feeding programs, and the Food Stamp program all contribute to a larger demand. However, their major objectives are undoubtedly the improved welfare of the recipients rather than the welfare of farmers. Nevertheless, farmers and their representatives can easily support these programs because their earnings will be supplemented in addition to achieving welfare goals.

The current U.S. price support program for major farm commodities uses all four of the latter methods of price support. For corn, wheat, and cotton, deficiency payments, purchases, and production controls can simultaneously be used to achieve the support price. When market prices are above the support prices, as they are at the present time, none of the procedures are in effect.

OTHER FOOD LAWS

There are several other "categories" of legislation and rules that bear upon the structure of the food and fiber system. These policy categories include: (1) consumer protection policies, (2) antitrust policies, (3) market regulations, (4) taxation and business association policies, (5) land and ecological policies, and (6) farm labor policies.

Consumer Protection Policies

Policies focused at the welfare of the U.S. food and fiber consumer are multi-agency in scope. Policies relating to consumer income are both part of the Department of Health, Education, and Welfare and the U.S. Department of Agriculture. Policies relating to the protection of consumers from health hazards associated with individual products are provided by the Food and Drug Administration, and protection for the consumer in regard to misleading information is provided by the Federal Trade Commission. Many such agencies exist at state levels as well.

Antitrust Policies

The antitrust policies of the United States are also multiagency in terms of enforcement. In addition to the antitrust division of the Department of Justice, the FTC and the USDA play important roles in defining and enforcing the antitrust policy relevant to U.S. food and fiber systems. The major concern of the antitrust enforcement bodies and the courts has been the anticompetitive *conduct* that can result from concentrated market structures rather than an attempt to discourage structural developments themselves. The notable exception to this philosophical tendency has been with merger policies, which are designed to maintain competitive markets in regard to firm size and number.

The cooperative exemption from the antitrust laws has received attention in recent years, given the major organizational developments (and the subsequent market conduct) of highly concentrated agricultural cooperatives, particularly in milk and fertilizer.

An interesting structural result has come about as a result of the extensive expansion of agricultural-cooperative fertilizer manufacturing and distribution in the United States in recent years. At the present time approximately 40 percent of the fertilizer sold to farmers is handled by a single agricultural cooperative (C.F. Industries, Chicago) and its regional agricultural farm supply cooperative members. At times this cooperative has sold its fertilizer to farmer members at prices considerably below world market prices and has served as a *low* price leader of private firms in the fertilizer manufacturing sector.

The net impact of the agricultural cooperative exemption has been to encourage concentration in agricultural markets by cooperatives. This is evidenced by the decreasing number of local and regional cooperatives in the United States and increases in their size and scope of influence.

Market Regulation

There exist a large number of individual pieces of legislation at federal and state levels that regulate market transactions or license individual firms operating in farm supply or farm product markets. The apparent impact of these laws is the discouragement of entry or the encouragement of exit of those firms that do not meet basic technical qualifications or financial conditions or that have engaged in various anticompetitive practices in previous marketing activity. Among the more important agricultural laws are the Commodity Exchange Act, the Packers and Stockyards Act, and the Perishable Agricultural Commodities Act. The Commodity Exchange Act regulates trading practices on the commodity exchanges. The Packers and Stockyards Act regulates rates and business policies in stockyards, and it enjoins the use of fraudulent and discriminatory practices in the meat industry. The Perishable Agricultural Commodities Act enjoins similar types of practices in the marketing of fresh fruits and vegetables.

While it might be argued that such policies are healthy and are not severely restrictive, it should be noted that the continuing morass of legislation at a variety of levels has made it increasingly difficult for firms to determine where and to whom they may market their product and what standards have to be met. This tends to increase the cost of business operations and may be burdensome for the small firm.

Taxation and Business Association Policies

Agricultural taxes by federal, state, and local governments may be grouped into three categories: (1) income taxes, (2) real and personal property taxes, and (3) estate taxes on intergeneration transfer. Farmers historically have received special treatment both with respect to themselves as individuals and as organized agricultural cooperatives.

In general, the income position of the farmer has encouraged the federal government to allow special credits for land improvements and to support enterprise development by giving special tax exemptions to a variety of types. Property tax treatment has similarly favored farmers, but estate taxes at both federal and state levels generally have not given favor to the farming community.

The effect of favored tax treatment, of course, is to encourage nonfarm interests to engage in agricultural activities so as to take advantage of any tax privileges granted this particular industry. The result has been an increased number of "tax-loss" business entities formed as cattle operations, land-holding companies, and so forth. Because most of these entities are formed using sophisticated legal business organization structures, such as corporations or limited partnerships, increased state legislation has been developed to prohibit or severely limit the activities of farm corporations and limited partnerships from engaging in agricultural activities and/or taking advantage of tax laws written primarily for the benefit of bona fide farm operators.

Land and Ecological Policies

Most of the land and ecological policies in recent years have dealt with land use problems at the interface between urban and rural areas or have considered pollution control problems that relate to agricultural production activity.

Land use regulations have been primarily concerned with the problem of accommodating urban development at the expense of agricultural production. Agricultural land has largely been treated as a vast resource that is continuously available for urban expansion projects of all types. Given such a philosophy, there has been an expansionary effect in the nonfarm urban residential and business area. But there has also been a settlement concentration which has an increasing impact on agriculture by virtue of the fact that it draws farms and farm land out of agricultural production.

Ecological problems associated with agricultural production and food processing have been resolved largely by imposing abatement procedures at the expense of farms or food and fiber processing firms. The proposed effect is to keep the environment free of various types of impurities.

Farm Labor Policies

There has been a substantial increase in legislation arising out of the concern for the wages and working conditions of farm laborers. In addition to serving as a basis for an increased number of labor organizations operating in the agricultural community, this increased legislation has also created and provided a substantial increase in labor and fringe benefits costs that have to be incorporated into agricultural production costs overall.

SUMMARY

Agricultural marketing may be subdivided into descriptive marketing, marketing analysis, and marketing policy. Descriptive marketing involves summarizing the economic characteristics of the marketing system in an effort to understand how the system operates. Marketing analysis is primarily concerned with explaining *why* the system operates as it does. Analysis necessarily involves described facts that the system and economic theory which lists identified relationships gained through the study of many market environments over the years. Marketing policy refers to the business or governmental strategies that are employed to change the marketing system from what it is to some normative ideal that is specified in terms of goals. The goals may be fashioned out of our past experiences or analytical models.

A frequently used norm in marketing is the *perfect market concept*. This concept states that a perfect market is desirable and that it can be identified as having the following characteristics:

1 A large enough number of firms so that no individual firm can control price.

2 A product that is sufficiently standardized so that purchasers do not distinguish among sellers because of supposed or real product attributes.

3 All buyers and sellers possess a substantial amount of knowledge regarding prices, costs, and product availabilities.

4 There exists freedom of entry into and exit from all markets.

5 All prices are equal except for transportation cost, storage cost, or processing cost differentials.

6 No firm is able to establish artificial restrictions in buying inputs or selling its outputs.

However, the realities of marketing policy have encouraged legislation to give market power to those who do not possess it, namely farmers. This must be justified on the grounds of a concept of countervailing power—meaning that power should be given to those competitors in the market situations so that they are on equal footing with fellow competitors.

Agricultural marketing policies include those with the perfect market as its normative ideal and those with the concept of countervailing power as its normative basis. Perfect market policies include those policies that attempt to assume atomisticity of power, homogeneity of product, locational equalization, nondiscriminatory pricing, free entry and exit, and perfect knowledge and certainty. Countervailing power policies include agricultural cooperative exemptions from antitrust laws and the existence of market orders and agreements.

Price and income policy in the United States has been directed to the resolution of two major income problems. The first problem is that of severe income instability caused by highly fluctuating prices for many farm commodities. The second problem is the tendency of farm prices to decrease over a long period of time, creating lower incomes than what could be earned in the nonfarm segment of the economy. Income disparity and instability have brought forth agricultural policies which support prices at a level that discourages severe price fluctuation in extremely low prices in any one year. Support prices can be achieved through one or a combination of procedures: (1) import controls in certain cases, (2) deficiency payments, (3) governmental purchases of products, (4) production and/or marketing controls, and (5) a number of demand expansion programs. In addition to price supports, demand, expansion, and supply control programs are used in an effort to bolster farm prices.

Other food laws include consumer protection policies, antitrust policies, market regulations, taxation and business association policies, land and ecological policies, and farm labor policies.

QUESTIONS

1 Describe how beliefs and values influence the goals of agricultural market and price policy.
2 Why are many governmental policies in agricultural markets as well as others directed to making the markets more competitive?
3 Distinguish between the goals of parity income and parity power in agricultural market and price policy.
4 Discuss some of the considerations or factors that would determine whether deficiency payments or governmental purchases are selected as a method of price support.
5 Under what conditions would import controls be used as a method of price support for a commodity? What would be the factors to consider for selecting between a tariff or a quota as the means of import control?
6 Many of our agricultural market policies can be defined as perfect market policies. Why and in what respects are they perfect market policies?
7 What are some of the goals or objectives of agricultural market and price policies? What influences a society's selection of these goals?

BIBLIOGRAPHY

Abridged List of Federal Laws Applicable to Agriculture, Office of Information, Mimeograph 2, 1950.

Bain, Joe S.: *Industrial Organization,* Wiley, New York, 1959.

Clodius, Robert: "Opportunities and Limitations in Improving the Bargaining Power of Farmers," Agricultural Adjustment Center, Iowa State College, Ames, Oct. 1958.

Consumer Report, Sept. 1960.

Dismark, Marshall: *Business and Government,* Holt, New York, 1953.

Dykstra, Gerald A.: *Cases on Government and Business,* Callaghan, Chicago, 1948.

Gibbons v. Ogden 9 Wheat, 1 (1824).

Lanzillotti, Robert F.: "The Superior Market Power of Food Processing and Agricultural Supply Firms—Its Relation to the Farm Problem," *Journal of Farm Economics,* vol. 42, no. 5, Dec. 1960.

Markham, Jesse W.: "Changing Structure of the American Economy: Its Implications for Performance of Industrial Markets," *Journal of Farm Economics,* vol. 41, no. 2, May 1959.

National Labor Relations Board v. Jones and Laughlin Steel Corporation, 301 U.S. 1 (1937).

Sosnick, Stephen A.: "A Critic of Concepts of Workable Competition," *Quarterly Journal of Economics,* Aug. 1958.

Taylor, H. C., and A. D. Taylor: *The Story of Agricultural Economics in the United States,* Iowa State College Press, Ames, 1952.

U. S. Department of Agriculture: *Compilation of Statutes Relating to Marketing Activities of the AMS,* Agricultural Handbook 130, Jan. 1958.

———: *Developments in 1957–1958,* Marketing Research Report 352, July 1959.

———: *Grade Names Used in U.S. Standards for Farm Products,* Agriculture Handbook 157, Feb. 1960.

———: *A Legislative and Judicial History,* Marketing Research Report 188, July 1957.

United States v. Aluminum Company of America, 148 F. 2d 416(1945).

United States v. Hartford Empire Company, 323 U.S. 386(1945).

United States v. United States Steel Corporation, 251 U.S. 417(1920).

Works Projects Administration: *Comparative Charts of State Statutes Illustrating Barriers to Trade between States,* Marketing Laws Survey, May 1939.

Chapter 15

Marketing, Pricing, and Economic Development

INTRODUCTION

The focus of considerable development work in agriculture is on the basic farm production unit. How can the productivity of agricultural resources of a country be increased to meet the food needs of an expanding population and simultaneously provide excess savings for investment in the nonagricultural sectors? Achievement of a "green revolution" for any country involves more than finding or developing a technology of crop production that makes "two blades of grass grow where one grew before." On the one hand, it requires additional marketing facilities and institutions to move the additional products into consumption. It also usually requires additional market demands for food products. On the other hand, the green revolution requires new and additional inputs. These include fertilizer, insecticides, herbicides, water, fuels, machinery, and credit. The interdependence of farming and marketing increases as development occurs. Marketing institutions that meet the needs of agriculture as it currently exists will not meet its needs when techniques of production are altered and output is expanded. Thus, researchers have come to conclude that poor market performance can limit increases in agricultural productivity, or that increasing agricultural productivity can cause marketing problems, or both.[1]

Although the degree of the marketing and pricing problems for the less developed countries (LDCs) is greater than for the developed countries, the basic problems are identical. That is, is the marketing system providing the inputs for farm production and providing outlets for the products in the most efficient manner possible? This involves questions of operational efficiency in the performance of marketing services and pricing efficiency in regard to the use of resources and the allocation of products. The tools for analysis of these problems are those of supply, demand, and market analysis that have been used in the preceding chapters. In effect, there is no unique theory or method of analysis of agricultural markets and prices for the less developed countries.

The preceding statement does not mean that the conditions surrounding U.S. development or other developed countries are replicated in most other countries of the world. In many countries, population density is great and the availability of resources is limited. Many people have limited or no employment opportunities and the accumulation of capital resources has not been possible. U.S. economic development took place gradually over a time span of nearly 200 years; the country was rich with natural resources; the spark of invention was everywhere; and the population was small relative to land size and food and fiber production opportunities.

Regardless of the degree of the agricultural marketing problems and the environment in which they occur, the marketing problems are numerous. The following section describes the nature of some marketing problems for both product markets and input markets in developing countries.

PRODUCT MARKET PROBLEMS

Probably the most complete listing and discussion of kinds of problems that less developed countries face in marketing agricultural products was compiled by J. C. Abbott.[2] Some of his examples may be out of date; however, the problems still exist for most LDCs. The following is based on his discussion.

Determination of the Marketing System for Types of Farming

Subsistence-type farming is characteristic of much agriculture in LDCs. Farms are geared to producing food crops for their own consumption and possibly for payment of rent and taxes in kind. Little marketing machinery is needed to deal with these operations. Even where farmers may be producing some surplus, it

---

[1]Eldon Smith, "Agricultural Marketing Research for Less Developed Areas," *American Journal of Agricultural Economics,* vol. 54, no. 4, Nov. 1972, p. 666; Richard Norris, "A Framework for Analysis of Agricultural Marketing Systems in Developing Countries," *Agricultural Economics Research,* vol. 21, no. 3, July 1969, pp. 78–85; J. T. Bonnen, C. K. Eicher, and A. A. Schwind, "Marketing in Economic Development," in V. L. Sorenson (ed.), *Agricultural Market Analysis,* Michigan State University Press, East Lansing, 1964, p. 43.

[2]J. C. Abbott, "Marketing Problems and Investment Programs," in *Food and Agricultural Organization of the United Nations,* FAO Marketing Guide 1, Rome, 1958.

may be marketed locally. Thus, simple and limited market facilities may be quite adequate.

Abbott describes situations where eggs are brought to market.

> . . . without reliable indication of size, freshness, or other quality aspects—[the eggs are] brought into town by the wives of local farmers; such eggs are mainly the seasonal surplus output of small flocks of hens kept as a domestic sideline. From more distant villages, eggs are collected weekly by small country buyers who have little control over quantity and quality. The result is that many consumers prefer eggs imported from the specialized European exporters. Real improvement in the marketing of home-produced eggs is difficult so long as they are drawn from many suppliers, each resistant to change, and none dependent on egg sales for their main source of income.[3]

Many LDCs have had modern marketing systems operating with traditional systems for many years. Those have been the single major export crop economies—coffee, cocoa, tea, rubber, bananas, and so forth. The modern marketing facilities may only partially meet the needs of an expanding agriculture for domestic markets.

Transportation and Communication Problems

Transportation is still an important problem in numerous LDCs. Improved roads connect only a few of the important cities in a country. In some cases, they extend only a few miles from the main city. Other roads may be passable only during the dry seasons. Railroads reach only more important parts of the countries.

Because of the lack of adequate and low-cost transportation, regions of LDCs are restricted to producing for needs of the local villages. In the Philippines, subsistence crops such as corn and rice are grown instead of more profitable Manila hemp because of problems of transporting the hemp to the market.[4] Wide markets for highly perishable crops depend upon efficient and rapid transport systems.

The development of adequate transport facilities for agricultural marketing is a multidimensional problem. It requires expansion of road systems, acquisition and development of equipment that meets the needs of the commodities (refrigerated transport may be needed to expand the market for perishable commodities), scheduling and dispatching that ensures transportation when it is needed, and provision of transport services at lowest possible cost. The impact of transport cost on location and comparative advantage in production has already been described. Development efforts should be directed to ensuring optimum location of production and maximum possible competitive advantage in production.

---

[3] Abbott, op. cit., p. 43.

[4] J. C. Abbott, "The Role of Marketing in the Development of Backward Agricultural Economics," in C. J. Miller (ed.), *Marketing in Economic Development,* University of Nebraska Press, Lincoln, 1967, p. 12.

Storage

Provisions of cold storage facilities could expand the markets for many perishable commodities in LDCs. It can extend the marketing season for seasonally produced commodities. It may also expand demand in that consumers can be more readily assured of quality products.

A program of developing reliable storage facilities can reduce marketing costs. If facilities are such that risk of insect damage and spoilage are high, merchants are likely to require higher margins to compensate for the risks involved. Development of facilities to reduce those risks should reduce costs.

Size of Marketing Enterprises

Middlemen in LDCs often operate on a very small scale. This small scale may be quite sufficient for a traditional or subsistence-type of agriculture. However, the needs of expanding production and increasing commercial demand may create problems for the small merchants or opportunities for larger operations. Larger volumes of product can provide for specialization in the use of labor. Modern labor-saving and cost-saving equipment may require much larger volume. Larger business enterprises may have access to more credit and lower-cost credit. Larger businesses may be able to make use of skilled management and technical personnel, both of whom may contribute to more efficient marketing.

If the above advantages exist, it means that small merchants should be replaced to reduce marketing costs. What is the best method for obtaining this size? Cooperative marketing ventures have proved successful in many countries. They provide a means to obtain necessary size and, at the same time, avoid some monopolistic tendencies that result as the number of firms is reduced.

Monopoly

Local-buyer monopoly has often been a charge leveled against merchants in LDCs. It may be maintained because of the credit role played by the merchant, collusion to exclude potential market entrants, or government-granted monopoly. The monopolies can and do charge excessively for their services.

The breaking of monopoly power may be very difficult. Trade associations, market associations, or the government (municipal and national) may be dominated by the merchant class. Abbott described a situation where monopoly was eliminated. The old Hong Kong fruit and vegetable market was controlled by families who dominated the market for generations. Marketing margins were 30–40 percent of wholesale prices. A new market was established with control over charges and activities. Producer-wholesaler margins dropped to 10 percent.[5]

Grades and Standards

Lack of grades and standards for agricultural products can limit the expansion of commercial markets. When products are marketed locally and producers deal directly with consumers, the development of standardized grades and standards

[5]Abbott, "Marketing Problems," pp. 88–89.

may be of little value. For commodities which are distributed throughout a national or an international market, an acceptable and workable system of grades and product standards is crucial. The advantages of grades have been described in an earlier chapter.

Until effective grades and standards are developed, market expansion may proceed slowly. This may be because buyers find it difficult to ensure adequate quality for themselves; producer prices may be lower to reflect minimum quality only, and it is difficult to reflect consumer desires to producers without grades or specifications.

Market Information

Lack of market information has several consequences. Wide divergence of prices occurs through the supply-demand areas. Some producers may receive lower prices than the market will bear. Without information on current production, stock prices, and outlook, production planning becomes more difficult. Price and supply fluctuation will be greater than if this kind of information is available and used.

Transmission of market information on agricultural production, stock prices, and outlook is probably the easiest part of the task. Radio, television, and newspapers are available in most countries and in all parts of the country. Marketplaces exist where buyers and sellers can exchange knowledge as well as products. The problem is to obtain representative market information. This requires skills in statistical sampling and analysis that are typically in short supply. Outlook requires not only this information as an input, but skills in economic analysis and forecasting. Again, these kinds of skills are in short supply in most LDCs. It seems obvious that technical training is an important part of expanding market information.

Marketing Taxes

Governments of LDCs often levy a production tax on farm products moving through commercial markets. In fact, this may be a major source of the government's revenue, particularly where agriculture employs a large part of the population. The method of taxing is attractive because it is easy to enforce and the costs of administration are low. This usually requires that producers pay a tax based on the sales price of fruit, vegetables, cereals, and livestock products sold through wholesale markets. The effect of the tax is to reduce net product price to producers and discourage production where economic planning objectives are to increase production.

INPUT MARKET PROBLEMS

The green revolution in agriculture involves new and increased resource use. Many resources are provided through commercial markets: fertilizer, machinery, herbicides, insecticides, fuels, and hybrid seeds. The existing marketing systems must adjust or new systems must develop to provide these inputs.

Some of the problems described in the preceding section on product markets are relevant to input markets. Lack of good roads and transport facilities hampers expanded use of new inputs. Information on input supplies, use, and availability may not be adequate. Inefficiency in handling and/or monopoly may be causing excessive costs. Any or all of these will result in less than optimum resource use from the point of view of the national economy.

Timing of delivery has been found to limit use of some inputs. In Tunisia, lack of storage facilities in rural areas and government policy on fertilizer imports have been cited as factors that cause handlers to ship most fertilizer when farmers begin to apply it. The transport system then becomes overburdened, and farmers who would use more fertilizer at the going price are unable to obtain desired quantities.

Credit is an important aspect of obtaining production inputs in modern agriculture. Abbott lists three aspects of this problem: (1) high interest rates cut into net returns for products and blunt the effect of price incentives for increased production; (2) borrowers are often obligated to sell their product to the merchants who provide the credit and are thus at a disadvantage in searching out alternative and higher return markets; and (3) use of traditional merchant credit places producers under pressure to market products immediately after harvest when prices are normally at their low level.[6]

Perhaps as important as the preceding credit problems is that credit availability from traditional merchant sources may not be adequate to meet the needs of agriculture for adopting new techniques of production. Long-term capital investments are required and purchased variable inputs become a much larger share of total product costs. The development programs of many LDCs now include programs to increase credit availability. It may be the promotion of cooperative rural credit systems or the establishment of government-funded credit agencies. Nevertheless, insufficient credit continues to be a brake on agricultural development of LDCs.

PRICE AND NONPRICE CONSEQUENCES OF AGRICULTURAL MARKETING IN LDCs

Many of the marketing problems manifest themselves in products and/or input prices. Inefficiency in marketing farm products and taxes on products lead to lower producer prices and higher consumer prices. The incidence of the costs depends upon the relative elasticities of supply and demand. The highly seasonal nature of production with inadequate storage, processing, and capital limits the ability to hold products and sell them during the low production periods. This leads to large price variability. Uncertainty and risk of price change adversely affect farm production. Monopoly elements mean that the price to producer may be lower and the price to consumers higher than would be the case without monopoly. As a consequence, quantities demanded by consumers are reduced and quantities supplied by farmers are reduced.

[6]Ibid., pp. 107–108.

The nonexistence of necessary product marketing facilities and institutions means that product demand cannot be accurately reflected back to producers. Unless producers in a locality can participate in a broader national market or an international market, increased agricultural production may be impossible. It would only mean lower prices in the local market.

Insufficient input market facilities and institutions limit the ability of farmers to adopt new production techniques even if new and expanded product markets develop. Production will expand using traditional techniques, but the expansion may be considerably smaller than would be the case with the best technology.

MARKETING AND PRICE POLICY FOR AGRICULTURAL DEVELOPMENT

In order that marketing does not inhibit expanded food production, international development agencies and government economic planning agencies should devise policies to ensure:

> **1** Reasonably stable prices for agricultural products at a remunerative level. Unless they have confidence that prices will bear some minimum relationships to costs, farmers will hesitate before incurring additional work or expense to increase their output or raise its quality.
> **2** Adequate marketing facilities. The marketing system should ensure that growing urban demand, stabilized prices, and differentials for quality at the processing or consuming level are actually reflected in cash incentives to the producer and are not lost en route.[7]

The policies should also ensure the availability of production inputs and the credit system to provide operating funds.

The actual programs or activities needed to achieve the objectives may be numerous and diverse. They include market stabilization schemes through government acquisition and sales of stocks, government-sponsored and government-funded marketing agencies to provide services not now offered, creation of lending agencies to provide short- and long-term credit to farmers and marketing firms, investment in roads and communication, training of market and price analysts, and subsidization of production inputs. Governments may also critically evaluate their current policies regarding prices and markets. Because consumers often have a strong voice in national policy, and because high and rising food prices threaten social and political stability, governments of many LDCs fix prices of food products. The short-term benefits may be apparent, but the impact on food production should be known. To modify somewhat the effects of low food prices, governments are subsidizing inputs, particularly fertilizer and irrigation water.

[7]Abbott, "The Role of Marketing," p. 5.

SUMMARY

Unlike economic development in the United States, the marketing and pricing systems in the less developed countries of the world are initiated to solve unique and difficult problems. The most significant problem faced by most LDCs is producing and distributing an adequate volume of food and fiber to feed and clothe a population that is too large for the resources processed by these countries.

Even where adequate food supplies are not a major concern, there are several product market problems that must be addressed:

1 Determination of the right type of marketing system to handle the varied types of farming.

2 The attempt to move farm products under poor road, rail, or water transportation situations.

3 Development of storage facilities that can balance temporal supply-demand variations.

4 Creation of marketing firms of a size adequate to achieve some cost advantages without instilling monopoly power.

5 Development of meaningful systems of grades and standards for food products to ensure adequate marketing information for producers and consumers.

6 Creation of a system of taxation that does not discourage farmers from producing more than their subsistence needs.

In the same way that farm commodities are difficult to distribute in many LDCs, inputs used in agricultural production are underutilized due to transport, storage, information, or credit problems.

Farmers in LDCs have more productive capacity than is being utilized. This is partly the result of severe marketing problems. But lower levels of production are also caused by a lack of price stability in the markets and the existence of product prices unfavorable to farmers' costs of production.

QUESTIONS

1 You have been requested by a regional development agency to assist them in surveying the needs, costs, and potential of increased production of a new crop in the region, for example, sunflower seeds, peas, or any crops that have not been previously grown in the region. You are asked to consider the marketing sector. What factors would you consider and what kind of information and studies would you need to respond to your task?

2 Among the objectives of agricultural development in many LDCs are the following: low food prices to consumers, increased levels of agricultural output, and positive contribution of agriculture to the nation's balance of payments. What are some of the conflicts between these objectives?

3 Frequently, the objective of development programs is the maximization of agricultural outputs or the achievement of self-sufficiency in food production. Economists

will agree that this is often a very costly method of meeting food needs. Describe the nature of their argument.

BIBLIOGRAPHY

Abbott, J. C.: "Marketing Problems and Investment Programs," in *Food and Agricultural Organization of the United Nations,* FAO Marketing Guide 1, Rome, 1958.

————: "The Role of Marketing in the Development of Backward Agricultural Economics," in C. J. Miller (ed.), *Marketing in Economic Development,* University of Nebraska Press, Lincoln, 1967.

Bonnen, J. T., C. K. Eicher, and A. A. Schwind: "Marketing in Economic Development," in V. L. Sorenson (ed.), *Agricultural Market Analysis,* Michigan State University Press, East Lansing, 1964.

Norris, Richard: "A Framework for Analysis of Agricultural Marketing Systems in Developing Countries," *Agricultural Economics Research,* vol. 21, no. 3, July 1969.

Smith, Eldon: "Agricultural Marketing Research for Less Developed Areas," *American Journal of Agricultural Economics,* vol. 54, no. 4, Nov. 1972.

Index